TRUMAN'S TRUSTED FRIEND

TRUMAN'S TRUSTED FRIEND

Charlie Ross and
His Remarkable Sisters

JOHN B. ROSS

Copyrighted Material

Truman's Trusted Friend: Charlie Ross and His Remarkable Sisters

Copyright © 2024 by West Oak Associates, LLC. All Rights Reserved.

No part of this publication may be reproduced, stored in a retrieval system or transmitted, in any form or by any means—electronic, mechanical, photocopying, recording, or otherwise—without prior written permission from the publisher, except for the inclusion of brief quotations in a review.

For information about this title or to order other books and/or electronic media, contact the publisher:

West Oak Associates, LLC
westoakllc.com
info@westoakllc.com

ISBNs:
979-8-9885475-0-1 (hardcover)
979-8-9885475-1-8 (eBook)

Printed in the United States of America

Cover and Interior design: 1106 Design

For my wife, Patti, and for our children,
David, Shannon, and Katherine

CONTENTS

About the Author	ix
Author's Introduction	xi
1. Memories of Dew-dewey	1
2. The Ross Clan	11
3. Going West (1870–1880)	19
4. The Early Years (1885–1896)	31
5. The Klondike and Charlie Meets Harry (1897–1901)	51
6. School in Independence (1890–1901)	69
7. A Girl Can Be Smart (1901–1905)	85
8. Charlie's College Years (1901–1905)	101
9. Charlie Is Launched, and the Ross Women Carry On (1905–1921)	113
10. Newspaperman and Professor (1909–1919)	135
11. The Writing of News	157
12. The Going of JB Ross	175
13. The Kechuwa Way	195
14. Mr. Ross Goes to Washington	217
15. I'm Going to Live with My Daughters	239

16. Charlie at the *Post-Dispatch*	263
17. A Lady and a Scholar	297
18. Charlie Gets the Call	327
19. The Friend of My Youth Is Gone	365
20. Helen's Final Days	401
21. The Four Sisters and Florence	419
Parting Thoughts and Epilogue	445
Acknowledgments	449
Endnotes	455

ABOUT THE AUTHOR

John B. Ross was the grandson of Charles G. Ross, who was a prominent journalist and Harry Truman's boyhood friend and lifelong trusted advisor.

Throughout his life, John was an avid reader of biographies of lesser-known people who made a significant contribution to history. Over the years, he became intrigued by the story of his own famous grandfather. Using his access to family letters, unpublished memoirs, and interviews with family members, he began to craft a book about Charlie Ross. As he wrote, there emerged a larger story that included Charlie's six sisters and their remarkable lives as independent and accomplished women in mid-twentieth-century America.

John was an attorney in Winston-Salem, North Carolina, and in Baltimore, Maryland. He was Corporate Counsel at MNC Leasing and Financial and General Counsel at Williams Scotsman, Inc., until his retirement in 2008. John was born in Washington, DC, and grew up in Jacksonville, Florida. He graduated from Georgetown University in 1970 and after college was an officer in the U.S. Navy and served in the Vietnam War. He later earned a master's degree in economics from Georgia State University and a Juris Doctorate from Wake Forest University. While writing this book, John and his wife, Patti, lived in Baltimore and Hedgesville, West Virginia.

During the COVID-19 pandemic, John worked tirelessly to finish the book. He wrote the last chapter in the summer of 2022 and hoped to have completed the epilogue and have the book ready for publication within a few months. However, John was diagnosed with gastric cancer in September of 2022 and passed away in May of 2023. The book is published posthumously.

The author hoped that his book would inspire others to research and write about their own family histories. John was sometimes asked why he worked so long and hard on this book. His reply was always, "History, unless it is recorded, evaporates."

AUTHOR'S INTRODUCTION

The creation of this book has its own story. The idea to write about a specific generation of my Ross relatives evolved over the years. I now realize there were many nudges along the way. Indeed, the initial nudges came from my mother.

Of my two parents, my mother, Anne Moore Ross, was the more talkative and outgoing (my father was neither), plus Mom enjoyed and cared more than anyone in our household about history, particularly family history. (Dad showed no interest in either.) Somehow Mom sensed that, among her four children, I most closely shared her penchant for learning about our relatives. She dearly loved and respected her father-in-law, Charlie Ross, the main character in this book, and, by all accounts, the feeling was reciprocal. Moreover, she thought highly of his sisters, particularly Helen Ross, another central figure in our story. So, I never found it surprising that, when I was a child, Mom related interesting anecdotes about a relative to my eagerly awaiting ears.

Mom's second prompt occurred in 1966, when she encouraged me to contact three of my great-aunts (on the Ross side) who lived in Washington, DC, where I was attending Georgetown University in the fall. That seemed natural enough to me, as they lived close to campus—so why not?

Mom's final push occurred in the early 1990s, shortly after my dad passed away, when she moved out of our long-time family home. Over the many years, she had kept family memorabilia: letters, newspaper and magazine articles, photographs, a homemade genealogical chart, and even her mother-in-law's "Wedding Journal" from 1913. She had placed these items both in red-tie folders and in a couple of corrugated-cardboard liquor boxes and gave them all to me. (I've since learned that such a gift, often a bequest, is known as *the Box*—as in "Oh, you inherited *the Box*.") At that time, I was busy pursuing my career, supporting my family, and making time to be "Dad" to my young children, so I only superficially glanced through the boxes and then stored them away in my attic.

The next impetus came in 2008, when I retired from my career and the workaday world. By then my father and mother had passed away (1989 and 1994, respectively), and my three adult children had all moved on with their lives. So, I began reviewing the contents of *the box* and soon found myself saying, "I didn't know that," and "Isn't *that* interesting." I wanted to learn more.

Shortly before my dad died, my parents had sent a significant amount of family-related information about my grandfather to the Harry S. Truman Library (HSTL) in Independence, Missouri. Knowing about my parents' donation, I contacted the HSTL and set up an appointment to visit on November 30, 2010.

In fact, two reasons led to my going to the HSTL that November day. The first, of course, was to learn more about my grandfather. The second was that my visit coincided with a basketball game in Kansas City between my Georgetown Hoyas and the University of Missouri Tigers. My son, David, who, like many in our family, was a Georgetown alumnus, had invited me to the game. The HSTL is in Independence, Missouri just 10 miles east of Kansas

City—I could do both! So, on November 30, the day prior to the basketball game, I visited the library.

The East Entrance to the Harry S. Truman Library. Independence, MO, 2023. (Photo/Harry S. Truman Library)

As I pulled into its parking lot in my rental car, I was impressed by the HSTL's size, simplicity, and understated grandeur. When I walked in, I was cordially greeted—there was even a visitor's badge waiting for me. It turned out, as the grandson of a significant figure in the Truman Administration, I was treated as something of a celebrity. Mike Devine (Director) and Ray Geselbracht (Assistant Director), cordially greeted me, while Randy Sowell (Archivist) patiently responded to my every request. In all, I spent two days reviewing selected files at the library and getting to know the town of Independence, where I stayed. Mike and Ray told me about the history of the library as well as some new things about my grandfather, e.g., prior to marrying my grandmother, Charlie was deeply in love with another girl . . . and the girl's picture was hanging in the library! The second day, Mike and Ray took me to a local restaurant for lunch. "I've always thought someone should write a good book about your grandfather," hinted Ray after lunch as we were waiting for the check to arrive. That was in 2010 and the thought of writing a book had never occurred to me. Ray's suggestion sparked my curiosity, and I began to wonder whether such an undertaking would be worthwhile—or even feasible.

I returned home with my interest piqued. I began locating and reaching out to various relatives, mostly cousins, to determine what more information they had about my grandfather. Pieces of information began to surface, much more than I had previously known about. For example, I learned that two of my grandfather's sisters had written memoirs about their experiences as children in Independence, Missouri. Through my cousins' generosity, I was given copies of the unpublished memoirs, and I soon found they shed a broader light on the story. As I read these memoirs, I began to realize that my grandfather, although the most famous relative of his generation, wasn't the only Ross with an impressive story. Indeed, his six younger sisters had their own perspectives about growing up in the late 1800s and early 1900s in Independence, Missouri. Learning about these women and their lives shifted my focus—broadened it, actually—to the larger story that became this book.

My grandfather, Charlie Ross, and his second-oldest sister, Helen Ross—a highly regarded psychoanalyst—are the central figures of this story. However, the other sisters have not been overlooked, and I trust they will forgive me for the lesser amount of ink devoted to their lives. In many ways, this is also a portrait of that remarkable generation, fashioned in the Progressive Era and tested by two World Wars and the Great Depression.

This book, admittedly, has been slow to come to fruition. (The research began in earnest in 2010, more than a dozen years prior to the publication date.) Like many, my life hasn't progressed in a straight line over the past decade. It is sometimes said, "Life often gets in the way." Stumbling blocks have included my health (an unexpected quadruple-bypass operation and a knee replacement) as well the joys of a growing family. Offsetting these delays, however, have been many rewarding discoveries, such as friendly and helpful cousins and relatives, who provided useful information and encouragement. My explorations took me to new places, such as Independence and Columbia in Missouri, as well as the tiny hamlet of Michigamee on the Upper Peninsula of Michigan.

Lastly, the reader should note that this book, like all others, has its limits. It doesn't purport to be an exhaustive study of the lives of Charlie or Helen or their siblings. Rather, it's the most accurate picture I could draw about one generation from the credible evidence—family letters, unpublished memoirs, published articles, and, in a few noted instances, "family lore." This book evolved from the journey I took to discover more about my grandfather, Charlie Ross, and it ultimately led to my learning (and appreciating) more about the lives he and his sisters lived. In any event, I hope you, the reader, find this story interesting, and perhaps useful as a stepping stone on the road to a similar journey of your own.

John B. Ross
Baltimore, Maryland
August 2022

1

MEMORIES OF DEW-DEWEY

Standing upright on the plush back seat of the large automobile, with my young face pressed against the side window's cold glass, I was spellbound by the massive airplane parked next to us on the tarmac. "There's Dew-dewey! See Dew-dewey!" my mother's voice called out. Peering past the long, metal propellers, I saw a line of men walking up the metal stairway and into the belly of the aircraft.

"He's the man wearing the hat!" her voice instructed. My focus turned to the tall man in the middle of the queue as it inched up the stairs. One man stood out—my grandfather, a tall man wearing an overcoat and a brown businessman's fedora. His walk appeared steady and purposeful, as if he'd done this dozens of times before. As soon as he disappeared into the plane, I knew there was nothing else important to see, so I playfully collapsed onto the car's cushy back seat.

Grandfather Charles Ross (1950)

The year was 1950. My ride was in a White House limousine, one used that day to take Harry Truman's Press Secretary, with a few of his family members, to Washington's National Airport, where he boarded the President's plane, the *Independence*, to go about our country's business. Although I had seen him many times before, this one sighting remains as my sole memory of him. I was two years old, my grandfather 65. My life was just beginning; his would end suddenly a few days later.

"Dew-dewey" was my family's nickname for my paternal grandfather, Charles Griffith Ross. That moniker had been created by my older brother, also named Charles Griffith Ross, who,

President Harry S. Truman seated with Charles G. Ross Jr., grandson of the Presidential press secretary Charles Ross and the author's older brother. March 19, 1948. Harry S. Truman Library.

as a toddler, used this instead of the word "Granddaddy." In my family, "Dew-dewey" was not only a term of endearment but also one to differentiate my older brother from his namesake. To most people outside of our immediate family, my grandfather was known simply as "Charlie."

Dew-dewey died in December 1950. Time and circumstances didn't permit him to play an active role in my life, and this one memory of him is all I have retained. When I was growing up, my family spoke about him only sparingly, mostly because my father, his oldest son, was a reticent man who seldom spoke of his upbringing or his parents. Indeed, my father struggled to express his feelings about *anything* personal. Nevertheless, over time, I learned bits and pieces about Dew-dewey. I learned he'd graduated *Phi Beta Kappa* from the University of Missouri; he became one of the original professors in its trailblazing School of Journalism; he wrote the first journalism textbook; he won a Pulitzer Prize; and he served as the Press Secretary to President Truman. These stories placed him on a pedestal, but he could never be an active figure in my life.

As a boy, I sometimes daydreamed: *What would it be like if Dew-dewey were still around?* Seeing his framed picture among those of other relatives lining the long hallway of my boyhood home helped keep his memory alive. I often wished I knew more about him. *Did he have a sense of humor? Was he a generous person?* I always imagined him as an ally—someone who would have been supportive of whatever I chose to do. *Could he have given me practical advice about my education or about a career?*

To satisfy my curiosity, I sometimes searched for information about Dew-dewey. For example, whenever I saw one of the many books about his longtime friend, Harry Truman, I immediately would open it, turn to the index, and look up "Ross, Charles G." Then, I'd read everything the author had written about my grandfather, devouring every word. Also, I would ask relatives who knew him the general question: What was he like? The answers that came back were always positive and complimentary, yet vague and unsatisfying. His wife, my Grandmother Ross, gave me the strong impression she didn't want to talk about him, and she quickly dismissed my question by saying, "He was goodness itself," and then, she'd change the subject. I took this to mean that she didn't want to relive the past; perhaps she didn't want to revisit the loss she had suffered. My mother, the parent who was most interested in family history, said: "He was just wonderful. He really treated me as if I were his own daughter." I, perhaps incorrectly, took these terse responses to mean that I was hitting on painful memories, so I generally refrained from asking more questions. As a result, this curiosity remained latent throughout my childhood.

My Great-Aunts

"When you are in Washington, you have to go and visit your great-aunts," my mother announced shortly after I'd opened my college acceptance letter from Georgetown University. "They'd love to see you, and they are very interesting women."

"What great-aunts, Mom?"

"They are Dew-Dewey's sisters, and they are all very accomplished women in their own right," Mother said.

"Sure—what the heck. I'd be glad to meet them." As one of the more gregarious family members, I always enjoyed meeting new people, even elderly relatives.

"Well, I'm sure they'd like to meet you, and I know you'd enjoy meeting them." Mom continued, "Your Aunt Hi is a psychoanalyst. She's a close friend of Anna Freud, Sigmund Freud's daughter. Aunt Virginia is married to your Uncle Carl Weston, who had a distinguished career in the Justice Department in Washington. Your Aunt J.B. is a history professor who taught at Vassar College."

"Okay, Mom," I replied, the promise quickly slipping to the back of my mind as I mused on the upcoming independence of going to college away from home.

This conversation occurred in the spring of 1966. It was the introduction to my great aunts: Helen (known to family and friends as "Hi"), Virginia, and James Bruce (known as "J.B."), named after her father, who wanted a boy.

The dynamics and logistics of my family had kept many relatives out of our lives. In 1952, my father became Medical Director of the Jacksonville Blood Bank, so, in 1953, our family moved from Washington, DC, to Mandarin, Florida, a semi-rural suburb south of Jacksonville. When we moved the 800 miles south to Florida, we left our family, friends, schools, and all the rest behind. It was shortly after my fifth birthday.

Keeping the promise to my mother, in the fall of 1966 after I'd settled into college life at Georgetown, I telephoned my Aunt Virginia (Ross) Weston. (I shortened the more cumbersome "great-aunt" title to the more economical, albeit technically incorrect, title of "aunt," and I use this convention throughout this book for all of those relatives in my grandfather's generation.) She had expected my call and seemed happy to hear from me. We agreed on a time for me to visit on a Sunday afternoon, when her two sisters, Hi and J.B., could join us.

The Westons' modest home on Hawthorne Street in Northwest Washington, a short taxicab ride from Georgetown, was nestled into a shaded lot with many leafy trees and a fieldstone walkway leading to the front door. I rang the doorbell and was warmly greeted at the door by Aunt Virginia, a short, friendly lady with an aging yet animated face. She ushered me into the living room and introduced me to my Uncle Carl (Charles H. Weston) as well as to my aunts Hi and J.B. Immediately, I saw these were unlike other relatives I'd met; they were short in stature. (My father and my brother each stood six inches taller than me, while my mother and sisters were roughly the same height. I had somehow gotten the "short genes" in our family.) But now I was standing in a room of relatives of kindred size; despite the age difference, I felt an immediate connection. *My people!* I felt at ease, as if I'd discovered I had a new home.

After the introductions, I was seated in a comfortable chair and offered lemonade. I recall I drank more than one glass of Aunt Virginia's excellent lemonade (freshly made from real lemons and far better than the frozen concentrate I'd grown up with). Although I don't remember our exact conversations, I recall being asked about my family in Florida. A recap of my responses: *Everyone is well. My father left the blood bank a few years ago and currently is in private practice by himself. He had had a bleeding ulcer, but he's recovered now and is back at work. Mom continues doing volunteer work in Jacksonville, especially with the League of Women Voters. Charlie [my older brother] is now at the University of Pittsburgh working on a degree in Urban Affairs. Mary Anne [my older sister] is at Trinity College across town, and Margaret [my younger sister] has just entered high school in Jacksonville.* They listened intently and asked thoughtful questions, showing their depth of interest, particularly about my mother, whom they clearly held in high regard.

During the visit, I began to form impressions. Physically, the women all looked like sisters, although slightly different from one another. Aunt Hi, the oldest at 76, was the most serious. She wore a slightly loose-fitting, dark-blue dress with a subtle polka-dot pattern on it. Her impressive gray hair was short, yet neatly combed back. She gave me the impression that she absorbed everything that was said. She spoke the least, but when she did, her voice had an authoritative quality. She mainly sat, listened, and took it all in.

Aunt J.B., the youngest at 64, also sported a short hairstyle, which accented her shiny, silver hair. She wore a sprightly blue dress with a flowerlike pattern of alternating dark- and light-blue hues. Hers appeared to be a newer, fresher, and more stylish dress than those worn by her sisters. Her soft voice had a girlish lilt to it, making her seem younger than her years. Her diction and demeanor were all very proper, as would be expected of a college professor. She impressed me as the most cheerful of the sisters.

Aunt Virginia, at age 69, was the more energetic and assertive of the sisters, probably because it was her house, and she was the hostess. Her practical pageboy cut accented her salt-and-pepper hair. She was more direct and outspoken than—in my opinion—her more reserved and measured sisters. In our conversations, Aunt Virginia would occasionally state her opinion, which, although strong, was not voiced in an objectionable way. As she moved about the room performing her hostess duties, she displayed a confident, animated demeanor. She impressed me as having a very practical, down-to-earth approach to life.

Uncle Carl, a short man with a wiry build, let the rest of us do most of the talking. In his early 70s, he sported a short haircut; he mostly sat in his favorite chair next to his ashtray, smiling while smoking his pipe. Occasionally, he would offer an insightful comment or humorous remark. My most vivid memory of Uncle Carl was his high-pitched, raspy voice. The first time I heard Uncle Carl speak, I thought, *Oh my, that's unfortunate!* Yet with that voice, he somehow became chief of the appellate section of the Antitrust Division of the US Department of Justice, an impressive achievement under any circumstance. Over the course of several visits,

I grew fond of Uncle Carl, who occasionally offered a contrary opinion to that of his wife and sisters-in-law, adding an additional perspective to the conversations.

During my four years at college, I visited my great-aunts and Uncle Carl a number of times, probably twice a year. Over this period, we discussed a wide range of topics, including religion (the sisters were all agnostics), politics (everyone was a Democrat), and current events (all were against the Vietnam conflict, were for women's rights, and felt uneasy about the "hippie movement" of the 1960s, which they thought was too short-sighted and unrestrained). Although they were reluctant to talk about themselves (which to them would have been bragging or "blowing your own horn,") they told a few anecdotes about their upbringing in Independence, Missouri. For example, Aunt J.B. referred to her father, who was often absent from the family on account of unsuccessfully prospecting for precious metals as a "self-taught mining engineer" (my father had characterized him to me as "a ne'er-do-well".) Also, Aunt Virginia recounted the time in Independence when she had been "taken to the river" by a local church to be "baptized." She recalled being dunked in the cold water as, "the worst experience of my life."

By the time I'd graduated from college and left Washington, DC, for the next phase of my life (the U.S. Navy), I had learned from our conversations some of the rudiments of the lives of Dew-dewey's sisters:

- "Sis," the oldest of the sisters and two years younger than Dew-dewey, had died in 1951.

- Hi, the next oldest, had never married. She remained busy lecturing at such places as the University of Pittsburgh

Medical School. She also had a twin sister, Louise, who lived in Arizona.

- Louise, Hi's twin, was married, lived in Arizona, and her health was slowly failing. Hi kept in touch with her and visited her in Arizona on occasion.

- Virginia, the next oldest, had lived in Washington for decades and was active in civic affairs. She and Carl enjoyed traveling; they particularly enjoyed hiking and spent some time touring in Guatemala. They had one son (Charlie) and two daughters (Amy and Burnsie.) Charlie was working on his PhD in political science, Amy lived and worked in DC, and Burnsie was married and lived with her husband in Tappahannock, Virginia, where they owned a furniture store.

- Frances, the next oldest, was married to Lowell Leake, a man the sisters clearly didn't care for; he never held down a job for long and had a drinking problem. Frances and Lowell had three sons, two of whom (Charlie and Bud), operated Camp Kechuwa in Michigan.

- Aunt J.B., the youngest, wasn't married. She had taught history for years at Vassar College but was now retired. She traveled a great deal, particularly to Europe, where she did extensive research for the books and articles she'd author.

In addition to the updates about family members, I recall getting reports on two places that the sisters, particularly Hi and J.B., regularly visited. The first was Lake Michigamee on the Upper Peninsula of Michigan, where, in 1914, Hi and Sis had founded

Camp Kechuwa, which was originally a summer camp for girls. The camp had been turned over to the nephews, Charlie and Bud Leake, who now operated it as a summer camp for boys. Hi and J.B. had retained Footprint Island in the lake and a rustic cabin there that they used as a summer place. The second was Captiva Island on the Gulf Coast in south Florida, where they had a beach house and spent much time during the winters.

Visits with my great-aunts and Uncle Carl gave me a welcomed, fresh perspective about the Ross side of my family. These were interesting relatives about whom I had known almost nothing. They impressed me as people about whom I'd like to know more.

Unfortunately, that interest took a back seat to the practicalities of my life and lay dormant while I worked to establish a career and to support my family. Once I retired, I had time to learn more about my grandfather, Charlie Ross, and his remarkable sisters. The following is the product of that pursuit.

2

THE ROSS CLAN

The Highlands of Scotland

For Charlie, the family narrative began in the rugged Highlands of Scotland, where his great-great-grandfather, Hugh Ross, was born in the mid-1700s. Orphaned at about age six, Hugh's early welfare was entrusted to a nobleman.[1] Although the facts about the deaths of Hugh's mother and father remain unknown, many Highland children lost parents during that brutal and turbulent period of war between the English and Scots.

For centuries, the Ross Clan had lived in the Highlands just above Inverness in north-central Scotland.[2] The Highland clans operated for hundreds of years in a feudalistic social and economic system. Typically, the clan chieftain, owner of all of land within his domain, rented large tracts to a "tacksman," who parceled the land out to smaller tenants. The tenants, often living in isolated glens, hunted in the thick forests, farmed where the rocky soil allowed, and raised livestock. They also served as the chieftain's military force when battle with other clans or with the English required. The tenants generally adopted the last name of their clan chieftain.

Laws imposed in the Highlands by the English monarchy in the 1700s undermined and weakened the clan system; their enforcement, often implemented with callousness and brutality, led inevitably to conflict. On April 16, 1746, the English-backed army, led by the Duke of Cumberland, soundly defeated—then slaughtered—an army of Highland clansmen at the Battle of Culloden near Inverness. This effectively ended the thousand-year-old clan system, allowing a series of laws, known as The Clearances, to be carried out. These laws reduced the Highland Scots to second-class citizens, dislodged the clans from their lands, and outlawed many of their cultural identities, such as wearing kilts and playing bagpipes. Ultimately an estimated 85–90% of the Highlanders were removed from the land, and vast swaths of forests were cleared for large sheep farms and grazing land.

Amid this turmoil, Hugh Ross was apprenticed by his nobleman to a tailor. Hugh learned his craft well and was reputed to be "a fine workman." He began his trade in Edinburgh, in southern Scotland, and then moved to Sutherlandshire, a county in northern Scotland above Inverness. Around 1760, Hugh married Margaret McDonald, a descendant of Robert Bruce, the 14th-century Scottish king and national hero. The young couple had five children: two boys (Donald and Hugh II) and three girls (Margaret, Jane, and Katherine). Hugh II was Charlie's great-grandfather.

In the early 1770s, Hugh and Margaret made plans to emigrate with their children to the American colonies. Perhaps Hugh's business could no longer support his growing family, or, perhaps he ran afoul of the pro-English authorities. He also certainly saw that there would be adventure and opportunity in America that he did not have in Scotland. In the months just before the signing of the Declaration of Independence, Hugh and Margaret made their gutsy move. The young family boarded a creaky wooden ship and sailed to America, eventually settling in Anson County, North Carolina, just east of present-day Charlotte.

Even though many families had made similar decisions and similar journeys, the courage demanded by a voyage across the Atlantic in a wooden ship was remarkable. In Ross family lore, there is a legend of a kidnapping of one member of the family during the voyage—by a pirate or suspicious authority? Whether true or not, we do know everyone arrived intact.

Although Hugh's personality has been lost to history, I imagine him as a tough and canny Scot. Losing his parents at a young age had to toughen him emotionally, but that shock was counterbalanced by the nurturing of the kind nobleman. His mind proved nimble and disciplined enough to learn and practice a trade and later plan for the family's relocation to the New World. Ultimately, he succeeded in his quest for a better life, despite the uncertainties and hardships. I've always considered him a great relative who set a favorable stage for the ensuing generations.

North Carolina

Like many colonial newcomers to southeastern North Carolina, the family settled into its strange, adopted homeland, where Hugh soon began to acquire land. Everyone worked hard and adapted to the new surroundings. The family likely raised livestock, including sheep and swine, grew wheat and corn, and cut and sold timber. They attended the local church, probably Presbyterian, and sold livestock, crops, and timber for cash. By 1790, Hugh owned one slave; by 1800, that number had increased to four.[3] The Ross family became particularly close to the neighboring Lacy family. Tom Lacy, the head of that family, was a local magistrate and prosperous landowner. In time. three of Hugh's children wed three of Tom's children: Hugh Ross II married Lucretia Lacy in 1797, and, about the same time, Katherine Ross married Stephen Lacy, and Jane Ross married Thomas Lacy II.

The Ross-Lacy newlyweds weren't satisfied working in the shadows of their successful parents when so much promise—and land—lay westward. In about 1810, the three young families migrated west, ending in Hickman County in middle Tennessee, about 50 miles southwest of present-day Nashville. Like many other settlers to that region, they used their experience in farming to support their families. Hugh II, who I imagine as a Davey Crockett-like figure, and his pioneer wife, Lucretia, found frontier life to their liking. They bore ten children: six boys and four girls.[4] One of their sons, Griffith Lacy Ross, born in 1812, was Charlie's grandfather.

Tennessee

Although Hugh II's family settled in Tennessee, not everyone remained in Hickman County. Griffith Ross and his brother, Stephen, two years younger, eventually moved 50 miles west to the village of Jack's Creek, Tennessee, near Henderson, in the southwestern part of the state. Here the brothers cleared land and established contiguous farms each 640 acres in size.

During the 1840s and '50s, the brothers' farms and families prospered. Griffith, known as "Griff" to family and friends, married a Virginian, Dianisha Hamlet. They raised five children: two boys—Stephen (who died at age seven) and James—as well as three girls—Keziah, Betty, and Ada. By 1850, Griff's family owned 15 slaves.[5] On the Ross farms—then referred to as "plantations"—crops, including cash-generating cotton, were grown and livestock raised, particularly horses. Griff, widely known as a "sport and a gentleman," owned fine horses. In the parlance of the day, a "sport" was a man with strong interest in leisure activities, particularly horse racing and gambling. Griff stood an imposing six feet, two inches tall, was active in his community and in local politics, but he never joined any church[6]. I can easily picture him as a dashing character from *Gone with the Wind*. Griff's family grew and prospered on their plantation—until 1861.

The Civil War

The Civil War changed life forever throughout the South, including Jack's Creek, Tennessee. At age 49, Griff signed on as a captain in the Forked Deer Volunteers, a Tennessee regiment of the Confederate Army. He went off to war but returned home after a year when "his health failed." Despite his infirmity, he managed to serve in the Confederate Congress. While he was away, the family home was looked after by his wife, daughters, and young son, James Bruce Ross, who would become Charlie's father.

James, known then as "Jimmy," was nine years old at the outset of the War. An older brother, Stephen, had died seven years before, leaving Jimmy the family's only male child. Growing up, Jimmy received much favorable attention. In sparsely populated western Tennessee, his closest companion and playmate was an African-American boy, most likely one of the family's slaves. For schooling, he attended a local "Academy," but his formal education was, at best, uneven.

The Civil War affected Jimmy and his family directly. At the beginning of the War, when Griff was away, the women of the family, young Jimmy, and a few slaves were left to run the plantation as best they could. Later in his life, Jimmy often told the following Civil War story to his children.

One day news came from a neighbor that Federal troops were approaching. The family scurried to hide its food and treasures before the Yankees reached their home. The slaves dug a large pit on the edge of the woods. The women prepared the potatoes, apples, and root vegetables for burial. First to go into the pit were the family treasures—the tiny wedding rings, earrings, brooches in a little box, and then a big box that Jimmy's ancestors had brought with them when they left the Highlands, now filled with family silver. On top of these, the vegetables and apples were placed. Dirt was thrown back into the pit, and leaves and branches were raked over the hiding place. The family had worked against time—and won. Jimmy and his younger sister, Betty, were stationed on the two stone pillars that marked the entrance to the plantation.

"When you see a cloud of dust, run and tell us," said their mother. "That will mean the Yankees are almost here."

The children waited proudly on the two pillars most of the afternoon. At last, the cloud of dust was seen, and Betty ran home with the news. Jimmy, feeling brave, waited, and watched. Finally, the troops arrived. The officer drew up his horse and signaled to the foot soldiers behind him to stop.

"Good day, boy. We're going through. You live here?" he asked. Jimmy admitted he did.

"Nice place here. We're tired and thirsty. A good spring here? And, say, boy, you don't have some apples, do you? I'll give you a silver quarter for that cap of yours full of apples. What about it? It's a good deal, eh?"

The questions came too fast for answers. A silver quarter in the South at that time was not easily turned down. Jimmy reasoned that the apples were on top of everything in the pit and would be easy to get.

"Well, my men will be resting awhile. Think about it, boy. I'll join my men," he added as he rode back to the group.

Jimmy thought some more. He could get the apples in a few minutes, and his mother would be glad to see a silver quarter. Why not? He raced to the pit, shoveled out the dirt with his hands, filled his cap with apples, threw back the concealing leaves and brush, and ran to his place by the entrance post.

The officer came up, took the apples and gave Jimmy a silver quarter. Several soldiers came with him, too. They had followed Jimmy straight to the pit and had already emptied it out. All was gone. Jimmy cried. His mother tried to comfort him. "It's not your fault, Jimmy. It's war." The officer and his men moved on.[7]

At the end of the Civil War in April 1865, Jimmy was 14 years old. The family remained on the plantation. But it was in ruins, and the social and economic structure on which the plantation stood had changed forever. The war had diminished Griff's capabilities and resources. Young Jimmy, who struggled to find his place in the depressed environment, lacked the inclination—and most likely the ability and vision—to forge the plantation's future. He taught at the local school for a time but didn't care for that, either. His attention turned to the glamorous stories of easy riches in the mountains of Colorado. When he turned 21, Jimmy left the plantation and headed west to find gold in Colorado.

3

GOING WEST
(1870–1880)

Go West, Young Man

By 1873, Jimmy knew he didn't want to shoulder the burden of running his family's Tennessee plantation, which, after the Civil War, the family referred to as its "farm." His life growing up as the only male child on a prosperous plantation was idyllic, but a farmer's life in Tennessee after the Civil War was dramatically different—and more difficult. Pressing questions had no easy answers: What crops should be planted? Who would plant and harvest the crops? How would the family's property be restored after much of it had been taken or ruined in the war? How and when would the war-torn economy get back on its feet? Jimmy simply didn't want to struggle with these dilemmas not of his making. The spirit of the times showed Jimmy his path. In 1871, Horace Greeley of the *New York Tribune* extolled the virtues of westward expansion—the extension of the country's *Manifest Destiny*—when, in an open letter, he advised a young friend to "Go West!" This enticement became a siren song for many young men, particularly those from the war-torn South. Jimmy knew that earlier generations of his family had moved west; now it was his turn. The decision was an easy one: leave the dreary business of the family farm behind and seek your fortune where the nation's tide was flowing. Jimmy's cousin, Hugh Ross, was a year younger, lived on a neighboring farm, and shared Jimmy's thirst to find a better opportunity. The two young men, then in their early 20s, decided to adventure out together—to go to Colorado to find gold.

On their way west, Hugh and Jimmy, who'd recently changed his nickname to the manlier "JB," stopped in the town of Independence, Missouri, where some distant relatives resided. Located in far western Missouri, about ten miles east of Kansas City, Independence was the county seat for Jackson County, named after President Andrew Jackson. Founded in 1827, Independence was the point of origin for the Oregon, California, and Santa Fe Trails used for decades by settlers heading west; many referred to it as the "Queen City of the Trails." The town was built on a hill just south of the Missouri River at the point beyond which steamboats heading west could no longer travel. Families heading west by boat would have to disembark at Independence and continue their journey by horse or wagon. Between 1848 and 1868, the town's economy flourished by outfitting the pioneers heading west. In Independence, horses and wagons were bought, sold, and traded; bridles, saddles, and harnesses were made and repaired; pots, pans, kettles, and bowls were acquired; and foodstuffs and other provisions for trail life were brought to market and sold. It was a bustling commercial center and a welcome stop for thousands of westward-heading pioneers. However, in 1873, Independence was undergoing profound changes. Four years earlier, the railroads had constructed a bridge across the Missouri River at Kansas City, causing commercial activity to gravitate to that upstart town. But this change gave no pause to the adventure-seeking cousins who were just passing through.

James Bruce Ross, Independence, MO, 1880.
(Photo/Ross family collection)

On to Colorado

The cousins had heard that there was still gold—and plenty of it—in the Rocky Mountains in the Colorado Territory even though the Pike's Peak Gold Rush of 1859 had long ago petered out. It would require hard work, but they were hopeful they could extract a fortune out of the rugged mountains and streams by placer mining, which required little equipment or capital. Panning for gold, as it was generally called, required the miner to scoop the stones and sand from the bottom of the stream into a large metal pan, and then sift through it to find any precious ore. Recently, the gold fields region had become accessible by train when the Denver & Rio Grande completed 70 miles of new track south from Denver to Colorado Springs. Miners were able to travel by train to the foot of the Rocky Mountains in the shadow of Pike's Peak. What could be easier?

Upon arriving in Colorado Springs, the cousins found suitable horses and immediately set out riding through the nearby Garden of the Gods—a majestic expanse of red-rock formations. This trip ended back in Colorado Springs with little to show for their efforts. They made lemonade with some lemon sugar mixed with the "water of the grand old spring," and considered their next move. They then decided to hook up with an old prospector and a hunting party that took them around the base of Pike's Peak to the area of Cripple Creek. After several days on the trail, the party camped near Cheyenne Falls in a snowstorm. The next day JB, for some unexplained reason, walked into the town barefoot while snow was on the ground. None the worse for wear, he had fallen in love with the mountains and the outdoor life and was determined to make his fortune in Colorado. Over the next few years, he spent most of his time prospecting in central Colorado—from Denver southwest to Del Norte—looking for that ever-elusive gold.[8]

Raised on a plantation, JB had received little formal education. However, he showed an aptitude for making do and for fixing things. Before long he developed the practical skills needed for living outdoors. He learned to cook. Later in life, he would admonish his children, "Don't eat the first griddle cakes. Let the greedy people have them." He traveled easily by horse or mule, did carpentry work, hunted, and learned placer mining.[9] During evenings spent around a campfire, he honed the craft of storytelling, and his mining trips gave him a deep reservoir of material. Some of his stories were amusing, like the one about his first autumn in Colorado. According to JB, he was with a group scouting the wilderness for a promising mining spot. One morning, the group camped near Pike's Peak, and their food was running short. For JB it was a chance to show his Tennessee hunting skills. As he crept among the rocks and trees, he noticed a dark object suddenly move. He raised his rifle and fired. The movement stopped. JB walked cautiously toward his target. He leaned over and he saw his kill; it looked like a squirrel, only it was all black, not gray. He returned to the camp puzzled when the miners told him it indeed was a black squirrel, which was common in Colorado. JB laughed, "I just killed the first black squirrel I ever saw."[10]

JB also learned to respect the risks taken by prospectors in the Rocky Mountains. One day in the early spring, JB came across the frozen corpse of a young man with blond hair who had gotten caught in a deadly snowstorm. His body was now exposed by the spring thaw. After emptying the pockets, JB dug a grave, buried the body, and then marked the grave. A picture of a beautiful young woman was with some papers that also gave the name and address of the dead man's mother in Germany. JB wrote to the mother, sent her the picture, and told her where her son was buried. In reply, he received a sad letter of thanks and a man's ring set with a huge amethyst stone. JB kept the ring and later gave it to his wife. The ring—and the story—remained in the family for generations.[11]

The likelihood of deep snow made prospecting in the Colorado Rockies hazardous from November until April, so JB, like other placer miners, left during those cold months. He initially went home to Tennessee, but as time went by, he spent the winters in Independence, Missouri, where he enjoyed himself more and could find work.

Independence, Missouri

Before the Civil War, Independence thrived by serving the pioneers heading west. However, beneath this layer of economic prosperity, social unrest was coming to a boil. Most families that settled in western Missouri around Jackson County were farmers and slave-owners; they were ideologically rooted in—and economically committed to—slavery. Sympathies were quite different just across the Missouri River in neighboring Kansas, where New Englanders and others with abolitionist leanings were the primary settlers. By the 1850s, armed conflicts broke out between the pro-slavery Missourians and the abolitionist Kansans, most occurring within a 75-mile radius of Kansas City. These bloody skirmishes, with punches and counterpunches delivered by both sides, came to be known as the Border Wars. One example occurred in May 1856, when armed pro-slavery Missouri ruffians invaded Lawrence, Kansas. They killed two men, burned a hotel, destroyed printing presses, and robbed homes. Three days later, abolitionist forces from Kansas retaliated for this "Sacking of Lawrence." John Brown, in a raid later known as the "Pottawatomie Massacre," led a group of armed men into Franklin County, a few miles south of Lawrence in the Kansas Territory, where they attacked and killed five pro-slavery settlers. Writing for the *New York Tribune*, Horace Greeley coined the term "Bleeding Kansas" to describe the violence.

The Civil War did little to sooth these hostilities. There were only two military battles that took place in Independence during the war (one in 1862, the other in 1864). However, guerrilla raids by armed gangs were common. Pro-Union bands known as "Jayhawkers," sometimes led by "Jim Lane and his Redlegs," raided Missouri families at will. William Quantrill, a pro-slavery marauder turned Confederate soldier, frequently led bloody raids into Kansas. Even though a Federal Provost Marshal (a military policeman meant to deal with the civilian population) was headquartered at the Independence jail for much of the war, the bloodshed continued. In August of 1863, Union General Thomas Ewing, Jr., the area's military commander, declared martial law and issued the now-infamous General Order No. 11.[12] This order applied to Jackson and three nearby Missouri counties and required a citizen to take an oath of loyalty to the Union. Those who did "to the satisfaction of the commanding officer" were allowed to remain in the area. Those who failed to "prove their allegiance" were forced to move. In January 1864, five months after it was issued, the order was rescinded by General Ewing's successor. However, the damage had been done, and many people lost their homes, livestock, and property. This left a bitter taste in the mouths of residents, particularly those who had Southern leanings.

Independence after the War

The Civil War took a toll on Independence, and it never returned to its position of commercial prominence. The scars of the Border Wars were slow to heal, and the violence that took place in western Missouri before and during the war worried the government. It was doubted that the local sheriff alone could keep the peace. By this time, the small Independence jail was also seriously over-crowded. Another county jail was established ten miles away in Kansas City, a city that was now booming. In 1871, the Missouri legislature established the position of County Marshal for Jackson County. The Marshal was responsible for criminal matters within the county, the sheriff was now relegated to less dangerous civil affairs.[13] This meant that the local sheriff now just oversaw the security of the county courthouse, which consisted mainly of transporting prisoners to and from their courthouse hearings.

The caution shown by the Missouri Legislature proved well-founded. Jesse James and his brother, Frank, were Confederate soldiers who had served alongside two of the most notorious leaders in the Border Wars, William Quantrill and "Bloody Bill" Anderson. From them they learned to hate all Yankee soldiers and developed skill in the art of killing. It didn't take long for the James brothers and their band to take the law into their own hands. On December 7, 1869, they robbed the Gallatin, Missouri, bank, and Jesse shot and killed its banker.[14] Gallatin was just 70 miles north of Independence. Now known as the James Gang, they had prices on their heads—dead or alive. Some Missourians thought the James Gang were simply outlaws that needed to be brought to justice. Others saw them as Robin Hood characters—taking from the rich (mostly Northern-controlled banks and railroads) and giving to the poor. Despite scant evidence to support the giving-to-the-poor part, Jesse James reached folk-hero status in post-war Missouri. From 1866 to 1882, the James boys joined forces with Cole Younger, and the band became known as the James-Younger Gang. They were responsible for over 20 bank and train robberies and countless murders throughout the midsection of the country. In 1882, Jesse was shot and killed by a member of his own gang. The myth of the James brothers stirred the emotions of many Missourians around Independence long after Jesse's death.

Despite this lawlessness, post-war Independence was evolving from its boom-town days into a stable and mature community. With its strategic railroad bridge over the Missouri river, nearby Kansas City was now Jackson County's boom town. Independence became a pleasant and closely knit small town where many families saw their future.

Ella Stone Thomas

Hugh and JB found living in Independence more comfortable as time went on. Through their connections, they were able to secure temporary work that tided them over until the next mining season out west. The bachelor cousins soon found their way into the town's social life. Hugh met an eligible young lady, Ella Thomas, whose family was in the livery business. They saw each other a few times, but nothing came of the relationship. However, when JB was introduced to Ella, things took a different path. JB was drawn to the attractive Ella's poise and level-headedness. She was impressed by this tall Tennessean's Southern manners and entertaining stories. It wasn't long before a courtship began.[15]

Ella Stone Thomas was born in Independence, Missouri, in 1856.[16] Her father, Charles Thomas, had come with his family from Kentucky decades earlier to make his living as a livery stable keeper.[17] Ella's mother, Frances Stone Thomas, known as "Fannie" to the townspeople, had been born in Virginia. During the Civil War, the Thomas family was "removed" from their home by the hated Order No. 11. Ella and Fannie had to move temporarily to Kentucky, where they spent dreary months living with a couple of elderly bachelor relatives.[18] After the war, Fannie became a highly regarded schoolteacher who founded Independence's first elementary school. After her own grammar-school education, Ella enrolled in Woodland College, a two-year, local women's college, where she took fine-arts courses and received her degree in 1879. She was also an accomplished musician and pianist.[19] By the late

1870s, soft-spoken, educated Ella had many *beaux*, but JB Ross, with his easy charm, cut too romantic a figure for her to ignore.

Ella Stone Ross, Independence, MO, 1880.
(Photo/Ross family collection)

On December 14, 1880, JB and Ella were married in an evening ceremony in The Christian Church by its progressive minister, Rector Alexander Proctor. Ella's family was one of the founders of the church. JB, a non-churchgoer like his father, respected Rev. Proctor and generally approved of The Christian Church, which didn't espouse any specific creed and left its members to interpret the Bible and its teachings in their individual ways.[20]

The young couple traveled to Tennessee for their honeymoon and visited JB's family, who were now struggling on the farm without his help. The homecoming did not go particularly well. Strait-laced Ella was taken aback by the "drinking and dancing" of the Ross family. JB's sisters, particularly Betty (to whom he was closest), resented Ella for keeping JB away from the farm, where he was desperately needed.

Upon returning to Independence, the couple moved in with Ella's parents to begin their life together. Ella called her mother "Mammy." JB called her simply "Mrs. Thomas." Ella's father—undoubtedly "Mr. Thomas" to JB—was in failing health and stayed mostly at home; he passed away a few years later on January 1, 1883.[21]

As a married man, JB felt the pull—much of it surely from his new wife—to work closer to home rather than on faraway mining trips. His marriage caused him to rethink his career as a prospector and led him to build a new life in Independence. He found work locally, but that didn't mean he would shun adventure altogether. He was known around town as an excellent horseman, a quality which caught the notice of the town's Marshal. On September 7, 1881, Jesse James and his gang robbed a passenger train three miles outside of Independence at a spot known as The Blue Cut on the Chicago & Alton Railroad line. JB suddenly found himself deputized and riding with the Marshal's posse in pursuit of the robbers. The posse was able to apprehend a few of the gang but none of the leaders. No stolen items were recovered, either. JB, always the storyteller, told his children years later that his posse had captured Jesse James at "old man Milton's farm" and taken him to the Independence jail. JB claimed that Jesse probably hid the loot at the farm, but no one could find it. Unfortunately, this entertaining tale didn't comport with the facts. Jesse James, in fact, was never captured, although this was his last train robbery. A few months later, in April 1882, he was shot and killed by Robert Ford, a newer member of the gang, who decided it would be easier to collect the bounty on Jesse's head than it would be to keep riding with him. "Old man Milton's farm" has been lost to history. It was Jesse James' final train robbery and an adventure for JB. It likely led him to his next career—law enforcement.

JB and Ella didn't have long to adapt to married life before their family began to grow. Their first child, Frances Rogers Ross, was born on October 5, 1881. "Little Fannie," as she was called, was named for her grandmother, in whose house she was born and where her parents resided. Less than two years later, the couple gave Little Fannie a playmate, when, on August 5, 1883, her sister, Emma Dianisha Ross, was born (her middle name came from the Ross side of the family.) The young family lived happily together until a diphtheria epidemic stormed through Independence in the winter of 1885. The outbreak claimed the lives of both the Ross children: Fannie on January 7th and Emma two weeks later, on January 22nd. In this era before the advent of antitoxins, such tragedies were all too common. JB and Ella—who until now had experienced only the joys of their young family—faced the abject pain of the deaths of their two small children.

4

THE EARLY YEARS
(1885–1896)

Charlie's Birth

My grandfather, Charles Griffith Ross, was born on Monday, November 9, 1885, in the home of his maternal grandmother, Rebecca Thomas, on North Main Street in Independence, where his parents then resided.[22] Named after his two grandfathers, Charles Thomas and Griffith Ross, he was the fulfillment of his father's wish for a son and his mother's hope for restarting the next generation of the new family. Everyone called him "Charlie."

The Ross family remained in the Thomases' modest home for the first four years of Charlie's life. For Charlie, it was a loving environment with his mother and grandmother both caring for him. There was also no shortage of aunts, uncles, and assorted relatives to provide more support. The Thomas family had run a livery business since before the Civil War and was well-known and respected in Independence.

Charlie Ross as a young boy, about two years old. Independence, MO, 1887. (Photo/Ross family collection)

Grandmother Thomas

Charlie's grandmother, Rebecca Frances Rogers, was born in Pittsylvania County, Virginia, in 1827 and moved with her family to Independence, Missouri, in 1849. Her father set up shop as a tanner, making leather from animal hides. Young Rebecca met Charles Newton Thomas, a native of Kentucky, who worked in the livery business in Independence. He had two children from a previous marriage. Charles and Rebecca married shortly thereafter and began their own family with the birth of their daughter, Ella Stone Thomas, who later became Charlie's mother. Ella was raised and educated in Independence, where she had many Thomas and Rogers relations throughout the town.[23] Ella enjoyed a close relationship with her mother, who she called "Mammy."

Rebecca Thomas, known throughout Independence as Miss Fannie, was a well-respected member of the community. Her parents were among the founding families of The Christian Church in Independence. The Christian Church is part of the Disciples of Christ movement and has many similarities to the Congregational Church in New England. The Church espoused a simple New Testament Christianity following the teachings of the Bible and it allowed its members to interpret those teachings independent of any strict dogma. She remained a lifelong member of the local congregation.

Outside of the church, Fannie was the town's first schoolteacher. She initially "kept the first private school in her home," and moved the class into a one-room building after a few years. This schoolhouse eventually became the first public school in Independence. She not only educated the town's children in that small, wooden classroom, but she also "opened the door and swept out the room, fired the stove and shoveled the snow in the winter months."[24] She was one of those many dedicated, strong-willed women that brought formal schooling to the pioneering communities west of the Mississippi.

Upon her death in 1894, Fannie Thomas left behind several faded little notebooks containing outlines for lessons and precepts for teachers, as well as assorted Bible verses. Among other things, her notes showed a dedication to grammar that she defined as the "science and art which teach how to speak and write correctly."

She developed her own approach to teaching children which she outlined in her notebook; it contained the following six admonitions for a teacher:

1. The teacher must understand the nature of the child.

2. The subject must be adapted to the pupil.

3. The pupil must proceed from the known to the unknown.

4. The practical must precede the theoretical.

5. All instruction must be an uninterrupted progress from the easy to the difficult.

6. All instruction must reach the understanding.

Her notebook reflected her lifelong teaching experiences by which she developed strong beliefs about the qualities a teacher must possess. On its final, dog-eared page, she wrote the following, which had been noticeably traced over, as if reread and pondered many times:

Teacher should be:

1. Moral and upright

2. Attentive to personal appearance

3. Careful of feelings of children

4. Scrupulously honest

5. Prompt in all things

6. Studious

7. Devoted to her work

8. Deliberate in counsel

9. Cool in temper

10. Clear in statement

11. Just in judgment

12. Firm

13. Patient

14. Eschew evil.[25]

A formal photograph of her, most likely taken in the 1870s, shows a serious woman with dark hair, pulled back, and parted in the middle. Her smooth skin is belied by the deep lines around her mouth and eyes. Charlie remembered his "grandmother as a woman of great strength of character, with strong, well-cut features—the kind of face that goes with our conception of the pioneer women of the West."[26] Despite her exacting standards and severe demeanor, she enjoyed a loving relationship with her daughter Ella. Indeed, shortly after her mother's death, Ella lamented that whenever something new or exciting happened in her life, her first thought was that she must "go tell Mammy."

Grandmother Rebecca Thomas, known by everyone as "Miss Fannie." Independence, MO, 1880. (Photo/Ross family collection)

Charlie well remembered his Grandmother Thomas, who first introduced him to academic discipline. He would later say: "My earliest memory is of going to school to my Grandmother Thomas in an upstairs room set apart for this use. She had been a schoolteacher, and so when I reached the age of 5 or thereabouts, she undertook to instruct me in the work of the primary grade. This she did for a year, following closely (as I believe) the regular first-grade course of the public schools, with the result that when I entered the old North Side School in Independence, I was placed in the second grade." Charlie absorbed thoroughly this early instruction. He said, "I have the impression also that she had a strict sense of justice. Certainly, despite the firmness with which she held me to my school tasks, I retain only the most affectionate memory."[27] This one-on-one instruction gave Charlie an important head start when he entered grade school and catapulted his intellectual growth.

Within the Ross family, Grandmother Thomas was deeply respected and loved, even by her free-spirited son-in-law, JB Ross. While he called her the rather formal "Mrs. Thomas," he was devoted to her. JB and Ella lived in the Thomases' house for their early married years. Later in life, JB noted to one of his children, "I admired your grandmother . . . but she could be stern." He went on to say, when "your grandfather [Thomas] was moaning in his last illness, your grandmother told him to control his feelings."[28]

Grandmother Thomas influenced her grandchildren's lives, even after her death. One of her granddaughters, Virginia Ross, born a year after Fannie's death, wrote: "she was no stranger to me—she figured in everyday conversation. She read her Bible, taught her grandchildren, wrote articles for a religious paper, was a fine needle-woman—and had great dignity." Even after her death in 1894 at 68, Grandma Thomas remained an indelible influence. Charlie wrote, "I well remember my grief at her death." Three of Charlie's younger sisters, born after her death, recalled her constant place in everyday conversations as well as her imposing portrait, which hung over the family mantle.[29]

1887—A Growing Family, a Career Change, and a New Home

The year 1887 brought two major changes in Charlie's life. First, on November 24, a little more than two weeks after his second birthday, the first of his six sisters was born. Named after her mother, baby Ella was given the nickname "Sis" to avoid any confusion. Her birth was without trouble, and she provided a welcome addition to the family.

Ella Ross, oldest sister of Charlie. She was always known as "Sis," to avoid confusion with her mother, Ella. Independence, MO, 1891 (Photo/Ross family collection)

Second, Charlie's father, known universally as JB, accepted a position as Deputy to the County Marshal for Jackson County.[30] JB was an accomplished horseman and man of the outdoors. His experience on the posse chasing after Jesse James also likely played a role in his selection by the Marshal.

The Deputy County Marshal served primarily as the jailer for the town of Independence, which was the County Seat for Jackson County.[31] The Deputy oversaw the local jail and occupied the "Marshal's Residence" within the jail building and was commonly referred to as the Jailer.

Up until this point, JB had spent most of his adult life trying with very limited success to make his living mining for gold out west. When back in town, he earned money working for a variety of local businesses but never found a steady source of income. This new position allowed him to remain in Independence and to support his growing family. The unusual requirement—that he (and his family) live at the jail building—was accepted by him and Ella. She wanted him closer to home, and a steady income was sorely needed. If living in a jail be the price, so be it.

Jackson County Jail

JB, Ella, Charlie, and Sis moved into the Jailer's residence a short time after the baby Sis was born.[32] The Independence Jail was completed in 1860 and was located on the east side of Main Street. Viewed from the street, the building (as it still looks today) is a symmetrical, two-story, red brick building of Federalist design. At each end of the building are single-door entrances with several white-framed, double-paned windows in between. The upper floor has similar windows neatly placed all along the front. The building served two main purposes. There was a residential section where the Ross family lived; these rooms were located along the street-side wall. On the first floor was JB's office, a dining room, and some family living spaces. On the second floor, just above, were more living spaces and the bedrooms. The actual jail section was buried at the back of the building away from the street, like a hidden dungeon. It was a classic jail cell with thick limestone walls and heavy iron doors and windows.

Just north of the building stood a long wooden platform for unloading and offloading. It was used mostly by prisoners for their work details and chain-gang duties. Several yards beyond this platform, and further back from Main Street, stood a large gallows area with high surrounding walls for hangings. (Only two recorded hangings took place in Independence during JB Ross' tenure as Jailer.) During the day when the prisoners were away on work details, the Ross children would use the platform as a play area for foot races and games.

Living and working in a jail must have been a challenge for a woman like Ella. Ella was a well-respected, thoughtful, and kind woman; one of her daughters recalled her exceptional capacity for "forgiveness."[33] The new position also required Ella to be "Jail Matron." Ella was responsible for preparing the meals for the prisoners as well as any jurors and visiting lawmen. This position earned Ella a few extra dollars a month. Sometimes selected prisoners, known as "Trustees," would assist in the daily chores of operating the Marshal's office and jail, and Ella would supervise them. Charlie also performed some minor chores, which was expected for a young son of the Jailer. On one occasion, he passed some tobacco to a prisoner who gave him a carved-bone knife in return.

1890—The Twins Arrive

On March 16, 1890, the Ross family took another step forward when twin girls were born in the Marshal's residence. Louise and Helen were healthy from the start, and their birth was the talk of the town. Ella soon started calling Helen, the eldest twin, "Hi" (purportedly from Robert Burns' poem "Yon High Mossy Mountains"). Throughout Helen's life, family and close friends would call her "Hi," while others would use the more formal "Helen." Louise simply remained "Louise."

Ella spent most of her time tending to the infant twins, while Mammy helped with four-year-old Charlie and two-year-old Sis. The family slept in the large bedroom on the second floor of the

Twins Helen Ross and Louise Ross as infants, Helen is pictured on the left as viewed by the reader. Independence, MO, 1891.
(Photo/Ross family collection)

Marshal's Residence. JB worked in his office on the first floor, and Ella, as Jail Matron, worked primarily on the lower level as well. There was a lot of togetherness in these close living quarters, which was helped some when Mammy began tutoring sessions for five-year-old Charlie. Mammy would also take three-year-old Sis as her helper during the many hours when she was sewing.

When the twins became old enough, they were allowed to play on the flagstone sidewalk just outside the Marshal's residence and on the platform next to the building. Years later, Helen recalled that they largely "played pretend" by using their imaginations to make up games and envision traveling to faraway places. Their few toys and dolls helped keep them busy, as did racing each other along the platform. Helen, later in life, reflected that she and Louise operated "as a collective" by their constant sharing, by playing, eating, and even bathing together. Helen believed this was an advantage; like any child, she was developing a sense of self. She was also becoming part of another, unique unit known as, "the twins."[34]

The family seldom got away from the responsibilities of the jail. They never took any family vacations and never traveled except for an occasional Sunday outing to the Missouri River. As Helen remembered, ". . . the old carriage loaded with father, mother, the four children, the pug dog, Mack, a huge, covered pail of water with its own dipper, and a basket of Saturday sugar cookies made its usual weekly excursion to see the powerful, muddy, sometimes acrid-smelling Missouri River, often swollen and turbulent." This was the family's only getaway from its day-to-day routine. Helen recalled "lots of space and grass to play in, trees to climb, maybe even some water to swim in." Indeed, her imagination contained a far different picture. "Clear water with the blue of the summer sky in it was in the child's dream. And lots and lots of children to play with, to make up games with, to 'pretend' with."[35]

JB's storytelling provided the children with a view of a larger and more exciting world. Helen loved his stories, "the trips we loved to hear about the most were Dad's as a very young man, when he left the Tennessee plantation, ruined by the Civil War, to go looking for gold in Colorado." Even though he never traveled with his children, he developed in them a thirst to see the world.

Charlie's Pre-School Tutoring

While the rest of the family lived as normally as possible in their quarters in the town's jail, Charlie spent a good deal of time learning from his Grandmother Thomas. He was being personally tutored by Mammy, who by then had retired as a schoolteacher. About this experience Charlie, later in life, wrote, "I kept for many years the large thick tablets of coarse paper in which I did my writing exercises she set for me, and I may have them yet, stored away among other old papers."[36]

Charlie from an early age showed his penchant for studying and the written word. He regularly attended the family's church. When he was six years old, the *Sunday-School Evangelist*, published by The Christian Church, printed the following letter:

> "**Independence, Mo.**—I am six years old. I have learned to write, and can read **The Evangelist**, too. I go to Sunday-school every Sunday that I am well, never forgetting to take a nickel or a penny. I can repeat every one of the Golden Texts we have had since Christmas. Miss Mollie Hughes is our teacher. We love her nearly as well as we do our mammas. Bro. Proctor is our preacher. Please print this in the paper.
>
> *Charles Griffith Ross*"[37]

Charlie at School

Charlie started school in 1892 at the Ott School (also called the North Side School).[38] The Ott School was referred to in the family as "Mammy's School" because it was the successor to the one founded by Mammy. The family wanted Charlie to start his education there. Charlie had already learned the curriculum required for the first grade from Mammy and could read and write. Thanks to his grandmother's tutoring and influence, he skipped first grade and began his academic career as a second-grader.

From his earliest days, Charlie enjoyed learning and especially loved the written word. He quickly grasped that a word represented a single concept, a sentence a complete thought, and a paragraph a body of information. He discovered that stories could be told through written words, so he learned to read. From an early age, he read constantly; he was seldom seen without a book in his hand. His family was keenly aware of his affection for books, so every Christmas he received at least one as a gift. Not only did he read everything available; he *remembered* what he read.[39] According to local lore, by the time he'd completed high school, he had read every book in the town's library.

Charlie, with Mammy's help, was also drawn to writing. She had him write short compositions that she read and critiqued. He enjoyed learning new words, parsing the meanings of words, playing with words, and creating sentences. Charlie liked it all. Mammy taught him that punctuation helped the reader navigate sentences. Punctuation marks gave the reader directions. Writing became his preferred way of expression.

Mother Jerome and Mammy

Mammy retired from teaching in the late 1880s, sold her home, and moved into the jail's living quarters with the family. She helped with the children, spent much time with the family, and even contributed to the lives of the prisoners.

During her years in and around the jail, Mammy began working with Mother Jerome, the head of the local Sisters of Mercy Convent, to improve the lot of the inmates. Mother Jerome Shubrick was born Alicia Shubrick in 1830. When Alicia was in her late teens, her father, to whom she was very close, and two of her brothers all died suddenly and unexpectedly. These tragedies motivated her to a life dedicated to works of mercy and service to others. In 1853, Alicia entered the Convent of the Sisters of Mercy and took her vows two years later as Sister Mary Jerome. By 1884, she'd established the Convent in Independence and was known as Mother Jerome. She became widely known for her personal visits and ministrations to the inmates at the jail.[40] Before long, Mammy and Mother Jerome became friends and organized their efforts to "start the first 'charity' in the small community."[41] They supplied the inmates with supplemental food and reading materials and wrote letters for the prisoners to send to their families and friends. Her work at the jail was deemed so important that Mother Jerome was given her own key.[42]

Working with Mother Jerome, however, raised eyebrows in Mammy's family—Mammy's sister "thought it odd . . . that she had any truck with Irish Catholics."[43] But Mammy's keen sense of right and wrong paved the way for her—and her strong ally, Mother Jerome—to lift some of the inhumanity from the shoulders of the jail's inmates.

Sis often accompanied Mammy on periodic visits to the Convent on charity business. The twins were jealous of these visits because

Sis often brought home "beautifully made gifts" from the nuns. This enhanced Sis's uniqueness to the twins. Ella encouraged this, when, after Mammy died, she told her children: "Mammy told me once she thought the Sisters at the Convent baptized Sis when she was a baby. One day when she was talking to Mother Jerome, the nuns . . . [took] Sis with them for a while." This story was followed by Mama's laugh, but it did make Sis special in the twins' minds and "added to Sis' reputation as an arbiter."[44]

Mother Jerome and Rebecca Thomas both died in Independence in 1894, the former on February 5th, the latter on June 10th. Mother Jerome is buried in the local Woodlawn Cemetery, and her grave marker bears the inscription: "The Prisoner's Friend."[45] Rebecca's funeral was followed by a large reception, to which relatives and many friends brought food and expressed their admiration for the effect "Miss Fannie's" works, particularly her teaching, had on their community.

Family Relationships

By the time he entered school, Charlie had three younger sisters. His feelings for his mother and grandmother were always consistently strong and positive, and, later in his life, he would become devoted to his sisters. However, as a young boy, Charlie wasn't so protective of his sisters. A family friend related the story of how young Charlie arranged a boxing match between Helen and Louise and sold admission tickets to a few of his friends to get some spending money. The fight, perhaps on the platform next to the jail, apparently didn't last long. Louise, the more athletic of the two, decked Helen after one or two punches, and the fight was called.[46] Charlie's parents couldn't have been pleased, but fortunately the twins didn't hold it against him.

Little is known about the relationship between Charlie and his father. Charlie noted little about him, except to quote a distant relative's impression of JB in 1890, "He married a most excellent young lady and is in every way a promising young man."[47] One of Charlie's sisters recalled the time Charlie defied his "Mother's injunction to wear his overcoat—it was plaid green and blue." JB heard about this and took a switch to him.[48] This event was remarked upon because JB was normally a kind and deliberate man. The punishment was typical for the time, and Charlie himself never referred to this incident, or to his father, in a negative way. From every indication, their relationship appeared to be appropriate for the era, but not particularly close.

Sis

Sis tried to be the glue to keep the family together. Much of her early years was spent with Mammy, learning from her and, in part, taking on her perspective. She inherited Mammy's "wisdom" and directness. When Mammy died in 1894, seven-year-old Sis cried at her funeral.[49]

After Mammy's death, Sis was often tasked by Mama to look after the boisterous twins, three years Sis's junior. Sis kept the twins when Mama went to a funeral or any "reception" outside the home.[50] She was generally responsible for the young twins and did so competently, dutifully, and without fail. She did this despite being overshadowed by her "perfect" older brother on one side and the boisterous twins on the other. Helen, years later, acknowledged that she, along with the rest of the family, took her older sister for granted.

Sis maintained a prominent place in the twins' upbringing. For the twins she became the arbiter of what, and what not, to do.

"She always seemed to know what we should do and when. We did not question why. This knowing came from . . . Grandmother [Thomas] . . . Sis has a special communication, we felt, with right and wrong."[51] Indeed, her sense of propriety was so respected in the family that even "Charlie strove for Sis' traditional approval."[52]

Most of Sis' advice to the young twins was sound, for example, "You never speak to people on the street you don't know."[53] However, some may have been a bit on the creative side. Explaining the reason her beautiful baby doll, with its finely stitched outfit was named "Sister Jerome," Sis told the twins: "You always name the dolls for the person who gives them to you." This was accepted by the twins "without question of its suitability." However, this became much more awkward when Mr. Kessler, Papa's political boss at the jail, gave the twins identical dolls dressed in pink. Since a doll named "Mr. Kessler" was out of the question, a conference with Mama was held. After much discussion, an exception was made, and Sis informed the twins that their new dolls could be called "the pinky dolls," a solution readily accepted by the twins.[54] Sis' role as Mama's main support and arbiter for the children served the family, with its paucity of material resources, well. However, her contributions were somewhat under-appreciated by her siblings, perhaps because her delivery was often authoritarian and a bit too direct.

Departing the Jail

By 1897, JB and Ella had grown weary of their nine years in the jail. Ella had stoically served as the Jail Matron, a role that went against her grain. Serving as the Jail Matron undermined the status she enjoyed in the close-knit community. According to one daughter: "Mother was always hurt by this living at the jail, tried to deny its very existence." Indeed, she never spoke to her children, either when living at the jail or afterwards, about the prisoners or about their father's duties at the jail. While they lived at the jail, she made every effort to keep her three young daughters away from the jail cells.[55] Fortunately no incidents occurred between the daughters and inmates, but Ella was leery of living so close to Independence's prisoners. She was sure that as the girls got older, it was just a matter of time before something bad would happen.

Sis, like her mother, intensely disliked the jail and considered it a social stigma. No doubt she heard snide remarks from her classmates at school. Residing in the town's jail left an emotional scar on Sis for the rest of her life. She seldom mentioned the fact that the family had once lived in the jail, nor would she allow her sisters to mention it in her presence.[56] Helen, however, recalled that she and her twin, Louise, thought of the jail as just another place to play. The prisoners were mostly somewhere else and not considered a threat.

In contrast, Charlie never showed any ill effects of living in the jail. Sometimes he was with his grandmother. At other times he was doing chores such as "bringing in wood, starting the fire, taking out ashes, cleaning the kerosene lamp globes, or beating rugs." The fact that the prisoner gave him a knife suggests that Charlie got closer to the inmates than his sisters did. Of course, he understood the social stigma of living in the jail. Later in life, he would petulantly call the twins "the jail birds" because they were born in the jail building. To Charlie the jail was simply home, not only for his family but also for their two beloved dogs, Mack and Slicky.

During JB and Ella's eight years living at the jail, several things occurred that signaled to them it was time to move on. On one occasion, JB came to Ella carrying a suspicious-looking bag full of new children's shoes and asked her to have their three girls try them on to see which ones fit. Ella reluctantly took the bag and found the girls. A little while later, she returned the bag to JB and told him, "none of them fit." Church-going Ella wasn't about to have any of her girls wearing shoes stolen by some inmate.[57] In addition, Ella was worried that as Charlie grew older, the prisoners might become an influence. Shortly before the family left the jail, Helen overheard a conversation between her mother and father: "Charlie (now 11 years old) is noticing more now; we must get away soon," followed by, "Yes, Mother, I know, I know. If only we could get enough money together to explore that lode in Colorado."[58]

All evidence suggests that the Rosses had performed their duties at the jail very well, but they were ready to leave. JB and Ella wanted to move on, Ella for the sake of her children and JB because he wanted to strike it rich ("Mama, you'll be wearing diamonds yet."[59]). JB, at age 44, wanted more for his family. Although he was good at the job (one inmate called him "the best boss I ever had"), it had become routine, and it failed to feed his adventuresome, romantic yearnings. There was also insecurity about the job since it depended on two elected officials: the town's sheriff and the Marshal. His work at the jail was always in the public eye and subject to scrutiny and criticism, something that didn't sit well with JB. Most importantly, he was looking for adventure, and he held out hope he would someday strike it rich and provide lavishly for his family. The presence of Rebecca Thomas also held him in Independence, but that, too went away upon her death. By the early winter of 1897, JB left his job as the Deputy Marshal. He had decided to return to mining. He left town before the end of March on a new trip west, where he hoped to find his fortune.[60]

5

THE KLONDIKE AND CHARLIE MEETS HARRY

(1897–1901)

The Winter of 1897

By the late winter of 1897, JB—now "Papa" to his children—had set out on a mining trip to seek his fortune in Alaska, where the Klondike Gold Rush had just begun. Meanwhile, Ella—now six months pregnant with what would be their fifth child—had moved the family and all their belongings from the jail into a large, brick rental house in town. JB's absence altered the family dynamics by leaving 11-year-old Charlie as the sole male in the house. With Papa's steady income a thing of the past, financial strain bore down on the family. Charlie felt it keenly. When he was told Mama was going to have another baby, he mournfully replied, "Poor Papa. He already has enough to support."[61]

Papa must have felt he had the freedom to chase his dream, because he knew his resourceful wife would handle whatever came the family's way. Ella had the benefit of her family's network—her half-sister, Sarah Thomas Sweringen; her brother, Charles Thomas; several cousins; and many good friends living locally.[62] Ella's connections within the Christian Church, where she remained active, could provide additional help. JB took advantage of Ella's support network as well as her resourcefulness, organizational abilities, and common sense to chase his dream. On some level, she must have agreed with her 46-year-old husband that he had no time to lose if he was going to strike it rich.

The Family's First House

In early March 1897, JB was gone and the growing family had a new start in the spacious rental house. One cold, rainy evening in the middle of the month, just after the twins' seventh birthday, the children had dressed for bed, and the family was about to retire when they smelled smoke—the house was on fire! Much confusion followed. Mama scurried through the rooms, attempting to save what furniture and clothes she could, but to little avail. When the flames appeared and the plaster began to fall, she abandoned the house. The girls scampered out helter-skelter. Quickly, the flames grew. *Where are my children?* Mama agonized. The twins had become separated. The neighbors came to help and restrained Mama, now six months pregnant, from going back into the house, but she couldn't be consoled until all her children were found. Charlie rushed out of the burning house dressed for school with the family's dog under one arm and his schoolbooks under the other. Sis appeared outside unharmed. Charlie found Helen and asked in his matter-of-fact voice, "Where's Mama . . . and where's Louise?" In the confusion, Louise ended up at a neighbor's house, huddled behind a door, crying, "God save Mama, God save Mama." In short order, the fire reached the five cords of wood, the next winter's fuel, stacked on the back porch. Mama and the children could only watch as the house was engulfed in flames. The walls of the house collapsed, leaving a pile of embers that slowly crumbled as daylight came. Only Mama's beautiful, square Knabe piano was somehow saved, along with a few other valuable items. The local firemen, who were reportedly drunk following a St. Patrick's Day celebration, were of little help. The beautiful baby clothes that Mama had hand-stitched for the new baby were found, ruined, among the rubble, although eventually replaced by friends. Charlie's rescue of the family's dog had elevated his status to heroic in the eyes of his sisters. He had now become the man of the house. Several months later, Mama gave birth to another daughter, Virginia, whom the family dubbed "the fire baby."[63]

After the Fire—Miss Reddy's House

After the fire, Ella and her children, minus most of their belongings, soon found another house in town to rent—or at least part of one. The family rented and moved into about two-thirds of a house in town that was also the home of a "Miss Reddy." This house, forever known in the family as "Miss Reddy's House," was located on South Pleasant Street. It was "ramshackle and in need of repair" but had some iron beds and other worn furniture that, when added to "the bits of furniture left from the fire," became the makings of a home. In the eyes of the Ross children, their new home's large yard made up for the shortcomings of its interior.[64] Its wide lawn, fine maple trees, and old fruit trees attracted children of all ages who joined the eager Ross children. They played "hide-and-go-seek, give-me-a-wink, croquet, and all the new pretend games" the children made up.[65] It was a grand experience for the family to have a real yard in which to play; gone were the days of the limited flagstone steps and the jail's long platform.

The May 1897 birth of the fourth daughter, Virginia Celeste Ross—"the Fire Baby"—weighed on the family and monopolized

Mama's time and attention, the more so because Virginia had colic.[66] However, the Ross girls didn't let this dampen their spirits. During the late-summer afternoons and into the evenings, the twins would remain outside and "watch a bedroom window to see when the silhouette of Mother rocking the baby would disappear, and then go home in the hopes the baby would stay asleep."[67] But that proved to be only a minor annoyance, as the children were happy staying outside, playing with neighborhood children "of all ages."[68]

Following the first summer at Miss Reddy's house, the twins were enrolled in the first grade at the local South Side School, better known in the area as The Noland School. Charlie, too, attended that school. As the elder brother, Mama had him to escort his sisters to their "first day at school" so they would arrive on time and enter the right classroom. Although happy to be escorted by their brother, Helen recalled years later that, "Charlie thrust us in the door and bolted for his freedom in the sixth grade, above stairs."[69] Nevertheless, the twins had "a golden experience" that day. Their teacher, Miss Effie Whaley, was, to Helen, "a vision of beauty in a red satin tight-fitting blouse and a long black skirt that touched the floor and swooped gracefully between the aisle of 'double seats,' hair done high."[70] She was like so many elementary-school teachers of that era: prim, forthright, and fiercely dedicated both to her students and to her profession, following Mammy's example set decades before.

Evolving Family Alignments

As they entered elementary school, Helen and Louise remained "a collective" because they looked alike, wore the same outfits, and were with one another continuously. Over time, however, the twins began to develop different interests. Helen, like Charlie, learned to read very quickly—Louise, not as quickly or enthusiastically. Helen liked school and did well, Louise less so. Louise became stronger physically, enjoyed making things with her hands, and was more social and outgoing. "Louise learned to use her hands well, to sew, to do acrobatics"; Helen "read endless stories . . . [while] . . . Louise . . . pretended it was a bore to learn reading and spelling."[71] Like most twins, they remained competitive, though not to any unusual degree. But as their interests began to diverge, a shift in alliances within the family likewise occurred.

Helen Ross and Louise Ross at six years old. Helen is pictured on the left as viewed by the reader. Independence, MO, 1896. (Photo/Ross family collection)

Helen began gravitating toward Charlie, Louise toward Sis. Charlie had always liked to learn, to read and write, and enjoyed school (most years he had perfect attendance). He told his sisters, in exhaustive detail, various stories he'd learned in school from Greek mythology, and Helen absorbed it all. "Every new word or information Charlie brought home from school, I tried to make my own," Helen recalled years later.[72] As a child, Helen identified so closely with her brother that he became "the greatest love of which I was aware."[73]

Louise, by contrast, gravitated to the skills practiced by Sis, including sewing, baking, cooking, and helping with the household duties. Sis had learned to sew at her grandmother's knee and was taught to cook and bake by her mother. When asked, "How do you make a good cake?" Louise, later in life, said: "Never follow the recipe exactly; always add to the eggs and butter and sugar it says in the book." The family all agreed that Louise's "cake was the best." Louise also became more socially outgoing than Helen. Many times, when the twins went to a neighborhood party, Louise would step in, take over, and direct the games for the children to play, many of which she worked up herself.[74]

The Church

The family continued to attend the local Christian Church regularly. All the Rosses were members, except for JB. He was not demonstrably against religion. ("Papa never talked about God and Church at all."[75]) He did attend church, albeit rarely, when prompted by his wife. In contrast Ella taught at the Sunday school and made sure her children attended too. The curriculum was taken largely from the Golden Texts, a series of religious stories and Bible lessons popular in the late 1800s. Each Sunday afternoon, Ella would rehearse with her children the lesson she would teach the following week in Sunday school. Despite their father's indifference, the Ross children all learned the fundamentals of the Christian faith at an early age.

The Family Adjusts

With Papa mostly away from home, more responsibilities fell to Mama. Her friends commented that Ella "organized her family life well" and they observed how "the children were polite and friendly."[76] On a more fundamental level, Ella instilled in her children the family's core values: "to be well nourished, clean and sensibly dressed, and to be educated."[77]

Mama now depended on Charlie to take a leading role in the family, perhaps even more than his sisters liked. Mama held many traditional beliefs about the roles of the sexes. To her a male "was associated with being smart, intellectual, [while] femaleness with taking care of people and being kind." Mama's attitude toward Charlie, according to Helen, was "like the British Navy, he did not have even to be described; he was perfect, though even that word need not be said; it was understood and accepted."[78] Helen believed Mama put her son in that special category ("perfect") and thus never criticized him. Charlie also showed great prowess in his studies, a value that Mama held most dear. She knew that, with a good education, Charlie wouldn't have to settle for work as a jailer, a mining prospector, or a store clerk like her husband. Mama said: "It was my mother's fondest wish that he go to a great university. Mammy often predicted: 'Ella, he'll make his mark.'" Mama added to this her hope that: "He'll help us later with the younger children."[79]

Although a good son, Charlie wasn't perfect. His favorite form of exercise was taking long walks. When he was about 11 years old, he took a hike along the tracks of the Missouri Pacific Railroad and came to a trestle—something he'd been told to avoid. As he walked across the bridge, his foot slipped, and he fell through an opening in the cross ties. The fall gave him a torn and bloody lip but luckily no other injury. Mama was there when he returned home, and she immediately demanded an explanation. Put on the spot, he blurted out, "I was drinking water out of the spring and a frog bit me." That answer apparently satisfied Mama. He recalled years later it was the only lie he ever told her.[80]

By the late 1890s, the center of Independence was the Town Square. A rectangular plot, a double city block in size, it was the focal point of the community. The county's courthouse stood alone in its center. Its western side faced Kansas City, ten miles away; its eastern side faced St. Louis, 230 miles due east. The county jail sat diagonally across and just beyond the Square's northeastern corner. Shops and stores faced the Square on its north and east sides. A stretch called "up town" along the south side of the Square harbored the town's saloons and other less-than-savory establishments and could have been right out of a Western movie.

In his adolescent years, Charlie looked after his sisters and took a more protective attitude toward them, due in part to the absence of their father. He knew things about the town that his young sisters did not. He knew about "up town" in Independence with its long row of saloons, which the Ross girls were advised to avoid. Charlie also shared many things he'd learned in school with his sisters. Indirectly, this sharing helped prepare his sisters for their future schoolwork. (When the twins irritated him by hiding his books or homework, he denounced them as Trojan soldiers, and referred to himself as the Greek army.) Occasionally, he entertained them by reading classic tales, such as Aesop's fables. When they were old enough to read, he suggested books for them by notable authors such as Edgar Allan Poe and Charles Dickens.

Charlie stepped into the role of "older brother" when the circumstances warranted. The family never had the resources for travel or entertainment. For fun they would make ice cream in the basement. Charlie supplied the muscle to laboriously turn the hand crank of the manual ice-cream maker with all his sisters watching.[81] When Mama went to visit relatives or shopping in nearby Kansas City, she'd sometimes bring back a one-pound bag of chocolate drops for her children. She gave the bag to Charlie to divide equally, which he judiciously did, using his inmate-made knife. This was challenging for him because he had a sweet tooth and was eager to do it quickly.[82] The sisters watched him closely with great anticipation. Complaints were never heard, because his dividing was always fair; Mama knew she could depend on him.

1899—A New Baby and Another Home

JB began a *modus vivendi* by which he'd leave on a mining trip, and then, a few months later, return home and regroup, only to find another mining "opportunity" and depart again. This remained his pattern for many years. In 1898, Papa returned from the Klondike Gold Rush with little to show for his efforts. In February 1899, the fifth daughter—Frances Bruce Ross—was born.

Although the family, particularly the girls, enjoyed the larger yard and many neighborhood friends who came to play at Miss Reddy's house, the home on South Pleasant Street was getting cramped. On one of JB's trips home in 1899, he declared that his family had outgrown Miss Reddy's house. As told years later by his daughter Helen:

"Then one day, Papa said he couldn't stand it at Miss Reddy's any more. We needed extra room for Charlie, now too old to be with the girls; two little girls, Virginia and Frances, had added to the crowded rooms, and Miss Retty and her deaf sister, Miss Jennie, didn't like the noise. So, wonders of wonders, Papa found a house on South Main Street and bought it for $4,000 with some unexpected income from a mining venture, and we moved! Into a brand-new neighborhood where the houses were far apart. Next to us on one side was a big open pasture; on the other a lot grown up with weeds. In the yard was an old carriage house and barn approached by a built-up ramp, 'with 3 stories.' We screamed with delight, as we made our way up to the hayloft and down on the lower level to stalls. Such a play place this became for us and the neighbors! No prospect of horses or cows, we knew. Mama said it could be just for us, and every child in the neighborhood soon came to love the barn as much as we. It was wonderful for plays; the audience would sit outside and we slid the big door back and forth for a curtain. . . . We used the barn for a play house, setting up 'rooms' and special places for possessions; it was fine for 'hide and go seek' and 'Burglar,' and a good place to 'take care of the babies' in. Louise built 'pens' for them and set them up in one of the stalls, where we could teach them and still have fun. The barn as much as anything was a forerunner of the camp which later made our living."[83] There is no evidence that Charlie spent any significant time in the sisters' new barn-turned-playhouse. It became their domain; Charlie pursued other interests.

Charlie at School

Charlie loved school and always encouraged his sisters in their studies. In grade school, he suggested to his twin sisters that they learn at least one new word every day to increase their vocabulary. Later, he recommended that in high school they study Greek and Latin as he had. He explained that those languages contained valuable root words used in English. As noted earlier, Helen embraced Charlie's love of reading and writing.

Charlie Ross as a schoolboy about six years old. Independence MO, 1891. (Photo/Ross family collection)

Charlie made friends easily at school. A year before Charlie entered the second grade, a local boy who wore thick glasses and lived in another part of town began his elementary education in

Independence. This boy's family lived west of the town's Square, while Charlie lived north of it. After his initial year at the Ott School, Charlie transferred to the South Side School (also known as The Noland School).[84] One of his fellow students that year at South Side School was the bespectacled, round-face boy, who was friendly and, like Charlie, a serious student.[85] They immediately liked each other. Over time, they learned they had many common interests. These two elementary-school classmates would remain friends for the rest of their lives—that other boy was Harry Truman.[86]

Harry S. Truman as a schoolboy in Independence, MO, circa 1897. (Photo/Harry S. Truman Library)

Harry Truman

Charlie and Harry had much in common. Charlie's family attended The Christian Church, while the Trumans attended the local Presbyterian Church.[87] Both had encouraging mothers who appreciated the advantages that schools offered; both were eager and receptive students; both developed a love of reading. (By the time he graduated high school, Harry, like Charlie, had read every book in the town's public library.[88]) "In and out of class they were the closest of friends. Charley [sic] was a natural student. He loved books, and he and Harry always had their head in books. Both liked reading better than sports," wrote one observer of the two.[89] And one schoolmate, Henry Chiles, observed that Harry, like Charlie, "didn't tear around and ride fast horses like the rest of us."[90]

But they had differences, too. Charlie, a year and a half younger than Harry, was a thin, studious child; Harry was stout and wore glasses. Harry loved playing the piano, while Charlie never showed any interest in music.

Harry was the oldest son of John Anderson Truman and his wife, Martha Young Truman. His parents, who married in 1881, were both from slave-owning families who moved to western Missouri from Kentucky before the Civil War. Both his parents' families made their living as farmers, belonged to the Baptist Church, and, like most rural Missouri families, sympathized with the Confederacy during the Civil War. John Truman's family, who lived in Platte County, Missouri, just north of present-day Kansas City, took the family's few slaves to Kansas shortly before the Civil War and set them free. The Trumans remained largely untouched by the cross-border violence in the area.[91]

Harry's mother's family, who lived just south of present-day Kansas City, had a different experience during the Civil War. In

1861, on a day when Martha's father was away from home, the family's homestead was raided by the notorious Jayhawkers, Jim Lane and his Red Legs. They killed the hogs and chickens, burned the barns, tortured family members, and stole the family's silver. To add insult to injury, Union troops confiscated the Youngs' livestock and property on four different occasions. As southern sympathizers, the family was mandated by Union Order No. 11 to relocate, and their house was burned to the ground. They eventually made their way to unaffected Platte County, where they spent the duration of the Civil War.[92] (It is little wonder that Harry's grandmother, for the rest of her life, reviled Abraham Lincoln.)

Soon after their wedding on December 28, 1881, Harry's parents moved to Lamar, Missouri, a small town about 100 miles south of Kansas City, where they purchased a small farm, and John went into the business of trading livestock. The couple's first child, Harry S. Truman, was born there on May 8, 1884. The baby's name reflected a family compromise; Harry was for Martha's brother, Harrison. The letter "S" was an abbreviation for both "Solomon" (Martha's father's first name) and "Shippe" (John's father's middle name). This explains why Harry's middle name was simply the letter "S."[93] John soon saw that he could not make a living for his growing family in Lamar and they moved north to Jackson County. Sometime later, John agreed to manage the farm of Martha's aging father, Solomon Young, in Grandview, Missouri, just south of Kansas City. In 1890, at Martha's prompting, the family left her parents' farm and moved to nearby Independence, then a town of about 6,000, so that her children could get a first-class education in the school system first begun by Rebecca Thomas.[94]

Martha Truman, like Ella Ross, was better educated than her husband. Martha was an alumna of Central Female College in Lexington, Missouri, where she had studied art, music, and literature.

She was a talented amateur artist, played the piano, and enjoyed English literature, particularly the work of Alexander Pope.⁹⁵ Charlie's mother had received a similar formal education at Woodlands College, a small women's college in Independence at the corner of Waldo and Union Streets. Ella also played the piano—well enough to give lessons later in life—and carried an appreciation for art and literature.⁹⁶ Each woman strove to have her children receive the best education and cultural advantages available, and each was pleased with and supportive of the educational system of Independence.

The Racial Milieu of Independence, Missouri

Like most, if not all, of the Southern-leaning towns after the Civil War, Independence, Missouri, clung to a racially binary social order. The Ross family, firmly embedded in that community, were affected by the inherent prejudice, and that included the impressionable Ross children. In her memoir, Helen reflects on one of her earliest memories, playing on the flagstone walkway next to the town's jail. One of her brief recollections highlights the town's racial divide.

> "Occasional red and blue flagstones offered many choices in our made up games. At election times they could represent the Democrats and the 'black Republicans,' or they could be negroes and whites. Republicans and negroes were then the only minorities we knew in this Missouri town, whence our grandmother's family once had to flee to Kentucky during the only war we knew about, the Civil War."⁹⁷

The term "black Republicans" was a pejorative phrase used in that era to portray the Republicans as the party which sought to elevate Blacks at the expense of the Whites. By implication, it depicted Blacks as inferior beings, unfit for participation in the democratic process.

Helen's recollection reveals the community's systemic racial prejudices, still strong decades after the Civil War. These prejudices were an integral part of the community's milieu—and the Ross children weren't impervious to them.

In her memoirs, Helen recounts an event involving "Slicky," the family dog, who she, Louise, and Sis dressed up in a doll's pink dress and then paraded around in a baby's carriage. Slicky had acquiesced to this dubious arrangement "until he saw Sassy, a skinny little negro girl on whom we three girls had lavished all our secret, hidden hates." The dog "true to his training leapt from the carriage and chased his prey [Sassy] before she could run into Mr. Perry's livery stable."[98] The outcome of this sad episode eluded Helen's memory when she recalled it years later. ("The end of this story is gone—faded into the limbo of childish guilt."[99]) The Ross children were subjected to the community's prevailing prejudices from a very young age, about which Helen, years later, lamented: "We did not feel the smallness of our world."[100]

Nowhere in her memoirs—nor in any other family writings—did Helen or any of her siblings give any indication that their father or mother acted with prejudice. Indeed, their father, in his role as jailer, worked regularly with Black prisoners, who made up an estimated 40% of the jail's inmates.[101] Helen, who was born and resided in the jail for more than six years, recalled: "The prisoners were kindly treated as far as we knew."[102] The more trustworthy and helpful inmates were known as "trusties."

> "Trusties, mostly negroes, helped in the kitchen, scrubbed the hall floors, swept flagstones, cleaned Papa's office, but never came into our living room and bedroom. In these

pursuits, we saw them daily, called them by name. Indeed, some of them we loved and admired for some peculiar prowess. Old Alec could cut an apple in two parts in points, so that you could fit them together again and keep the apple whole until you were ready to eat it, point by point."[103]

Alec, the trustie, enjoyed a good relationship with Helen's father, his jailer. Helen quoted Alec years later as saying: "Mistah Ross is the best boss I ever had."[104] This was consistent with JB's personality. For all his shortcomings, JB maintained the reputation in town as someone who would unselfishly help a friend or struggling neighbor. Ironically it may have been his "goodness" that, according to his wife, made "him a poor competitor in the business world."[105] Although the Ross children were exposed to the town's pervasive racial divide, their parents never allowed this to metastasize into the cancer of prejudice and hatred.

6

SCHOOL IN INDEPENDENCE
(1890–1901)

The Public Schools of Independence

Ella ardently believed that a good academic education was the pathway for a better future for her children. Charlie, who had readily taken to Mammy's pre-school tutoring, thoroughly enjoyed school and took full advantage of it. His mother and grandmother held aspirations that, someday, despite the family's poor finances, he'd attend "a great university."[106] Mammy's belief in education, accepted as dogma by her daughter, instilled in the Ross family the importance of doing well in school and getting a good education.

The public schools that Charlie and Harry attended in Independence, by all accounts, had excellent teachers, as well as their share of serious students. According to Miss Tillie, one of Harry's and Charlie's favorite high-school teachers: "In those days, the students didn't come to school for extra frills of education. We didn't have frills. Every boy and girl thought seriously about what he or she would do after high-school graduation. They worked toward their careers."[107] This was made easier in an era without the distractions of radio, television, computers, or the internet. Charlie passed this focus on learning down to his sisters, who followed him in the years to come.

The teachers were predominantly single women who were paid a subsistence wage of about $40 per month.[108] Charlie's grandmother, Fannie Thomas, taught and hired many of the teachers in town and set lofty standards. Charlie's exposure to competent and effective teachers, which began at home, continued through high school. The typical teacher in Independence at that time may be pictured as conservatively attired in a long, dark dress with a pleated top, or perhaps a long-sleeved blouse with a skirt that skimmed the tops of her shoes. Her hair would have been pulled back or cut in a short, practical style. These were intelligent, conscientious ladies who took their callings seriously.

Report Cards and Tests in Elementary School

The public schools Charlie and Harry attended in the 1890s consisted of seven years of elementary education followed by three years of high school. Charlie, who entered the North Side School in the second grade, remained there through the fifth grade. The report cards and tests saved by Charlie's mother reveal a great deal about the curriculum of that time. His elementary-school report card from the school year 1895–1896 shows that Nannie B. Wallace was his teacher and that there were three terms in that academic year. No grades were recorded for work done in the first term; however, the second and third terms show the following subjects with the respective grades, all under the general heading of "SCHOLARSHIP":

Subject	Second term grades	Third term grades
Spelling	90	91
Reading	90	95
Writing	85	96
Geography	95	96
Language	92	95
G.A. [General Arithmetic]	90 1/3	95
WRIT. AR. [Written Arithmetic]	90	97
Drawing	78	80

The remainder of the report card shows that, during the two final terms, Charlie's attendance was good (Days Absent ½ and 3) as was his Deportment (90 and 93). He wasn't particularly gifted in Vocal Music (75 and 85) or in athletics (Calisthenics 80 and 80).[109]

During that 1897–1898 school year, his teacher was Miss Phelps. Two of Charlie's final examinations, which were preserved by his mother, show the rigor as well as the practicality of the curriculum. The final examination in "Grammar" was given on May 23; the next day, the final examination for "Arithmetic" was administered. Both the questions and answers for the examinations were written on simple lined paper in Charlie's handwriting, presumably because he copied the questions from the blackboard and then wrote the answers beneath the questions.

The first three of the twenty questions on the Grammar examination are emblematic of the type of questions on the exam—and reflect the thinking of a 12-year-old boy living in a southern-leaning Missouri small town:

Question 1:
Write a complex sentence containing the three forms of the adjective term.

Charlie's answer: *Vicksburg, the strong position of the Confederates, surrendered to General Grant, who had been besieging the city.*

Question 2:
Introduce an adverbial clause of manner by as. Introduce a relative clause by as.

Charlie's answers: *The slave did as he was commanded. I will give you such as you gave to me.*

Question 3:
Use a noun as an objective attribute. Use an adjective as an objective attribute.

Charlie's answers: *He compelled his slave to call him master. He polished the silverware bright.*[110]

The above answers were all graded as correct, and he went on to receive a grade of 100% on the exam, also shown by the letter "E," handwritten in at the top of the page.

Charlie took an Arithmetic Exam the following day. Like the Grammar examination, all of the questions and answers were written in Charlie's handwriting. His calculations or written explanations were written below the question, presumably so that the basis for any mistake would be apparent.

The first question simply asked: Write a negotiable promissory note.

Charlie's answer:

$350 *Independence, Mo.*
May 24, 1898

Three months after date, I promise to pay to RW. Smith, or order, three hundred and fifty dollars, for value received, with interest at 8%.

Chas. G. Ross

Some other examples from the 17 questions on this exam:

Question 4:
If Missouri 6% bonds are 16% below par, what sum must be invested to obtain an income of $960? (Analyze)
Charlie's answer: $13,440.

Question 7: A bought a bill of goods; the merchant's terms were $5400 cash or $5565 in 4 months. Which offer should he [A] accept, money being worth 9%?
Charlie's answer: The first offer is better for the buyer.

Question 9: A gardener having 6241 strawberry plants set them in rows, putting as many in a row as there were rows. How many plants did he put in a row?
Charlie's answer: 79 plants in a row.

Question 15:
How much will it cost to cement the bottom and sides of a cylindrical cistern that is 10 ft. deep and 8 ft. in diameter, at 20 cents per square yard?
Charlie's answer: $6.70208.[111]
Charlie's grade on this exam was 99%, with a letter grade of E—for "excellent"—written at the top. The one point taken off was for his mistakenly putting an extra ".1" at the end of a calculation, causing the answer to be off by $.40.

These exams show how practical and rigorous Charlie's education was in Independence, and how it was designed to prepare students for the working world.

Leaving The Noland School—1898

After graduating from seventh grade at The Noland School in the late spring of 1898, Charlie was ready to enter Independence High School in September. That summer the townspeople, like most throughout the country, followed the excitement of the Spanish-American War. The newspapers—the main sources of news—had seized upon the dramatic and mysterious sinking of the *USS Maine*, an American battleship sent to Havana Harbor to oversee the protection of American interests in Cuba. Two major newspapers, Hearst's *New York Journal* and Pulitzer's *New York World*, published a number of sensationalist—and largely inaccurate—stories about the Cuban nationalists' uprising and later the sinking of the *USS Maine*. These stories swayed public opinion against Spain and toward the Cuban nationalists, and eventually led the United States into the struggle. The United States declared war on Spain on April 25, 1898. Major events of the war such as the Battle of Manila Bay, the Rough Riders taking San Juan Hill, and the destruction of Spain's Caribbean fleet at the Battle of Santiago were publicized throughout the summer. A few months later, in August, an armistice was declared, which ended the hostilities. The Spanish-American War officially concluded in December, when both countries signed the Treaty of Paris. Charlie noted the exaggerated tone of many of the newspaper articles and experienced the impact that "the news" had on people and their everyday lives.

With his father away on "mining trips," Charlie carried his share of the household chores. He also indulged in his favorite pastime—reading. While his sisters enjoyed settling into their newly discovered barn-playhouse, Charlie sought out the companionship of the neighborhood's boys.

The Waldo Street Gang

Near Waldo Street, where the Truman family lived, there was a pond and a field where a group of local boys played games, particularly baseball. During that summer they began calling themselves The Waldo Street Gang. Tall, thin Charlie wasn't a natural athlete, and he never showed much interest in baseball. Like Harry Truman with his glasses, Charlie was more of a spectator than a participant. Some of the other members of the gang included Elmer Twyman (the son of a local physician), the three Wallace children—Frank, George, and Bess (something of a tomboy, who later became Mrs. Harry Truman)—as well as brothers Peter and Forrest Allen.

Forrest Allen was nine days younger than Charlie. When he yelled on the field, his voice sounded like a foghorn and the boys began calling him "Phog." Phog later attended the University of Kansas and played basketball there. After college, he became an osteopathic physician. However, basketball was his true love, and he returned to Kansas to become its basketball coach. His success was legendary, and he led the team to three national championships. In Forrest's honor, the University of Kansas in 1955 built a new basketball arena named Allen Fieldhouse. Four years later, in 1959, he was inducted into the Basketball Hall of Fame.

Charlie's and Harry's Adolescence

Charlie and Harry were classmates and friends throughout their school years and shared many interests. There were also marked differences. Charlie was tall and thin, and eventually grew to 6' 2"; Harry was short and more solidly built, at 5' 8". Charlie, at that point in his life, was less self-assured than Harry. Julia Rice, a high-school classmate, noted "when Harry [later in life] went before the microphone to accept the vice-presidential nomination, the announcer described him as squaring his shoulders and stepping up to speak." She went on to note:

> "It was so characteristic of the way he used to recite in his classes. He always got clear out of his seat and squared his shoulders before reciting. Now, Charlie Ross was different. He could never recite without hanging onto his desk, and the teachers used to remind him that the 'desk couldn't get away.'"[112]

Although accepted by his peers, Charlie received his share of teasing. Throughout his grade-school years, he had been the son of the local jailer and, to make it worse, his family had lived in the jail building. *(Charlie, how was the prison food this morning? Charlie, what time do you get locked up at night?)* His love of reading and his academic success surely didn't go unnoticed. *(Charlie, what do bookworms eat anyway? Charlie, your nose is going to fall off if you don't take it out of those books!)* Perhaps worse than such barbs, was the one he often got that was related to his name: *Are you the long-lost Charley Ross?* During this period, the name "Charley Ross" was well-known—and not in a good way.

Before the kidnapping of the Lindbergh baby in 1932, the most notorious kidnapping receiving national attention was that of Charley Ross. This sensational crime occurred in a suburb of Philadelphia on July 1, 1874. Two boys, Charley and Walter Ross, ages four and six, a few days before, had been given some candy by two men they didn't know. On the day of the kidnapping, the men again approached the boys, who were playing in front of their home, and told them to climb into their buggy with the promise to buy them firecrackers if they went along. The boys boarded the buggy, which drove off toward the city of Philadelphia. As the buggy drove farther away, Charley said he wanted to go back home and began to cry. The men stopped in front of a store and gave Walter twenty-five-cents to go in and buy some firecrackers. While Walter was in the store, the men and Charley drove away. Charley was never seen again. Various ransom notes were received from purported kidnappers, and the Pinkerton Detective Agency became involved. Eventually a possible suspect was apprehended, but there wasn't evidence to convict him. The story made national news and became a warning to parents throughout the country. Over the next several decades, dozens of would-be Charley Rosses appeared, but none was proven to be the kidnapped boy. The dramatic case spawned such phrases as "Don't take candy from strangers!" The Charley Ross Project was a missing-persons list that was named after him. So, it isn't surprising that Charlie Ross got the question: "Are you the long-lost Charley Ross?" In later years, my grandfather said that, as a boy, he often wished his parents had given him a different first name.

Independence High School

In September 1898, Charlie entered high school at age 12; he would be 13 that November. Independence High School's academic program lasted three years; each school year was divided into four quarters of nine weeks each. During the three years Charlie and Harry attended the high school, "Professor" William Lewis Collins Palmer (called W. L. C. Palmer) served as its principal. Professor

Palmer was a highly regarded teacher and administrator. He not only led the school's first-rate faculty, but he also taught many of the courses, including Greek and Zoology. The other teachers were women, all well-educated, dedicated, and unmarried. Ms. Amanda Ardelia Hardin, a teacher who taught at the high school, had to discontinue teaching in 1900, when she married Professor Palmer "because there was a rule against married teachers in the school."[113]

The high school's curriculum was divided into six "branches of study":

| Mathematics | Civics & History | Latin |
| Science | English | Greek |

In his first year (1898–1899), Charlie studied Latin (Ms. A. A. Hardin), English (Matilda C. Brown), and Zoology (W. L. C. Palmer); he took one Mathematics and one Civics & History subject as well. In his second year (1899–1900), he took Algebra during the first two quarters and completed the Mathematics curriculum that year by taking Inventional Geometry—an introductory geometry course based on the 1876 book written by mathematics teacher William George Spencer. In the second year he took English History, Rhetoric, Caesar's Gallic Wars, and Greek Exercises. In his final year (1900–1901), Charlie took Geometry (most likely plane and solid) from Ms. Jennie McDonald; Greek (most likely Xenophon's *Anabasis*) from Professor Palmer; English Literature from Ms. Matilda Brown; Physics from Professor Palmer; and Latin (Cicero) from Berta Entrekin. Unfortunately, the school's records were destroyed by fire, and we don't know Harry Truman's high school coursework. Harry undoubtedly took most, if not all, of the same courses as Charlie. Two aspects of Charlie's performance in high school stand out from these report cards. First, all of Charlie's grades were between 95 and 100%, except for Inventional Geometry, where his two quarterly grades were 89% and 90%. Second, his attendance was perfect; he never missed a day of classes during his high-school years. His mother was proud of his high-school achievements, and she kept his report cards among her personal papers until her death in 1925.

Final Days of High School—1901

One of Charlie's and Harry's favorite high-school teachers was Matilda Brown—"Miss Tillie" to those who knew her. She schooled the students in history, but her *forte* was English, which she taught each year. Her younger brother, James Terrell Brown, was also in the Class of 1901. Teaching was Miss Tillie's calling. When she entered her classroom each day, she reminded herself: "Put off thy shoes from thy feet, for the spot on which thou standest is hallowed ground."[114] Some of her students may have snickered at her enthusiasm. But her dedicated efforts bore fruit because "she was a genius at making us appreciate good literature," Harry would say years later.[115]

Charlie, who occasionally wrote poems, held Miss Tillie in the highest regard. On behalf of the Class of 1901, he wrote her the following:

TO MISS TILLIE

Thou will be crowned with garlands fresh and bright,
With radiance shining, not in jewels seen,
And every leaf in warmth of placid green
Telling a soul by thee reclaimed from night
To dwell in realms of pure, enabling light—
A shade of what is thine. On thee we lean
For kindly help, to so ourselves demean

> That we may stand not all unworthy in thy sight
> Thou'st taught us now at Shakespeare's shrine to kneel,
> Milton's grandeur to revere, to Scott's sweet lay
> And wild, with thrilling pulse our ears to bend,
> The magic spell of Tennyson's song to feel,
> But more than all—be it spoken while it may,
> Thou'st taught us how to honor thee, our friend!
>
> Chas. G. Ross[116]

This handwritten tribute, dated May 21, 1901, was cherished by Miss Tillie long after her retirement from teaching in 1920.

The Class of 1901 wanted to make its mark on Independence High School, which had recently settled into its permanent home in a new building. The building itself gave the Class some impetus—the stained-glass window over the front door proclaimed the Latin phrase *Juventus Spes Mundi* ("Youth, the hope of the World"). The Class decided to publish its own book—today known as an "annual" or "yearbook"—to leave something of itself behind for future classes. The name "The Gleam" was chosen to reflect the Class's hope, optimism, and sense of duty. "The Gleam" came from Alfred, Lord Tennyson's Idyllic poem, *Merlin and the Gleam*, the ninth and last and most emblematic stanza of which includes the following:

> Launch your vessel,
> And crowd your canvas,
> And, ere it vanishes,
> Over the margin,
> After it, follow it,
> Follow The Gleam.

According to Miss Tillie, those "boys and girls loved *Merlin and the Gleam*." She admitted that she "always tried to impress them with the idea to go on, follow on, not be stopped but keep eternal progress." The yearbook's name, taken from the material she taught, remained a source of pride with her. It had a cover that showed Lynette riding into the distance followed by Gareth, the knight, the youngest of King Arthur's nephews. Little wonder that so many in that class moved beyond small-town Independence, Missouri, to make their mark—following the Gleam as they saw it.[117]

Writing, editing, proofing, and finally publishing *The Gleam* kept Charlie, Harry, and the other staff members busy in their final year of high school. Charlie enjoyed the creative challenge of writing and editing. This also gave him an opportunity to use his literary capabilities to make a mark, to delight his teachers and parents, and to leave something for the school. It was a fitting ending to his distinguished high school career.

By April, when the work on *The Gleam* was mostly complete, Charlie, Harry, and another classmate, Elmer Twyman, all lovers of Latin and Roman history, got together and whittled a wooden model of the bridge that Julius Caesar had built over the Rhine to pursue his northern conquests. The boys extrapolated the dimensions of the bridge from Caesar's *Commentaries*. Given that these boys, like most boys of the day, carried small pocket knives—useful for practical things such as nibbing a quill, sharpening a pencil, or cutting string—the act of whittling was a normal exercise, and all they needed were a few sturdy branches of wood to get started. It is unknown whether this effort ever was completed (most likely not), but it kept them harmlessly busy waiting for the summer to begin. (Fortunately for the Romans, Caesar was more successful in completing the actual bridge.)[118]

Independence High School senior class picture. Charlie Ross is on the first row, farthest left. Harry Truman is on the back row 4th from the left. Independence, MO, 1901. (Photo/Harry S. Truman Library)

The photograph of the Class of 1901 shows a clean-cut, well-dressed group of boys and girls lined in rows on the school's steps. All are dressed up for the day and, in those days of segregation, all were white. Charlie, one of the taller boys at more than six feet, somehow got placed in the front row, sitting on the grass just off the steps. He appears to be bemused, perhaps because the young man behind him has his hand draped over Charlie's right shoulder. Harry Truman, several inches shorter, stands in the back row with a serious look on his face. (He uncharacteristically removed his glasses for this picture.) In the second row on the far right on the steps sits Bess Wallace—the future Mrs. Harry S. Truman—with a happy, even perky, smile. It's an interesting, yet unexceptional photograph of the period, except for one unidentified lad sitting in the middle of the second row, surrounded by girls, wearing a derby hat and a feigned look of seriousness on his impish face.

Graduation Day

On Thursday, May 30, 1901, the Thirteenth Annual Commencement of Independence High School was held at 8:00 p.m. in its auditorium. The printed program was saved by Charlie's mother. It lists the names of the 11 boys and 30 girls who graduated in the class. In its Honor Roll section, the program listed Mr. Charles Griffith Ross as First in Scholarship because he had the highest grades in the class. Other students—Miss Laura M. Kingsbury, William Lloyd Garrett, and Mary B. Anderson—also received honors, and Miss Mary C. Taylor was the "Elected Valedictorian." The Program featured instrumental pieces and readings by members of the class. Charlie gave an oration about William Shakespeare. Charlie's sister, Helen, who adored him, had helped him practice his speech. That evening, she sat in the audience and recited under her breath the exact words she'd heard him practice so diligently.[119]

Toward the end of the evening, Miss Tillie Brown, in appreciation of Charlie's fine performance in her classes, his work on *The Gleam*, and the poem he penned in her honor, went on the stage and kissed Charlie squarely on the cheek. Harry Truman, seeing this and standing nearby, said to Miss Tillie, "Don't I get one, too?" Without hesitation, she responded, "Not until you've done something to deserve it!" These were words that Harry never forgot.[120]

The Next Step after Graduation

In May 1901, the month they graduated, Harry turned 17 years old. Charlie, then 15 years old, wouldn't turn 16 for another five months. Members of the Class of 1901, like high-school graduates before and since, went in separate directions. Harry, whose father had suffered serious financial reverses, chose to stay close to home, continuing his piano lessons, attending Spalding's Commercial College in nearby Kansas City, and eventually helping in the family business. Another classmate, Elmer Twyman, son of the town's physician, was headed to the University of Missouri in Columbia, where he would eventually follow in his father's footsteps and study medicine. Charlie wanted to attend college, but the family's lack of money stood in the way of making him the first Ross to receive a higher education. Plus, there was another barrier: his father had other ideas.

Charlie was the oldest in his family, and, at the time of his graduation, he had five sisters, two of whom were younger than five years old. JB earned no steady income and resisted spending any more money than necessary. He thought it was time for Charlie to "go to work" and help support the family.

"But what would he do?" decried Charlie's mother, "Clerk in a store? My brother did that. No, it was my mother's fondest wish that he go to a great university. She used to say, 'Ella, he'll make his mark.'"

Her husband countered with the idea that there were other children who needed to be clothed, fed, and educated. How was Charlie going to contribute to the family?

With a sigh, Charlie's mother replied, "He'll help us later with the other children."[121]

7

A GIRL CAN BE SMART

Homelife Changes in Independence

On the day Charlie graduated from Independence High School, no one knew *if*—not to mention *where*—he would go to college. Mama remained determined that Charlie should go, despite JB's opposition.

She had a strong supporter in the principal of Independence High School, "Professor" W. L. C. Palmer. He graduated from the University of Georgia in 1879 and pursued a career in education. He moved to Kansas City in 1888 as a public educator and was eventually assigned the position of principal of Independence High School in the early 1890s. Prof. Palmer made contacts at the University of Missouri and, over time, convinced the admissions group that the quality of education at Independence High School was of a very high caliber. So, when Charlie Ross, the top-ranked student from its Class of 1901, applied, his application was accepted without any further examination requirement. The University even provided a modest scholarship, which was enough to cover Charlie's initial fees. Fortunately, the tuition at the University was modest—"almost free"—for in-state students.[122] Eventually, Ella mysteriously found more funds when she "called in" a previously unknown loan of $300, to get the balance of the money for Charlie to go, and made her dream a reality.[123] When the University of Missouri, located about 100 miles east of Independence in Columbia, began its fall semester in 1901, Charlie Ross was in the freshman class.

Charlie's leaving for college changed the dynamics in the Ross household. Papa was usually away on his "mining trips," and they were now without Charlie. The household was now exclusively female. This didn't lead to any noticeable problems because the resourceful Ross women quickly adjusted and carried on their lives much as usual. The girls continued to grow up, although their lack of financial resources limited the things they could do.

The family wasn't destitute, but, in their situation, every penny counted. The girls' clothes were homemade because they couldn't afford to purchase many "store-bought" items. Mama earned some money giving piano lessons, although these earnings were little more than supplemental. Their groceries were mostly purchased on credit from the local grocer, and, upon JB's return from his mining trips, he would settle the accounts, only to start the process over again with his next trip. The Ross women became very proficient at saving and reusing things, a habit that remained with them for the rest of their lives. (When Helen died decades later, she left among her possessions what appeared to be a softball-sized ball of yarn, labeled "pieces of string too short to use."[124]) There was no money for dance lessons, music lessons, or party dresses. They couldn't have any fancy parties, or the finer things enjoyed by well-to-do young women in town.[125] The girls stayed close to home and kept busy with chores, taking care of one another, and, for amusement, creating their own games and activities. It was a tight-knit family. They continued to attend church and were expected to do well in school.

Mama's "Fall Crop"

The relationship between Mama and Papa remained steady and positive, albeit unconventional. There's no record of any note of discord between them. Mama didn't protest, at least not outwardly, about JB's mining "career." Mama well knew that JB was not a good businessman. His kindness, ability to fix things, positive and outgoing personality, and gift for storytelling made him well-liked. But his lack of good business sense held him back and limited his ability to provide. Later in her life, his daughter, Helen, said about her father, "Dad was good, we were sure, but we did not know for a long time that his kindness made him a poor competitor in a business world."[126] His wife mostly focused on JB's kindness and "maleness" and gave him a pass for his lack of financial success. Things were simply the way they were, and they both seemed satisfied with their arrangement—and it certainly didn't get in the way of their active sex life.

During this period there came what Mama called her "fall crop" of children. They were born after, what one would expect, were her normal childbearing years. The fall crop began with Virginia (the "fire baby"), born just after Mama's forty-first birthday in May 1897. She was followed by Frances Bruce Ross in 1899. Just after Mama's forty-eighth birthday in 1902, her sixth and last daughter was born and named James Bruce Ross (the unusual name to be explained shortly).[127] Clearly, Mama and Papa engaged in more than just casual affection when he returned from his mining trips. JB would typically go off in the spring to some remote place in the West where he thought there was opportunity. He would remain for months until the job was finished, or the weather turned bad; then he'd return home. As Papa departed for these long absences, usually six to nine months at a time, he would often leave Ella with a child in the womb. Upon his return, he would learn that the family had grown.

As the family story is told, just prior to the birth of the final baby—Papa (and everyone else) foresaw that this would be their final child. JB declared, "I don't care what the baby is—it will be named 'James Bruce Ross'!" Even though the child was born a girl, he got his wish. (There was no "junior" attached to her name, likely

James Bruce Ross, the sixth and last Ross daughter. She was given the name James Bruce by her father and was always referred to as J.B. by her family and friends. Independence, MO, 1904.
(Photo/Ross family collection)

because she was female.) This, of course, led to confusion—*Which, James Bruce Ross are you referring to?* The family tried to resolve this by calling her "Jamie," a nickname that stuck until she was in her teens. Later she dropped that nickname and simply went by the initials "J.B.," just as her father had. In the end, Papa got the namesake he wanted, even though the name proved chronically awkward for its recipient.[128] [From this point on, the author refers to the daughter as J.B.]

Mama, while very efficient and organized, wasn't invincible. After Virginia's birth, she began to have headaches which dogged her for years. At one point, she went to a local doctor, who recommended that she have an operation on the bridge of her nose. JB refused to allow it because he didn't believe it would work—and the medical fee was too high. So, Mama just lived with the pain. Eventually the headaches went away as the babies got older.[129]

Papa had his own health concerns. About the time he resigned as the county's jailer, he began to have trouble with his eyes. This was recorded by Helen in her memoirs:

> "Something else Mother hid from us was Dad's failing eyesight, which was disturbing her even when he left the jail. Later knowledge made me think this was Glaucoma, but to us children, it was simply, and sadly, "poor eyesight." Mother read the papers to him, we might have observed, and helped him with the blueprints he would bring home from the mining trips. Slowly it seeped into our unwilling consciousness that Dad really did not see well. One day he asked me to stand in a certain place and made the same request some half year later after a long trip, this time to Mexico to look at silver mines. And then, I understood, though still a little schoolgirl, that Dad was measuring his sight."[130]

Despite his failing sight, the family didn't stand in the way of his mining trips, probably because they were so important to him.

Sis' Role

Due largely to birth order, Sis held a unique role within the family. She was the second of the seven Ross children. Charlie, the eldest and only male child, was two years older and received special treatment. Although Sis and Charlie loved and respected each other, they were never especially close. Sis was followed by the twins who were three years younger. Sis was expected to assume care-taker responsibility for her twin sisters. This expectation continued when the fall crop of girls followed, much later. Although she got along well enough with her siblings, Sis was something of an island unto herself. She was stationed between her older brother and her younger sisters, and, in a sense, between her mother and her younger sisters as well.

Sis followed Charlie in school and graduated from Independence High School in 1904. While Charlie was a star student and teacher favorite, Sis was less of a standout. Although her grades have been lost to history, she was reputedly a good student and was awarded the prize for the "best essay" at graduation.[131] Sis also contributed to *The Gleam*, and, in her senior year, she became its copy editor.

It wasn't in the cards for Sis to go to college. However, after high-school graduation, she was rewarded with a train trip to Tennessee to visit one of her father's sisters, Aunt Lou. She visited the old Ross plantation near Henderson, Tennessee, then in a shabby state. She was also introduced to some of her Tennessee relatives, who, although friendly, referred to her as a "Yankee." Sis sensed they still held a grudge against her mother for keeping JB from returning to Tennessee after the marriage.[132]

The visit was interesting but short, and, afterwards, Sis returned to Independence to spend the next decade supporting Mama and the rest of the sisters. Given the family's circumstances, Sis' time and talents were vitally needed. She was Mama's main support with all the housework—sewing, cooking, shopping, cleaning—and she continued to care for her younger sisters, who largely underappreciated her efforts.[133] Helen recalled that, during this period, Sis "learned to make bread, she was the best cake baker in the neighborhood . . . [and] . . . she got all the younger children off to school."[134] Sis developed a lifelong interest in food, particularly its nutritional value, and she became adept at caring for the needs of children.[135] Her efforts helped keep her cash-strapped family together—and her brother and sisters in school—and she made these sacrifices at the expense of her own education.

In terms of personality and perspective, Sis inherited much from Grandmother Thomas. From her earliest days, Sis would spend a lot of time upstairs in the jail with Mammy sewing and learning. Sis absorbed some of her grandmother's personality from these experiences. To her younger sisters, she was the family's conscience. Her sister Helen recalled: "She always seemed to know what we should do and when. We did not question why. This knowing came from upstairs, where Grandmother was. Sis had a special communication, we felt, with right and wrong."[136] Sis' opinion about propriety was so highly regarded that all the children accepted it. "Even Charlie strove for Sis' traditional approval."[137]

Perhaps it was Mammy's influence that enabled Sis to willingly sacrifice years of her life for her family. This selflessness provided much-needed support for her mother and sisters. It also served as the catalyst that allowed others in the family to succeed. As explained by Helen years later:

"Sis must have taken into her marrow much of Mammy's surety of right and propriety: in behavior as well as grammar. The essential importance, the imperative of learning, of education, surely reached her, too. I wonder how Mammy had she lived, would have influenced Sis' conflict, which became the family's: help with the present demands of seven children, a submergence of self within the group, or aggressive pursuit of the family ambition: to get a good education. I was chosen, not Sis, for the "education" when High School was finished."[138]

Whether Sis made her choice cheerfully or otherwise is unknown, but, in the broader sense, that is not important. Through her personal sacrifice, she helped her family during these critical child-rearing years when she was direly needed. Her service helped her family in the short run and strengthened its fabric for years to come.

The Twins' Path Diverges

Helen and Louise were 11 years old in 1901 when Charlie left for the University of Missouri. By then, the family had settled into their own home at 1001 South Main Street. Sis mostly stayed close to the house and usually didn't participate in the events staged by her younger sisters; she enjoyed reading alone.[139] Helen and Louise, who, particularly in the summer, were responsible for entertaining their younger sisters, created their own entertainment. As told by Helen:

"The summers in the South Main Street house found us usually in the pasture. Mama would give us lunch in a basket and a bottle for the baby, and with our improvised carts and baby carriages, invented by Louise, who was always putting old things together in the barn, we transported the babies and the dog to our favorite place to play, a knoll in the pasture crowned by a beautiful, wide-spreading maple tree with wide-spread branches, just right to climb. In the midst of my first geography book, we sought names for our shrine, and the tree became Buddha. Sometimes Louise and I took the role of Buddha, too; we invented rites and demanded obeisance of all the younger neighbor children who loved our authoritative play. If they did not conform, we mildly "tortured" them behind the sumac bushes, pinching and tickling or pretending we would do "something terrible"; though tearfully they often ran home, they invariably reappeared. Higher and higher limbs of Buddha beckoned us, and the little band of faithful below would scream with delight. Mama's "sewing window" was just down the slope and always in her range of view."[140]

Helen's attitude toward education became more firm, more serious as time went on. These summer and other experiences planted the seeds in Helen's mind that, someday, she would be a teacher, like her Grandmother Thomas and, eventually, operate a school of her own. She expressed it years later:

"But the mantle of Mammy first fell on me. Mama thought I should be a teacher, that I should have "the education" after Charlie. Whether she spoke this out loud to us, I do not recall; only that I knew from those South Main Street days that I would "teach school" and inside, I knew I would have a school of my own. The bean patch in which this resolve was made belonged to the South Main Street house."[141]

Helen performed well in school, where she remained a serious student at the top of her class. In contrast, Louise was more outgoing and less serious about school. She enjoyed socializing and developed more traditional skills like sewing and baking. The divergence increased when Louse, in her early teens, developed "eye problems" like her father. As recalled by Helen:

> "Louise had been taken out of school because of an eye difficulty the local doctor called "grandulated eyelids" and treated with a brutal scrubbing that made her cry and look sad, and Papa said he couldn't stand it any longer and took her to a doctor "in the city" [Kansas City] who advertised a "wild-medicine cure," and said she should come for treatment every day. The cost of the car fare was even a strain then and Mama thought she should not go alone, and asked Cousin Emma to go with her. Louise rebelled, with my cheers, and came home each day with tales of her experiences on the "electric car" and in the city, while my envy seethed, in spite of the advantage of being in school. "The twinship now had to undergo a new shift. I was "getting ahead" in school."[142]

Although clearly exacerbated by Louise's eye difficulties, the divergence of the twins also progressed along a more natural path. As reflected upon years later by Helen:

> "Dominance in even so small a social unit as twinship must be gained, and twins learn to find their own spheres of superiority. I learned quickly to read, and read endless stories to Louise who pretended it was a bore to learn

reading and spelling. Louise learned to use her hands well, to sew, to draw, to do acrobatics, and I admired her for these accomplishments. We did not transgress on these individual domains, but built them up in each other. As we went together to a "party" and approached the house of the celebrating friend, Louise would always secretly whisper, sometimes adding a pinch, "Remember you do the introducing, I'll tell them what to play." And she did, with imaginative games I often wondered how she conjured up. Always with a new twist to an old favorite, she would make the afternoon successful . . ."[143]

Louise had to drop out of school for two years while she got her eye difficulties under control. During this period "Louise's defensive scorn of books increased" and, in these days before radio and television, Helen ended up on occasion reading to her for entertainment such popular pieces as Sherlock Holmes stories.[144] The twins, despite their divergent paths, remained close, but they didn't do as much together as they once had. In 1907, Helen graduated from Independence High School, where she, like Charlie, was editor of *The Gleam* and graduated with the highest marks in her class.[145] After that she immediately went to college at the University of Missouri, where her brother had already blazed a trail. Louise graduated from Independence High School, but two years later, as a member of the Class of 1909. She greatly enjoyed her final high school years where she "had fun" and got by academically largely on her family's reputation.[146] After high school, Louise remained at home for a few months until she was cajoled into traveling to Arizona to help take care of her nearly blind father on one of his mining ventures.

Mama's Talent

Mama's hands were full following the birth of "Jamie" in 1902. Maintaining a large household was difficult in that era—the buying, preparing and cooking of food; the washing, ironing, and mending of clothes; the bathing, organizing, and caring for the children of different ages—all without the help of modern-day conveniences. Not only was Mama in charge of it all, but, during this period, Mama had a decreasing amount of money to spend.[147] And to make matters worse, Mama was often tired "and was subject to terrific headaches which had started even at the jail." These headaches were later (after 1900) accompanied by "chills and nausea."[148] Mama was under extreme pressure to maintain the household, and she also experienced considerable physical pain.

One of Mama's key talents, though, was that she was "organized." She assigned chores and responsibilities to all her children. She got Sis to stay home after her high-school graduation and help out. The birth of her last child in 1902 was particularly difficult, and she quickly assigned Helen to take over the baby's care. Fortunately, Helen had become very attached to the baby and relished this new responsibility. In Helen's words:

> "What powers [of] capitulation an adolescent of thirteen has: this was my child at once and immediately I took over with such energy and assurance of proprietorship it soon came not to be questioned. 'Helen will take care of the baby,' Mother would say to Sis and Louise, and they in turn each adopted one of the others, so that soon there were three big girls looking after three little ones, and the little ones accepted this as if it had been ordered. Louise

put Virginia to bed. Sis took over Frances, and I basked in the baby's appreciation of my ministrations."[149]

Thus, in a single maneuver, Mama gave each of the older girls responsibility for one of the younger sisters. Thereafter, in the family, they were known as "charges"—baby Jamie became Helen's charge, Virginia became Louise's charge, and Frances became Sis' charge. Each older girl now had almost complete responsibility for making sure that their charge was bathed, had clean clothes, got to bed on time, did her chores, etc. Helen describes her relationship to Jamie ("the baby") as follows:

"She was mine. Mama was willing indeed to give over much of the care [of] this, her ninth child, and often said to me, "Time to take your baby out," or "Your baby is calling you." And in the night would wake me up to warm the bottle and give it to the baby."

But having Helen, at age 13, taking over the responsibility for an infant was not without its pitfalls. As recounted by Helen:

"One night when I was deep in sleep, Mama patted me gently to say the baby is fretting for her bottle and sleepily I crept out to the kitchen but forgot to empty the soda water Mama left in the bottles 'to keep them sweet.' But the baby knew and tossed the bottle out of her crib, improvised from an old baby carriage, onto the iron wheels and into smithereens. Already asleep again, I was gently aroused by Mama, only to discover there were no more ready bottles at all. . . . What to do? Mama said go to the cellar and find a suitable bottle. Then it had to be washed, and condensed milk prepared while the baby protested. In the morning, I heard Mama telling the story to a neighbor, laughing that I found a bottle of Lydia Pinkham's Vegetable Compound, of which Mama 'took' many bottles. Lydia Pinkham was associated with having babies in my fantasy, and I could not think the night's episode very funny."[150]

Helen's linking Lydia Pinkham's Vegetable Compound with having babies wasn't just her fantasy; the compound's advertising tagline was: "There's a baby in every bottle." Mama, who generally eschewed drinking and dancing, regularly took Lydia Pinkham's Vegetable Compound. Its original recipe, as first marketed in 1875, contained 20% alcohol, a level Mrs. Pinkham claimed was needed to preserve the mixture of the herbs before bottling. This "herbal medicine" was sold as a "woman's tonic" and a remedy for menstrual and menopausal problems. Its aggressive marketing soon led to it being memorialized in a variety of drinking songs, such as "Lily the Pink," which included ribald fantasies about what this "woman's tonic" might indeed cure.[151]

These sisterly ties became lasting relationships. The younger girls received support from the older girls for years to come. For example, Helen paid for Jamie's college and university education. On occasion, the younger charge would help out her older sister. Virginia's family put up Louise's son so he could attend college during the Great Depression. Mama created these pairings to solve the immediate problem of raising her young family; she probably couldn't have guessed that the bonds would last decades.

Another Family Value Is Born

As previously mentioned, the standards instilled by Ella in her children—"to be well nourished, clean and sensibly dressed, and to be educated"[152]—stood as core values for the family. From these, the sisters never wavered, even as the family's financial circumstances tightened. Beyond these, it is also clear that they did without things that would have been considered as "advantages" such as dance or music lessons, store-bought clothes (rather than making their own), and having a family carriage as a means of transportation.[153] These, the family simply couldn't afford.

While always clean and properly dressed, the Ross sisters weren't the prettiest girls in town (a fact mentioned by Helen in her memoirs[154]). At this time in Independence, a town with vestiges of the Deep South, the conventional norm was for a girl to get married after her high school education was completed, rather than go to college. It was best that she not only be physically attractive but also that she have other advantages to help attract a future husband. In the Ross family, which was just getting by financially, this was a challenging situation.

The family's shortcomings were brought into high relief by a visit from Ella's sister-in-law, Della Thomas, whom the children knew as their Aunt Della. Ella's only brother, Charles Thomas, a successful businessman who lived in nearby Kansas City, was Ella's closest family member, one whom she very much loved and respected. His wife, Della, however, was decidedly not a family favorite, but rather a to-be-tolerated relative who from time to time dropped by the Ross home for a visit. One such visit unexpectedly changed the Ross girls' perception of their future and added to family lore. As told by Helen, this is what happened:

> "'So many girls to marry off,' Aunt D. sighed one day. This made mild Mama answer back, "And there are other things for girls to do nowadays, Della, besides marry. They can go to college and teach school," though Mama, I knew, was wondering how college could be managed.

"'I'll see that my boys marry money,' was another pricking remark. How would anybody want us, if money were necessary? And I thought we were all far from pretty. When Mama questioned her assurance, Aunt Della proudly replied. 'I shall expose them only to girls whose fathers are rich.' If a girl could not be beautiful or rich, what could she be? Mama had often given the answer, 'She could be smart.' So, a new value was born. To Aunt Della, I owe much."[155]

Aunt Della's visit surfaced another, formerly latent, family value: A girl can be smart—and, albeit implicitly, make it on her own. Eventually "being smart" became one of the Ross girls' "advantages." To do well in school, to solve problems independently, to forge her own way (without the necessity of a husband), and to find her own way in the world. This is what Mama wanted for her girls to know and to do, and Aunt Della had forced her to articulate it. This value was ingrained in the Ross girls as they were growing up in Independence—and it continued for future Ross generations to come. So, thank you, Aunt Della!

8

CHARLIE'S COLLEGE YEARS
(1901–1905)

A Great University

Ella was delighted when Charlie was accepted into her state's flagship institution, the University of Missouri. Founded in 1839, the University stands as the oldest university in those states carved from the Louisiana Purchase. A particular advantage was its location—only about 100 miles east of Independence—and its accessibility by train and ground transportation. But most of all, it was affordable. Charlie's modest scholarship, plus the money his mother scraped together, was enough. Charlie only needed money for out-of-pocket expenses, which he managed to obtain by getting part-time work at the University.[156] After years of hoping and praying, Ella's wish had come true: her son was going to get a college degree from a great university.

Charlie's excitement and anticipation more than matched his mother's joy. He was now able to continue his education away from his female-dominated home. He could make new friends—a test for his natural shyness—and be forced to adjust to a new setting without the familiar comforts of home. He was eager to take this big step. He yearned for a fulfilling life, to "follow the Gleam," his own gleam, which went reaching far beyond that of the store clerk his father thought he should be.

Freshman Year

When Charlie arrived at the University in September 1901, he was only 15 years old, two months shy of his 16th birthday.[157] At this impressionable age, the university must have been overwhelming. There was the imposing main building, the new Academic Hall, which stood at the south end of the University's main quadrangle.[158] (It was later named Jesse Hall in honor of Richard H. Jesse, the University's dynamic president during Charlie's undergraduate years). Walking north from Academic Hall through the large quadrangle toward the town of Columbia, Charlie saw six Ionic columns that stood by themselves. These pillars, then a bit of a curiosity, were a stark reminder of the devastating fire that nine years earlier had destroyed the first Academic Building, of which they were a part. Over time, they became a favorite symbol and testament to the resilience of the University.[159] Still, Charlie was confident he would find his place among the 1,300 students he saw scurrying about and making ready for the academic year.

Charlie enrolled in the Academic Department, which awarded Bachelor of Arts degrees to undergraduates. Its curriculum consisted of the traditional academic subjects such as mathematics, languages, history, and philosophy. Thanks to his work with Professor Palmer, the University gave him a full year's credit for his high school's Greek courses.[160] Charlie took the standard freshman courses in English, Latin, and German as well as courses in history and math. In addition, he took (and passed) the pass-fail physical-education course. His high-school training served him well—his marks for the year ranged from 90 to 98. Although academically talented, he didn't stand out as an "egghead." Instead, he was just one among many well-prepared students who were interested in learning and in getting ahead in the world. He made new friends and gravitated toward like-minded young men with similar interests. One of these was Harris Merton ("Harry") Lyon, with whom Charlie took several classes his freshman year. Both Charlie and Harry were creative and bright—and they both loved the written word, especially poetry. In class they often sat near each other, and, when a lecture became uninteresting, they would entertain themselves by writing doggerel back and forth. Charlie might write the first line to a limerick and then pass the paper to Harry, who would write the second line, and then Harry would pass it back to Charlie, and so forth. They found much entertainment with this game and became quite good at it. In time, it led to a strong friendship and foreshadowed their professional careers.[161] By the end of his freshman year, Charlie had become acclimated to his new home, made many good friends, and continued to learn more about the world and about himself. His love affair with the University of Missouri had begun.

Sophomore Year

In his second year, Charlie began to blossom. He pledged and joined the *Sigma Chi* fraternity, which provided him with room, board, and a social network. With the close male companionship—far different from his female-centric home in Independence—a new confidence began to replace his natural shyness. As one of 21 members of his fraternity, he was both challenged and supported by his new "brothers," young men who were as ambitious and motivated as he.[162] For the rest of his life, he would remain a proud and supportive brother of that fraternity. At reunion events, he would often lead the *Sigma Chi's* in the singing of their signature song, the "Sweetheart of *Sigma Chi*."

Group photograph showing Charlie Ross as a college man (front row 4th from left) with a group that are probably the Sigma Chi Fraternity at the University of Missouri, 1904. (Photo/Harry S. Truman Library)

Charlie was named Class Historian for his sophomore year (1902–'03).[163] While not the most important of the class-officer positions, it shows that his classmates knew and approved of him. It also reflected his understanding of history and his ability to write.

In the winter of 1903, Charlie and Harry Lyon, along with five of their classmates, formed a group known as The Asterisks. Their purpose was "to promote a higher standard of literary production at the University of Missouri." This small group shared a love of creative writing and believed there wasn't enough original student work published at the University. The Asterisks set about creating a literary booklet containing poetry and other literary pieces written by its members, often under a *nom de plume*. The first booklet was published in 1903 and was distributed on the campus, a few issues following irregularly after that. Although The Asterisks' publication wasn't sustained over a long period, the writing and distribution of the publication harnessed the efforts of these young men, who enjoyed writing and seeing their works published. This set the stage for the future careers of several of the members. Harry Lyon authored two books of short stories so promising that a literary critic referred to his as "De Maupassant, Jr." Unfortunately, he died in his early thirties in 1916, much too early to establish his success. Homer Croy became a famous regional writer who wrote many novels about Missouri, including *West of the Water Tower* and *They Had to See Paris*. Herbert Carl Crow wrote a series of books about China, Japan, the Philippines, and South America. One about China, *Four Hundred Million Customers,* became a bestseller. James H. Craig wrote novels about the rural communities of Missouri, including *Kettle Drums and Tom Toms,* while he pursued a career in advertising. Robert W. Jones, after graduation, received an LL.B. degree from the University of Missouri School of Law. He became a journalist and wrote professional books, including *Journalism in the United States* and *Law and Journalism*.[164] Only one member, Daniel H. McFarland, did not publish after graduation, but pursued only business interests.

During his sophomore year, Charlie carried a full load of academic courses: German, Latin, and English as well as English History, English Literature, and American Literature. His extracurricular activities must have taken a toll, because, in the first semester, he received three A's, one B, and a lone C (his only one, ever—in English History). He bounced back a bit in the second semester when he earned two A's and four B's. Although these marks were hardly an embarrassment, they were below his standards and must have left him disappointed.[165]

Junior Year

In his junior year (1903–'04), Charlie remained active in *Sigma Chi* and with The Asterisks. He also found time to become the business manager for the University's yearbook, *The Savitar*.[166] (The word *Savitar* comes from the Hindu religion and refers both to an important god as well as the sun in its life-giving aspect.) From his work in high school on *The Gleam,* this was familiar territory for Charlie. It took a great deal of time and diplomacy to handle the business side of getting this annual publication funded and published.

Despite this demanding extracurricular schedule—and perhaps stung by that "C" during his sophomore year—he didn't let his grades slide. He earned A's in all of his courses during his junior year. It helped that he took only four courses each semester in his junior year. By contrast, in his first two years, Charlie took either five or six academic courses each semester. It should be noted that he began the first semester taking five courses, but he withdrew from Elementary Economics.[167] [Author's Note: In 1967, when asked by my Grandma Ross, Charlie's widow: "What is going to be your major in college?" I told her that I was going to major in economics. She replied: "Your grandfather always said he wished he'd taken more economics courses."] Nevertheless, earning straight A's for an entire year was an impressive accomplishment.

Senior Year

Charlie's senior year was busy and rewarding. His social life flourished, and he remained active in his beloved fraternity, with its events and characteristic camaraderie. As noted earlier, Charlie took many on-campus jobs to help cover expenses. In his senior year he found employment off-campus at the local weekly newspaper, the *Columbia Herald*, as a general worker and a student-reporter covering the University. This was more challenging work than his earlier odd jobs. However, he managed to carry a full academic schedule and took five courses each semester. These included a variety of history, English, Latin, and sociology courses, plus one course in logic. During the first semester his marks were two A's and three B's, and, in his final semester, he earned all A's. This final flourish of top grades was duly rewarded, when late in his senior year, he was elected into the *Phi Beta Kappa* Society.[168]

In 1905 the University of Missouri's chapter of the *Phi Beta Kappa* (PBK) Society had been in place for only four years. The PBK Society was founded in 1776 at the College of William and Mary to "celebrate excellence in the liberal arts and sciences."[169] Since its beginning, it has acknowledged only the top students at qualifying institutions. The University of Missouri was the 53rd college in the United States to qualify for a PBK charter. Charlie considered this a great honor, and his Phi Beta Kappa key became one of his most prized possessions.[170]

Charlie's election to Phi Beta Kappa wasn't the only honor he received his final year. He was also elected to the QEBH, an "Alma Mater society" unique to the University of Missouri. Only a few upperclassmen were elected each year. Those elected were students who, during their undergraduate years, had furthered the welfare of the University and whose deeds reflected the spirit of their Alma Mater. Charlie understood it was a compliment to be elected a member, and he accepted this honor as such.[171]

A Bit of Good Luck

The main reason Charlie accepted part-time employment at the *Columbia Herald* was because he needed the money. But along with his wages, Charlie also stumbled into a bit of good luck. Later in life, Charlie, with his characteristic modesty, would tell his sons: "I owe much of my success in life to good luck." Clearly, he'd had his share of good fortune: early home schooling from his wise grandmother, his supportive family, and the good public schools he attended in Independence. The *Columbia Herald* was led by a dynamic editor named Walter Williams. He introduced Charlie to the complex operations of newspapers and gave him a chance to test his writing skills as a reporter. This opportunity turned out to be one huge turn of good luck.

Walter Williams

Walter Williams was born Marcus Walther Williams on July 2, 1864, into a family of modest circumstances in rural Boonville, Missouri, about 20 miles west of Columbia. He was the youngest of seven children. His formal education began in 1871 in public school, although his attendance was spotty. Nevertheless, he was issued a diploma from Boonville High School just before his 16th birthday in 1879. Despite his irregular attendance, he developed a love of reading and devoured everything he could find, which fortunately was a great deal, mostly from the ample libraries that friends and neighbors kept in their homes.

While he had a strong intellect, he was not physically impressive. On his 12th birthday it was noted he "was still a smallish lad, frail, slender, and somewhat effeminate, with a high squeaky voice and a childish beauty."[172] To his credit, he didn't let his physical presence stand in his way. When he was 11 years old, in 1875, he began working as an apprentice at a small newspaper in his hometown, *The Boonville Topic*, where he started as a "printer's devil," mixing tubs of ink, fetching type, and performing other menial tasks. As his talents became recognized, he advanced to reporting and writing stories, and eventually to editing. Over the next nine years, he continued working, learning all facets of the trade, and honing his newspaper skills at *The Boonville Topic*. Then, in 1884, that paper was acquired by a local competitor, the *Boonville Advertiser*, where he carried on as an editor.[173]

The next chapter of this Horatio Alger story began when, at age 20, Walter traveled to a meeting of the Missouri Press Association in nearby Columbia. He was impressed and soon became a member of the association. By this time, he began thinking beyond Boonville about the reach and potential of newspapers generally. The following year, in January 1886, he was given the opportunity to acquire part ownership in his employer, the *Boonville Advertiser*, which he eagerly did, becoming a part owner at age 21. Despite the demands at the *Boonville Advertiser*, he remained active in the Missouri Press Association and impressed its members so much that, in 1889, they elected him president.[174]

After an ill-advised three-month stint in a politically appointed position in Missouri state government, Walter Williams moved to Columbia, and joined the large E. W. Stephens Publishing House. The firm had almost 100 employees and printed books, community newspapers, and assorted other publications. One of its major holdings was the *Columbia Herald*, and its owner, William Edwin Stephens, was looking for a top-notch editor. Walter Williams filled that bill and immediately set out to make the *Columbia Herald* a "model weekly newspaper."[175]

Over the next 15 years, Walter Williams' energies were directed toward his work, his family, and advancing journalism from his newly adopted town of Columbia. Under his guidance, the *Columbia Herald* modernized, improved, and became a highly successful weekly newspaper. In 1892, he married a local lady, Hulda Harned, and, over the next six years, they had three healthy children.[176] Between 1895 and 1902, despite his high-pitched, squeaky voice, he led a popular and inspirational Bible School on Sundays at the local First Presbyterian Church, which attracted, among others, many non-Presbyterians.[177] In addition to these demands, Walter Williams remained a guiding force in the Missouri Press Association. Using his leadership role in that organization, along with impressive public-relations skills, he was able to entice many dignitaries from foreign press organizations to attend the St. Louis World's Fair (also known as the Louisiana Purchase Exposition) in 1902.[178] Charlie knew Williams' reputation and put his best foot forward when the then-40-year-old Mr. Williams interviewed him for that initial newspaper job in 1904.

As noted earlier, Charlie's part-time position at the *Columbia Herald* turned out to be a huge stroke of good luck. It gave Charlie the opportunity to learn the newspaper and printing business from the ground up, and also placed Charlie under the tutelage of one of the leading forces in the complex, fast-moving, and growing newspaper business.

Charlie always remembered his four years at the University of Missouri as among the best of his life—and no wonder. When he arrived at the University in 1901, he was a skinny, shy 15-year-old boy who'd never traveled far from Independence. Four years later, he was leaving as a dependable young man who was well-liked by his peers. He demonstrated that he was a top student and a gifted writer. Additionally, thanks to his position at the *Columbia*

Herald, he discovered an interest that would become his calling. He graduated from the University of Missouri a more mature young man and more confident than he had ever been. He felt he was ready to take what the world had to offer—he was ready for life's next step.

9

CHARLIE IS LAUNCHED, AND THE ROSS WOMEN CARRY ON
(1905–1921)

1905—After Charlie's Graduation

Charlie's graduation from the University of Missouri was the fulfillment of Ella's dream—and her mother's dream—that he should complete an education at a great university. Not only did he graduate, but he was celebrated for his exceptional performance. He now stood as the first Ross to graduate from college. (Prior to this, Mama had come the closest when she attended Woodland College, a two-year school for women in Independence.) Charlie's success validated Mama's belief that college was the right avenue for him. It also enhanced the family's stature in town; they were now fortified with "a college graduate."

Charlie's graduation also sent a signal to his sisters that they, too, could aspire to an education beyond high school. If their sibling could go to college, then why couldn't they? After all, they, too, were successful high-school students, and women were now going to college; some had graduated with Charlie at the University. A college education was now within reach of Mama's "smart" girls.

The constant lack of financial wherewithal would be a hindrance, but the prospect had been introduced: If Charlie could get a college education, why couldn't his sisters?

There is no record of JB's reaction to his son's college graduation. His mining trips left JB largely absent from the family's day-to-day life. Presumably, he was proud of his son's accomplishment, although he may not have viewed a college diploma as a life-changing event. He kept struggling, in his own quixotic way, to provide his family financial security. He probably didn't see college as a pathway to financial success, at least not to the level he was seeking. His main interest now was in seeing just how Charlie would contribute back to the family's finances. Mama had told him that Charlie would "help us" support his sisters once college was completed, and Papa was surely looking forward to that help. JB's main emotion must have been one of relief when Charlie graduated from college and began making his way in the world.

Charlie's Career—A Rocky Beginning

Upon his graduation, Charlie sensed the direction he thought his life's work might take. Growing up in small-town Independence, he was aware of the types of jobs most young men pursued, *e.g.,* store clerk, grocer, banker, teacher. Plus, he'd had summer jobs during college, which he later referred to as "casual work," such as serving as a water boy for a mining crew in Colorado (a job no doubt secured for him by his father). None of these appealed to him as a career. However, that final job he'd had in college working at the *Columbia Herald* was stimulating and enjoyable. That was the work he liked best.

After his graduation, he remained at the *Herald*, continuing to learn the trade under the watchful eye of his mentor, Walter

Williams. However, after several months, Charlie decided he needed to move on; he was ambitious and wanted to "follow the Gleam." Within a few months of his graduation, Charlie, with a recommendation from Walter Williams, applied for and accepted a position as a reporter at one of the most prominent newspapers in the state, the *St. Louis Post-Dispatch*. So, he packed his bags, left familiar Columbia, and relocated to St. Louis, where he began working for this large, big-city newspaper. Only a few days after he'd started work, the newspaper's management got spooked by the threat of an economic downturn and decided to lay off expendable employees. As a very recent hire, Charlie was let go, although with the promise that he'd be rehired as soon as a suitable position became available. This abrupt turn stunned idealistic 20-year-old Charlie. He needed money and a job right away.[179]

Most likely through JB's connections, Charlie quickly secured another newspaper job. This was in the boom town of Victor, Colorado, just a few miles southwest of Colorado Springs. It was in the Cripple Creek area, where JB had maintained local contacts from his early days of mining. Serving this booming mining community was the *Daily Record*. Grateful for a job but nervous about his new employer in this faraway place, Charlie cautiously purchased a round-trip railroad ticket from St. Louis to Victor. The return-trip portion of the ticket would expire in three months if not used by then.

Charlie's new job at the *Daily Record* didn't go well. After a few weeks, he wrote a postcard expressing his disappointment to a friend back in Missouri. Its message was brief: "Out here to carve a fortune out of the west, so the books say. The books prevaricate." The job did pay a meager salary, and he was there long enough to send some of his wages home to Independence for his sisters' support. Although he tried to give the job at the *Daily Record* a chance, he soon realized it wasn't what he wanted. The day before his return-trip ticket expired, he (again) packed his bags, said his farewells, and boarded the train back to St. Louis. In a stroke of good luck, fear of the economic crisis had subsided, and he was

Charlie as a young man getting started on his career. Missouri, 1911. (Photo/Ross family collection)

rehired by the *Post-Dispatch* upon his return. He could now pursue his dream of a career in journalism with a big-city newspaper.[180]

Learning at the *Post-Dispatch*

At the *Post-Dispatch*, Charlie quickly got past the bitter layoff episode and dug in to make the most of his opportunity. As a local reporter, he spent hours on assignment in the courthouse building as well as at other places in and around St. Louis. His boss was the City Editor, a legendary figure named Oliver Kirby ("O.K.") Bovard, who maintained tight control over the reporters and the gathering of news, particularly local news. One of his fellow editors at the *Post-Dispatch* described O.K. Bovard as "a classic example of the stuffy, high-hat, supercilious, cold-blooded, know-it-all type of executive"—but also admitted that Bovard "got results."[181] Others on the staff more charitably referred to Bovard as a "one-man school of journalism." Ultimately, it was Charlie's good fortune to work under Bovard—although not always a pleasant experience. On one occasion, Charlie was sent to the southwestern reaches of St. Louis to report on an incident where a painter had been injured by falling from a smokestack. The event happened well beyond the limits of the streetcar line, so Charlie had to walk a long way on an uncomfortably hot day to get the story. Charlie finally found the smokestack, gathered the facts he believed he needed to write the piece, walked back to the streetcar line, and returned in the late afternoon sweaty and grimy to the office. He wrote up his account of the accident and submitted it to Bovard for his edits.

A short time later, Bovard asked Charlie: "How tall was the smokestack?"

Taken aback by the question, Charlie replied, "Quite tall."

"*Tall* is a relative term," responded Bovard. Then he added: "I want you to go back and find out the exact height."

Charlie did as he was instructed and returned to the newsroom late that night, but this time with the exact height of the smokestack in feet and inches. It was a lesson he never forgot, and he often repeated this story when talking about the requirements of a good reporter.[182]

Lured to a Rival Newspaper

After about a year at the *Post-Dispatch*, Charlie's reputation around St. Louis as an emerging star in Bovard's talented team had grown—so much so that he began to receive job offers from other local newspapers. Always on the lookout for additional funds to send home, Charlie couldn't refuse a lucrative offer from the *Republic*, an understaffed rival St. Louis newspaper looking for talent. The position also allowed Charlie to become a copyreader, the person who edits pieces written by others. This often involved shortening the "articles, if necessary, to fit space requirements, to examine each piece of copy carefully for errors in fact, in style, in grammar and spelling."[183] It also required creating the headlines for the articles. Charlie soon showed he had the talent to be a copyreader—so much so that, within a few weeks, he was promoted to chief copyreader or news editor. Charlie was just 22 years old and now held a top job at a major newspaper in the fourth-largest city in America. The duties of the chief copyreader are described as follows:

> "The chief copyreader, often called the news editor, is usually responsible for the makeup—that is, the display of news in the paper. Each day the newspaper has available to it, from its reportorial staff, its wire services, press releases,

and other sources, several times more material than it can possibly use. It is the news editor, often after consultation with the managing editors and others, who decides not only what can and cannot be printed that day, but also the style and size of headline to be assigned to each individual article. And then, under deadline pressure, he grades the stories once again to determine which properly belong on the front page, the second page, and so on."[184]

Charlie was now doing responsible, demanding newspaper work, and was moving up in the growing business. His career had taken off. He was on his way.

The Ross Women Carry On

Mama, always deferential to the males in the family, now had a house dominated by the concerns of her daughters. As usual, JB would return periodically to Independence from his latest mining trip for a few weeks or months. These comings-and-goings were unsettling for his daughters, particularly the younger ones. However, with Papa usually away, the girls banded together—and thrived.

As in many families, there were "understandings"—be they expressly articulated or not—as to the roles each person would play. Mama came to an understanding with Papa that he could pursue his dream to make a fortune mining in the West. In return, he agreed that Charlie would go to college—and the family would support him as best it could. This was the reciprocal accommodation made between Mama and Papa to keep peace in the family, and, despite the economic squeeze it would place on everyone, it was seen as the best path forward. This put a large burden on the shoulders of Mama, but it was one she willingly took on.

To make their parents' "grand bargain" work, the Ross women took on new roles. As mentioned earlier, Sis stayed home and became a primary caretaker. Each of the three older sisters took on responsibility for one of the three younger "fall crop" girls. With Charlie off at college, helping one another became imbued in the fabric of the Ross women. Under Mama's direction, they successfully managed the household and developed their own paths forward.

Helen—Following in Charlie's Footsteps

Helen always felt a special kinship with Charlie. She took very seriously all the advice Charlie offered, particularly about learning. For example, she recalled:

> "Charlie said Latin was important 'to teach you about words' and I believed him and faithfully learned my Latin grammar. Words were precious to him always, and he transmitted this value to me. When I was still in the grade school, he insisted I should learn ten—*at least* ten—'new' words every week, and I carefully compiled a list from books and newspapers and struggled to make them my own. A favorite family story was told by Louise of one day coming home from school when we were still in the second grade, and I had said, 'Well, we did not have a copious rain today.' 'Copious' was on my list for the week. Any rain on any occasion thereafter was likely to bring from Louise, 'And do you think this will be a copious rain today?'"[185]

Helen didn't share Charlie's shyness as a young student. Rather she, like Harry Truman, wasn't afraid to speak in public. She recounted an episode from her elementary school days:

"I took part as a third grader in a "Contest," when children chosen from four different schools in town would 'speak a piece' in the High School Auditorium. Chosen to represent my grade, I was coached by the teacher, stout Miss Bridges, who selected a dreary poem, "The Heavenly Guest," hardly understood by me and Louise, who drilled me many times a day. Since I had demonstrated I was the best speaker of pieces and the best reader in my grade, I was poorly prepared for the award to go to a little boy who spoke a funny piece. Indeed, I was broken hearted and embarrassed myself as well as Mama and the family by bursting into bitter tears when the prize was announced. It did not seem possible that that silly little boy would win. I had little appreciation of the humorous [sic] in verse. Poetry was serious and beautiful even if you could not understand it. The judges in the contest I could not agree with."[186]

Helen navigated her way successfully through the Independence schools and matched Charlie's achievements. She entered Independence High School in 1904 and recounted years later:

"I was expected to get the best grades in my High School classes, to win the final prizes that Charlie won, and I did. Sis had won the essay prize at her graduation, too, but I had to do better than she and as well as Charlie, never better."[187]

Helen served as the lead editor of *The Gleam* in 1907, her senior year, and she received the first-in-scholarship award as well. And, like Charlie, after high school, she entered the freshman class at the University of Missouri.

When Charlie left for college in 1901, the household became "an increasing sorority."[188] For the Ross girls, the feminine charms were never an emphasis, but they became more conscious of their physical appearance. At the parties she went to later in college, Helen said she "danced poorly."[189] and "I thought we were all far from pretty."[190] While physical beauty was not in the cards for the young Ross women, they strove to be clean, healthy, and "smart."

Also, during these formative years, Helen began to realize that women could and should do more with their lives than was then generally expected. She later expressed this as follows:

". . . a little girl of the 1890's already had a Janus face. There must be some way to combine adventure into the mind with the inherited job of taking care. Suffrage for women was still unknown. We heard of a woman doctor who wore pants; well, grandma had done the same when she went to open the door of school in the winter. A woman was Queen of a great country, Queen Victoria, who Mama loved to talk about. What wonder that in High School, Olive Schriner's "Stories of an African Farm," and Elbert Hubbard's "Little Journeys to the Homes of Famous Women" caught my eye, and created a restlessness that had to wait. Mary Wolstonecraft [sic], a whole new idea of women; Mary Shelley, who spelled a new kind of courage."[191]

As Helen got older and began to read more, she began to sense that perhaps she shouldn't look to the past for a future role to play. Rather she should consider her future to be broader and more flexible than was the norm in Independence at the time.

Charlie Provides Helen's College Support

Helen graduated in 1907 from Independence High School at the top of her class. Although she enjoyed growing up in Independence, Helen saw her future beyond it. ("Boy and girl parties took place in the neighborhood and Sunday school picnics and an occasional 'entertainment' at the Old Music Hall, but these to me had little to do with the future."[192]) However, she keenly felt the family's deteriorating financial condition. ("The 'future' became increasingly important as the family economics declined, visibly, year by year, with Dad's failing eyesight. . . . It became harder and harder to find the nickels and pennies we took to Sunday school.")

Mama was able to provide only meager financial help for Helen. However, Charlie was employed now and felt an obligation to help his sisters have the opportunities he'd been given. So, he provided a substantial part of the tuition and fees for Helen to attend the University. He also sent her some additional spending money. This support was the beginning of what would be a chain reaction within the family for years to come. Each of the older children helped the younger ones with their college expenses.[193]

Scarlet Fever

Unforeseen events sometimes intervened to undermine the Ross sorority's well-being. Illnesses which today seem minor were especially feared before the advent of antibiotics and similar "wonder drugs." The family dealt with bouts of whooping cough and scarlet fever. Helen, in her memoirs, told how dreaded scarlet fever gripped the Ross household for several weeks.

"Four . . . children had Scarlet Fever, Sis, Louise, Virginia and Frances, all at once and I was kept from school because of quarantine and Mama's need for help . . . Six weeks of no school for me was trial enough, but I did my lessons and whispered to the baby that we would be different—no Scarlet Fever for us. Virginia's illness was severe and she cried in pain in her fat little rheumatic hands. It was a bad time. I would try to comfort her with the beautiful gelatin and puddings that the neighbors brought to the front door and then fled in the face of the orange quarantine sign with its big black letters. Cousin Etta, who lived up the street, would come to the sewing window every day several times, shawl over her head, to ask about the children and how Mama was holding up. No one would come help in a home with Scarlet Fever, then a dread disease, and 'trained nurses,' unknown to us then, would have been beyond our strained resources. Illness brought good neighbors, all busy households themselves, and when they dared not enter the house, they brought 'good things' to the door."[194]

Fortunately, Mama, Helen, and her sisters all survived with no lasting ill effects. Helen recalled, "Mama praised me to the neighbors and the teacher complimented me on the lessons done at home, so I added to my stature in my own eyes, even though I envied the attention the sick received."[195]

Louise

As noted earlier, Louise didn't enter high school at the same time as Helen. On the advice of a medical doctor, she stayed home and "rested her eyes," only periodically traveling to nearby Kansas City for eye treatments.[196] This wasn't a psychological blow for Louise, who was never as enthusiastic about formal schooling as Helen and Charlie. This setback didn't prevent her from contributing to the family's well-being. During these two years, she continued to contribute to the family, and kept monitoring Virginia, her "charge."

Around the house, Louise mainly sewed and cooked.[197] She used her newfound time to work on her sewing skills, for which she had a natural aptitude. She became adept at sewing and made so many items for family members that her skills improved to a professional level. Sewing became Louise's major contribution to the family, particularly after her eyesight improved—she made all of her sisters' clothes through their high school days.[198] The family was thrilled at her creations and all agreed "no children looked nicer."[199] She even made many of Helen's clothes just prior to college. In Helen's words:

> "Louise . . . sewed all that summer before I started to the University so that I would be 'presentable' in her words. Some of those clothes I recall: a black and white checked 'Peter Thompson,' a blue skirt with several 'waists,' mostly dark colors because of laundry, a pink mull dress with a square neck outlined with lace insertion for parties and [a] short blue reefer with brass buttons."[200]

In addition, Louise, along with Sis, did the cooking for the family. Both sisters learned to cook—and became very good at it. Their cakes were deemed to be among the best in the neighborhood.[201]

Louise reputedly became "the most popular of the six sisters at their home in Independence."[202] She enjoyed entertaining at neighborhood parties, particularly those for children. She had one memorable routine where she would go to a children's party dressed like a witch, carrying one of her pet chickens hidden inside a gunny sack; she would then enter singing the lyrics to Stephen Foster's song *Old Black Joe*, putting emphasis on the chorus piece: "I'm coming, I'm coming." At the conclusion of the song, Louise would open the sack and release her pet chicken into the audience. The skit was always a hit.[203]

Louise also enjoyed entertaining her girlfriends. One way she did this involved the parlor game known as "table-tapping"—which is akin to holding a seance or using a Ouija Board—where the participants allegedly communicate with deceased persons. One memorable session was recounted more than 70 years later by Louise's sister, Virginia.

> "Only her best friends, about half a dozen, were ever allowed at her table-tapping sessions, which she held in our little-used, chilly parlor. Younger sisters were sent off to bed but didn't always stay there. Frances and I crept to the dark hall and put our ears to the door frame and our eyes to the key-hole. The table tapped and the girls oh-ed and ah-ed and Louise kept them entertained. The questions centered around school and boys. One spirit at a time tapped out his name (1-A, 2-B, etc.) and then answered the questions (1 tap for "yes" and 2 for "no"). One evening the name that came in was O-L-I-V-E-R B-R-Y-A-N-T. "Dr. Bryant," they screamed, "No, I saw him today," "He's alive," "He's our doctor" "No" "No".
>
> The noise brought my mother running. With a firm "this has gone far enough, no more of this," she pushed the table and chairs aside and ended the session. Believe it or not, the next morning Mama told us that her friend, Oliver Bryant, had died in the night. No more table tapping sessions, at

least no more in our home, but Louise's reputation with me and with her friends soared."[204]

Louise, like Mammy and Mama, was openly supportive of the less fortunate, probably more so than her siblings. Louise often helped needy people in a personal way. Her sister, Virginia, cites a couple of examples:

"One neglected little girl was occasionally brought home from school by Louise for a bath and hair-brushing, and when Louise sent her back to her shiftless mother, she was sweet-smelling and happy. I remember another unfortunate child for whom Louise made a gingham dress and how proud I was when she took me with her to 'try it on.'"[205]

Louise sometimes found a way both to instruct her charge *and* to help the less fortunate. Virginia, years later, still recalled one episode:

"One day she took me 'up-town to the square.' I had five cents to spend and was happy with the thought. We reached the square and there was a beggar, holding out a tin cup. Louise told me to put the nickel in the cup and I refused, saying that I was going to buy an envelope of Japanese water flowers. We argued, back and forth, yes and no, as we started away from the beggar. She clinched the argument by saying that I would never be happy with the water flowers. Such was her power over me that she was right—and I knew it. In went the nickel."[206]

Louise's eyes improved after her two-year hiatus from school, and she returned to Independence High School, where she was placed in a class two years behind Helen. It now became even more apparent that "she had not the slightest interest in books or study." She often "played hooky," was behind in her assignments, and was indifferent to the grades she received. To make it worse, Louise "made fun of her teachers, and in general was a rebel."[207] Despite her aversion to school, Louise retained her sense of humor and her popularity. She graduated in 1909; it was commonly acknowledged that she "squeaked through on her family reputation."[208] In the 1909 issue of *The Gleam*—for which she, unlike her older siblings, was *not* an editor—next to her senior picture was stated: "Louise Ross: 'An example of how Wisdom, and Folly Meet, mix and unite.'"[209] According to Helen, "Louise's high school years were happier, I'm sure. She retired from the intellectual contest and 'had fun,' as she often boasted."[210]

Following high school, Louise remained in Independence and helped raise her younger sisters. She continued carrying on an active social life and had no shortage of boyfriends—each of whom her family referred to as her *beau*, in the custom of the day. She also carried on a varied social life with her many friends in town. One friend was Bess Wallace—later, Mrs. Harry Truman—who, like Louise, liked the outdoors. Louise said years later:

> "Bess loved sports, especially hiking and tennis. We used to go on early hikes to a spring three or four miles outside of town. We'd try to get there and have a drink of water before the 6 a.m. whistles. Afterwards we'd go to someone's house for breakfast."[211]

Louise Goes to Arizona

Louise remained in Independence until 1911. Her mother had recently returned from Arizona after spending several months taking care of JB, as he by then was almost blind. He had made friends in the desert town of Parker, Arizona, near where copper and some gold had been found. He was happy in Parker and had no interest in joining his family in Independence. The plan evolved that Louise would go west and join her father and spend the winter taking care of him in that small, remote town near the California border; she reasoned that the "thrill of the West" would make up for the rugged life.[212] Louise signed on for this adventure, and thought it was just a short-term plan.

Ginny

Louise willingly took responsibility for Virginia, whom the family called "Ginny," as her charge. Later in her life, Louise fondly told Ginny about the day of her birth.

> "Ginny, I remember the day you were born. Sissy, Helen and I spent the day at Aunt Nannie's and when we came home there was a new baby. Everybody was so happy and the church bells were ringing."[213]

Of course, Louise and Ginny experienced temporary highs and lows. For example, Helen recalled the following testy exchange between them:

> "Don't be so bossy," Virginia complained.
> Louise shot back: "I'm just telling you what to do and how, now listen."[214]

In time, Ginny accepted Louise's mentoring as well as the discipline and instruction that came with it. As they grew older,

Ginny became thankful that she was Louise's charge. Their bond evolved over time, and it remained strong throughout their lives, lasting eight decades.

Virginia went through the Independence public-school system. She was an excellent student, who, in 1915, graduated with high marks where she, too, was an editor on the staff of *The Gleam*. In that issue, under her picture, the following is stated:

VIRGINIA ROSS

"Gin," the fifth member of the Ross family to graduate from I.H.S. leaves behind her an excellent record in schoolwork. She made her mark in "The Rivals," was the Alumni Editor of the *Gleam* and discovered her calling in substituting as Latin teacher.[215]

Frances

Responsibility for Frances fell to Sis. No record has survived on the specifics of their relationship. However, family lore points to no serious problems or conflicts. Frances must have been a cooperative charge, because her husband made the following observation later in her life: "When Frances is in her home, she manages everything, but when she's with you sisters, she's just that little Ross girl, doing what you say."[216] On balance, Frances' and Sis' relationship was not unlike the other older sister-charge arrangements; it lasted nearly five decades, until Sis' death in 1951.

Frances, like her siblings before her, was educated in the Independence public-school system. She, like her other siblings, lived at home. She graduated from Independence High School in the

Class of 1917. None of her academic records have been preserved, although she reputedly was an excellent student. Perhaps the most memorable event occurring during her time at Independence High School was when she had a leading part in a school drama. In one scene she played a bride getting married, the groom being played by a student named Lowell Leake. Eventually, they turned that fantasy into reality when they were married in 1921.

The Baby Girl—James Bruce Ross

James Bruce Ross was the youngest daughter and last of the "fall crop" of Mama's children. As the baby, five years younger than Virginia and two-and-a-half years younger than Frances, she soon became a favored child in the all-female household. It didn't hurt her cause that she had sparkling blue eyes and a cherub's face.

As JB reportedly said: "I don't care if it's a girl or not. That child is going to be named James Bruce!" Presumably, his wife went along with this—probably to placate him—and the baby's name legally became James Bruce Ross.[217]

However, a deeper investigation into family history reveals that it might not have been as cut and dried as that story. In an undated letter postmarked four months after the baby's birth, Virginia Ross, then five years old, sent the following hand-printed letter to Charlie at the University of Missouri.

DEAR CHARLIE—

THIS IS SUNDAY AND I WILL WRITE YOU A LETTER. WE ARE ALL WELL. HOW WOULD YOU LIKE TO MOVE TO CARTHAGE? PAPA IS TALKING

ABOUT MOVING DOWN THERE. WE ARE GOING
TO NAME THE BABY MILDRED.
GOODBYE

FROM
VIRGINIA ROSS

Perhaps there was more than a little discussion—and disagreement—within the family about the baby's name. In any event, her legal name never became "Mildred." It was "James Bruce Ross." Baby J.B. began her education in the Independence public-school system. However, she didn't finish there. She would finish in another school system, many miles away.

Mama and Papa

Mama had no interest in leaving Independence, where she had many close-by relatives and where her children were in school and doing well. Independence was familiar—and it was home. Papa, as suggested in Virginia's letter to Charlie, wanted the family to relocate and become part of his mining life. With his eyesight failing, he probably wanted more care, but Mama wasn't willing. Yet, despite this, all indications are that they remained a loving couple, who, in their own ways, were devoted to one another. Mama agreeing to give the baby girl a boy's name showed that Mama still deferred to her husband. In 1904, JB was devoted enough to take Ella on a once-in-a-lifetime vacation to the Louisiana Purchase Exposition in St. Louis (informally known as the St. Louis World's Fair).[218] This must have been a welcome second honeymoon for them both.

While Mama would not budge from living in Independence, she had shown she was willing to move periodically within the town.

Shortly after Frances was born in 1899, Papa was able to purchase the house on South Main Street, where the children turned its barn into the neighborhood playhouse. The Ross Family then built and moved into a new home at 214 South Spring Street, after Charlie graduated from college in 1905. Virginia recalled years later:

> "We moved to the 'new house,' 214 North Spring Street when I was about eight years old. The building of the house was the time I remember my father best. It was his last effort to provide for his family. Mining operations must have had a period of financial success—the finished house was without any mortgage, although we had to wait a couple of years for wall paper. It was a big brick house with many rooms, on a deep lot in one of the best parts of town. Papa made almost daily trips to the building site. . . . Frances and I accompanied him and played in the orchard, a part of the property. With a reading glass in hand he studied the architect's plans and made many suggestions to the builders."[219]

Papa's longer trips to search for gold in Colorado, Alaska, and Mexico became a thing of the past, as his eyesight deteriorated. In 1902, he pursued less-glamorous, but closer-to-home, mining opportunities in southwestern Missouri, in the area near Carthage and Webb City, where lead and zinc were mined. These efforts brought some modest success and allowed them to build the house on North Spring Street. As was JB's pattern, that success was short-lived. Not long after the house was built, Virginia recalled "great concerns about water in the mine" as well as a stream of tax bills and collection letters from establishments in southwestern Missouri, where her father had stayed.[220]

When Virginia was about ten years old, Papa, now with creditors in pursuit, heard of an opportunity in Arizona, just across the border from California in a desert town called Parker, where copper was being mined. To Papa this sounded like a good opportunity, so he once again headed out on another "mining trip" to seek his fortune. Mama remained in Independence, steadfast in her belief that the best place for her and her girls was in her hometown, and she didn't budge—at least not then.

10

NEWSPAPERMAN AND PROFESSOR
(1909–1919)

Good Times in St. Louis

As a lead copyreader at *The Republic*, Charlie, at age 23, knew his career was on the rise. Both the newspaper industry and the city of St. Louis were fast-paced and growing. His professional life had become fulfilling; he now had the intellectual stimulation of critically reading and writing, a steady salary, and the energy and dynamics of a big-city newspaper. He was also able to send money home to support his family. He had quelled his father's objection about not "helping the family"—something his father still struggled to do.

During his off-hours, Charlie enjoyed the social life of vibrant St. Louis. Joining Charlie from the *Republic* were Jim Craig, one of *The Asterisks* from his college days, and Sam Hellman, a humor writer, who later would become a highly paid movie writer in Hollywood. Charlie's circle of friends also included men employed by other newspapers in town. They would often dine at Faust's or at Lippi's restaurant, and sometimes meet at one of the old beer gardens in south St. Louis, drink beer, and sing along with the music of a polka band. These were good times for these up-and-comers.[221]

It was during these halcyon days that Charlie began to smoke cigarettes. Starting in the late 1800s, tobacco companies began mass producing cigarettes. By 1900, they realized that heavy spending on advertising increased sales and they particularly targeted younger people. The result was that more and more cigarettes were sold, and more and more young adults bought and used them. Charlie's

A young Charles Ross is shown typing at his typewriter in an office. Location and date unknown.
(Photo/Harry S. Truman Library)

enjoyment became a habit, one which sadly lasted him the rest of his life. Like his weakness for candy, he had little resistance to the lure of tobacco. At the time, cigarette smoking seemed harmless enough; it wasn't until later in his life that it would ruin his health. Had he known this at that time, he may have not indulged so readily.

Charlie was professionally satisfied and socially engaged in St. Louis, and it seemed unlikely that anything could cause him to veer from this path. However, time and events have a way of changing things.

Yellow Journalism

Toward the end of the 19th century, as the population of the United States grew, newspapers became increasingly influential and lucrative. In New York City, a rivalry began between two papers: the *New York Journal*, owned by the wealthy Californian William Randolph Hearst, and the *New York World*, owned by the brilliant, scrappy Joseph Pulitzer.

Once Hearst arrived in New York in 1895, the rivalry began. The main goal for each was to increase circulation, which meant more money from the sale of papers as well as from advertising. Both papers used provocative tactics: bold headlines, aggressive news gathering, eye-catching illustrations and cartoons, and particularly dramatic crime and human-interest stories.

Hearst's *New York Journal* began to focus on the uprising in Cuba against the Spanish government's control; Pulitzer's *New York World* followed suit. Soon, concerns about Cuba increased dramatically in the United States as the two newspapers traded more on rumor and sensationalism than on fact. This type of news coverage was dubbed "yellow journalism." The origin of that odd term is explained as follows:

Starting in 1895, Pulitzer printed a comic strip featuring a boy in a yellow nightshirt, entitled the "Yellow Kid." Hearst then poached the cartoon's creator and ran the strip in his newspaper. A critic at [a rival newspaper] the *New York Press*, in an effort to shame both newspapers' sensationalistic approach, coined the term "Yellow-Kid Journalism" after the cartoon. The term was soon shortened to "Yellow Journalism."[222]

The sinking of the *U.S.S. Maine*, coupled with sensationalistic accounts of alleged atrocities by the Spanish, ushered the United States into that conflict. The Spanish-American War officially began in April 1898, and it lasted only 6 months, with fewer than 400 Americans dead. After the war, it appeared to many that the conflict was unnecessary and avoidable. For the two rival newspapers, the sensationalist coverage used to promote the war undermined their credibility and stature. To put it in more colorful terms, yellow journalism gave the newspaper business a black eye.

Hearst remained unmoved by the damage the war had done and even accepted responsibility, crowing about "*The Journal's War*" while the conflict was still going on.[223] Pulitzer, on the contrary, felt a sense of shame and remorse, so he decided to spend part of his fortune to improve the professionalism of the country's newspapers. To that end he offered Columbia University in New York City two million dollars to start a school of journalism. But the university's administration and conservative faculty were wary, as the excesses of Yellow Journalism were still fresh in their minds. It would take years before Columbia University would relent and accept Pulitzer's proposal; in the meantime, momentum was building for such a school at the University of Missouri.[224]

Walter Williams Advocates for a School of Journalism

By the time Charlie left the University of Missouri in 1906 to pursue his post-college career, Walter Williams, then 41 years old, had established himself as a force in the newspaper publishing world. As a past president and an active member of the Missouri Press Association, he kept strong professional connections within the state.[225] As the president and substantial shareholder in the locally published *Herald*, he ran a well-respected weekly newspaper, which served as an important voice in the community.[226] Through his political connections, he had been appointed to the influential Board of Curators, a civilian board created by the state government to oversee the operations and needs of the University of Missouri. Shortly after his appointment, Williams, with the help of the University's long-serving president, Richard Jesse, was elected chairman of that Board's executive committee.[227] Williams, who had barely graduated from high school, now began to focus on something he felt passionate about: creating a school of journalism at the University of Missouri.[228]

The idea of a collegiate-level school devoted only to journalism was not new. The concept had been percolating in Missouri since as early as 1884, when it was advocated by E. W. Stephens, owner of the large printing company which included the *Herald*, and who initially had hired Williams as that paper's editor and Charlie Ross as an intern.[229] However, the idea languished for years. But now in the wake of the public scandal caused by "yellow journalism," Williams was well-positioned to create a new school dedicated to raising journalism's professional standards.

Growing up in the newspaper business, Walter Williams had experienced firsthand the haphazard methods by which journalists were trained. Essentially, it was an unofficial apprenticeship system closely aligned with the printing business. Before the twentieth century, anyone with a printing press could start a newspaper and if that entrepreneur sold enough copies and garnered some advertising, it could be a good business. There were few standards or restrictions concerning the quality of the content. To Williams, the value of a newspaper was too important to suffer this degree of laxity. The plea for higher standards in journalism—and for a separate school devoted to teaching journalists—gained momentum. This was noted in *Collier's,* a popular magazine at that time:

> "To the physician or the dentist we may not go but once a year. The teacher may be forgotten a month after commencement. The lawyer may not serve us more than once in a lifetime. But twice every weekday and again on Sunday most Americans turn to the newspaper; and a magazine of some sort is on every reading table and in every farmhouse living room. Then why isn't it at least as important to train writers as to train engineers, dentists, or lawyers? Edmund Burke, told of Three Estates in Parliament, commented that in the reporters gallery there was a Fourth Estate far more important than all three."[230]

As for the separate school devoted to journalism at the University, Williams advocated:

> "Our school seeks to do for journalism what schools of law, medicine and agriculture have done for those vocations. Previous to the existence of those schools, training in those fields was obtainable only in a lawyer's office, the doctor's office and on the farm. But now professional schools have taken the place of such individual training.

They have obtained their high development by the application of the laboratory or clinic to their . . . programs. The School of Journalism is to be conducted on the same plan . . . ."[231]

As soon as Williams' involvement in the Louisiana Purchase Exposition of 1904 concluded, he turned his energies to this and became not just an advocate, but an evangelist, for a School of Journalism.

A Professional School Is Born

As chairman of the executive committee of the Board of Curators, Williams' diplomatic skills served him well—he was a master at working the system. Through his friendship with President Richard H. Jesse, he was appointed to a three-person committee to examine the advisability of creating a school of journalism at the University. This committee consisted of J. Carleton Jones, A. Ross Hill (who would soon succeed Jesse as the University's President), and Walter Williams, all of whom were generally in favor of such a school. Not surprisingly, the committee recommended the establishment of such a school, and its findings were approved by the entire Board of Curators. Specifically, the report, dated December 13, 1906, recommended:

1. "That a College of School of Journalism be established as a department of the University, co-ordinate in rank with the departments of Law, Medicine, and other Professional Schools.

2. That the School of Journalism be provided with adequate laboratory equipment for practical journalistic training.

3. That the course of study be at least four years in length and that the entrance requirements to be at least equal to those of the Academic Department . . . ."

The approval of the Missouri legislature soon followed with funding, assuring the school's academic standing and financial support. However, before the school could begin, it needed a dean to lead and operate it, not an easy task for this first-of-its-kind academic institution.[232]

There was no front runner for the job. A number of prospects, including established newspaper editors, were asked, but their interest in the position was tepid in light of the fact that the school was "speculative" and the salary was only four thousand dollars a year, considerably less than first-rate newspaper editors were making at this time.[233] In April 1908, after a number of months with no success, Richard H. Jesse and A. Ross Hill asked Walter Williams if he would take the deanship.[234] This was an unusual and risky request because Williams was not a college graduate, and he had obvious conflicts of interest, including his position on the Board of Curators and his association with the *Herald*. However, in other ways, it was a natural fit for Williams, given his journalism experience, his organizational and diplomatic skills, and his deep desire to make the school a success. After some negotiation, Williams decided to accept the position, but in doing so he had to resign from the Board of Curators and "retire" from editorial control of the *Columbia Herald*. So, finally, in July 1908, the new dean was in place, allowing the legislature to confirm the approval of the new School of Journalism—and the operating funds began to flow.[235]

Williams pushed for the classes to begin in September, two months after the final approval, so he had to move quickly. One of his first communications was to Charlie Ross, who he asked to join the faculty as an instructor at a nine-month salary of $1,500, certainly a lot less than Charlie was then making at the *St. Louis Republic*. If Charlie hesitated at all, it wasn't for long.[236] Charlie loved his undergraduate years in Columbia, and returning there and to the academic world was very appealing. Charlie admired and respected Williams from working for him at the *Herald*. This also was an opportunity to teach—in Charlie's family teachers were revered—and he, like many successful students, loved the idea of becoming a teacher. The opportunity was irresistible. So, at 23 years of age, Charlie left his promising career at the *St. Louis Republic* and joined the first faculty at his *alma mater's* new School of Journalism.

The summer of 1908 moved along rapidly for those organizing the University's newest professional school. Charlie left St. Louis and moved his belongings to Columbia. Williams,[237] who would serve as both the dean and a lecturer at the school, soon hired a third faculty member, Silas Bent, from the city editor's desk at the *St. Louis Post-Dispatch*. This third and final member of the initial faculty gave it three experienced journalists. Williams acquired office space in the stately Academic Hall and began creating the school's curriculum. He also attended to the myriad administrative tasks needed to begin classes in September.

The Beginning

Williams, reflecting his personal zeal for good and ethical journalism, chose to teach a primary course: *History and Principles of Journalism*. The other courses listed in the first-year catalogue included:

- Newspaper Making

- Newspaper Administration

- Magazine and Class Journalism

- Comparative Journalism

- Newspaper Publishing

- Newspaper Jurisprudence

- News-gathering

- Correspondence

- Office Equipment[238]

Despite the school's novelty and its untested faculty, 97 students registered that September. This was a respectable showing; there were only 2,307 students in total on the campus in September of 1908.[239] The new school's headquarters was placed inside an existing building, Switzler Hall, and classroom space was provided in nearby Academic Hall, both of which were centrally located on the campus quad.

On September 14, 1908, Charlie met with his Correspondence class for the first time at 8 a.m. in a makeshift classroom in the basement of Academic Hall. Already anxious and still uncomfortable speaking in public, he stood before his first class, many of whom were not much younger than he. Suddenly, a large stream of warm water spurted out of one of the large overhead pipes in the ceiling and cascaded on his head in full view of the class.

"This might be an omen," he said to his students, grinning. "I hope it is the last time I am in hot water with this class.

"Even so," he said, "we must begin."[240]

This baptism turned out not to be a bad omen at all, as he would spend the next ten years on the faculty, introducing young minds to the craft of journalism in the first academic institution in the United States dedicated to it. Over time, the University of Missouri School of Journalism would become one of the leading journalism programs in the world. It still is to this day.

The *University Missourian*—Cornerstone of the Experience

At this time, journalism mainly meant newspapers. Newspapers were the primary and most influential means by which people received the news. Magazines were becoming popular, but were not as widely read as a general source for news. Williams took seriously his charge to provide an education "as thorough and as technical as that given to engineers, physicians, dentists, teachers, or lawyers."[241] To do this, he created a fully functioning newspaper—the *University Missourian*—which reported news from the University and from the town of Columbia. They also reported national news using telegraph links with national news services. The *University Missourian*, an eight-page newspaper published five days a week, was designed as the cornerstone of the School of Journalism experience.

Two Initial Growing Pains

The Journalism School had a couple of rocky episodes early on, which were handled by Williams. The *University Missourian's* entry into the local newspaper market riled the two local weekly newspapers, the *Columbia Statesman* and the *Columbia Herald*, which feared the upstart newspaper would cut into their advertising and circulation. The matter was quelled over time by Williams' skillful diplomacy. He moved the *Missourian's* printing operations off-campus and set up a separate non-profit corporation to operate it. All the while, he kept it the core of the school's curriculum.[242]

The second difficulty arose when Williams determined that Silas Bent was not "fitting in" at the school. As two men with entirely different personalities, Williams and Bent clashed. "Bent's urbane wit and irreverent manner, added to a love for fast living and lively parties, did not at all suit Williams, whose approach to life and to his pioneering, evangelistic mission was deadly serious."[243] Charlie tried to intercede, but neither of these two strong-willed men would give ground, so Bent tendered his resignation, which was accepted at the end of the first semester.[244] Williams replaced Bent with Frank L. Martin, whom he had known for many years. Martin worked at the *Kansas City Star*, where he had risen to the position of associate editor and editorial writer. He turned out to be a highly competent and agreeable individual who fit in well and soon became "a superb colleague."[245]

The Required Steps to Earn a Journalism Degree

A feature article in the September 2, 1911 edition of *Collier's* magazine described the process for earning a degree from the School of Journalism. It was written three years after the school's founding and outlined the required steps to a degree:

1. The Liberal Arts as an Academic Foundation: The first two years of study entailed essentially the same courses as for someone pursuing a standard Bachelor of Arts degree.

The *Collier's* article explained the rationale as follows:

> "Because of the value of a liberal academic education for writers, the student of journalism, in the first two years at

the university, takes much the same work as the candidates for the degree of Bachelor of Arts."[246]

2. The Journalism Coursework: In the second two years, journalism courses became the focus of the coursework. The courses listed in the *Collier's* article, many the same as the original ones, were presented as follows:

"But in his last two years, more than half of his studies are courses that are distinctly professional, such as these: *History and Principles of Journalism, News Gathering, Newspaper Making, Reporting, Copy-reading, Newspaper Administration, the Editorial, Advertising, Magazine Making, Newspaper Jurisprudence, Agricultural Journalism, Comparative Journalism, the Press and Public Opinion, Professional Terminology, Bibliography.*"[247]

The article further noted that these courses were taught with the same degree of professionalism as were courses in the medical, law, and engineering schools, and supplemented by the students' work on the *University Missourian*.[248]

3. Newspaper Experience: To learn the practical application of the newspaper, the students rotated through the stations of the *University Missourian*, akin to departments of a large newspaper, where they performed the hands-on work required at that stage of the process. These were:

Station I: The Assignment Desk

At the beginning of the workday, a designated number of students would line up at Prof. Frank Martin's desk to get their reporting assignments.

The process is described in *Collier's* as follows:

> "Just as on the city daily, the reporter's work here is systematic and exacting . . . for each reporter has work and destinations as definite as a postman's.
>
> All morning squads of reporters are coming to Professor Martin's little office, which is just off the larger room that resounds with typewriters. One after another, he calls their names and they appear for assignments. One is to interview the dean of the school of agriculture on the menace of the tenant-farmer; another is to see what news the jail and the hospital can furnish; another is to cover hotels; one of the young women in the class is to get the year's basketball schedule and 'write a line or two' about the sophomore girls' fudge party. As soon as they have collected their information, they are to return to the office and write their stories.
>
> (In the slang of the newspaper world, *everything* the reporter writes is a "story," from the description of a runaway to the Rev. Mr. Kuhl's interview denouncing peek-a-boo shirt-waists.)"[249]

Station II: The Typing Room

After a student (reporter) gets the story, it must be typed. This typing is performed at the school in a separate room, one with many typewriters. The *Collier's* piece vividly describes the area as follows:

> "That pitter-patter of typewriters! That paper strewn everywhere on the floor! The cub reporter sweating and biting his lips while he punches letter after letter with one finger of each hand! Now the patter rises to crescendo; now it subsides until the tick-tick of the cub's typewriter seems to

be as loud each time as a whack. Someone angrily wads up a sheet of copy paper and throws it on the floor. Then the crescendo of ticking again and the telephone bell jangles frantically.... To the writer who loves his trade, this scene, so jumbled and harsh to the ears and eyes of the outsider, is a picture of life that is truly worth living."[250]

Station III: The Copy Desk

Armed with the newly typed story, the student reporter would take it to the semi-circular copydesk where Charlie supervised their editing. This process was described as follows:

"In the room next to Professor Martin's office is the class in copy-reading.... In one corner is a semicircular table, the shape of a half disk of pineapple, with the professor [Ross]—another of those newspaper faces!—sitting in the hole where the core used to be.

Grouped around the head copy-readers table, in chairs which have arms like those in dairy lunchrooms, sit the student copy-readers. They are editing, rewriting when necessary, posting directions to the printers, and scribbling proper headlines for the manuscripts furnished by Professor Martin's classes in reporting. The business of Professor Ross's class is to prepare the copy for the printers. They must be as quick to discern errors and discrepancies in facts as in grammar and spelling."[251]

Station IV: Printing

After the stories were edited at the copy desk, the final copies were assembled, and taken to the printer shop (located in the town of Columbia) where the newspaper was printed. The students had little to do with the *University Missourian's* printing and circulation, although it was open to them for observation. The *Collier's* article described it as follows:

"From the copy-reading room a basketful of copy starts for the printer's. Follow that basket and you go downtown to publication offices of the '*University Missourian*,' an address with the businesslike sound of 'Broadway and Eighth Street.'

Three men are hired by the university for the mechanical department of the paper. The student has a chance to see as much as he wishes, the way the wheels go round and how the type is set; and he may ask questions to his heart's content. The shop has its own linotype and a duplex press, which prints from rolls of paper just as city dailies do, and which, if necessary, can finish 5,500 eight-page copies in an hour."[252]

4. Real World Work Experience: At the School of Journalism, all students had the opportunity to work at an actual newspaper before graduation. Walter Williams' industry connections were critical here. The *Collier's* article described this opportunity as follows:

"Before graduation each student is given a try-out on a newspaper in St. Louis, Chicago, Kansas City, or Omaha. The result is that most of the graduates have assurance of jobs before commencement time. This is the third year of [the operation of] the school. It has increased in attendance far more rapidly than any other department on the Missouri campus. A gain of twenty-five percent last term. Its students are enrolled from eighteen states this year, all the way from New York and New Jersey to California."[253]

This hands-on method of teaching journalism proved popular, and, by all indications, it was an idea whose time had come. It was essentially an internship program, like those common today in professional schools.

Williams had quickly created a rigorous program for the practice of journalism, one that gave its graduates a practical nuts-and-bolts education and set them up for success in the newspaper business.

Charlie Falls in Love: Mary Paxton

When he accepted Williams' offer to join the faculty at the newly formed School of Journalism, Charlie prepared for his move to Columbia. As part of his transition, he visited his family in Independence, where he explained the reasons for and ramifications of his career change. Despite his drop in income, he assured his mother he could continue sending money home for the family's support. He also continued to support Helen's education, who had just completed her first year at the University.

During this visit, Charlie saw Elmer Twyman, a good friend and high-school classmate, who encouraged Charlie to take a local girl, Mary Paxton, on a date.[254] Mary was less than two years younger than Charlie and was Bess Wallace's good friend and next-door neighbor. Although Mary and Charlie had both grown up in Independence, they didn't know each other. This, in part, was because their families attended different churches; Mary's family belonged to the Presbyterian Church, while the Rosses were members of The Christian Church. Mary's parents were well-to-do, and her father didn't want her to attend the public high school. She was sent to Manual High School in Kansas City[255] and then to Hollins College in Virginia. Later she spent several years at the University of Chicago. Eventually she decided she wanted to study journalism, but the University of Chicago didn't have that curriculum. She then learned the University of Missouri was opening a journalism school, so she left Chicago for her home state to enroll at its new school.[256] She, too, was visiting Independence during the summer of 1908, when Elmer Twyman introduced her to Charlie.

On their impromptu date, Charlie and Mary spent an enjoyable afternoon together at Fairmont Park near Kansas City, where, among other things, they rode a popular ride, the "shoot-the-chutes." At the end of the day, Charlie, as per the etiquette of the day, got Mary home before dark. Although the outing was a pleasant time for both, they parted with no plans to see each other again. Charlie's visit to Independence soon ended, and he moved to Columbia to prepare for the upcoming semester.[257]

A few weeks later, Charlie and Mary met again, this time in Columbia, when Mary registered for her courses at the journalism school. In so doing, she not only became one of the first women to register for the program, but she also learned, to her surprise, that her blind date from Independence was now one of the professors. Apparently, neither had talked about their careers on that first date! By the spring of 1909, they began dating again, this time steadily.[258] Charlie was an eligible bachelor, and Mary was "pretty, bright, and lively."[259] Charlie soon learned that dating a student had its share of drawbacks. Mary had joined the Kappa Kappa Gamma sorority. When Charlie picked her up for a date, a sorority member would meet him at the door and yell, "MARY, HERE'S PROFESSOR ROSS."[260] Despite these awkward moments, they became engaged to be married. It was the summer of 1909, a year before Mary was to graduate. This relationship by then had become a cause célèbre throughout the school. This caused Charlie such professional concern that, in Mary's final year, he wouldn't allow her to take his Correspondence course because, in her words, "everybody knew we were engaged, and he was afraid the other students would think he was partial."[261]

In the spring of 1910, Mary became the first woman graduate of the School of Journalism. Just before graduation, Dean Walter Williams, who genuinely liked and respected her, sought her advice on an unusual matter. As the story goes:

> "As graduation approached, Williams gave Paxton the honor of selecting the color of the journalism school's graduation tassel because she would be the first female graduate. Williams asked her what color she would like, and Paxton replied, 'Any old color as long as it is red.' The journalism school's tassel remains red to this day."[262]

While they were happily engaged, neither was in a hurry to marry. Charlie had not saved enough money to support a wife, mostly because he helped his family. Also, he didn't want his wife to have a time-consuming job outside the home. Mary, by contrast, wanted to put her journalism education to use—and she wanted excitement in her life. "There's so much to see, so much to do" she said.[263] So, after graduation, Mary took a job at the *Kansas City Post,* where she became the first female journalist in Kansas City. Her articles stood out—one was on the sport of ballooning, based on her airborne ride in one; another involved a tour through Kansas City's notorious red-light district. Not surprisingly, she became a success as well as something of a celebrity.[264]

As a result of their differences, not to mention the distance between Columbia and Kansas City, Charlie and Mary drifted apart and eventually ended their engagement. They parted amicably and remained friends. They each enjoyed a stellar career in journalism and eventually married someone else—she became Mary Paxton Keeley. But their fondness for one another never completely ended. They kept their friendship alive and wrote hundreds of personal letters to each other for more than four decades after their engagement ended. At the University of Missouri, their star-crossed romance remains part of the folklore of the School of Journalism.[265,266]

The Journalist's Creed

Even with the School of Journalism's early success, Walter Williams felt something lacking. Somehow, the school's stated mission—the education of future journalists—remained incomplete. Fundamentally a religious man, Williams cared deeply about man's relationship to God as well as man's duty to his fellow man. He felt that guiding moral principles were lacking in the profession of journalism. After all, medical students were guided by the Hippocratic Oath, and law students were guided by a Canon of Ethics, so shouldn't journalism students also have a core set of beliefs? In his inimitable style, he set out to do something about it.

By 1914, Williams' statement of principles for journalists was complete. Williams named it "The Journalist's Creed." It immediately became part of the *Deskbook of the School of Journalism*, the manual developed by the faculty for the *University Missourian*. It was also integrated into the courses and the student classroom work. To reinforce its importance, all students were required to commit it to memory, and they would be tested on it before the end of their academic careers.[267] It reads as follows:

THE JOURNALIST'S CREED

I believe in the profession of journalism.

I believe the public journal is a public trust; that all connected with it are, to the full measure of their responsibility, trustees for the public; that acceptance of lesser service than public service is a betrayal of this trust.

I believe that clear thinking and clear statement, accuracy and fairness are fundamental to good journalism.

I believe that a journalist should write only what he holds in his heart to be true.

I believe that suppression of the news, for any consideration other than the welfare of society, is indefensible.

I believe that no one should write as a journalist what he would not say as a gentleman; that bribery by one's own pocketbook is as much to be avoided as bribery by the pocketbook of another; that individual responsibility may not be escaped by pleading another's instructions or another's dividends.

I believe that advertising, news and editorial columns should alike serve the best interests of the readers; that a single standard of helpful truth and cleanness should prevail for all; that the supreme test of good journalism is the measure of its public service.

I believe that journalism that succeeds best—and best deserves success—fears God and honors man; is stoutly independent, unmoved by pride of opinion or greed of power, constructive, tolerant but never careless, self-controlled, patient, always respectful of its readers but always unafraid, is quickly indignant at injustice; is unswayed by the appeal of privilege or the clamor of the mob; seeks to give every man a chance and, as far as law and honest wage and recognition of human brotherhood can make it so, an equal chance; is profoundly patriotic while sincerely promoting international good will and cementing world comradeship is a journalism of humanity, of and for today's world.[268]

Soon after it was published, The Creed became well-received and widely distributed. It was disseminated by graduates of the school, by editors of many newspapers and even by members of the International Press Congress, with whom Williams had ties. Over time, it would be published in more than one hundred languages and would be posted in newspaper offices around the world.[269]

There is no record that Charlie Ross played any meaningful role in the creation of The Creed. He may have been consulted by Williams or asked to review a draft, but that is only speculation. The religious tone of The Creed was not Charlie's style, and, at that point in his life, he was not vocal about his religious beliefs (his family understood him to be an agnostic)[270]. He most likely let Williams create and propagate this on his own. Likewise, there is no reason to believe he would have opposed it, because his belief in the fairness and objectivity of journalism was totally consistent with that in The Creed.

11

THE WRITING OF NEWS

Charlie's Book

As part of his duties at the newly opened School of Journalism, Charlie was assigned to teach, among other things, a course in "Correspondence." (In the jargon of journalism, a "correspondent" meant—and still means—an on-the-scene reporter; thus, the term "correspondence" meant the written product of news reporting, *i.e.,* the stories published in newspapers.) This course drew on Charlie's strengths; he was a good writer who had worked as a reporter and at the copy desk at multiple newspapers.

As a pioneer teacher of newspaper writing, Charlie was tasked with creating this new course's curriculum from scratch, lecture-by-lecture. He was certain he'd be asked to teach it more than once, so he kept the original notes, which, as time went along, he amended and refined. At that time newspapers were haphazardly training most of their own reporters, and he began to realize that a wider need existed for this content. He decided to use his notes to write a textbook on news writing; and he hoped it would be both useful and a money-maker for him personally. By 1910, he had collected and organized enough information that he was well on his way to writing a book. Eschewing the newspaper jargon of "correspondence," he titled his book *The Writing of News*. It was published in 1911 by Henry Holt & Company. It was a 230-page book that sold for $1.50 per copy (or $1.62 if you bought it by mail directly from the publisher).

A cover shot of a reprint of Charlie Ross' book, *The Writing of News*, published by Kessinger's Legacy Reprints. (Photo/Ross family collection)

On its inscription page, *The Writing of News* says, "To My Mother." Charlie's mother always supported his academic advancement, and theirs was a very close relationship. Helen, however, considered this inscription differently. She says in her memoirs: "Though dedicated to Mother, it is a monument to the pedagogical talents of Mammy in her stiff black dress."[271] Since his mother was alive at the time the book was published (and Mammy wasn't), it seems unlikely he would have had it any other way.

By design, the book was organized so that it could be used either in a classroom or independently by a working reporter wanting to learn his craft. Charlie encouraged this broad usage; the book's preface stated he "hoped the book will prove helpful either as a laboratory guide in the school room or as a textbook for home use." For Charlie, then living on a modest faculty salary, sales of the book beyond the School of Journalism would be most welcome.

For the book's initial printing, the publisher's brief promotional piece stated:

> THE WRITING OF NEWS
> By Charles G. Ross
> Assistant Professor of Journalism
> in the University of Missouri

A practical manual that every man who wishes to write for the papers should have, and that contains much of interest to the general reader.

The author was trained on a newspaper and is now assistant professor of journalism in the University of Missouri. His book is equipped with helpful exercises, shows how to rewrite faulty matter, is full of practical examples of "Heads," "Bromides," etc.

The chapters include: Newspaper Copy; The English of the Newspapers; The Writer's Viewpoint; The Importance of Accuracy; News Values; Writing the Lead; The Story Proper; The Feature Story; The Interview; Special Types of Stories; The Correspondent; Copy Reading; Writing the "Head"; Don'ts for the News Writer; Newspaper Bromides.

The first eight chapters of the book provide definitions and broad principles of newspaper writing. The final seven chapters deal with the various elements of a newspaper's content. The book is loaded with practical examples as well as an exhaustive list of "Don'ts for the News Writer" (*e.g.*, "Don't hesitate to repeat a name for sake of clearness" and "Don't use 'state' for 'say.' A statement is formal. Most persons merely 'say' they are going fishing."). The second, third, and fourth chapters contain the three most enduring aspects of the book: (1) the quality of writing in a newspaper, (2) the perspective (viewpoint) of the reporter in writing the story, and (3) the importance of accuracy.

Simplicity, Clearness, and the Terseness of Style

In the book's second chapter, entitled "The English of the Newspapers," Charlie takes exception to the criticism then leveled at newspapers that their use of the English language was inferior. The term "Newspaper English," he asserted, is a term that has been "hurled indiscriminately at all newspapers, the good as well as the bad . . . ." He agrees that, for "loosely edited newspapers the criticism is just." However, he countered, "No defense is needed of the style of writing in the well-edited modern newspaper." He went on to explain that the "reporter writes his story for all readers of all degrees of intelligence—for the man whose only reading is newspapers and the man of cultivated tastes." To accommodate this variety of readership, Charlie concluded, "a good news story is *clear, concise and forceful.*" Charlie laid out the three elements not only for good "newspaper English" but also for good writing in general—for him there was no difference between the two.

Charlie advocated in the book for "clearness," saying that writing should be simple: "Simplicity of structure and diction implies clearness." Second, to emphasize "conciseness," he references a command frequently heard in working newspaper offices: "Boil it down!" From his newspaper experience, Charlie argued: "The hurried reader has no time for the story clogged with unnecessary words and trivia detail; the newspaper has no space for it." Last, Charlie believed a reporter's writing should be forceful. He asserted: "Force grows out of simplicity, clearness and terseness of style." He instructed the reader that the "active voice is usually more forcible than the passive." He also emphatically gave the following rule of thumb to the novice reporter: *"In seeking force, choose the Anglo-Saxon word instead of its foreign equivalent unless clearness demands the latter"* [Italics in original text]. All three of these characteristics of good writing were reflected in Charlie's own terse, straightforward writing style.

The Writer's Viewpoint

In the third chapter of the book, "The Writer's Viewpoint," Charlie articulated the gold standard for the reporter's point of view in writing a newspaper story:

"The ideal news story, apart from the questions of style, has these qualities:

1. It is written without prejudice. It is fair, both in spirit and in detail.

2. It is written from the impersonal, objective viewpoint.

3. It is written in good taste.

4. It has originality."

The Importance of Accuracy

Charlie devoted an entire chapter of his book to accuracy. In its first sentence, he emphatically states: "The first essential of good news writing is accuracy." He tells of placards posted "on the walls . . . in some [newspaper] offices where, with laudable brevity, this motto is urged upon the staff:

> ACCURACY
> TERSENESS
> ACCURACY"

In this chapter, he goes on to explain that accuracy means more than "mere grammatical correctness" and more than "stating every fact with precision." For a story to be accurate, it must contain "the spirit as well as the letter of the truth."

The Book's Influence

No record exists of the sales of *The Writing of News,* or the royalties Charlie earned from the book. (He said that the money he made "wasn't much.") Nevertheless, Charlie was proud of it, and it was one of the first textbooks on journalism written in the United States.[272] It was used at the School of Journalism for several decades and made its way into newspaper offices around the country. Charlie's advocacy for clearness, conciseness, and force in writing was later espoused by others. An example was the *Kansas City Star*, a major newspaper approximately 100 miles west of Columbia in Missouri. In 1915 it developed the "Star Copy Style sheet" as a guide for its reporters. It gives many of the writing principles found in *The Writing of News* (*e.g.,* "Use short sentences," "Use vigorous English," "Eliminate every superfluous word," and "Avoid the use of adjectives"). Ernest Hemingway, whose trademark was the economy of his words as well as the strength and vigor of his writing, worked at the *Kansas City Star* as a reporter in 1917 and 1918. He used that newspaper's style sheet and "remarked to a reporter that the admonitions in this style sheet were the best rules I ever learned in the business of writing."[273]

In her memoirs, Helen Ross referred to Charlie's book, but mistakenly called it *The Elements of Style* instead of *The Writing of News*. This was an interesting mistake, because, at about the time Helen was writing her memoirs in the 1950s and 1960s, a textbook entitled *The Elements of Style* by Strunk and White was widely used to teach writing (and still is). *The Elements of Style* is a short, pithy textbook that gives rules for writing lucid English prose. For emphasis, its rules of grammar are phrased as direct orders. Like Charlie's book, it focuses on those rules most commonly violated, such as the misuse of "bromides," and contains numerous examples of the "do's and don'ts" of good writing. Prof. Strunk, like Charlie, advocated clear, concise, and "forcible" writing ("Vigorous writing is concise. A sentence should contain no unnecessary words, a paragraph no unnecessary sentences . . .").[274] Of course, it would be presumptuous to argue that somehow Strunk and White copied Charlie's ideas for their own textbook. However, it does show that Charlie was at the vanguard of the effort to improve the writing of prose from the florid, verbose style of the 19th century to the more crisp and direct style of the twentieth century.

The Writing of News set a standard for professionalism in journalism. It demonstrated Charlie's mastery of the essentials of efficient and effective writing, as well as his understanding of what makes quality in newspaper writing. It would be the only book he'd write. However, it would not be his last writing project to earn him some additional money while at the University.

Helen at the University

Helen's expectations about her college experience were heavily influenced by Charlie, who, in college, had worked hard and enjoyed college social life as a member of his beloved *Sigma Chi* fraternity. Since high school, Helen had believed "it was in the stars for me" to be a teacher, like her grandmother Thomas, so she put herself on an academic track to pursue the "pedagogical courses." Upon her arrival on campus, she was assigned to live in "Reed Hall, the one girls' dormitory." Perhaps she should have seen it as an omen that she was paired with a lackluster roommate whom she described in her memoirs "as plain as I could imagine."[275]

The Unnamed Sorority

Years later, Helen recalled that her first major disappointment was the "rejection by the sorority to which Charlie thought I would be invited." She had assumed that becoming a member "was just a part of going to a university." However, during the selection process, she realized "my little reefer with the brass buttons and my hair ribbon and my plain clothes were no decoy to a sorority," and she was not invited to join—and that rejection stung. She later recalled that "for the first time, I felt 'left out.'"

After this setback, Helen settled into life in the dorm for the remainder of her freshman year with "feelings of utter inadequacy, until an older group of girls took me up and began to treat me as someone worth noticing."²⁷⁶ They accepted Helen and appreciated the interest she showed in their lives. Perhaps it was during this period Helen first realized she had a talent for listening and counseling. She knew she "liked the attention and tried to live up daily to new expectations of combined wisdom and shyness." Although her stated goal was to be a teacher, this newly appreciated skill of listening and giving suggestions to others would help her in the future, in ways she had yet to realize. Like many college freshmen, Helen not only learned the academic lessons but also discovered things about herself and how she might contribute to the larger world.

The following year (1908), shortly after Charlie joined the faculty at the School of Journalism, that same unnamed sorority, perhaps with encouragement from Charlie, invited Helen to join. She did not want to disappoint her brother, and, with much trepidation, she accepted. Helen's introduction to sorority life was predictably unsatisfying because she discovered "it meant little except trying to be an acceptable member of a group primarily concerned with fraternity parties." In her memoirs, she expressed her anxiety about the social demands of the sorority life:

> "For this [attending fraternity parties] I was unready and timid and sad about it, too. I must go to fraternity dances, I was told, and I did go to the Sigma Chi's, who asked me because of Charlie, groaning inwardly at the failure I expected to make. I danced poorly; Mother and Mammy had not 'believed' in dancing so . . . I . . . learned self-consciously and awkwardly, [but was] never able to surrender to the rhythm and the fun."²⁷⁷

In time, Helen learned to adjust to sorority lifestyle. After her second year, she moved into the sorority house. Her sorority sisters tried to make her "popular" though soon abandoned that idea. Nevertheless, they accepted her and became "content as I helped to keep up the average grades of that organization."[278] Although not "popular" for social events, she soon found herself sought out "as a confidante by the love-lorn, a new role" which, in her words, "brought me as much information as satisfaction."[279]

Helen's excellent grades and ability to listen apparently made her respected enough that the chapter appointed her its delegate to a sorority convention in Bloomington, Indiana. To attend it, Helen took the train, a memorable trip that resulted in her first night in a "sleeper car." It wouldn't be her last.

Although she had little in common with her sorority sisters, she remained a member through graduation. She became so respected that, in her final year, she was elected the sorority's president. She found the position's title was more impressive than the actual duties, some of which reinforced her feelings of inadequacy. As she later expressed it, as president of the house, she "was supposed to watch [the members'] decorum, [and] to send the steady beaux home if they stayed too late at night, a masochist's job for one who longed not so much for the man as for the feeling she could get one."[280] Although she remained a dutiful sorority member, her overall distaste for the sorority experience kept her from mentioning its name in her memoirs, written three decades later.

Two Memorable Relationships

Although Helen initially struggled to remember much from her college years (I "recall so little except determination to get through and to work"), her memoirs later recount two noteworthy adventures.

One episode involved the daughter of a saloon owner, the other the daughter of a wealthy man.

Agnes O'Brien

In Helen's freshman dorm, Reed Hall, there were several older students who belonged to no sorority. Agnes O'Brien, who also happened to be from Independence, was one of these women. Her father was "an Irish saloon keeper" and Agnes was "from 'a good Irish Catholic family, but people we never knew.'"[281] Agnes was "the youngest in a big family of mostly boys [and] had the independence and security of being her father's favorite and the only one he could afford to send away to school."[282] Agnes was a self-assured, impressive-looking young woman—"narrow hipped, long legged, she strode across the campus, her blue eyes always seeming to see far ahead, her light brown hair hanging in a careless braid, looking for some justice to be done."[283] Helen soon learned that "Agnes could smell injustice afar off and no matter what the context, felt called as an avenging angel to right the wrong."[284]

In one episode, Agnes was brought before the University's Disciplinary Committee, (made up of male professors) for refusing to take a "shower-bath" after gym class. Helen accompanied her to the hearing. Helen recalled sitting in the anteroom as a potential witness for Agnes, caught up in the indignation of the incident, while failing to "see the utter ludicrousness of a solemn meeting of the professors" about this "injustice."[285] Fortunately, the Disciplinary Committee never asked for Helen's testimony. Agnes was disciplined by the committee and had to leave school. Soon a St. Louis newspaper learned of Agnes's refusal and "made a big story of the event, with headlines, 'Coed expelled because she won't take a bath.'"[286] Agnes believed she was victorious because "she left the University to show them she would live a life of her own."[287] Helen later admitted that she "was caught up into the fervor of the leader" and that she "was there [at the hearing] in obedience to feelings, not rational judgment."[288] After the episode, Helen came to realize that by befriending Agnes and joining her crusades, she had jeopardized her own college education—something that left her unnerved for the rest of that year.

Irene W. and Her Father

During Helen's senior year, she still lived in the sorority house. Across the street was a newly built apartment house. Two of its first tenants were a father and daughter, whom Helen guardedly refers to only as Mr. W. and Irene W. Irene and Helen were the same age, although Helen was a senior and Irene was only a freshman. Apparently ill health had kept Irene out of school for several years. Irene and her father "kept house, a novel arrangement, to my mind," Helen later reflected. Mr. W was "middle-aged, highly intelligent, sophisticated, polite but bantering, his conversations spiced with bits of his life in the consular service under [President] Cleveland."[289] This father-daughter pair was independently wealthy. Irene wore beautifully tailored clothes, had a weekly delivery of boxes of chocolates from Boston, and "two colored servants to take care of the apartment."[290] Irene ruled over her indulgent father, who went to great efforts to avoid angering his daughter.

Helen was fascinated by the sophistication of the Ws. They had the first Victrola (a phonograph record player) Helen had ever seen or heard, and they played a wide range of records, particularly operas such as *La Traviata, Madama Butterfly,* and *Rigoletto.* It became an oasis for Helen, who would enjoy "a beautiful, quiet dinner in their home, a frequent refuge from the din of the chapter-house dining room."²⁹¹ Because Mr. W was often away, tending to his "farms" in southern Missouri, Helen essentially moved into the apartment with Irene. Because of the Ws' sociability and sophistication, Irene "developed a little salon of young professors who were charmed by her hospitality and her father's urbanity."²⁹² In her memoirs, Helen mentioned three of the men—an ambitious law-faculty member, a mathematics instructor, and a tall, lively professor—and was flattered by the attention they paid her though none led to any romance. Such was not the case with Mr. W, who, unbeknownst to Helen, was taking a liking to her.

After her graduation in 1911, Helen left Columbia and returned to Independence to teach, but she remained friends with Irene. The physical separation and change in circumstances understandably tempered their relationship. However, this was only temporary, as Helen would see Irene—and her father—again.

Charlie and Helen at University

Charlie joined the faculty of the School of Journalism just after Helen had completed her freshman year, and they both benefitted from this favorable turn of chance.

As noted earlier, Helen's rejection by the sorority was reversed after Charlie arrived on campus. Perhaps it was due to Charlie's intervention, or perhaps Helen had acclimated to college life and became more acceptable to the sorority, or perhaps there was some other reason. Certainly, Charlie's presence on campus gave Helen enhanced status with this sorority. ("Charlie . . . was unmarried and my popularity with the girls in the chapter increased.")²⁹³

Charlie's academic advice for Helen continued in college just as in high school: "Charlie had expected . . . [me] to go on with the Classics and I read Horace and Plautus and Terrance and Livy with much more difficulty than Caesar and Cicero in High School." Helen's transcript shows many Classics courses: Greek Mythology, Horace, Roman History, Roman Life (Latin), Roman Drama (Latin), Latin Prose, and Latin Literature, to name a few.[294] Charlie's financial support was welcomed, and he provided the "weekly check to care for my expenses, usually ten dollars was enough."[295]

Although Charlie had fostered in Helen a love for words, he subtly discouraged her from pursuing a career as a journalist or a writer. Shortly after the journalism school opened, Mary Paxton offered Helen a position on the "student staff." Flattered and seeing this as an opening to a potential career, Helen accepted, albeit "with a flood of anxiety."[296] Asking Mary for guidance, Helen was simply told she should find something interesting and write about it. Helen became completely at a loss to find a topic: "I knew few people, I was bewildered by a new society in which popularity, dates, and fraternities made demands I could not fill." Too embarrassed to seek any further help, she wrote nothing—and resigned. This ended any further thoughts of a newspaper or writing career.[297]

Helen Earns Her Degrees

Helen's academic performance at the University was exceptional. At the end of her four undergraduate years, she had earned two degrees: a Bachelor of Arts (B. A.) as well as a Bachelor of Science in Education.[298] At that time, areas of concentration (*i.e.,* majors) were not used. Her B. A. was the general college degree—awarded for successful completion of the undergraduate program. Helen's B. S. Ed. Degree enabled her to work as a schoolteacher. Like Charlie, she was elected to the *Phi Beta Kappa* society.

Commenting on her college years, Helen recalled her "determination to get through and to work."[299] In her memoirs, Helen admitted she relied on studying to get through the awkwardness she experienced: "I was no athlete, I was no social success, so I turned to study, much of which was dull."[300] She found her education classes particularly dull: "'Education' courses—I had to get a teacher's certification someday—flattened out into a few platitudes, which seemed familiar enough to one who had lived so intimately in a family group where one was always learning or teaching."[301]

Helen earned the degrees she wanted when she entered the University, and that was the main reason she went to college. Her college years did not stand out as an enjoyable time. Her awkwardness colored her experiences, and she was mostly relieved when her undergraduate years ended. During my conversations in the 1960s with Helen, Virginia, and J.B., there was little mention of their college experiences, except to say that the University was "almost free" and that they were happy to get a degree. By contrast, Charlie's undergraduate years at the University were among the happiest of his life, and he was forever devoted to *Sigma Chi*.[302]

Helen Returns to Independence

After her graduation in June 1911, Helen returned to Independence. She felt obligated to support her mother and four sisters (by then, Louise had gone to Arizona to take care of their ailing father). By this point, many loans incurred by JB's various mining ventures kept the family in debt. Helen was committed to helping her family and supporting her sisters so they, too, could one day earn a college degree.[303] When Helen returned home, she was delighted to find that Independence High School needed an additional teacher. She was immediately hired. Over the next five years, she taught Latin, English, and history at the high school she and her siblings all attended.

A Marriage Proposal

When Helen returned to Independence, she happily left college behind as the next chapter in her life unfolded. However, she remained in touch with Irene W. Within a few months after Helen's return to Independence, Irene wrote Helen and unexpectedly invited her to spend her Easter vacation with Irene and her father in New York City, all expenses paid. Helen readily agreed. How could she pass up a free trip to New York?

Helen took leave from school, boarded a train, and met Irene and her father in New York. Irene and Mr. W treated Helen to a first-class experience. Helen recalled that they "stayed at the old Hotel Majestic on Central Park West for a week" and "went to the theatre or a concert every night." They saw Ethel Barrymore in *Slice of Life*, which Helen admitted was her "first encounter with irony on the stage." The threesome also ate well, enjoying "oysters and baked Alaska and mushrooms, [and] Chicken-ala-King." They drove through Central Park in one of the old hansom cabs, visited the Metropolitan Museum, and saw the sights. In her memoirs, Helen recalled the week as an eye-opening, exhilarating experience that showed her a totally different side of life.[304]

A few years after their New York City sojourn, Irene became engaged "to a young lawyer her father did not choose." The wedding took place at Mr. W's residence "in a great white southern house." Helen served as the maid of honor and wore "a lovely silk dress brocaded with pink rosebuds." Mr. W gave Helen red roses to carry, which Helen soon realized was Mr. W's "way of telling me of his affection." Shortly after the wedding and when the reception had concluded, Mr. W unexpectedly proposed marriage to Helen surrounded by those luxurious trappings: "White dresses, with plenty of servants to wash and iron them, rose gardens, silver, [and southern] hospitality." Helen was taken aback, but also tempted to accept, mainly because it could mean an end to her family's financial struggles. But she eventually declined. In her memoirs, she cryptically says: "The lure was there, but the fantasy broke under the realism of the love-making of a sophisticated middle-aged man. Only the fantasy was ready." So, there must have been a sexual issue, either in fact or in Helen's imagination, that made the physical relationship unappealing. (In that Victorian era of sexual repression, one can only speculate.) She further acknowledged that the age difference was too great; she simply could not envision the marriage working. She eventually rejected his proposal and ended the relationship. Although Helen never married, she had at least this one opportunity to do so.[305]

After five years at the high school, Helen realized she wanted to do more with her life than teach high school at a woefully modest salary. She decided it was time to pursue her dreams beyond Missouri.

12

THE GOING OF JB ROSS

Papa's Comings and Goings

During the years JB spent away from home chasing his mining dreams, he periodically returned home to Independence. His visits, as recalled by Virginia, were times of both joy and sadness.

"Papa's home-comings were happy events. The 'girls' dressed 'the children' in their best to greet him. It was a long way from the railroad station to our house, and he always arrived 'grip' [a suitcase] in hand, stepping from a 'hack' [a hired carriage]. The children called the conveyance a 'funeral' because hacks were black and principally served funerals. Papa brought presents for everybody. Once I received a silver birth-date [charm] . . . . Another time he brought me a tiny gold ring. I can see it now and feel a tingle of joy—I put it on my finger at once. And in one of my childhood tragedies—I lost it the same day. Papa took me to the 'square' in the late afternoon, and when we stopped at the drug store, his friend,

Mr. Yantic gave me a cigar box. I carried one present in the other, but only the cigar box arrived home."[306]

Virginia and her sisters loved their father and looked forward to seeing him when he came home. It was a different feeling when he went away on one his "mining trips." Those departures left a sadness, almost a bitterness, reflecting the emotional gap between JB and his children. Virginia, even years later, recalled his departures:

"Goings were not happy events. Going meant that Frances and I each got a 'talking to' which was an admonition to 'help your mother' and 'be good' and a gentle extraction of a promise to do just that. Of course, 'the girls' were too grown up to get 'talking to's'—there was a vast difference between the 'girls' and the 'children.' [Baby] J.B. was just too young, and Charlie was already away.... I did not like the 'talking to.' Nor did Frances. It was too solemn."[307]

In his later years, J.B.'s family became increasingly concerned about his well-being, particularly with his failing eyesight. Virginia recalled:

"This was about the time Papa's sight began to fail. On visits home one of the children accompanied him, holding his hand, when he went about the town. We held his tools and passed them to him when he did his small jobs about the house. How he got along away from home remains a mystery."[308]

By this time, most of his trips were to Carthage in Missouri. But this was not making things any easier, and his family could sense that. It was what he wanted, and the pattern continued of his "comings and goings." With the deterioration in his eyesight, his earning power decreased even more, and this further undercut the family's circumstances.

JB's Final Stint in Missouri

In the summer of 1906, the Ross family moved into its newly built home at 214 Spring Street in Independence. Some might cynically characterize this mortgage-free, mostly finished (except for the wallpaper) house, as a "day late and a dollar short." However, it was the high-water mark of JB's accomplishments. His less-exotic mining ventures in southwestern Missouri had at least modestly paid off.

In 1906, Charlie was a year out of college and on his own. He never lived in the Spring Street house. Mama and all six of Charlie's sisters happily moved in. Helen was entering her senior year at Independence High School; Louise remained at home to undergo her eye treatments; Virginia and Frances (ages nine and seven, respectively) were in elementary school; and four-year-old "Jamie" remained at home. As usual, Papa was mostly away, doing his mining work in southwestern Missouri.

JB acquired an ownership interest in several Missouri mines—one was called the Log Cabin Mine[309]—and he "frequently acted as a consultant for prospective buyers"[310] on others. Although he'd had no formal education in mining, he'd been in the mining business for more than 20 years and had "developed a good, practical, if not scientific, judgement of mining property values." Putting their father's professional experience in a positive light, his daughters, years later, would refer to him as "a self-taught mining engineer."[311]

After the Spring Street house was completed, problems at the sites in southwestern Missouri began to snowball. His mining operations had deteriorated, and there was "a great concern about water in the mine—where would he get the money for pumping it out?"[312] Notices also arrived at home telling the family that taxes were overdue.[313] Letters began arriving about unpaid bills from hotels where JB had stayed. (Virginia recalled: "One letter sadly ends 'with much love, but that doesn't buy shoes or petticoats.'")[314] With his eyesight failing and his Missouri mining operations struggling, JB began looking for a change, for another business opportunity, which would get his wife those elusive diamonds he had promised her years ago. Before long, he found what he believed he had been looking for, a new situation on the remote western border of the Arizona Territory—in a place called Parker.

Parker, Arizona Territory

In 1871, Arizona was only a U. S. Territory, and Parker had just been established as a remote post office location to serve the Indian agent for the Colorado Indian Reservation. Located on the eastern bank of the Colorado River, overlooking California's Mojave Desert, it took its name from General Eli Parker, the first Native American to be appointed to the office of Commissioner of Indian Affairs. The Colorado Indian Reservation had been created by Congress in 1865 for all Native Americans living along the Colorado River; those peoples were members of the Navajo, Mojave, Hopi, and Chemehuevi tribes.[315]

In 1905, the railroad ran its tracks through the middle of town, and Parker became a railroad stopover, watering, and shipping station. Soon, the town developed from a railroad service area into a trading and shipping center for agriculture and mining in the region. Gold, copper, iron, and silver had been mined in this remote area for years. For decades, entrepreneurs had also had visions of turning this part of Arizona into an agricultural empire, but various attempts to irrigate the land had all failed. While nothing had as yet "taken off," the promise of Parker remained—and speculation only increased with the coming of the railroad.[316]

In 1908 the town of Parker was incorporated and formally laid out in an effort to attract more settlers. The design was a grid pattern of streets that formed blocks, with twelve 50'-wide lots in each block. In 1910 the federal government began auctioning off these lots to new residents. A small community began to take shape that scratched out its existence providing supplies and services to the nearby Indian Reservation and to scattered agricultural and mining operations.

JB Discovers Parker, Arizona

We don't know how JB first became interested in Parker, Arizona. Possibly he heard it word-of-mouth through his mining contacts, or perhaps he read about it in a newspaper. But it must have come as a shock to Ella when he first proposed to go there. Parker was a thousand miles west of Independence in the remotest part of the American desert. In his younger years, he had traveled such distances, but in 1908 he was 56 years old, no longer a young man, and going blind. Somehow, this wild and godforsaken place had an irresistible allure for JB, who still refused to believe he couldn't strike it rich. There was mining near Parker, which was JB's business. It was a warmer climate, with almost year-round sunshine, undoubtedly a draw given his aging body and poor eyesight. The federal government was promoting the area, and it was just across the Colorado river from California, the Golden State. JB calculated that Parker was a place that needed his skills, would be more amenable for his health, and he would find that elusive fortune which he knew was just one stroke of good luck away. He was also more than happy to leave those dark, damp, disappointing lead and zinc mines in southern Missouri behind—not to mention the local creditors.

How did JB possibly persuade his wife to agree to this sudden decision—and to this crazy location? How did he explain it to his children? Apparently, this wasn't terribly difficult for JB. Ever the storyteller, he easily wove a tale of future riches. Ella had long since condoned JB's peripatetic pattern. It's easy to imagine Ella rolling her eyes when first hearing JB tell of this new "opportunity." The children were led to believe that "Parker was to provide our college educations, our financial security, even some luxury."[317] So long-suffering Ella agreed to let him take this new adventure, though she must have harbored serious reservations.

JB's first visit to Parker went very well, and he immediately fell in love with the isolated outpost. ("Papa went there to spend a few months and it became 'home,'"[318] Virginia recalled.)[319] He returned to Independence for the summer and relayed his excitement to Ella. Ella, a few months later in 1908, and with five-year-old "Jamie" in hand, skeptically accompanied JB to Parker for the winter.[320] Ella quickly realized that Parker wasn't a good place to raise a child, and its hot, dry, and dusty isolation had no appeal for her. However, JB had made his decision. Ella acknowledged that "it was a safe place for a man who was almost totally blind, and it provided the interest that he needed."[321] After serving out the winter in Parker, Ella gratefully returned to Independence with Jamie. JB was now determined that the "spot in the sand in the Mojave desert" would become his home.[322]

With his engaging personality, it didn't take JB long to win over the Parker community. He purchased a few of the town's lots and "invested a few hundred dollars on the Arizona side of the bridge on the Colorado River." He became a well-known and respected member of this community of fewer than 500 people. He took on a few public-service jobs, such as Justice of the Peace (drawing on his prior background in law enforcement) and president of its school board. While he cultivated community life in Parker, there is little evidence he engaged in the mining business or earned any significant extra income. Meanwhile, the family continued to worry about him living by himself with his failing eyesight.

After graduating from Independence High School in 1909, Louise remained in town to continue helping out the family. According to her sister, Louise had "many friends and several beaux" and "visited her twin at the University" and generally "had a good time" for that entire year after graduating high school.[323] In July 1910, the family encouraged Louise to go to Parker and to look after JB. Louise saw this as an exciting adventure and agreed. Thus "Papa and Louise went West on the several-day train trip with stops at Harvey Houses for meals."[324] Arriving in the fall, after the worst of the summer heat had subsided, Louise learned firsthand about the difficulties of life in the Arizona desert. As recalled by Virginia:

> "Life in Parker was hard. They lived in two houses (little more than shacks) which were joined at the property line to satisfy homesteading requirements for two lots. Heat, even in the fall and spring, was above 100 degrees. Frequent sandstorms left the flimsy houses with heaps of sand that had to be shoveled out. Water was brought in by the barrel and in short supply. No plumbing. No luxury of any kind, except sunshine. Small comfort."[325]

Louise adjusted to life in Parker and to taking care of her aging father's home and other needs. Little did she know what was in store for her.

Louise Becomes a Teacher

Not long after she arrived in Parker, Louise received quite a surprise. Her reaction to this unexpected turn of events was vividly captured years later by her sister Virginia:

> "No sooner had they settled in their homestead shacks than Louise was waited upon by a delegation of leading citizens. The schoolteacher had just left, and term was about to begin. Miss Ross would have to take over the one-room school. No, she told them. She did not like school, could not teach, did not know how long she would be there, had plenty to do in taking care of her father and the homesteader shacks in which they lived. Definitely, no. Under no conditions. The delegation left, only to return the next day. She was the one unmarried woman in the town and she would have to take the school job. Again, no. Finally our father persuaded her to try it, temporarily. Louise, the reluctant servant, gave in. Of course, said the school board, after she gave in, she would have to pass a little examination to satisfy the state law, but that would be no problem. And it wasn't."[326]

School-hating Louise became Parker's only schoolteacher in its one-room schoolhouse. It's easy to imagine she didn't take kindly to her father's finessing her into this situation. However, as it turned out, she became a very good teacher and enjoyed the work for several years. In the process, she earned a reputation as one of the finest teachers in Arizona.

Charlie Becomes Smitten—Again

By 1912, Charlie was a respected member of the School of Journalism's faculty, and he'd published a groundbreaking textbook. His engagement to Mary Paxton had ended when she moved on to Kansas City to pursue her own career. With Mary gone, Charlie felt a void in his life. He realized he was getting older, and he missed the female companionship he'd had with Mary. However, he now knew he wanted a partner who would support his work and career, not someone who pursued an independent path.

Florence Marie Griffin

Florence Marie Griffin was born in 1894. The Griffin family fled Ireland's Potato Famine in the mid-1800s and settled in St. Louis. Her father, John J. Griffin, was raised in a crowded household with a brother and six sisters. They all attended the local Catholic grade schools. In 1893, John married Jeannette K. Cooley, two years his junior, who had been born of pioneer parents in the Dakota Territory. After their marriage, the young couple settled in St. Louis, where their two daughters, Florence and Estelle, were born.

As a young man, John started out in various clerk jobs and eventually worked for the Assessor's Office for the City of St. Louis. In 1900, his employment prospects improved when he joined *The St. Louis Republic,* then a major newspaper, where he eventually rose to manager of the circulation department. When Florence was in high school, he managed to purchase a home at 4134 Labadie Street in a mixed German-Irish neighborhood. The family attended nearby St. Matthew's Catholic Church, and they were devoted members. As a child, Florence was unusually close to her proud father, who took her to political and social events where most of the married men were accompanied by their spouses.[327]

Florence excelled in school. In January 1906, when she was 12 years old, *The St. Louis Republic*, where her father worked, featured a story highlighting her success. It related how the principal of her grammar school proudly announced that Florence Griffin had performed well enough on her final examinations to be promoted to study at newly built Yeatman High School (soon to be renamed Central High School). This made her the youngest person at that time to ever attend public high school in St. Louis.[328] Four years later, on January 10, 1910, Florence graduated from Central High School as the youngest person in her class. Her family was proud, her father robustly so. An article in *The St. Louis Republic* read in part:

> "Miss Griffin displays unusual talent for art, is a musician and a writer of essays. She has perfected her handicraft under the tutelage of Francis Oakes Sylvester, director of art at Central High School. Some of her products in hammered brass, tooled leather and jewelry are now in the possession of her friends, upon whom she bestowed them as presents.
>
> Miss Griffin will take the course at Teachers College, after which she will matriculate in the State University, at Columbia, Missouri, where she will take up journalism. Miss Griffin is the winner of a second prize for a story which appeared in the High School magazine a year ago."[329]

This article reflects Florence's penchant for art and handicrafts, subjects not typically associated with academics in today's world. However, these practical skills were highly valued at the time. Florence relished showing off (and talking about) her skills.

Bright and confident, Florence was on a path to college. It is unknown whether she attended Teachers College in St. Louis after high school as the newspaper article suggests. But 18 months later, on September 18, 1911, she did enter the University of Missouri in Columbia as an undergraduate student. At that time, her father wrote to D. J. McAuliffe, an editor at the cross-town rival *St. Louis Post-Dispatch*, and asked if he could have someone at the University call on Florence to welcome her to the University. Mr. McAuliffe didn't know Florence's father, although both men had attended St. Brigit's grade school at about the same time. A bit perplexed, he wrote to Charlie Ross, the person he knew best at the University in Columbia. Mr. McAuliffe asked Charlie if he could find someone "to give her [Florence] some courtesy and attention." In response to this rather unusual request, Charlie, who couldn't think of anyone else to carry out the favor, called on Florence himself.

Despite their difference in age (Charlie was nine years older than Florence) and in their status (he was a professor, she a first-year student), something clicked between them. Florence was bright and self-assured, and she enjoyed—often sparked—lively and interesting conversation. Charlie's personality was fundamentally reserved—a thoughtful man more comfortable with writing than speaking—yet he had an easy manner and was a good listener as well. He appreciated interesting and unusual people, and Florence had those characteristics, plus she enjoyed talking and seldom hesitated in articulating an opinion. They hit it off immediately and continued seeing each other in the months to come. Charlie's reluctant "helping Florence get settled" in the fall of 1911 became the beginning of a long relationship.[330]

Surprisingly, Florence's academic performance at the University was disappointing. In her first semester in college in the fall of 1911, her transcript shows she enrolled in five courses, with the following results: B (Superior) in English Composition; C (Medium) in Elementary French; C (Medium) in English History; D (Inferior) in English Literature; and F (Failure) in Gymnasium—due to her withdrawal from that course. It is difficult to believe, given her past academic record, that the courses were too challenging for her. More likely, she lost interest in studying and became preoccupied with her courtship with the young journalism professor.

Her performance deteriorated further during the following semester in 1912. Her transcript shows she took only three courses, with the following results: F (Failure) in General Botany and withdrawals from Introduction to Psychology and from Elementary Sociology. Then at the end of that semester, the bottom of her academic career fell out, when she received a handwritten note on her transcript, dated May 13, 1912, stating "Dismissed by Dean."[331]

Charlie and Florence Wed

On May 25, 1912, less than two weeks after Florence's dismissal, Charlie proposed under a large tree on "the links," the University's golf course. She accepted immediately. It was a happy day for them both, and Florence immediately began making plans for the wedding. Florence was always highly organized, so she kept a detailed "Wedding Book" where she filed and labeled memories of the wedding and the honeymoon. Her book reveals that a small family wedding took place on Wednesday, August 20, 1913, in the parochial residence (rectory) of St. Matthew the Apostle Catholic Church in St. Louis. Florence's sister Estelle served as the maid of honor. The marriage took place in the parish rectory rather than the church building because it was, in the parlance of the day, a "mixed marriage" (a Catholic marrying a non-Catholic). Charlie was never a Catholic and declined to convert to one. (As noted earlier, Charlie considered himself an agnostic.)[332] Helen Ross attended, representing Charlie's family, but most of the attendees were friends of Florence and her family. The couple were given a

Wedding picture of Florence Griffith Ross. Independence, MO, 1913. (Photo/Ross family collection)

variety of modest gifts such as silverware and serving dishes. After the wedding, the couple traveled to Boulder, Colorado, for their honeymoon, staying at the Boulderado Hotel for a few days, mostly "loafing" (as Florence described it) and seeing some of the local sites. (It's likely Charlie chose this area based on his early days working at the newspaper in Victor, Colorado.) On their trip back to Columbia, Missouri, the newlyweds stopped off in Independence and stayed with Charlie's mother and sisters then living there.

It's hard to imagine Charlie choosing a wife less like his grandmother, mother, or sisters. The Ross women placed a high value on education, particularly at the college level; Florence showed little interest in college courses or a degree. The Rosses were all raised in The Christian Church; Florence was raised a Roman Catholic and remained one all her life. The Ross women were mostly thoughtful and analytical, and approached life cautiously. Extroverted Florence was quick to speak and give her opinion and loved being the center of attention. The Ross women had a distant relationship with their frequently absent father; Florence had a very close relationship with her opinionated, boastful father. The Ross women depended on and revered their well-organized and loving mother; Florence's relationship with her mother wasn't particularly close, and there is no evidence Florence viewed her mother with any sense of admiration.[333]

Why would Charlie have chosen a spouse so different from the women in his family? Although Charlie never gave reasons for marrying Florence, it isn't difficult to deduce a few. Florence was a lively, interesting, and attractive young lady. This made her an appealing prospect, particularly for a man striving to be a success. She was outgoing and social, which balanced against Charlie's natural shy nature. Charlie wanted a wife who would be happy to stay at home and maintain a family as he advanced in his career (the major obstacle in his engagement to Mary Paxton.) There may have been other reasons, but these certainly appear primary.

JB's Final Days

After his first couple of years in Parker, JB told the family he had no interest in returning to Missouri. His daughters remember him at that time promising Ella, "'Mama you'll wear jewels yet,' at which our mother only smiled."[334] Mama remained accommodating, although realistic—and pessimistic—about her husband's prospects.

JB had invested "a few hundred dollars"[335] in Parker and scratched out a living there, but hardly struck it rich. Due to his good nature, and outgoing personality, the residents embraced JB—and he embraced them. Known as "Parker's Senior Citizen," he became the honorary captain of the baseball team."[336] The income from his public-service positions, coupled with whatever funds he had from his meager savings and local investments, allowed him to remain happily in Parker.

In the summer of 1913, five years after arriving in Parker, JB contracted typhoid fever. Typhoid fever is caused by Salmonella typhi bacteria, which typically enters the body through contaminated food or water or close contact with an infected person. Today, there are vaccines to prevent a person from contracting typhoid fever as well as antibiotic treatment for infected persons.[337] Louise was living with JB when he first became ill. Others in the community also became aware that JB was ill. Louise soon noticed that she and her ailing father were not alone. As told by Louise's sister, Virginia:

> "Louise noticed one night when she went to the door for a breath of cool air that an old Hopi Indian was sitting on a

bench in front of the shack. She questioned him. 'Me here every night,' he said. 'Maybe my friend need me. No worry, Miss. Me stay here. Morning—go home. Sundown—come back.' And he did just that for several weeks. The old Indian sat through the night, dark to dawn, and disappeared when Louise came out in the morning. It was a long trip across the desert toward the mountain canyon where he lived. The Hopi never failed—he was befriending the friend who had befriended him."[338]

Unfortunately, there were no clinics or doctors in or near Parker that could treat JB.[339] By early September 1913, his illness had become so serious that he was taken to Mercy Hospital in Prescott, Arizona. After being hospitalized there for two and a half months, JB succumbed to the ravages of typhoid fever on November 16, 1913. Four days later, at the family's request, his body was transported to Independence, Missouri, for burial.[340]

JB's funeral, like many aspects of his life, was far from ideal. As told by his daughter, Virginia, who attended:

"The funeral was ghastly. Aunt Betty came and brought with her on the slow train from Tennessee a 'funeral arrangement,' which she had tried, but failed, to keep fresh. It was placed in front of the Regina music box . . . which played the great punch steel record . . . and they chose 'Don't You Make Those Goo-Goo Eyes at Me.' [Virginia] . . . refused to look at the body. And . . . [admitted] that adolescent that I was, I became hysterical and giggled uncontrollably, to my shame. We went to the Woodlawn Cemetery—in hacks."[341]

Funerals of Two Fathers

Florence's father, John, who stood proudly at her wedding, was 19 years younger than JB Ross, and generally in much better health. A month before the wedding, John, who enjoyed exercise, suffered "injuries to the ear caused by diving" while swimming. Although significant, the injury was not sufficiently serious to keep him from enjoying his daughter's wedding. A couple of months later, in early November of 1913, weeks after the wedding, he was back playing handball, something he did regularly with friends after work. In his final game of the day, he took a hard shot to that same ear he'd injured in the diving accident a couple of months before. This second injury was so serious he had to be taken to a local hospital for treatment. Surgery was performed to repair the twice-damaged ear, and the doctors concluded that the operation had been a success. However, while recovering in the hospital, he contracted pneumonia, "became delirious," and tragically died. This was a shocking ending for Florence's 42-year-old father, an otherwise healthy man who, before these seemingly minor setbacks, had enjoyed excellent health. His funeral service was set to take place in St. Louis shortly thereafter.[342]

In November, Charlie and Florence were back in Columbia, where he had resumed teaching, and she had settled into the role of a professor's wife. Unexpectedly, Florence was notified, most likely by telephone, of the sudden death of her father in St. Louis. That same day, Charlie received a telegram informing him of the death of his father in Arizona. In fact, the two men died one day apart.[343] Since JB had been in the hospital for some time, his death may not have been a complete surprise, but the news of John Griffin's death was a shock. Coming together on the same day, the news of the two deaths left the young couple dumbfounded.[344]

Charlie and Florence eventually got over their shock. The funerals of the two fathers had been scheduled to take place on nearly the same day. As a result, Charlie and Florence were required to travel in opposite directions—he to Independence, she to St. Louis—to attend the funerals of their respective fathers.[345] This was a sad time for the newlyweds, but, in the long run, these deaths would simplify some things in their lives.

Florence and John Griffin

Two letters John sent to Florence during her first year at college give us a sense for their relationship. Both are typewritten, clearly by someone using the hunt-and-peck method, and are replete with punctuation, grammar, and spelling errors. Two themes stand out. First, he reports in each about his playing handball. (Quoted verbatim: "Play handball till 6.15 every eve and the family raise Cain. Fine; the table is turned; no longer hungry; Dining room is cleaned out and we are getting thick.")[346] Second, he prods Florence about her spending. In December 1911, he began a letter with the salutation, "Dear Miss Spendthrift," and then commented on the price of the ticket to a college football game she reported attending. (Quoted verbatim: "You say 'The football game was worth every cent of that $2.00.' Should read, maybe 'The football game was worth every cent of your $2.00.'") In addition, the postscript of that letter included the following poem: "Rah Rah Rah?/Overcoat in pawn/Who's the fall guy/Poor old John." Then the following addendum is added: "The female of the specie is more expensive than the male; Kippling."[347]

Beyond their subject matter, these letters show a familiar, almost chummy, father-daughter relationship that was more casual than might be expected during that period. In addition, the letters highlight John's limited writing skills and the limits of his grade-school education. They also show John's scrappy, working-class background and values. Despite her father's rough edges, Florence managed to go to college. Ironically, she married a well-educated man who made his living by the written word.

Florence's mother survived her husband by more than 30 years. As noted earlier, she wasn't an important influence in Florence's life, particularly after Florence left home. In many ways, their relationship appeared to be more of a rivalry than a supportive mother-daughter relationship. Florence soon put aside the loss of her beloved father and became immersed in the demands of her new marriage, one which would last for the next 37 years.[348]

The Legacy of James Bruce Ross

The "almost blind" JB Ross effectively deserted his wife and family in 1908, when he relocated permanently to Parker, Arizona. This despite a long and loving marriage and the raising of seven children. JB was a man who loved adventure and dreamed of striking it rich in the West. This consumed him, and he never really adjusted to "normal" family life. He experienced firsthand the life of the "Old West" and had a front row seat to its history. In 1872, he was prospecting for gold in Colorado when that territory became the 38th State, and he was living in Arizona when that territory became the 48th State in 1912.

Perhaps the best recollection of him was written by Virginia. She penned the following and included it among the memoir pieces she wrote about her father. It reads:

> "This is a profile of my father. I think of him with respect and affection, also with regret that in an otherwise closely-knit

family, I did not know him well. He was a child of the Civil War, born to comfort and security, which vanished. Responsibility for a large family may have fallen too heavily, first on his wife, later on his children, but they all met that responsibility with a great devotion to family. I never heard a word of complaint from my father about his blindness. Friends and family praised his kindness and generosity. By some standards, he was a failure. His children, grandchildren, and great grandchildren number enough namesakes (Rosses, Bruces, and James in their combinations) to suggest he left something to carry on."[349]

For Virginia, her father's shortcomings allowed (or, more accurately, "forced") his wife and children to work together to fill those gaps left by his long absences. Instead of criticizing JB, Virginia focused on his positives, which were considerable and long-lasting for her generation.

There is an adage among lawyers: Death solves more problems than it creates. Certainly, this was true of the death of JB Ross. It lifted substantial weights from the family. His wife and children no longer had to worry about his health and well-being in faraway Arizona. It also lifted the prospect of further debts and financial blunders from their future. His death allowed everyone more freedom to take hold of their own futures and move on with their lives.

13

THE KECHUWA WAY

Helen Opens a Side Door

By the summer of 1913, Helen had completed her second-year teaching at Independence High School. She had to remain in Independence for the time being. Her three youngest sisters were still in school, and her family depended on her income to help pay off her father's debts.[350] But she also wanted adventure and to move beyond Independence. She envied her twin sister, Louise, who now lived in remote, exotic Arizona, with their father. Helen never forgot the stories her father told of his outdoor adventures in Mexico and Colorado, and she yearned for those types of adventures of her own making.

As a high-school teacher, she had the summer months free. This was an opportunity to find ways to supplement her meager teacher's income. (Helen made $70 per month at the time, which is roughly $1,940 in today's dollars.) She was on the lookout for additional money-making possibilities. Prior to the summer of 1913, she learned of an intriguing opening as a counselor at a place called Camp Michigamme on the Upper Peninsula of Michigan. So, Helen, together with her older sister Ella ("Sis") and a local friend named Barbara applied.[351] (Helen refers to Barbara by only her first name in her memoirs.) She described Barbara as "an earthy blond creature with high color and sky-blue eyes, and who had an aristocratic veneer of a year in a fashionable girls' school in Rome." Helen and Sis had little in common with the attractive Barbara. Helen says, "She was an orphan who lived with an inebriated aunt, and we came to know her through her cousins, some of our best friends."[352] Sis, then 25 years old, was also anxious for a change in scenery from her household duties. The rather plain Ross women and their stylish friend were all offered work that summer at Camp Michigamee.

In the late spring of 1913, Helen, Sis, and Barbara boarded a train and took the long trip north to Michigan's Upper Peninsula. They disembarked on a platform in the town of Michigamee. The camp had been founded only the year before by Mrs. Caroline S. Rowell, who had previous experience as a teacher and a camp counselor. Mrs. Rowell was a Christian Scientist—although she proudly asserted "her girls were of all faiths." The Rosses couldn't afford to send their girls to summer camp, and Helen and Sis had never been to a sleep-away camp. Their sense of adventure and the camp's rustic setting quickly overcame any apprehension. The camp was situated on idyllic Lake Michigamme, which is just a few miles south and inland from Lake Superior on the north shore of the Upper Peninsula.

It is one of the largest lakes in Michigan and is shaped like a short, squat, number 7. There are 95 miles of shoreline, 27 islands, and an area of approximately 4,300 acres. The pristine lake offers spectacular views of sunrises and sunsets. The small town of Michigamee rests on the western edge of the lake's north shore. Founded in the early 1870s to support local mining and lumbering operations, the town served as the commercial center of the area.[353] The main transportation artery was a railroad line, which ran through the town and along the lake's northern shore.

The Ross women settled easily into the routine. They were accustomed to hard work and caring for others, and they took to camp life. Helen fell in love with the lake and often went off to explore the surrounding woods. During these treks, she began to assess her future. Her childhood dream of starting her own school began to evolve. She now visualized how she could run a camp of her own, one that was better than Camp Michigamme. She studied her employer's operations and made detailed notes. She even recorded the name of the company that made the tents—the Carnie-Goudie Tent Manufacturing Company of Kansas City. As the ideas took shape in her mind, she began looking for possible sites around the lake. She found an ally in one of the local citizens, a Mr. Newett.

Unexpected Alliances

Mr. Newett, a widower, visited Camp Michigamee often and struck up a friendship with the Ross girls and Barbara, often taking them fishing on the lake. Eventually, Helen confided her dreams to Mr. Newett. He patiently answered Helen's questions and was a font of local information. As the summer wore on, it began to dawn on Helen that Mr. Newett had his own agenda—he was smitten with Barbara. As the camp's season ended, everyone said their farewells and returned home. Barbara and Mr. Newett would soon become instrumental in helping Helen realize the dream of their own camp.[354]

The Camp Takes Shape

In mid-November, a little more than two months after she returned to teaching, Helen learned that her father had died of typhoid fever in Prescott, Arizona. The day after she heard it, she decided it was time to make the dream of her own camp a reality. First, she signed Barbara on as a partner in her new adventure. She wrote to Mr. Newett, subtly trading on his attraction for Barbara, and asked if he would help them lease a property they had identified the summer before. His enthusiastic response came quickly, and the three formed an informal partnership.

Barbara made frequent visits to the Ross home during that winter and even stayed several weeks. Letters were exchanged among the three partners. Helen "became the confidante and collaborator," encouraging the relationship between Barbara and Mr. Newett. Each of the three partners "put in a few hundred dollars, which we borrowed."[355] Things moved quickly. Mr. Newett got the lease for a parcel that stretched along the northern shoreline. It faced on a small bay (originally known as Slaughter Bay) on one side and was open to the wider expanse of Lake Michigamee on the other. (The nicely shaped bay got the name "Slaughter Bay" because it was where butchers slaughtered cattle to feed local miners and loggers and dumped the carcasses in the lake. Helen later renamed the inlet "Kechuwa Bay.") It was agreed that Helen and Barbara would run the camp.

Planning and organizing the operation, as well as finding girls to enroll, all fell to Helen. Sitting at the small desk Charlie had left behind in Independence, she wrote the camp's initial brochure and application form, and began to contact potential campers. Barbara, all this time, exchanged "endless letters, much of them in code," with Mr. Newett. Realizing that Barbara's heart may not be in the venture, Helen appealed to Sis. Who better to run the camp's day-to-day operations? Sis initially resisted the idea as too risky. She was won over slowly, and then, in Helen's words, "fell into the fantasy with diligence, in her characteristic way."[356] The pieces were coming together.

In time, the camp's "booklet was printed and mailed out as widely as our acquaintance allowed"; it included a few picturesque snapshots taken by Mr. Newett. Helen traded on her reputation as a college-educated teacher with lifelong roots in her hometown of Independence. The booklets were designed to appeal to well-to-do families in neighboring Kansas City, St. Louis, and Columbia, Missouri. They promised an innovative, enjoyable, and unique adventure in a healthy outdoor setting. Her promotions worked, and girls began to apply.

Back in Michigan, Mr. Newett worked with a local carpenter to build a long-framed, one-story "bungalow," which would serve as the main lodge. It was situated on a high point overlooking the lake. Tents, beds, mattresses, dishes, pots, and pans were purchased with the partners' slim resources. Helen traveled to Kansas City to Carnie-Goudie, the tent manufacturer, where Mr. Carnie himself listened to her plans for her yet-to-be-opened camp. She informed him she needed ten tents with five-foot walls—higher than a standard tent—based on specifications she'd worked out during her previous summer. To further impress Mr. Carnie, she asserted the tents must be made of "the best Army duck . . . and to be fitted with a fly." Mr. Carnie smiled when she next asked him for credit until the end of the first summer.

"Do you think you will make a go of this?" he asked.

"Yes, Sir," she responded in her most confident voice.

"Then I'll make them up for you," he said.

At that moment, Helen knew that the Camp was real and permanent—and there was no turning back.[357]

Kechuwa

Helen's camp needed a name. The word "Michigamee" was taken, so Helen decided on Camp Kechuwa. Helen rarely divulged the meaning of the name. If a camper asked, she was usually given a vague answer by Helen or Sis, such as Kechuwa stood for "lasting friendship" or "friends forever."[358] However, that explanation wasn't exactly accurate. The true meaning is much more interesting.

Reading had been the main source of entertainment for the Ross girls growing up in Independence. Popular books, fairy tales (*The Arabian Nights*), classics (*The Iliad* and *The Odyssey*), as well as stories from magazines, like "The Adventures of Sherlock Holmes" from *The Strand*. One popular short story at the time was "The Love of Antelope" by Charles Alexander Eastman, a mixed-blood Sioux who wrote romantic tales about Sioux life on the plains in the old days. In "The Love of Antelope," the brave Antelope called his true-love, Taluta, "kechuwa" (meaning "dear love" or "darling")—a term of tender affection in the language of the Sioux.[359] This romantic story was read by Helen and

Sign at the entrance to Camp Kechuwa. Lake Michigamme, MI, date unknown. (Photo/Ross family collection)

probably by Sis. "Kechuwa" had an exotic ring to it that sounded just right to them. It had a connection with the Sioux, who originally inhabited the Upper Peninsula. It also reflected the sisters' love and affection for the camp.

The Camp Opens

Helen's recruiting efforts bore fruit as ten paying campers enrolled. By her calculation, the campers' tuition and fees should just cover their costs for the first year. The initial goal was simply to break even. Later, the camp's profits were considerable and dwarfed Helen's salary as a teacher. Helen and Sis kept an eagle eye on the finances, as they had learned to do at home from an early age. One longtime camper said that a strong motive for Helen's founding of the camp was "to make a buck!"[360]

In the late spring of 1914, Helen, Sis, and Barbara traveled north by train. Mr. Newett met them and took them to the campsite, where the new bungalow looked like "a barn . . . in its unpainted newness."[361] They spent the first night on the porch of Mr. Newett's cottage, picked at by gnats ("no-see-ums") and bitten by mosquitoes. Sis was openly miserable. But, the next day, they got to work pulling things together. Sis and Helen were both were very organized. They knew and respected each other's strengths, shortcomings, and preferences. Helen focused on working with the campers and counselors and scheduling the activities; Sis took over meal preparation, the day-to-day finances, and dealing with their many vendors. Helen later recalled with disappointment that pretty Barbara showed a greater concern for her blond hair than for the tasks that needed doing. The place hummed with excitement. Nails were still being driven into the tents' wooden floors when the train brought their very first campers. A "Chaperone" named

Miss Fox, also arrived. She was a middle-aged English teacher invited due to her age, and Helen immediately told her, "She was not expected to assume any authority"—a role she accepted and played to the fullest. (The next year she was not invited back as she "was regarded unnecessary.") Not surprisingly, Helen's former employer at nearby Camp Michigamme wasn't pleased. He called them the "soubrettes"—a term of reproach referring to coquettish maids or frivolous young women in a theatrical play.[362]

Soon the new campers settled in. The sisters worked flawlessly together: Sis managed the physical operation, while Helen supervised the camp's activities and tended to all matters directly involving the campers. The organization and division of labor remained this way for the next 37 years. Helen recalled how Camp Kechuwa began:

> "on borrowed money and 'down-payments' on equipment, it surprised us with its success. Camps were then a new idea in the Middle West. We started with a handful of older teenage girls and almost as many councilors . . . At first my sister and I were too young and inexperienced to be concerned with more than keeping the campers entertained and well-fed. Gradually we became aware of the camp as an educational institution."[363]

In those early years, the families paid a substantial fee of $250 (roughly $6,800 today) to send their daughters away for the eight-week summer adventure.[364] It's a credit to Helen's stature and sales abilities that so many families paid the fee and entrusted their daughters' welfare to the Ross sisters. This would not be the last time Helen's gumption, backed up by her ability, enabled her to make the seemingly impossible happen.

The Summer Camp Movement

One advantage—perhaps the only one that Sis and Helen enjoyed when they started Camp Kechuwa—was the rising popularity of "sleepaway summer camps." Summer camps for boys were first established in the 1880s and mostly in New England. They touted the healthy benefits of outdoor living away from the increasingly unhealthy cities, as well as Victorian convictions about the moral benefits of nature. They also benefitted from President Teddy Roosevelt's much-publicized interest in nature and in the rugged outdoor life. By 1910 there were several hundred boys' camps in existence, catering mostly to educated, Protestant, middle-to-upper-class boys.

Summer camps for girls took root in the early twentieth century for similar reasons and to foster a new, more self-reliant generation of young women. By 1910, college-educated women began opening camps for girls, and Camp Michigamme and Camp Kechuwa were part of that trend. By 1915, there were about 100 girls' camps in existence, and that number would increase with the demand for years to come. The timing of Camp Kechuwa could not have been more favorable.

The Ownership of Camp Kechuwa

Camp Kechuwa was never a hobby or fleeting fantasy. After breaking even the first year, Helen became confident it would be a success, and she treated it as a long-term investment. After that first season ended, she settled her account with the Carnie-Goudie tent company. In the next few years, she paid off her loan from the bank in Independence. Next, she bought out Barbara and Mr. Newett, which gave Helen and Sis control of the camp's operations. The sisters also made it a point to keep positive relationships with their suppliers and the local people who worked at the camp each summer.

Helen knew she couldn't be secure until they owned the land on which the camp operated. The camp's property lease continued through the first few years of the camp's operation. Once the camp's finances were strong enough, she made her move to buy the land. In January 1920, she and Sis purchased part of the leased parcel for $600 from its owner, William G. Mather, a highly successful iron, steel, and mining tycoon from Cleveland. After two more successful camp seasons, she was able to purchase the remaining parcel from Mr. Mather for $400. Thanks to Helen's and Sis' hard work and good management, the camp had become completely theirs.

Camp Kechuwa's Early Years

As Camp Kechuwa's good reputation grew, so did its enrollment. By 1920, Camp Kechuwa was serving 73 campers between the ages of 12 and 20, who mostly came from cities in the Midwest. The aides were young college women. Helen intentionally called them "councilors" rather than the more traditional term "counselors." (The word "councilor" means one who belongs to a council, while "counselor" refers to one who counsels or advises another.) Helen believed that the college women who worked most closely with the campers should be part of the camp's managing council, with influence over the program and events. In her view, while their primary mission was to improve the lives of its campers, she also wanted to help develop the young college women. This collaborative approach helped to attract highly qualified women to work at the camp. As a result, Camp Kechuwa was able to maintain a healthy four-to-one camper-to-councilor ratio over the years.

The promotional literature told the prospective campers (and their parents) that the purpose of the camp was "to provide healthful recreation for growing girls by means of pleasant and profitable activities, amid congenial companionship and under careful supervision." The literature also informed that the camp's activities included swimming, canoeing, tennis, basketball, volleyball, archery, shooting [with rifles] and hiking. And even though participation in the activities was voluntary, "Instruction in all sports is provided, and each girl is encouraged to become proficient in more than one." This mirrored Helen's belief—and Camp Kechuwa's practice—that learning and growing should be fun—and without a rigid schedule, as was then the case at most schools. The camp's brochures made things sound fun: "The conditions for swimming and canoeing are ideal"; "Each camper is instructed carefully in canoeing"; "A native guide conducts long and short camping trips" (both on foot and by canoe); and "A float with

Campers canoeing on the lake in front of the main building at Camp Kechuwa. Lake Michigamme, MI, circa 1933. (Photo/Ross family collection)

springboard anchored in deep water, and a chute add zest to the swimming hour."

Dancing, handicrafts, and nature study were offered, and campers were encouraged to read and write creatively. Each Sunday there was an open session called "Birch Bark" held in the large bungalow—known originally as the "Teyoteepee" (a Sioux word meaning "Council Lodge")—and then, over time, to the less-confusing word "Teepee." Here, in this large, open space, the campers read and performed their poetry, songs, jokes, and skits. Even though campers participated on a voluntary basis, this became one of the highlights of the week. The best of the work was published in a booklet, also called "Birch Bark," that the campers took home at the end of the year as a souvenir. Popular plays were also performed by the campers on a completely equipped theatrical stage. For those who wished it—and wished to avoid summer school—academic tutoring was also offered "in the usual branches" for $1 per hour; reading and conversation classes in French were open to all, free of charge.

Campers slept in single beds that rested on the wooden floors of the large, army-style tents. The canvas sides of the tents were raised during the day and lowered each night. The campers' clothes were stored in their foot lockers, next to their beds. A daily tent inspection was held to make sure each camper did her part to keep things clean. Healthy living was emphasized by Sis, who gave "special attention to underweight girls." The brochures touted an "able swimming master, an experienced woman physician, and a skilled dietician" as part of the Camp Council.

The campers' attire reflected the times, and, of course, no uniform was ever required. For everyday attire before 1920, the campers mostly wore baggy trousers gathered closely at the ankles (generally referred to as "bloomers") with long-sleeved blouses for athletics;

a similar full-cover garment served as the swimsuit. By the 1920s, bloomers had given way to fashion—and practicality—as most campers donned knickers and knee-length short pants for most activities and loose-fitting, one-piece bathing suits for swimming.

World War I and the Spanish Flu Pandemic

During Camp Kechuwa's early years, two events shook the United States. First, on April 6, 1917, the United States declared war on Germany. Our nation's involvement in World War I lasted 19 months, until November 11, 1918, when Germany surrendered. During this period, millions of men were drafted into the military, and major changes occurred in businesses, in the distribution of goods, and in American life. Few Americans were unaffected by the war.

Then, immediately following World War I, the country was struck by the Great Influenza epidemic, better known as the Spanish Flu. (Interestingly, Spain, a neutral country in the war, didn't censor its press and didn't bar reporting about the illness. So, because the initial news came from that country, it was mistakenly thought of as the source of the illness and it was called the Spanish Flu.) The first documented case of this deadly H1N1 virus in the U.S. occurred in Kansas, in 1918, where it was most likely carried by returning U.S. soldiers. In the United States alone, about 28% of the population contracted the virus, and there were more than 500,000 deaths. Eventually, the pandemic subsided, and, by the end of 1920, the crisis had effectively ended.

Ironically, these events had a positive effect on Camp Kechuwa, and the enrollment continued to grow. Although women were involved in the war effort, it was the male population, particularly through the wartime draft, who were most impacted. Also, because of increased government spending and heightened economic activity, most well-to-do families prospered during World War I. Fear of the Spanish Flu led many parents to send their children out of the cities during the summer to someplace less populated. Camp Kechuwa was a perfect choice.

The Camping Experience

By the mid-1930s, campers arrived at Camp Kechuwa on the Duluth, South Shore & Atlantic Railroad (the "DSS&A") and were dropped off on the platform located near the camp. New campers, mostly from large cities, were awed by the rows of tents, the outdoor equipment, and the various wooden buildings, all neatly nestled along the shoreline of crystal-blue Lake Michigamme. The spacious Teepee—with its large, screened porch running the length of the building—housed the dining room, a large stone fireplace, the kitchen, and a library (with hundreds of volumes). The large Playhouse was the hub for indoor activities: dancing classes, ping-pong, shuffleboard, tumbling, plays, and other rainy-day events. Other structures included the Studio (for modeling, painting, and art), the Shop (for woodwork and printing), and the Nurse's cabin "with dispensary and isolation room." There were three tennis courts, a basketball court, baseball diamond, archery range, and a deck-tennis court. The camp maintained a springboard and diving platform, floats for water instruction and games, twenty canoes, two (eventually increased to five) sailboats, plus various rowboats, paddle boats, and a motorboat. Beyond the view of the new campers were Footprint Island (owned by the camp) and Goats Lake, places where campers traveled on camping trips and stayed overnight.

The Camp was innovative and flexible. For example, in 1936, the brochure read:

"[The] elasticity of program answers a frequent and natural question of the girl fatigued from the regimentation of schoolwork: 'Do I have to do everything at a certain time every day?' All activities are voluntary . . . The activities are so diversified as to meet the demands of individual differences among campers and to give every camper opportunity for achievement and recognition in a favorite field."

Then the brochure outlined a "typical day":

- 7:30   Rising, morning dip (voluntary)
- 8:00   Breakfast, followed by care of tent; group or individual instruction in various activities: dancing, tennis, canoeing, sailing, etc.
- 11:00   Swimming and diving instruction
- 12:30   Dinner, followed by rest hour; tennis, canoeing, rowing, sailing, etc.
- 3:30   Swimming and diving; reading, short hikes, play rehearsals, etc.
- 5:30   Supper
- 7:30   In the Playhouse or Teypee for dancing, music, plays, games, etc.
- 8:30   Milk and crackers
- 8:45   Retiring

The Studio and Shop were open all day for individual work. Plays, music, and dancing were performed at a particularly high level. The Little Stage in The Playhouse was the scene of many memorable performances. The campers staged (and sometimes wrote) the plays, designed the sets, made the costumes, constructed the scenery, and printed the programs. Councilors helped coordinate and direct the more elaborate musicals. Gilbert & Sullivan operettas—such as *The Pirates of Penzance* and *H.M.S. Pinafore*—were performed every year and were one of the highlights of the season. Music was an integral part of the Kechuwa experience. Two pianos were available for learning and practice, and the campers sang around campfires and wrote original songs, which they printed in the songbooks they used. Dancing was taught in two forms: social dancing, such as the waltz and foxtrot, and Expressionist Dance (sometimes called "modern dance"), which was the "Mary Wigman type of dancing, conducted by a graduate of the Wigman School in Dresden, Germany."

By the mid-1930s, the camp was accepting about a hundred campers per year, ages nine to seventeen. Helen and Sis were able to keep the number at this level because of the variety and flexibility of the activities, and they continued to keep the impressive four to one camper-to-councilor ratio. Many of the campers attended for multiple years. In addition to the normal camp activities, the campers were offered confidential counseling sessions with Helen, by then a professional psychoanalyst who specialized in children. Helen's youngest sister, J.B. Ross, who sometimes worked at the camp years later, said of Camp Kechuwa: "Ours was one of the first camps for girls in the Midwest founded on the principle of giving them freedom of expression. There were no uniforms, no competitive teams."[365]

The Kechuwa Way

Helen wanted Camp Kechuwa to be more than a place to just have fun. She wanted her campers to grow mentally, socially, and physically, and become accomplished, confident women. Campers were encouraged, but not forced, to try activities that were new to them. Instruction was provided in positive, supportive ways. A camper's progress was usually measured against her own past performance rather than against the other girls. In archery, for example, a girl's score was recorded after each session. After a few sessions, the camper would see her progress. When a new level of proficiency was reached, the progress was recognized, often publicly at that week's Birch Bark. Although there were "no competitive teams," competition *was* used to encourage enthusiasm for individual events such as sailboat races and tennis tournaments.

Campers with Helen Ross at Camp Kechuwa in the later years. Helen was clearly revered by the young ladies. Lake Michigamme, MI, circa 1940.
(Photo/Ross family collection)

Helen recruited, trained, and mentored many young women from prestigious women's colleges such as Vassar and Smith. There was a rigorous training program for the councilors in the week before the campers arrived. These were talented and accomplished young women. Helen Hayes (not the famous actress), was a tall, athletic woman, and she ran all water sports. She was renowned for her convincing impersonation of Eleanor Roosevelt. In the 1930s, Maria "Madi" Bacon led the camp in staging plays and performing music. She was a graduate of the University of Chicago, a lifelong music educator, founder of the Madrigal Singers of Chicago, and one-time dean of Roosevelt University's School of Music. In 1927, Madi Bacon showed there was more to her than musical talents, when she dove into the Lincoln Park lagoon in Chicago to try to save a drowning man. Unable to rescue him, she told the newspaper that a group of men just stood by and watched without helping. "If any one of them had helped me, I could have saved a life," she said.

In 1945, Helen Ross wrote:

"With the passing of time, I have become more and more interested in what can be accomplished with both campers and councilors individually. In addition to private consultations with councilors, therefore, I have set up a sort of training school in the understanding and handling of problems in personality growth. Many of our councilors continue in educational and guidance work."[366]

Not surprisingly, many of the young councilors subsequently took up counseling and social work as careers.

Camp Kechuwa worked to build *esprit de corps.* Cooperation was emphasized, and campers were always encouraged to contribute to the group and to participate. Kechuwa's spirit was given a name, "WO-HE-LO," which was derived from the first two letters of "Work," "Health," and "Love." It was the secret code word all campers were supposed to yell if they were ever in trouble—anywhere, at any time. The campers joked that, if they were anywhere in the world and cried "WO-HE-LO," Helen Hayes would be there within minutes![367]

The camping experience was continuously enhanced over the years. They added a residential cabin for Helen and Sis, a recreation building for the councilors, a spacious playhouse (with all the equipment to stage plays and musicals), a small cedar-lined sauna building, specially made sailboats (each named after a Gilbert & Sullivan musical), and a large boathouse, to name a few. Fine china—Blue Willow made by Wood & Sons in England—was added in the dining room as was silverware with "Kechuwa" etched on the handles. Woolen blankets with the word "Kechuwa" stitched into the fabric appeared during the later years. Although the campers were attending a rustic summer camp, Helen and Sis wouldn't let these young ladies take a step backwards from the proper way of doing things.

The Local Workers

The day-to-day operation depended on the work of many of the local residents. Getting the camp ready in May and June and then shutting it down in the Fall were big jobs. Kechuwa had *no* electricity, so cooking depended on a regular supply of firewood. The wages they paid were never particularly generous, but the Ross sisters were respected for being good to their word and good to work for. The local people remained hard-working and loyal throughout the camp's long life.

The Campers

Beyond their economic advantages, the campers' families had high expectations for their daughters. Many former campers went on to lead productive and successful lives. One was Nancy Robbins, who, after she was adopted by her stepfather, Dr. Loyal Davis, became Nancy Davis. Later in life she married the actor Ronald Reagan. She eventually became First Lady when Reagan was elected President of the United States (1981–1989). She loved her five years as a camper at Kechuwa. "I went to camp, and I absolutely adored it," she told the delegates of the Second International Camping Congress in 1987. She went on to say, "I believe self-esteem gives children the strength to cope, not just to avoid drugs or alcohol, but with life itself."[368] J.B. worked at Camp Kechuwa when Nancy was there and recalled: "I remember her quite distinctly—a very pretty little girl, well-mannered, well-brought up. I'm sure she must have participated in the plays, because all of the girls did."[369]

Many substantial women were alumnae of Camp Kechuwa. Louise's daughter, Helen Holmquist, came from Phoenix, Arizona, as a camper and then became a councilor for many years. She graduated from Mills College in Oakland, California, and received her master's degree in psychology from Stanford University. She had three children and became a noted psychologist in Phoenix. Lee Wilcox, from Chicago, both a camper and councilor for many years at Kechuwa, went into television in the 1950s in Chicago and later became the editor of *House Beautiful* magazine. She remained a lifelong friend of Helen's and encouraged her to make a book of her memoirs, an event that, sadly, never came about.

Hallmarks of Success

Camp Kechuwa operated successfully from its founding in 1914 through 1950, its final year. It survived during World War I and the Great Influenza epidemic and maintained an enrollment of about a hundred campers and twenty-five councilors throughout the Great Depression and the years of World War II. It was a financial success for Helen and Sis.

As a girl in Independence, Helen Ross often dreamed of opening "a school." That dream eventually evolved into Camp Kechuwa. With her imagination and abilities, the camp was built into an effective and innovative educational institution that helped to shape and build the lives of countless young women.

14

MR. ROSS GOES TO WASHINGTON

Charlie and Florence

Charlie and Florence settled comfortably into married life in Columbia, and they were in love. Florence wasn't your typical 19-year-old bride. An active woman with high energy, she showed she was highly organized and driven. Florence enjoyed and embraced the "domestic arts" and all aspects of running a home. By study, focus, and practice, she made herself an excellent cook, a meticulous housekeeper, and an accomplished gardener. She kept scrupulous records—mostly notes and recipes. Her role was to take care of all things around the house. When Charlie came home from work, he had few, if any, domestic obligations, only a comfortable place to live. He was the breadwinner, she the homemaker.

Their different personalities enhanced their relationship. Charlie was thoughtful, reserved, and measured in his approach to things, while Florence was talkative, gregarious, and more impulsive. They ardently shared a common ambition: for Charlie to be a professional and financial success. He worked hard to advance within his profession. She worked equally hard to build a first-rate domestic life at home. She devotedly read the newspapers. Keeping abreast of current events became one of their common bonds, and they would eagerly discuss the news when they were together. They complemented each other and forged a good team.

Charlie and Florence in their early years together. They do appear to be a good team. Columbia MO, circa 1913
(Photo/Ross family collection)

The Couple Becomes a Young Family

After their honeymoon, Charlie and Florence moved into a rented house on Virginia Avenue, not far from the campus. Although it was acceptable, Charlie and Florence longed for a larger home where they could raise a family. Charlie's situation had improved since he joined the faculty five years ago, but building a house was still out of reach. The couple eyed a spacious lot on Edgewood Avenue. It was next door to the home of fellow faculty member Frank Lee Martin, whom Charlie liked and respected. Charlie and Florence enjoyed the company of the Martins and decided the lot next door was where they wanted to build their first home. "I want a big house, with lots of windows, just like yours," Charlie told Frank.[370] But Charlie needed more money to make that desire a reality.

About this time, Charlie, always an avid alumnus of the University, had agreed to serve as the Secretary of the University's Alumni Association. The Association had recently created a magazine, *The University Alumnus*, designed to serve as a primary link between the University and its growing number of graduates. The new magazine needed a strong editorial hand to guide it. Charlie agreed to become the managing editor of the magazine, which earned him a modest increase in income. During the summer months and in his spare time during the academic year, Charlie made the magazine more appealing to the University's former students. To do this, he focused on the success of the sports teams, especially football. Scores were posted prominently—particularly games Missouri won—and he featured insider stories about the team members, coaches, and staff. He also recruited talented writers who wrote short articles about the advantages of being a Missouri alumnus. One was fellow Asterisks member, Homer Croy, by then a humorist and published author. Charlie also asked the chairmen of various academic departments to contribute articles about innovations and successes. Charlie added an "Alumni Business and Professional Guide" section so alumni could network and trade business information. In addition, a standing request implored the readers to write to the magazine to "tell friends and classmates" of weddings, births "or anything else you believe one graduate wants to know about the other."[371] Charlie solicited articles, wrote short feature stories, and edited the submitted articles. He left no stone unturned in an effort make the magazine a success. Florence said years later, "Charlie created . . . *The Alumnus*, doing all the work himself & made $1,000 out of it, with which he bought the lot on which the house was to be built."[372]

With their newfound earnings, Charlie and Florence purchased the lot next door to the Martins, and construction began shortly thereafter. About the same time that the construction crew laid the foundation, Florence learned she was going to have a baby. This complication didn't prevent hands-on Florence from frequently visiting the construction site and inspecting the progress and quality of carpenters' and masons' work. The Martins looked over fearfully as their pregnant neighbor-to-be climbed the ladders and moved around the catwalks inspecting the construction. Fortunately, there were no unpleasant surprises, and the house rose to completion. On August 7, 1914, Charlie and Florence welcomed their first child into the family. They named him John Bruce Ross after his two grandfathers out of deference to both families.

Charlie's joy at the birth of his first child was on full display in a letter he wrote to Sis and Helen—who earlier that summer had opened Camp Kechuwa—and Louse and Virginia. On the stationery of The Columbia Club, where he presumably went for a celebratory drink, Charlie, whose preferred manner of communication was the written word, penned the following note:

"Friday

Misses Ella, Helen, Louise and Virginia Ross—aunts since 11:45 a.m., Friday Aug. 7 . . .

Details: Boy, big, fat, lusty, black hair, blue eyes. Name John Bruce, for 2 grandfathers.

Florence perfectly well and very happy. She's at the hospital here, where the boy was born. She got along beautifully.

They had not weighed the baby when I left, but the doctor said the weight was about 10 pounds. He surely looks it. Nurses said he appeared a month old already. They pronounced him a perfectly proportioned baby—big head and shoulders and a big fat body. F [Florence] was not hurt in any way. She looks like an angel.

Don't any of you fall into the lake.

Much love from
Charlie"

Always close to his sisters, they were the first to know of his overwhelming happiness and of the arrival of the first member of a new generation of Rosses.

Soon after the birth of their first child, Charlie returned to his routine of teaching while Florence learned the practicalities of motherhood. Even though much of her time was taken up with her newborn son, Florence kept up a social life. In her brief time as a student, she had joined the *Delta Gamma* sorority, and many of her sisters were still at the University. Florence much preferred the company of these young women to the older faculty wives, and often invited them over in the evenings after the baby was in bed. They talked, compared notes, and otherwise entertained themselves while Charlie worked in another room. This comfortable routine lasted for about nine months. Then Florence learned she was pregnant again.

Florence's second pregnancy was trouble-free, like her first. On December 29, 1915, she and Charlie welcomed their second son into the

Florence holding the Ross' first son, John Bruce Ross, who is the author's father. Columbia, MO, 1914.
(Photo/Ross family collection)

world. This time they chose a name honoring Charlie's mentor, who had become a friend to both. They named their second son Walter Williams Ross.³⁷³ This honor surely touched Mr. Williams, whose 19-year-old son and namesake had tragically died three years earlier of typhoid fever.

Charlie and Florence, now the parents of two young, healthy boys settled into their new home next to the Martins. They had a solid network of friends, and Charlie was engaged in a job he enjoyed with increasing prestige and pay. Their shared dream of a solid and comfortable home life had come true, and they seemed destined to be part of the comfortable college town for a long time. Soon, however, events came along that would uproot them from Columbia.

Charlie holding his sons. John is the oldest and Walter the baby. Columbia, MO, 1916. (Photo/Ross family collection)

Australia

Walter Williams' network had spread beyond Missouri to the national stage, as well as worldwide. He encouraged travel, and he kept his eyes open for foreign assignments for students and faculty, which he felt enhanced the school's reputation. In academic year 1915–16, he arranged a sabbatical for Frank Martin to serve as a news editor on the staff of the *Japan Advertiser*, an English-language newspaper in Tokyo.[374] Then, in the following academic year (1916–17), he contacted Charlie about becoming a sub-editor at the Melbourne *Herald* in Australia.

Williams was prepared to cover the travel expenses for Charlie and his family, but he believed that the *Herald* should pay Charlie's salary. Theodore Fink and J. E. Davidson, the *Herald's* chairman and managing editor, respectively, were hesitant. Before agreeing, they asked Charlie to write two articles about America on topics they thought would interest their readers in Australia. One was a piece describing the operations of a department of agriculture at a large American university, such as the University of Missouri. The second article would cover several Australian boxers then touring in the United States. Charlie was busy with his regular duties, and this was a taxing assignment. Nevertheless, he researched and wrote the requested pieces and sent them to the *Herald*. The stories were so well received that he was offered a job as a sub-editor anytime he wanted.[375] Charlie accepted the offer for the next academic year, and he and Florence began planning a new adventure. Dean Williams was true to his word and paid the family's travel expenses out of the School of Journalism's "Betterment Fund."[376]

Many wives in Florence's situation would have been reluctant to uproot a young family and travel to the other side of the world. But Florence saw immediately that this assignment gave Charlie *bona fide* international experience that would enhance his credentials and his credibility. She readily agreed to this new adventure. She was doggedly determined to make it work.

Preparing for the Long Voyage

The family left Columbia, Missouri, for Melbourne, Australia, in June of 1916. But before leaving, Florence needed to address how to safely feed her six-month-old son, Walter, during their weeks-long voyage. Going so long without fresh milk was a challenge in 1916. Highly organized Florence started to search for options and her inquiries came to the attention of a unique dairy in New Jersey.

The Walker-Gordon dairy was founded in 1891, originally as the Walker-Gordon Laboratory Company.[377] This company specialized in producing healthy raw milk at a time when most of the commercially available milk in the United States was pasteurized. The company's founder, a scientist named Gustavus A. Gordon, "came up with modified cow's milk in an effort to change cow's milk to closer resemble human mother's milk."[378] To control the process by which it could produce a "clean milk," the company in 1897 purchased 180 acres of farmland in Plainsboro, New Jersey. The milk products produced there "exceeded all the standards for that time" so it was "marketed [as] 'Guaranteed Milk,' which later became known as 'Certified Milk.'"[379] All the milk at Walker-Gordon dairy was produced under strictly controlled, hygienic conditions, which included the frequent cleaning of its herd of cows. The dairy's Grade A, whole milk traveled well and was "a renowned quality product hailed for freshness and longevity."[380] As a result, it had very loyal customers who believed the milk tasted better and was more nutritious than pasteurized milk, particularly for children. Later on President Franklin Delano Roosevelt, when traveling aboard ship, insisted that Walker-Gordon milk and cream be available, on-board, for the trip.[381]

The Walker-Gordon dairy sensed a marketing opportunity when they learned that Charlie, Florence, and their two young boys were going on a long ocean voyage to Australia. They contacted Florence and asked if she would feed the baby Walker-Gordon milk on the voyage. Florence did her own due diligence and became persuaded that Walker-Gordon's products were safe. So, a deal was struck. The Ross family, at no cost to it, would use Walker-Gordon's milk during their Pacific voyage. In return, if the products were as good as represented, the family, including its two "highly photogenic" boys, could be used by the company in its advertising. The Rosses' luggage, along with several cases of Walker-Gordon milk, were delivered to their ship (the *Sierra*) in San Francisco, and all set sail for Australia. Everyone arrived safely in Australia, and the milk, which little Walter eagerly drank during the voyage, proved to be as good tasting and healthy as advertised.[382]

The *Sierra* sailed on June 13, 1916. Traveling onboard was Miss Margaret Murphy, a recent graduate of the School of Journalism, who went to Melbourne "to be a reporter on one of the Melbourne papers."[383] The *Sierra* was a steamship that carried both passengers and cargo. She later related how one amenity for the passengers was a small, wooden, rectangular swimming pool with a canvas liner which stood on the deck. Its depth was approximately five feet and swimmers entered by means of a short wooden ladder. It looked much like today's above-ground, backyard swimming pools and was enjoyed by all the passengers. The voyage took over three weeks and ended in July, a cool month for Australia. Upon arrival, the family moved into a small, rented house at 31 Wanda Road, in Caulfield, Melbourne.[384]

Getting Along in Australia

From all accounts, Charlie enjoyed the experience. The *Herald* was one of the leading newspapers in Melbourne. Founded in 1840, it had been publishing for more than seventy-five years when Charlie first walked through its doors. It was the city's afternoon newspaper, noted for the quality of its editing, and it ran "ten to twelve pages daily."[385] Its front page mostly displayed editorial pieces, book reviews, poetry, essays and the like. The news articles were found on the inside pages, which were divided into sections: "women's pages, gardening notes, a motoring section, and . . . sports, then, as now, extremely popular in Australia."[386]

In 1916, World War I was on the mind of most Australians, whose men had been fighting in Europe since 1914. The *Herald* dispatched its own writers and even a cartoonist to the front lines to give its readers reports and updates they could relate to and understand.[387] However, the far-away fighting had little effect on Australians' daily lives. Charlie was well received at the *Herald*, where he served as a copyreader—a job he knew well—and he was given the title of "sub-editor" of the paper. In this position, he had ample contacts with the reporters and the rest of the staff. Charlie melded well with his newspaper brethren. "After hours, he enjoyed swapping stories, learning the colorful Australian idioms, and getting to know the staff."[388] Florence, too, fit in nicely. "Ross and Florence were well received in Melbourne, and came as welcomed guests to homes throughout the city.[389] Stanley Kingsbury, another sub-editor who worked with Charlie at the *Herald*, recalled years later: "The things I remember today are the quiet confidence with which he [Charlie] gave his friendship, the utter absence of any assumption of American superiority or of criticism of things Australian, the sincerity which stamped everything he said or did, and his happy knack of catching the other fellow's point of view."[390]

Charlie's Test

The editors at the *Herald* soon felt comfortable enough with Charlie to give him a challenge—or perhaps they wanted to test him.

Charlie, who had little interest in sports, was asked to cover the most important sporting event in Melbourne's year. First run in 1861, The Melbourne Cup was (and today remains) one of Australia's premier sporting events, typically drawing more than 100,000 spectators to the Flemington Racecourse in Melbourne. It's a national event run each year on the first Tuesday in November. The 1916 race was postponed from its scheduled date due to flooding rains and had to be held on the following Saturday. A three-year-old gelding named "Sasanof" from New Zealand won. Sasanof came in two lengths ahead of the second-place horse, missing the course record by just half a second. Charlie, who knew next to nothing about horse racing, managed to write the following piece, published on the front page of the *Herald*:

> "It was 'some' crowd, which being translated into the Australian language, means a bonza crowd. That is the most definite of the many kaleidoscopic impressions left me by the wonderful spectacle of the Melbourne Cup. I am told this is the greatest race that Australia provides, and I can well believe it. If you have any greater than this, and I am called upon to record my impressions again, I shall have to coin a new set of adjectives to do it justice. As it is, the adjective box is too small for the meeting I have just seen. The reader will have gathered that this is my first Cup; indeed, I must risk incurring the pity of Australians by confessing that it was my first big race meeting of any kind in this country or elsewhere.
>
> The crowd was the thing . . . A moving, colorful crowd, always interesting; there is nothing like it in the world to hold the eye, nothing like it in the peculiar humming sound that it makes. In its very immensity, the Flemington crowd

was tremendously interesting and impressive. In America our greatest crowds are in the World Series baseball games, and the big football matches, like those between Harvard and Yale. A gathering of 40,000 is notable for any occasion, the attendance being limited by the size of the parks. At Flemington apparently there is no limit. Certainly, the crowd on Saturday was more than twice 40,000; and I have been told that the Cup, in pre-war days, has drawn as high as 120,000. I was inclined to believe that this 120,000 crowd was somewhat of a myth, created for press-agent purposes; but, as the man from Missouri says, I have been shown."[391]

Here Charlie, given broad editorial license, showed that well-presented personal impressions and colorful writing can bring the facts alive.

While in Australia, Charlie maintained contact with another old boss and mentor, O.K. Bovard, at the *Post-Dispatch*. On several occasions, Bovard had asked Charlie to return to the paper, but Charlie always refused. Nevertheless, they remained friends. Bovard was intrigued by Australia's advanced and progressive labor laws. Were they a harbinger for future laws in the United States and elsewhere? Might this be a beginning for an enlightened social order, where wealth could be more evenly distributed throughout society? When he learned about Charlie's sabbatical, Bovard asked him to study the situation and send a detailed report back to the *Post-Dispatch*. Charlie, presumably, was paid for this work.

After researching the labor situation in Australia, Charlie wrote the requested article, which was published in the *Post-Dispatch*. In part, it reads:

"Much has been said in America of Australia's advanced labor legislation. Whenever a great industrial dispute arises, and there is public demand for a speedy settlement, Australia is almost invariably cited as a country in which arbitration laws are in successful operation. Intercollegiate debates arguing for the minimum wage are almost certain to point to Australia as a Utopia in which legislation has forever settled the age-old differences of capital and labor.

What are the practical workings of these laws?

Doubtless they have ameliorated the condition of labor, which, at one time in the history of the country, was cruelly exploited. Doubtless they have been the main factor in making this, as it is frequently called, 'the paradise of the working man.'

Comparative figures show that wages have been raised and that Australia, perhaps more than any other nation, is trending toward an equal distribution of wealth. There are few very rich people in Australia and few very poor. Slum conditions in cities are comparatively unknown. This sums up the case for Australia's labor legislation. On the other hand, critics of the system point to the undeveloped condition of the country; to the fact that the vast majority of Australia's 5,000,000 people are settled in a thin fringe around the seacoast, the astounding proportion of 40 per cent of the total being concentrated in the six capital cities; to industrial inefficiency and waste in many lines; to the fact that Australia, so few are her manufacturers, is utterly dependent for her existence on the outside world.

There are charges, too, that the unions stand for "slowing down" industry, that their tendency is to put a premium on mediocrity and discourage capital from embarking on new enterprises.

There is one outstanding fact, attested by observation, by reading of the newspapers, and by reference to the Official Year Book of the Commonwealth. That fact is that Australia's labor laws, whatever may be their other merits or demerits, most certainly do not prevent strikes . . ."[392]

On balance, it appears that Charlie wasn't a fan of Australia's labor laws at the time. Again, as he did in his piece on the Melbourne Cup, he showed he was a man from Missouri—and he had to be shown. It is interesting to note that these basic pro and con positions regarding organized labor have remained largely unchanged over the past 100 years.

Returning to the University

In the late spring of 1917, Charlie, Florence, and their two young sons departed Melbourne and boarded another steamship—although this time without the benefit of Walker-Gordon's milk. For Charlie, it had been one of the most happy and carefree periods of his life.[393] The long voyage home gave Charlie a chance to relax and evaluate his career and his family's future.

When Charlie returned, he quickly noticed how things had changed at the School during his year away. The United States had just joined the war in Europe, and many of the young men who would have been journalism students had joined the military. Enrollment was down nearly one half, from 305 students the year he left to 173 when he returned. While the number of female students remained constant, the male enrollment had dropped from 246 to 113.[394]

The draft for World War I affected young men in the United States, including Charlie. It required men between the ages of 21 and 31 to register with the government to be available for service in the armed forces. At that time (May 1917), Charlie was 31 and would turn 32 in a few months. Charlie fulfilled his duty to register, but not until he returned to the country on September 5, 1918, just a couple of months before the end of the war. Luckily, Charlie was not the profile the draft boards were targeting, and he was never a serious candidate for conscription.

Upon his return in the summer of 1917, Charlie found that teaching at the School of Journalism had lost some of its appeal. He'd been teaching for nine of the past ten years and the job was both predictable and not as exciting as he, at age 31, would have liked. As the breadwinner he was always looking for more income, and he was particularly sensitive to supporting his family, something his father had been painfully unable to do. Also, he found he enjoyed the pace and camaraderie of the newspaper life in Australia, which brought back the good memories of his previous newspaper work in St. Louis. He knew he was good at that job, and it could pay a lot more than he'd earn in academia. To unsettle things further, O.K. Bovard had extended an open invitation to him to return to the *Post-Dispatch* whenever he wished.[395]

Charlie's Next Step

However, Charlie felt obligated to continue teaching at the School of Journalism. His young family was well-situated in their recently built home; he was an accomplished teacher, and the school depended on him; and, upon his return, he was promoted to full professor. Most importantly, he didn't want to disappoint Dean Walter Williams, his boss and mentor who had given him the opportunity to work and live in Australia for a year. Years later his widow, Florence, said that his sense of obligation to Dean Williams was the "only reason he stayed."[396] Charlie, despite Bovard's offers to return to the *Post Dispatch*, felt he had to remain at the University.[397]

Charlie continued teaching through the 1917–1918 academic year, also a war year for the United States. One day in June, Charlie spent an unusual amount of time preparing a new lecture, taking the trouble to write it out to make sure the points were logical and well-presented. Charlie launched into the lecture, employing all the emotion and emphasis he knew the subject deserved. When he had reached a key part of the text, he looked up and saw one of his better students, Pauline Pfeiffer, absentmindedly staring out a window eating nonchalantly from a bag of candy. Charlie was stunned. He coolly completed the lecture, and class was dismissed—but for Charlie that was the last straw. In that moment, he had an epiphany that teaching was no longer what he wanted to do. Teaching journalism was a waste of his time—and his professional life. So, he walked out of the classroom, straight into town to the Western Union office. There he penned a short message to Bovard at the *Post-Dispatch* and gave it to the telegraph operator to send. The telegram read: "If you still want me, I am now available."[398]

For most of his life, Charlie never divulged, except to family members, the identity of the candy-eating student for fear it might embarrass her. Pauline Pfeiffer had been born into a well-to-do family in St. Louis, where she graduated from St. Louis Academy of the Visitation, winning the school's prize for English. Upon graduation, she entered the University of Missouri and graduated from the School of Journalism in 1918; Charlie's fateful lecture was one of her final classes before graduation. After graduation, Pauline pursued a career and moved up quickly in journalism, first as a copyeditor for the *Cleveland Press* and eventually on to the glossy magazines, *Vanity Fair* and *Vogue*. While on assignment for *Vogue* in Paris in 1925, she met Ernest Hemingway, whom she married in 1927, becoming his second wife. Their tempestuous marriage ended in divorce in 1940. Pauline passed away in California at age 56 in October of 1951 and is buried in the Hollywood Forever Cemetery in Los Angeles.[399]

Charlie and Pauline crossed paths in 1950, thirty years after the event. He told her the candy-eating episode and asked if she would mind if he told it publicly. She laughed and happily agreed, so the story was finally told. Charlie's sensitivity for Pauline's feelings was typical of his concern for others. He reputedly never made an enemy. Florence, for her part, kept the episode confidential until 1950. Years later, she added a quip, commenting mostly on Charlie's notorious sweet tooth. Florence wrote: "If she had only passed the candy to him! But she didn't. He liked candy!"[400]

Before the summer session began, Charlie informed Dean Williams of his decision to leave. It must have been a difficult conversion for both men, but it ended well—they remained friends the rest of their lives. Charlie moved on to talk about his new role at the *Post-Dispatch* with O.K. Bovard. During the summer of 1918, World War I was still raging in Europe, and, at home, the Spanish Flu was metastasizing into a major public-health catastrophe. Bovard knew these weren't ordinary times and that the country would change once the war ended. In particular, he saw that Washington, DC, had become the country's nerve center and was emerging as a vital news center. It was decided that Charlie should go to Washington to open a news bureau specifically for the *Post-Dispatch* and staffed by its own people. Management hoped this would help transform the reputation of the *Post-Dispatch* from a parochial, midwestern daily into a paper of national influence and a broader readership with more middle-American values.[401]

Mr. Ross Goes to Washington

Charlie started his new job on August 12, 1918, and was given the title "Washington Correspondent." Bovard instructed him to feel his way slowly in his new town. He was told to start by gathering only news related to Missouri and St. Louis, rather than reporting on national events. He spent the first few months learning about Washington, DC, and discovered how to gain access to the houses of Congress, the sundry agencies and bureaus, and even the White House. He was also making contacts of all types. He learned to adjust to the faster pace of this post-war boomtown, but he was blindsided by the high cost of living. He rented a small temporary apartment and started looking for a permanent place where he could live with Florence and his sons. They had remained in Columbia, with the intention of joining him shortly after the first of the year. The cost-of-living difference was a major stumbling block. Charlie had agreed to a salary from the *Post-Dispatch* that was more than adequate in Missouri; he realized now that it wouldn't go very far in Washington, DC.

During this period, Charlie kept a diary. It covered just over two months of his life. He attempted at other times to keep a diary, but sadly those attempts, too, were short-lived. Below are a few of the more interesting items:

- His sister, Helen, who at this time worked for the U.S. Railroad Administration, was in and out of Washington intermittently, and they had dinner together on occasion throughout January.

- On January 6th, Charlie noted, "President [Theodore] Roosevelt died today."

- On January 16th, Charlie made a note to remind himself to write "to Virginia, ill with influenza in the hospital."

- On January 17th, he noted: "Wrote to Virginia."

- Throughout January, there were entries about his informing Florence of his many attempts to locate a house to rent. The tight post-war housing market offered few affordable rentals in Washington, and many of the leads Charlie pursued fell through.

- On February 6th, he noted: "Florence wrote that Estie [Florence's sister] is to be married."

- February: There are entries about his need for a car, but that he couldn't afford one. He told Bovard, who instructed him to look for one anyway. Charlie found a Ford he liked, Bovard told him to buy it, and presumably the *Post-Dispatch* paid the cost. Charlie also noted that Bovard raised his monthly salary by $10.

- March 3rd: Charlie went to Keith's restaurant with Mr. Cochran and Roy Roberts. Roy Roberts worked for the *Kansas City Star* and was also living and working in Washington. Charlie and Roy, both with Missouri-Kansas roots, became good friends and remained such for years. Roy later became the editor-in-chief of the *Kansas City Star* and, after Charlie's death, married Charlie's widow, Florence.

- March 4th: "65th Congress ends. Shook hands with the President at the Capitol."

- "Florence & children arrived today. All went to Mount Alto Inn to live at $60 per week."

- March 12th: "Received letter from Mamma, who sold the house for $8,000." [His mother sold their home in Independence.]⁴⁰²

When his family joined him in Washington, Charlie had little spare time, and, sadly, the diary ends on March 12, 1919.

After Florence and the boys arrived, the couple continued to search for a new home. Charlie eventually found an apartment on Keokuk Court just inside the District of Columbia from Chevy Chase, Maryland. Charlie soon realized that, even with his recent raise, he simply couldn't make ends meet in the capital. He told Bovard and offered to resign, but Bovard wouldn't hear of it. Quickly, the *Post-Dispatch* came across with a generous raise that was enough for Charlie and Florence to purchase a home.⁴⁰³ A relieved Charlie accepted the new salary, and he and Florence found and purchased a recently built home about a mile north of Washington, just off Connecticut Avenue at 5 Primrose Street in Chevy Chase, Maryland. The family settled into their new neighborhood and made that house their home for the next 15 years.

Charlie had decided to leave his home and friends in Missouri behind to pursue his own destiny. It was a decision Charlie's forebears made time and again—sometimes it worked out and, as in JB's case, sometimes it didn't. Countless other Americans were on the move, too, in the booming years after World War I. His decision to chase his dream in many ways gave his sisters tacit approval to do the same. Would they? Or would they, like Mama did, remain in Independence? Time would tell.

15

I'M GOING TO LIVE WITH MY DAUGHTERS

The Ross children's roots on their maternal (Thomas) side ran deep in Independence, but their roots also contained the seeds for their departure. From their mother and grandmother, they inherited a thirst for education. From their father, their imaginations were kindled by his stories of adventure and travel. Their exits began slowly, with Charlie leaving for college in 1901, followed by Helen in 1907. Although not a sudden or mass exodus, a pattern began to emerge.

Helen's Restlessness

When Helen returned as a schoolteacher to Independence in 1911, she had the capacity and desire to do more than just teach. Shortly after her arrival, Helen was given the opportunity to teach a night class to Mormons at the Columbian School, a local public school that Harry Truman had attended as a child. For people growing up at that time in Independence, the word "Mormon" was a "term of social opprobrium." She recalled in her memoirs that "Mormons, to us, as children, were fun at school, but the association ended there."[404] The night course was designed for adults, with an emphasis on basic reading and writing. She taught for only one term because, as she stated, "I found I was instructing Mormons how to write for their religious magazines."[405]

Later in her life, Helen related one particularly unpleasant episode, when one of her elderly students attempted to convert her to Mormonism.

> "One little black gowned lady who always carried a big umbrella, rain or clear, would ask each evening to walk home with me, 'so that nothing can happen to you, miss,' and clutched firmly by a scrawny hand, I went home over old plank walks, my little guide busy telling me all the way that I had 'a great future in the Church, my dear, a great future.'"[406]

Although she wasn't about to join the church, she must have been well regarded as a teacher, because, at the end of the term, she was given a poem composed in her honor.[407]

As soon as the term at the Columbian School ended, Helen came across another opportunity. This time it would involve teaching an evening course in nearby Kansas City at a school run by a Mr. Billikopf. This would open her eyes to social-welfare programs, allow her to work with different types of people, and provide her with some useful managerial experience.

Jacob Billikopf

Born in Wilna, Russia, in 1882, Jacob Billikopf emigrated to the United States in 1895. When he arrived, he spoke no English, but he soon learned it well and graduated from high school as a promising student and a chess prodigy. With the help of scholarships, he went to college and earned a Bachelor of Philanthropy degree (Ph.B.) from the University of Chicago in 1903.

After completing his formal education, he became deeply involved in a variety of civic projects—especially ones that improved correctional institutions in the area—and he worked with non-profit organizations such as the Helping Hand Institute, which provided food, shelter, employment, and other support for homeless men. In addition, he founded a night school to teach English to recently settled Jewish immigrants.[408]

In 1912, Helen became a teacher at this night school, where she taught English for four years. At Mr. Billikopf's urging, she also became the director of the school in the final two years. Working with the socially conscious Mr. Billikopf, she became much more aware of how social issues affect people, and how they could be addressed. According to one account about Helen, "under the tutelage of Jacob Billikopf she experienced the impact of social problems and laid the foundation for [her] later interest in social work."[409] It was also a new experience for Helen to work closely with members of the Jewish community. Managing this school, albeit a modest evening school, under the direction of the dynamic Mr. Billikopf, not only opened Helen's eyes, it provided her an experience upon which she would later draw.

Paying College Forward

Money had always been tight in the Ross household. So, as was their hallmark, the whole family pitched in to help with the finances. A particular challenge was how the three younger girls were going to be able to afford college.

In May 1915, Virginia, the oldest of the "fall crop" of younger sisters, graduated from Independence High School. She was a very good student in high school and was eager to go to college. She was determined to be the third Ross go to the University of Missouri. Helen felt a keen responsibility, but simply didn't see a way to make it happen, at least not right away. As a graduation gift, Helen gave Virginia the following note:

"Gin, it is unnecessary, I hope, to tell you I am sorry we cannot give you something really beautiful and good for a commencement present.

The present that meant most to me when I graduated was a note from Charlie saying that I should go to the University in the fall. Then I dreamed I could bring you the same happiness today. But I cannot make the promise that you will go when we are facing such an uncertain financial outlook. I can do this—make a promise that I shall try to make four years of college work possible for you. You deserve it now, and you will have it sometime.

I want no thanks and I ask no praise, for we are all working together. More than anything from you I should appreciate a frank expression of yourself at all times in all things.

Affectionately,
Helen"[410]

This letter meant a great deal to Virginia, who for years kept it among her important papers. However, strong-willed Virginia did not want to delay, so she took the untested path of enrolling in a newly opened college, the Kansas City Polytechnic Institute. She lived in Independence and attended classes in Kansas City. She completed the following college-level courses: General Zoology,

Composition and Literature, Elementary Physics, Spanish, and Physical Training.[411] As it turned out, these courses would enable her to realize her dream and complete her education in less than four years at the University of Missouri.

1916—A New Start in Columbia

When Charlie was planning his sabbatical in Australia, he had to decide what to do with their recently built home on Edgewood Avenue in Columbia. Who would look after it for the year they were away? Helen, Sis, and Virginia all immediately volunteered to help.

Helen and Sis moved in when the house became available in early June. They wouldn't leave for Camp Kechuwa until later in June. After camp ended in late August, Sis and Helen returned to Columbia and lived there full-time. Helen got a job teaching at Columbia High School that paid better than her job in Independence, which was good news for the sisters.

The University of Missouri's fall semester began in mid-September. The determined Virginia enthusiastically joined her older sisters and enrolled at the University, hoping her coursework from the Kansas City Polytechnic Institute would transfer. The timing couldn't have been better. Back in Independence, Mama wanted the family to stay together. So, she encouraged Frances to move to Columbia; Frances agreed and enrolled as a senior at Columbia High School. By mid-September, the four sisters had settled into the house on Edgewood Avenue. Sixty-year-old Mama and fourteen-year-old Jamie would soon join them.

The thrifty Ross women were skilled at making ends meet. The profits generated from Camp Kechuwa's increasing enrollment were welcome new income. And, of course, the University was "almost free" in the words of Virginia years later.[412] There must have also been a few meager savings, scholarship funds, and income from part-time jobs. In any event, the Ross women cobbled together enough to make the transition from Independence to Columbia work—and work for *all* of them.

Once Helen and Sis returned from Camp Kechuwa in August of 1916, everyone settled into the new arrangement. While teaching at Columbia High, Helen began to audit two graduate courses at the University, one in sociology and the other in economics.[413] Sis likewise enrolled at the University, where she took three courses given by the Home Economics Department. These courses reflected her growing interest in food, nutrition, and health, which had been sparked by her work at the camp. Virginia enrolled in the School of Journalism, and, fortunately her coursework from Kansas City Polytechnic Institute transferred easily. This allowed her to enroll as a second-year student, on track to graduate after three years of coursework in Columbia. The family was off to a good new start.

1917: A Year of Transitions

As the year began, Sis continued managing the home and taking second-semester courses at the University. In May, she completed the second semester of the 1916–1917 academic year and was awarded high marks, all E's and S's. (At that time the grading system at the University consisted of the following scale, representing grades from highest to lowest: E=Excellent; S=Superior; M=Medium; I=Inferior; and F=Failure; in 1958, it was replaced by the now-familiar A, B, C, D, F scale.[414]) Sis showed that she, like her college-educated siblings, had the makings of a top student.

In June, Charlie, Florence, and the boys arrived back in Columbia after their long voyage from Australia and reclaimed their home. Sis and Helen turned the keys to their temporary home back to Charlie and Florence and then departed for Kechuwa, which was about to begin its fourth year. But Mama and her Fall Crop decided to stay in Columbia and moved to another house. Virginia continued with her studies at the University for her junior year. She'd developed aspirations of becoming a journalist, like her brother.[415] Frances entered the University as a freshman, two years behind Virginia. Jamie enrolled at Columbia High School.

1917—Helen Leaves Columbia

By the spring of 1917, Helen made the decision to leave the small world of high-school teaching and pursue a graduate degree full-time. She had been awarded the Susan B. Anthony Memorial Fellowship at Bryn Mawr College to do graduate work in social research. Her one-year scholarship started in September. The scholarship offered Helen a fresh opportunity to enter a world where women were making a difference. It would allow her to push the boundaries for women, showing that they could do more than they were currently permitted. So, after her summer at Camp Kechuwa, she boarded a train to Pennsylvania to begin her graduate work near Philadelphia at Bryn Mawr.

When Sis left Camp Kechuwa in the late summer of 1917, she took the train back to Columbia, where her family was waiting for her. She continued her studies at the University. Sis, like Helen, realized that she was ready for a change, and she began to plan her next move.

Louise Makes a Home in Arizona

All this time, Louise was in Arizona making her living teaching elementary school. After being finessed into becoming the town's schoolteacher, she was informed that the State of Arizona "required some examinations." Helen, years later, recalled:

> "And so it was, Louise wrote me to ask [for] some coaching in what the questions might be, and I set up a correspondence course. That she passed was due, I am sure, to her native wisdom and inventiveness. She became the teacher [in Parker] of eight grades, with some twenty pupils, the idol of the children on that great desert plateau, where every day was an adventure for Louise as well as for the school."[416]

Louise taught in Parker for two years (1911–1913). Then, in the summer of 1913, her world changed. Recalled years later by Virginia:

> "Louise and Papa were planning to leave Parker [in the summer of 1913] because he had contracted typhoid fever and had to be hospitalized in Prescott. [Then] came a letter from Mr. Loper, Superintendent of Schools in Phoenix, saying he had heard of her teaching on the desert and offering her a job. Somewhat bewildered, she accepted. Until our father's death that autumn, she taught in Phoenix and spent weekends with him in Prescott. Again, she was a success, and taught in Phoenix for several years . . ."[417]

Louise enjoyed those years teaching in Phoenix. She resided at Mrs. Bane's, an all-female boarding house, with several other schoolteachers. While there, she made lasting friends, including Jessie Creighton and Eva Bane. On weekends, the new friends often went shopping. Goldwater's department store, with its wide selection of quality merchandise, was a favorite. She also sent money home every month to her family. During those hot Arizona summers, she traveled to Missouri to visit them. She often brought a trunk full of gifts, sometimes also fabric, which she used to make clothes for the family. Her sister Virginia recalled years later:

> "There was something for everybody, most often a piece of fabric for a dress or a blouse or a coat or what-not. She had combed Goldwater's store for bargains, and found them. By the time she returned to Phoenix, we were wearing her creations. Goldwater's store was a sort of hallmark for the Rosses."[418]

Louise's unconventional teaching style often proved to be remarkably effective. While walking with Helen in her Phoenix neighborhood, years later, Louise recounted:

> "That man we saw just now knew I couldn't spell, so every day he asked me a new word and I'd just say 'Look it up; you'll remember it longer' . . . [But] . . . Sometimes I'd sneak into my cloakroom where I kept a dictionary hidden. Spelling isn't really very important, you know."
>
> "See that Mexican garage over there? Well, he [Jesu] was in the grade I taught at the Adams School, the second grade, and he had a paper route and got up early, so he was always tired at school and went to sleep as soon as he came [to school]. I waked him up at recess so he could have fun. Once . . . the superintendent came to visit, saw Jesu fast asleep at his desk and scolded me, but I just said, 'He needs his sleep more than spelling.' Just see how well he is getting along now; [he] owns the gas station."[419]

One teaching experience involved a young man from a prominent family in the area. When he first came into her classroom, he insisted on sitting backwards at his desk. Tactful Louise, who always sought to adjust to her students' differences, agreed to this odd behavior if it didn't disrupt the rest of the class. As it turned out, it wasn't a problem, and the student successfully completed the year and moved on to the next grade. His name was Barry M. Goldwater.[420] He would, later in life, became a U. S. Senator from Arizona, and in 1964, he ran for the office of President of the United States.

Sis Makes her Move

Sis began the wartime year of 1918 doggedly learning all she could about food and nutrition. She continued devouring the practical courses offered by the Home Economics department and also took an economics course (General Economics). In that same academic year, she audited two additional courses: Elementary Sociology and Urban Sociology. Her high marks show she was an outstanding student, earning six E's and one S.

In June of 1918, Sis departed again for Camp Kechuwa, now in its fifth season. After her summer on the shores of Lake Michigamme, she took the train south, but not to Missouri. She got off at her new home, Chicago, a growing, vibrant, multicultural metropolis. Sis (likely with Helen's advice) believed there were more opportunities for single women there than in the sleepy college town of Columbia. She found a large, comfortable apartment at 1151 East 56th Street, just outside the gates of the University of Chicago. This also became the off-season business address for Camp Kechuwa.

The deciding factor in Sis' relocating to Chicago was that she had been accepted for undergraduate work at the highly regarded University of Chicago, which had an impressive and progressive Home Economics Department. In her first term, she took a six-hour course in the Chemistry Department entitled "Research in Chemistry of Food." She earned an "A" in the course and was well on her way to a degree.

1918—Helen Leaves Academia to Become a "Doer"

When Helen left Camp Kechuwa in September 1917, she traveled to Bryn Mawr, Pennsylvania, where she spent the next nine months studying social research on a graduate level. She had become increasingly interested in social issues, particularly as they related to women. She realized that, at age 27, she no longer wanted to be a schoolteacher. In her memoirs she recalled her social-research work at Bryn Mawr:

> "During this year [at Bryn Mawr] I helped in a study, made for the Quartermaster's Department, of the conditions under which U.S. Army uniforms for World War I were being made under the contract system of giving out piecework to women to do in their homes in the slums of Philadelphia."[421]

Two aspects of her experience at Bryn Mawr stand out. First, she was becoming increasingly focused on the role of women in society, and second, she "made the acquaintance with the then famous Goldmark sisters." Pauline and Josephine Goldmark were born and raised in New York City in a large Jewish family, and both had graduated from Bryn Mawr College, in 1896 and 1898, respectively. A third sister, Alice Goldmark, also became known for promoting progressive causes. She was married to Louis Brandeis, a highly regarded judge who was appointed Associate Justice of the U. S. Supreme Court in 1916. Pauline and Josephine "helped brother-in-law Louis Brandeis in framing social legislation."[422]

Pauline stood out as a social worker whose talents as a researcher were crucial in many labor-rights initiatives. She pioneered methods in social research, such as investigating, accumulating facts, and presenting research in an effective way to lawmakers for the desired legislation.[423] In a similar vein, Josephine helped lay the groundwork for transforming labor laws early in the twentieth century. She became highly skilled at compiling data on working conditions, writing articles, and leading campaigns for labor reform.[424] Both women were important reformers in the Progressive Era, and from them, Helen learned perspectives and methods that she would use to try to improve the role of women in society. Not coincidently, Pauline Goldmark, during World War I, served as the U. S. Department of Labor's Commission on Women in Industry, where she managed the Women's Service Section of the U. S. Railroad Administration, supervising the work of thousands of women workers.[425] The U. S. Railroad Administration would soon play an important role in Helen's future.

By the end of the 1917–1918 academic year at Bryn Mawr, Helen, always an excellent student, was invited to continue into the Ph.D. program for social research. But she declined that opportunity. Perhaps she was tiring of academia. Or perhaps she wanted, as she later stated, to do something to help the war effort and perform an activity that traditionally had excluded women. In any event, by the time she left Bryn Mawr for the summer at Camp Kechuwa, she'd turned her career path in a different direction—away from the academic world.

In Helen's own words, written years later, she outlined her thinking in 1918:

"At the end of this year at Bryn Mawr [June 1918], I was awarded a further fellowship for study toward a Ph.D. in social research. However, I gave this up to take a position as a field agent for the U. S. Railroad Administration to study the working conditions of the vast number of women taken into all branches of railroad work following the drafting of men for World War I. This work, which continued for two years with time off to run the camp, took me over practically all of the United States."[426]

This explanation outlines the extent of her career change, but not the reasons for it. The opening paragraph of her memoir provides some insight into her thinking in 1918:

"Today I find myself looking at my hands. They are old hands and larger than they used to be . . . A Swiss woman, a nurse trained in psychoanalysis, and an amateur palm reader, once looked at my hands on a skiing holiday, nodded her head and said, 'A kind of strength and lightness put together' . . . [Also a] . . . German doctor . . . and a dabbler in palmistry [looking at my hands said] 'you might have been an artist; you are a doer.' [Helen then concludes] . . . Indeed I was."[427]

Helen realized she was a "doer"—she needed to accomplish tangible things. Unmarried and now 28 years old, she changed gears and took a hands-on job in the larger world, one which she hoped would also broaden opportunities for other women.

Helen Rides the Rails: The U. S. Railroad Administration

After the summer 1918 camp season, Helen joined Sis in Chicago. Chicago had become a primary hub for the railroad industry, thus making it an ideal base for her new job, which involved traveling by rail through all parts of the United States.

The United States Railroad Administration (USRA) came into existence during World War I to address the war emergency. It's difficult today to imagine the extent and importance of the railroads at that time. The nation had more than 250,000 miles of track, which was owned in separate pieces by more than 400 corporations. Most freight and passengers traveled by rail. At this time, trucks and automobiles were fewer and unreliable, but they were beginning to have an impact on the rail business. When war was declared, many railroads had become struggling, cash-poor businesses (with many in receivership). The country suddenly needed a surge in rail traffic to meet the demands of arms production and the transportation of munitions, men, and supplies across the country.

The Railroads' War Board was created to achieve a coordinated "railway system" to support the war, but this effort proved inadequate. So, in December 1917, President Wilson issued an order nationalizing the railroads. He then appointed the Secretary of the Treasury, William McAdoo, as Director General of the railroads. When this happened, Congress became alarmed that this might lead to a permanent, socialistic takeover. So, in March 1918, Congress passed the Railroad Control Act, which stated that, within 21 months of a peace treaty, the railroads would be returned to their owners, who would be compensated for the usage of their property.

Shortly after taking charge of the railroads, Director General McAdoo divided the sprawling USRA system into three divisions: South, West, and East. The USRA then organized unified terminals (one notably in Chicago), standardized locomotives and freight cars, centralized the purchasing of equipment and supplies, and pooled repair shops and maintenance facilities.

Passenger services were streamlined, eliminating a significant amount of non-essential travel, important during wartime. It consolidated ticket offices, created standard ticket forms and luggage rules, eliminated advertising, and standardized all statistical records. During its existence, the USRA ordered more than 100,000 new railroad cars and 1,930 steam engines—all designed to the latest standards—at a total cost of $380 million. As a result, the railroads were able to meet the increased demand brought about by the war. In compliance with the constraints of the Railroad Control Act, the railroads were returned to the owners and became private property again after the war, on March 1, 1920.[428]

As an integral part of the upgrading and modernizing of the railroads, Pauline Goldmark, in 1918, was made the head of the Women's Service Section of the USRA, which carried with it the responsibility of supervising the work of its more than 100,000 female workers.[429] Helen came under her supervision. When Helen joined the USRA, the wartime labor shortage had led the railroads to hire a large number of women. The vast majority worked in jobs traditionally held by women, including more than 73,000 serving in clerical or semi-clerical positions, and more than 10,000 as cleaners and shop workers; only a mere 872 performed track work, and approximately 100 worked in train service."[430] Helen, years later, described her job for the USRA:

"When World War I came and I was employed as a field agent of the Women's Service Section of the U. S. Railroad Administration, to check on the work women were doing because of [a] man shortage, a little yellow pass took me on every line in the United States, indeed everything that went on tracks, way-freights, handcars, locomotives even."[431]

As a field agent she observed, analyzed, and reported on the work women performed for the railroad. Implicit in her role were the questions: Could women do more than they then were allowed to do? Was the compensation for women on a par with that earned by men? What specific jobs might be open for women in the future? Although it was challenging for physically diminutive Helen, she found parts of the experience exciting. "Those two years it was often fun to think, as I rode across a prairie, maybe in the cupola of a caboose, about the time in Independence when 'travel' was only a dream."[432]

She vividly recalled how she, as a woman, was received—and occasionally accommodated—by sympathetic male railroad workers:

> "Most of the railroads treated me with respect, albeit some scorn that a 'little woman with a yellow card' could walk into an office and begin asking questions. On one line in the friendly Northwest, I was heralded on the Simplex telephone as the 'Junior Brakeman,' and to earn this title, I had often to pocket my timidity and hope that my vocabulary smacked a little of the road. Often the way-freight broke down on a long run; a hot box held us far from the scheduled town; night would come, and if I had eaten the chocolate bar I learned to carry, I was glad the brakeman would share the remains of his dinner pail with me. Pineapple pie was the only residue once, handed up to me in the cupola of a caboose, and pineapple pie remains forever associated with the sunset over billowing Kansas wheat fields."[433]

Helen's work also brought her face-to-face with the tragedy of the Spanish Flu pandemic.

"Sorrowful times there were too, for field agents, for those were the years of the devastating flu epidemic. I came to dread arriving at the little stations where so often a row of coffins would tell me that the flu had hit, and the weeping members of a family would come to greet an arriving relative or to go on their way with one or two or even three of the coffins. And Mother would write letters begging me to be careful. When I had a day or two with Mother and the girls, they would look enviously at my yellow pass and see only the glamor of travel I had dreamed of."[434]

Helen's two years as a USRA field agent allowed her to see more of America than most people would see in a lifetime. It also enabled her to visit her family back in Missouri and to drop in on Charlie as he settled into his new job in Washington, DC. It paid a good salary, and she was able to enjoy the big-city life with Sis in Chicago. She was also allowed to take the summers off so she and Sis could operate their beloved Camp Kechuwa. Sadly, in March 1920, the USRA was disbanded, and Helen's job came to an end. And although a new era—The Roaring Twenties—was beginning, 30-year-old Helen again found herself searching for a meaningful and challenging professional path to pursue. It would take a few years before her life's work would present itself.

1918—Louise Marries

Louise, as usual, was taking a very different path from her twin sister. In 1918, at age 28, Louise was enjoying life in Phoenix, where she had lived for four years. More outgoing than Helen, Louise had an active social life, and went to dances and other events with her close group of friends. On one of these occasions, she was introduced to a promising young man, Fred N. "Fritz" Holmquist. Fritz was one of the first professional engineers in Arizona and worked as the engineer for the city of Phoenix. Louise caught the eye of this reserved young man, and a courtship ensued. It didn't take long for them to realize that they were in love. When Fritz asked for Louise's hand in marriage, she accepted, and the couple was married on November 26, 1918.

Louise and Fritz settled in Phoenix and were eager to start a family of their own. This proved easier than it was for many, and their first child, Lars Holmquist, was born less than a year later in October of 1919. Three years after this, Lars was followed by twins, Fred Nels Holmquist, Jr. and Helen Ross Holmquist, born in November of 1922, carrying on the family's tradition of twins. Then, to complete the family, James Bruce Holmquist was born in July of 1924. Louise resigned from her teaching position to stay at home and raise their active children. Louise had chosen a very different path from Helen's, but one she found equally challenging and fulfilling.

1919—Virginia Graduates from the University

Virginia demonstrated that she was a solid college student who'd received a good education, with an emphasis on the social sciences. However, she never earned the lofty marks received by Charlie and Helen or achieved Sis' intense focus on a specific field. She earned her A. B. degree from the College of Arts and Sciences in April 1919.[435] During the years Virginia attended college, Mama and young Jamie lived close by in Columbia.

Virginia's college graduation—the family's third—pleased Mama. However, the sisters were hesitant to tell Mama that Virginia had graduated without any honors, like the *Phi Beta Kappa* keys awarded to Charlie and Helen. They broke the news to her one day when she was in her bedroom, sitting at her dressing table brushing her long hair. When she was presented with the news, Mama continued brushing her hair but didn't respond immediately. After a long delay, she slowly said, "Someday the University of Missouri will learn of its mistake."[436] Although Virginia didn't earn the same academic awards as Charlie and Helen, she certainly received the assurance that her mother thought none the less of her for it.

Mama's confidence in Virginia's academic abilities was not entirely unfounded. Virginia, as part of her economics courses, had written "a term paper on the National Consumers' League's Interest in Women in Industry."[437] This paper found its way into the right hands and helped her win a graduate fellowship to Bryn Mawr College, where Helen had studied two years earlier. This opportunity became a vehicle that would allow Virginia to pursue her growing interest in society and in women's concerns.[438] Virginia left Missouri, boarded a train, and headed east to Bryn Mawr, Pennsylvania.

Frances Bruce Ross—the Fifth Ross to Attend the University of Missouri

In 1916, Frances completed her high school education outside of Independence—at Columbia High School. Just before leaving for Columbia, she was in a play at Independence High that staged a wedding ceremony where she played the bride. Lowell Leake, the son of the new minister at the Christian Church, played the groom. He later recalled meeting "a chunky little girl named Frances Ross" at that mock ceremony shortly after his family had moved to town.[439] Lowell became so smitten with Frances that he kept in touch with her long after she and her family had moved from Independence to Columbia in 1916. Always a good student, Frances graduated from Columbia High School in 1917 and enrolled as a freshman in the College of Arts and Sciences at the University of Missouri.

In college, Frances, like Virginia, who was two years ahead, took a wide variety of courses. Like most other students, she completed the introductory English and Philosophy courses. She initially showed an interest in French, completing five courses given by that department. Like Virginia, she took a wide variety of courses in the social sciences, e.g., sociology, psychology, economics, and political science, reflecting a general humanitarian interest. Her grades were better than Virginia's, and she completed her coursework in the usual four years, graduating in 1921, and becoming the third Ross to receive a *Phi Beta Kappa* honor.[440]

Lowell L. Leake

Lowell LeVerne Leake was born in Prescott, Iowa, on January 2, 1898, the son of a protestant minister, Reverend Erwin Francis Leake. Lowell was the oldest child in a very large family. As a boy, Lowell's family moved every few years and scraped by on his father's meager earnings. Lowell took on many part-time jobs to earn money. In 1915, the family moved to Independence, Missouri. Lowell was immediately enrolled in Independence High School, where he met Frances Ross. After high school, he went to college at Drake University on a "working scholarship" and made his way onto the staff of *The Drake Delphic*, the campus newspaper. He transferred to Drury College in Springfield, Missouri, when his parents moved there. When war was declared in April, 1917, he, like many young men at the time, enlisted in the army. After boot camp, Lowell was sent to France, where he served in combat. In one battle, he saw a good friend "blown to bits," a sight which would haunt him for the rest of his life.[441] World War I ended on November 11, 1918, and he was discharged soon thereafter. He returned to Drury College. He was soon hired by the local paper as a part-time reporter, covering many local organizations and sports. Because of the quality of his sports reporting, he was offered a job as a sports reporter for the newspaper in Akron, Ohio, at $30 a week. He accepted the job and set out for Akron.

On his way to Akron, he stopped by Columbia to visit Frances, whom he had kept in touch with. He recalls a memorable conversation from that visit:

> "There, Frances and I walked on the mezzanine of the Daniel Boone Tavern, and coming down the steps, she announced to me the terms on which she planned to be married. 'The man must have $500 in the bank and making at least $50 a week,' she said. A lobby sitter heard her, winked at me, which embarrassed me, and caused me to remember the incident."[442]

Lowell's embarrassment must have been only temporary because he soon asked Frances for her hand in marriage. She accepted, and they were married on May 11, 1921, at the *Kappa Kappa Gamma* sorority house, with Lowell's father, Rev. Leake, officiating. The couple then traveled to Akron, Ohio, to set up their first home.

1921—The Final Exits from Columbia

The prior year (1920), Jamie, the "baby" in the Ross family, graduated from Columbia High School. Particularly studious and academic, she followed the familiar pattern and enrolled as a college freshman at the University of Missouri. However, Jamie's situation was to take a dramatic turn.

Helen, since Jamie's birth, had been her guardian sister—Jamie was her "charge"—and a strong bond remained between them. Helen saw that Jamie was an exceptionally gifted student, and she felt Jamie would benefit from a different college experience. After her experience at Bryn Mawr, Helen believed that a woman received a much better education at one of the top all-women "Seven Sisters" colleges on the east coast. Through her work with the NRSA and the success of Camp Kechuwa, Helen's financial situation was solid. Helen agreed to provide the financial support, and Jamie applied to and was accepted at Vassar College in Poughkeepsie, New York. A few months after Frances' wedding, Jamie traveled east to New York to begin studying with the serious, like-minded young women at Vassar College.

In the autumn of 1921, Ella was alone in Columbia. Her children were now spread out across the country. Most of Mama's friends and family lived 100 miles away in Independence. These people frequently asked, "Ella, where are you going to live once your children have all graduated from college?" Never without a plan—and confident of the love of her children—she always responded, "I'm going to live with my daughters, rotating among them." That is what she did for the rest of her life, and all her daughters happily agreed to it. Mama never became a burden to her children; they all welcomed her helpful visits, and she proved to be an ideal houseguest. Mama, too, would be leaving Missouri, the state of her birth, her education, and her family's values—and with no plan to return.

Ella in her later years when she no longer had a permanent home and rotated her time between her daughters. Circa 1922. (Photo/Ross family collection)

16

CHARLIE AT THE *POST-DISPATCH*

His Life's Work

Charlie once modestly told his son, John: "I attribute much of my success to good luck."

True, many things had gone his way—but it wasn't all by luck. Charlie had worked hard in his studies and had mastered the rudiments of journalism, which hadn't always been a painless process. Over time and with effort, he discovered he enjoyed investigating events, discovering the pertinent facts, and writing them down in a logical, terse, and understandable way so they could be understood by others. This is what a news reporter did, and Charlie, who always relied heavily on the facts, considered himself first and foremost a newspaper reporter.

However, as the years progressed, Charlie developed a talent for reflecting on what had been reported, to see those events with a broader scope, and to interpret them for readers so they, too, could see things more broadly. O. K. Bovard noted this in Charlie and helped bring it out, both to Charlie's benefit as well as to his readers'.

This trait was also noted years later by Harry S. Truman, when he said about Charlie, "He saw life steady and saw it whole." In Truman's view, Charlie "saw life steady" and knew how to dispassionately assess the individual facts and essential truths in a news story or event. However, unlike most reporters, Charlie also "saw it whole." He was able to see the big picture and view things beyond the hurly burly of the daily news.

The First Washington Correspondent for the *Post-Dispatch*

In his new job, Charlie learned how to get around his new city and how to navigate the halls of Congress, the White House, and the various departments and agencies of the federal government. He made useful contacts with fellow newspaper men: Roy A. Roberts, the well-connected newsman from the influential *Kansas City Star;* H. L. Mencken of the *Baltimore Sun* and the *American Mercury*; and Arthur Kroc of the *New York Times*. These, and other professional newsmen, had experience in Washington and became friends and sources to help Charlie find stories and open doors. Charlie also joined and eventually became active in several professional and social organizations, including the National Press Club and the Gridiron Club.

As Charlie's familiarity with Washington deepened, the *Post-Dispatch* began to allow him to broaden the scope of his coverage beyond just events related to Missouri. After a full year on the job, he was beginning to be looked on as a Washington "insider." So, in 1920, he was sent to San Francisco to cover a national story—the Democratic National Convention. Then, in 1921, he was told to cover the Washington Naval Conference held in Washington. This conference was an outgrowth of the Treaty of Versailles, ending World War I, and was attended by the major powers to try to de-commission many of the warships used in that war. The conference resulted in several treaties that reduced the number of warships and that remained in effect until the early 1930s. The conference also marked a milestone for Charlie, because his reports no longer contained the anonymous byline: "The Washington Correspondent for the *St. Louis Post-Dispatch*"; rather a new byline was used: "Charles G. Ross: The Chief Washington Correspondent of the *St. Louis Post-Dispatch*," reflecting his growing stature and his employer's confidence in his work.[443]

About this same time, the *Post-Dispatch* authorized Charlie to increase the staff at the Washington office. But this help didn't come all at once. The news never came in a steady flow, and, at times, Charlie was swamped. At first Charlie used a reporter named Nixon Plumber [of Pulitzer's] the *New York World* on a part-time basis[444] when the workload was heavy. Later he was allowed additional, permanent help. Overall, it was a challenging process to staff an office and maintain a steady flow of high-quality articles and pieces. Two of the more noteworthy hires were: Raymond P. "Pete" Brandt (1923), a Rhodes Scholar and one of Charlie's former students at the University of Missouri, and Marquis Childs (1926), a longtime, well-respected *Post-Dispatch* correspondent, who, later in his career, won a Pulitzer Prize. The office was desperate for administrative support, so Charlie recruited his tactful and talented sister-in-law, Estelle G. Welsh. She saw that the office ran smoothly and efficiently for many years to come.[445]

The Roaring Twenties

Following the carnage and futility of World War I, the major powers became united in their quest for a lasting peace—out of which emerged the idea of disarmament. This led to, among other things, the previously mentioned Washington Naval Conference. Both Charlie and the *Post-Dispatch* believed that their readers needed to know why disarmament was important for them. This led them to print a special supplement devoted entirely to the discussion of disarmament. It was on this piece that Charlie's name first appeared in a byline from Washington. Charlie's analysis of this broad topic was based largely on the costs involved. He highlighted the fact that, at that time, 90 percent of all federal tax dollars was going toward maintaining an Army and Navy and paying off the military debts left over from World War I. Charlie's approach to this potentially dry topic appealed broadly to the paper's readers and highlighted one of his trademark techniques: using "economic arguments on a question that is normally argued only in a social or political context." In this article, he showed that military armaments, whatever their other characteristics, remained an expensive proposition."[446]

The Unexpected Death of President Harding

Initially, Charlie thought well of President Warren G. Harding, who came to office in March of 1921. Harding, like Charlie, was a Midwesterner. He grew up in a small town in Ohio. He came across as personable, made himself accessible to the press, and maintained a dignified appearance—he looked like a U. S. President. Charlie covered the White House and believed the country was in capable hands with Mr. Harding.

In July 1923, a few months before the scandals of the Harding Administration came to light, Charlie boarded the train with Harding's presidential entourage on a trip west all the way to Alaska. On the return trip, there were reports that the President was feeling poorly. However, the five doctors who accompanied him dismissed the illness as a minor ailment, perhaps food poisoning. When the party arrived in San Francisco, Charlie, based on this information, filed a report that said the president's health issue was not serious. In San Francisco, Charlie stayed in the Palace Hotel, one floor below where Harding was staying. On August 2,

1923, shortly after Charlie had submitted his upbeat report on Harding's health, the President died unexpectedly, most likely from cardiac arrest.

Charlie rode the train back to Washington with the President's entourage, witnessing the people who lined the tracks along the way paying homage to their country's deceased president. Charlie wrote a reflective piece about the trip, which, in part, read:

> "A compound of motives one feels is behind this unprecedented outpouring of people. Curiosity plays a part; the spirit of conformity actuated some; others render homage merely to the highest office of the United States. The mass effect, whatever the motive or motives, is that of a nation mourning deeply and reverently. That is the effect, whether 10,000 stand together or one lad stands apart at salute, with tears running down his face, or a woman lifts a baby out of a carriage so that it, too, may see and someday relate that it saw the flower-banked casket of a President . . ."[447]

The day after President Harding died, the office of the presidency was transferred to the Vice-President, Calvin Coolidge, who became the 30th President of the United States.

President Calvin Coolidge

Everyone in Washington, particularly those who covered the White House, noticed the dramatic change from the outgoing, affable Warren G. Harding to the tight-lipped, reticent Calvin Coolidge. Even though President Coolidge (dubbed "Silent Cal" by many in the press corps) appeared at the twice-weekly press briefings, his answers were curt, and he was uncomfortable talking to the press.

Consistent with his personality, Coolidge was a fiscally conservative Republican under whom the government drifted in a more conservative direction. He disliked governmental regulation. As a result, the Federal Trade Commission and the Interstate Commerce Commission, two dominant regulatory agencies, remained largely passive during his years in office. He happily presided over generous tax cuts, which particularly favored wealthier citizens. He advocated reduced federal expenditures, and a substantial piece of the public debt was retired while he was in office.

During his time in office (August 1923 to March 1929), the country still felt the aftereffects of World War I. Coolidge's campaign touted such slogans as "A return to normal" and "Cool it with Coolidge," which were well accepted during the boom years of the Roaring Twenties. Charlie became more and more concerned that "the country was becoming mesmerized by its own prosperity." The *St. Louis Post-Dispatch* was a newspaper founded on the principle of rooting out injustices. In the Coolidge years, it began to unearth the scandals of Harding's presidency.

Scandals, Causes, and Investigations

The Washington office of the *Post-Dispatch* served as ground zero for the paper's reporting on these national scandals. The most notorious of the time, the Teapot Dome scandal, was investigated and brought to light by Paul Y. Anderson, a brilliant *Post-Dispatch* reporter who was assigned to Washington. He investigated and covered that scandal for six years, beginning in 1922.[448] The scandal involved a complex set of facts with many layers of shady dealing. But through Anderson's dogged determination, the story was unearthed and published, forcing the Senate to hold hearings. These led, ultimately, to the resignation of the Secretary of the

Interior, Albert B. Fall, who, among other things, was found guilty of taking bribes. This investigative journalism led to a Pulitzer Prize for Anderson in 1928.[449]

Other scandals with roots in the Harding administration came to light as well. Charles R. Forbes, director of the Veterans Bureau, was sent to prison for defrauding the government. Attorney General Harry M. Daugherty, who was President Harding's campaign manager, was twice subject to corruption investigations while in office and was forced to resign. These and other members of President Harding's team of insiders, known as the "Ohio Gang," while in office engaged in large-scale self-dealing for personal gain at the expense of the federal government. Most of this corruption came to light after the death of President Harding. Investigations revealed that he had been aware of some of the corruption but he simply decided to look the other way. He was evidently much more concerned with the political liability than in seeing justice served. To his credit, then Vice President Coolidge was never implicated in any of the scandals, and, during his administration, many of these wrongdoers were ushered out of office.

Charlie took up two other famous causes during this period—the Sacco-Vanzetti case and exposing Benito Mussolini as an enemy of a free press. Nicola Sacco and Bartolomeo Vanzetti were alleged to have killed a guard in an armed robbery in Braintree, Massachusetts, in April 1920. The *St. Louis Post-Dispatch* was perhaps the most vocal newspaper outside Massachusetts to express serious doubts about the proffered evidence against the two Italian immigrants. The case ultimately gained international attention, owing to its many irregularities, including: recanted testimony of witnesses, conflicting ballistics evidence, and a prejudicial pretrial statement by the jury foreman. In addition, the crime occurred at a time ripe with anti-Italian and anti-immigrant sentiment, particularly in the Boston area. Despite public and international pressure, the two alleged anarchists were convicted, sentenced to death, and eventually executed on August 23, 1927. Many people worldwide were dismayed by what was probably a miscarriage of justice. Charlie's was a voice among them, although the objections ultimately turned out to be a lost cause. Commenting on the protests, Charlie wrote a somber piece that concluded: "The fight was lost, but it was lost in distinguished company."[450]

In 1926, Charlie, after much research, wrote a long piece for the *Post-Dispatch* magazine supplement about Benito Mussolini's muzzling of the Italian press. Due in part to his sabbatical while at the School of Journalism, Charlie paid close attention to what was happening in journalism throughout the world. When he learned that a distinguished editor, Luigi Albertini, and his newspaper, the *Corriere della Sera* in Milan, Italy, had been subjected to the heel of Mussolini's fascist boot, Charlie couldn't keep silent and exposed the situation in a lengthy piece. His graphic description began:

> WASHINGTON—Suppose that the President of the United States, setting himself up as a dictator, should enter upon a campaign to gag or abolish every newspaper that dared express the slightest opposition to his politics.
>
> Suppose by ruthless suppression in some cases and by the purpose of stock control of his supporters in other cases, he should carry out his design until only the *Post-Dispatch* remained.
>
> Suppose that the newspaper, the sole-surviving guardian and exponent of free speech in the United States, should be subjected to frequent suppressions of its editions, to the heaping [of] insults and threats on its controlling editors

by the official organs of the President, to the throwing of bombs at its publications offices . . .

Suppose that finally, after a gallant fight, the editor should be forced out through a legalistic trick and the management and ownership of the paper be changed as to make it, like all the rest of the nation's press, completely subservient to the President's dictatorship . . .

Suppose that these unbelievable things, leaving the United States without a single newspaper to report and interpret opposition and sentiment to the country and the rest of the world, should happen—and you have a perfect imaginary parallel to a real condition in the Italy of Mussolini today . . .[451]

Two years after this article ran in the *Post-Dispatch*, Twentieth Century Fox was in Italy to film a motion picture, when its publicity agent, John Connolly, paid his respects to Mussolini. The dictator expressed a strong interest in getting membership in the National Press Club in Washington, DC. Many foreign dignitaries found that this club was an excellent forum for giving their views privately in a relaxed environment. Mr. Connolly, a member, agreed to present the club with the application for Mussolini with assurances that acceptance would be a mere formality. When the usually mild-mannered Charlie learned of this request, he became furious. He forced a special meeting of the Board of Governors and served as the spokesman for the opposition, many of whom attended the meeting with him; he said:

"You could have searched the whole world over without finding a man so totally undesirable for membership as this arch-enemy of free speech and free press . . . Mussolini is today the chief living foe of those principles which the American press pretends to cherish . . .

"By its title, the National Press Club appears to foreigners to have a national character, and is accepted in some degree as a spokesman for the American Press . . .

"We owe it to those who are attempting to maintain a free press in Europe to give no comfort or appearance to the man who has done more than all others to destroy the freedom of the European press."

After he said his piece, Charlie sat down. Soon the Board of Governors, which a witness described as appearing "thoroughly chastened," then voted and rejected Mussolini's application. And it never came up again, ever.[452]

Herbert Hoover

Calvin Coolidge in 1928 announced he would not seek another term as President, opening the door for Herbert Hoover to get the Republican nomination. Hoover was the experienced Secretary of Commerce who had served under both Harding and Coolidge and was untainted by the Harding scandals. He had an impressive resumé as an engineer and successful businessman. Coolidge, however, never endorsed Hoover, about whom he had reportedly said: "For six years that man gave me unsolicited advice—all of it bad."

Hoover won the nomination at the 1928 Republican Convention on the first ballot; his campaign platform was simply to continue the peace and prosperity then in place. Coming from an impressive, experienced, and untainted Republican, that innocuous theme carried the day—and Hoover won the 1928 election in a landslide.

This optimism, which propelled Hoover into the White House, lasted a little more than six months.

The Great Depression

The economic buoyancy of the Roaring Twenties continued until the latter months of 1929, when the chilly winds of an economic downdraft began to blow. Most historians agree that the first event of what would become the Great Depression began in late October of 1929, when the main stock market index, the Dow-Jones Average, fell dramatically over two days. On October 28th ("Black Monday"), it fell 12.82%; then, on the 29th ("Black Tuesday"), it fell another 11.73%—losing 23% of its value in those days alone. (The slide continued, although not as dramatically, over the next three years, as the Dow lost a total of 89% of its value.)

The nervousness felt by the investor community soon leeched beyond Wall Street when ordinary people began purchasing fewer goods and services. This led to factories, mines, and utilities producing less, and to the layoff of employees. This, in turn, led to people earning less money overall, which led to people purchasing even fewer goods and services. This downward economic spiral continued for years.

Statistics in the United States from 1929 to 1933 paint a stark picture—production at the nation's mines, factories, and utilities fell by more than one half; unemployment rose from 1.6 million Americans (1929) to 12.8 million (1933); and people's disposable income fell by 28%. At the Great Depression's height, 25% of all American workers were out of a job.[453]

At least equally important were the images the times produced. There were breadlines in many cities, ubiquitous soup kitchens feeding hungry people, the rise of a substantial hobo community (men with few possessions, traveling lightly while looking for work), financially broken men committing suicide. There were many bank failures where people lost their life's savings. Economic uncertainty and fear abounded, with no plan to stop the pain.

President Hoover first tried jawboning the railroads and utilities to increase spending on construction and maintenance. Then the Federal Reserve lowered interest rates to try to induce more investment. Congress produced legislation raising tariff rates and import duties on domestic products to protect American producers. But nothing worked. The downward spiral continued. The Great Depression preyed on most households, yet no one in authority, particularly President Hoover, could find the solution.

Charlie Investigates

Charlie had been reporting for more than a year on the various effects of the Great Depression—high unemployment, depressed sales and incomes, the stock-market contraction—in many one-off attempts to explain various aspects of it. Then, early in October of 1931, O. K. Bovard summoned Charlie to St. Louis for a meeting. Bovard was convinced that someone needed to synthesize all reporting to determine the causes and possible solutions to the pervasive economic malady. "He urged Charlie to start work on it immediately, with a view toward producing a far-reaching essay describing the type of leadership the nation needed to get back on its feet." Bovard wanted it ready for the beginning of the first session of the 72nd Congress, which was to begin on December 1, 1931.[454]

Charlie began working on the project. These types of articles were beginning to be called his "think pieces," and he was becoming well known for them. It took weeks of collecting information, reading, analyzing, and writing. Like the newspaper man he was,

Charlie met Bovard's deadline. The piece, entitled "Our Country's Plight—What can be done about it?" became the feature article in Sunday's *St. Louis Post-Dispatch* published on November 29, 1931. It filled 24 columns and ran about 18,000 words. It would change Charlie's career forever.

When he wrote it, Charlie was keenly aware of the timing and urgency of the piece. The essay is a systematic presentation of the many effects, problems, arguments (pro and con), and causes of the Depression. His points were supported by direct quotes from many highly regarded leaders, including Senator James Couzens of Michigan (who helped found the Ford Motor Company), Dean Wallace B. Donham of the Harvard Graduate School of Business, and Robert S. Brookings, a wealthy, retired manufacturer then serving as the President of Washington University in St. Louis. Charlie's analysis also relied heavily on statistical data provided by the U. S. government and other reliable sources. Given the topic's complexity, Charlie divided the article into eleven sections, so that it could be easily followed and digested by readers. The final section presents the article's well-thought-out and logical conclusion for how the country could find a path out of the Great Depression.

Our Country's Plight—A Summary

Due to the historical importance of this piece—as well as the insight it provides into Charlie's analysis and writing—the final section is summarized below, using many of his own words. The sections and headings below are identical to those presented in the original piece.

1. Hard times have produced hard thinking—The capitalistic system of government is on trial.

The economic downturn was more than a typical recession, which appeared every so often. It was atypical because of the magnitude of its dysfunction (e.g., extremely high unemployment and severe economic contraction) as well as the widespread suffering (e.g., breadlines and lower incomes) it caused, with no end in sight. The section boldly concluded "the capitalistic system is on trial," requiring "hard thinking"—the serious probing of one's beliefs.

II. We must know the facts if we are to deal intelligently with the depression.

Charlie warned against the "babel of tongues offering remedies," and urged: "We need to distinguish between the sham remedy, designed to meet the political expediency of the moment, and the remedy that strikes at the root of the disease." Thus, facts and logic were paramount. "That is, if we are to get anywhere at all toward the solution of our problems, we must know the root facts out of which they spring."

III. The distinction between the Government's depression and the general depression—Why the Government is in debt.

Charlie was careful to separate the notions of the federal government's depression from the general depression felt by the American people. The "Government's depression" stemmed from "its excess of outgo [expenses] over income" ("a deficit during the last fiscal year of $903,000,000"), plus the high level of its accumulated national debt. Charlie concluded: "The Government is head over heels in debt." In contrast, he defined the "general depression" as what the country's people were then experiencing: high unemployment, reduced incomes, bankruptcies, and the absence of hope for the near future. Charlie was careful to outline that these were different beasts and needed to be considered separately.

IV. The Economy in Government is a good thing, but it can't cure the deficit.

Charlie asked: "What can the Government do in order to balance the budget?" Using federal-government statistics, he showed that, at that time, 70 cents of every dollar collected went to national defense—either to pay the debt for "past wars" or maintain military readiness (for "future wars"). This left only 30% of every dollar to pay for the general administration of the government, e.g., the "promotion and regulation of commerce, industry, and agriculture" and "flood control and improvement of rivers and harbors, and the promotion of public health, public education, and scientific research." He concluded that "there can only be cheeseparing economies" to be gained by cutting the funds for the general administration of government.

V. Should the Government in this emergency depend on borrowing or on new taxation—How should the burden of new taxation be distributed?

This served as the pivotal section of Charlie's analysis with numerous subsections. It began with the proposition that any additional money must be found by taxation or borrowing to balance the federal government's budget. Charlie noted that some people advocated increasing taxes, particularly on the wealthy, while others wanted the treasury to borrow short-term until the recession ended.

This led to the question stated in the heading to the next subsection: **Who Is Going to Pay?** Charlie cited John Dewey in his book *Individualism, Old and New*, for the proposition "that all great political questions in Washington come back ultimately to problems connected with the distribution of income."

The following subsection, **Wealth's Distribution**, stated: "We reach the proposition that the Government, through its taxing power, cannot only cure its depression (that is to say, close its gap between receipts and expenses), but the radical use of that tremendous power can profoundly affect the whole economic and social structure of the country. It can help bring about a redistribution of wealth."

Using Treasury Department reports, the section continued to examine how wealth in the United States was being distributed. "Persons with incomes of $100,000 each, forming a little more than one-third of 1 percent [1/3 of 1%] of all those reporting, had more than 17 percent of all income."

The next subsection addressed its titled subject: **What the Poor Own**. To indicate how much—and how little—of the nation's wealth (as opposed to income) was in the hands of the less affluent, Charlie cited findings from the Industrial Relations Commission, which "estimated that the rich (2 percent) own 60 percent of the accumulated wealth of the nation, the middle class (33 percent) own 35 percent of the wealth, and the poor (65 percent) own 5 percent of the wealth."

To further stress the point, the next subsection, **Incomes of the Super-Rich**, examined the incomes and expenditures of those dubbed the "Super-Rich." It began: "The 504 super-millionaires at the top of the heap in 1929 had an aggregate net income, for taxation purposes, of $1,185,000,000. These 504 persons could have purchased with this income virtually the entire wheat and cotton crops of 1930—the two chief cash crops of the nation, representing the labor of 1,300,000 wheat farmers and 1,032,000 cotton farmers." After providing additional supporting statistics, this subsection concluded:

> "The point need not be labored. There is growing concentration of American wealth in the hands of few; there is steady accentuation of 'the widest spread between the extremes of wealth and poverty existing in the Western world.' More and more, thoughtful observers who by no stretch of the imagination can be described as revolutionary or radical are calling our attention to this condition and its dangers."

Charlie used the next subsection, called **Sources to Be Taxed**, to subtly target members of Congress. He noted "the various tax proposals coming before Congress may be grouped under two heads. On the one side are those who would 'broaden' the tax base by taxing more people, as with a new federal sales tax. On the other side are those who would use the taxing power for the double purpose of raising revenue and breaking up, to some degree, the vast accumulations of wealth revealed in income-tax statistics." The article then examined the types of taxation:

Income tax is "called by economists one of the fairest taxes ever devised, is large or small [for a taxpayer] according to capacity to pay." The article noted that following the lowering of the income-tax rates on the very rich after World War I, the average tax paid to the federal government by the wealthy group dropped from $1,326,645 (with an average tax rate of 64.65%) to $362,309 (with an average tax rate of 16.7%). The article pointed out that the British, by comparison, paid almost triple the income-tax rate as Americans, which brought in an additional $900,000,000 annually.

As for a *federal sales tax*, not then in existence, Charlie noted that it "bears inequitably upon persons of small means" and basically "is an income tax in reverse." Also, the article dismissed its possible enactment because it was "advocated at this time, manifestly, in an effort to avert higher levies on the rich."

As for the *estate tax* (also referred to as the "death tax"), the article noted that, in 1926, the estate-tax rates were reduced from 40% to a sliding scale ranging between 1% and 20%, which produced a corresponding reduction in revenue. (Also in 1926, the gift tax was eliminated altogether.) The two arguments from the Coolidge administration stated by Treasury Secretary Mellon for these substantial tax reductions were 1) "the social necessity for breaking up of large fortunes in this country does not exist," and 2) "in a few generations, any single large fortune is split into many moderate inheritances."

These two rationales were debunked in Charlie's article. The first of Mellon's assertions Charlie countered by quoting President Theodore Roosevelt: "In a message to Congress in 1906, Roosevelt advocated heavy death duties, with a primary object of putting 'a constantly increasing burden on the inheritance of those swollen fortunes which it is certainly of no benefit to this country to perpetuate.'" Charlie continued his argument by quoting Andrew Carnegie, who said of estate taxes: "Of all forms of taxation, this seems the wisest." Charlie countered the second assertion by tracing the inheritances flowing from the estates of John D. Rockefeller, Meyer Guggenheim, and Alexis du Pont, which revealed that all these fortunes increased rather than decreased for the successor generations.

As for the *gift tax*—repealed in 1926 also at the urging of Treasury Secretary Mellon—the article simply quoted Senator Couzens: "There is no logic in an estate tax when a man, through gifts in his lifetime, can evade the tax. The gift tax would enable us to collect on transfers of property whether they are made before or after the giver's death."

VI. Our general depression is homemade, and it is due fundamentally to the maldistribution of wealth.

Quoting various authorities and citing statistical evidence, the article explained there were warnings during the economically buoyant Roaring Twenties that the good times wouldn't last. But no one listened, "until the buying of shoes and groceries began to fall off and men were seen walking the streets in search of work." The article quoted Senator Couzens, who emphatically said, "Long before the crash our production had been outrunning our consumption. The workers were producing more than they could buy with the wages they received. Our predicament is primarily due to the inequitable distribution of the earnings of industry between capital and labor. I have not seen a single denial of that statement—even by the bankers who are urging wage reduction." Then the article refuted the notion that the root of the depression was due to foreign countries not purchasing American goods by showing that the "the shrinkage of foreign trade . . . amounts to only 2 or 3 percent of our total productivity." In other words, the domestic market for American-made goods produced far exceeded the foreign markets for those goods. While the economic downturn in the rest of the world may have exacerbated the Great Depression in the United States, it wasn't the cause.

VII. How the machine has accelerated the growth of this economic disease.

Using the term "machine" to mean the mechanized processes of production, the article identified those reasons the Depression occurred when it did. Although the Depression's root cause—the imbalance between profits from capital and the wages to labor—had been evolving, the current situation was exacerbated by "frantic advertising," which implored consumers to buy more, together with sellers of products overextending credit to buyers—a system which ultimately collapsed from overuse.

At this point, the article asked: "What is the remedy?" It then provided the following response:

"In the opinion of many thoughtful observers, there is only one possible answer: human greed must cure itself, or be curbed. There must be shorter work hours . . . and this change must be effected not at the expense of wages, but . . . at the expense of profits. It is not merely the wage scale that must be kept up, but the amount of wages that a worker receives over the course of a year. This . . . fundamentally, is a broader distribution of the profits of industry."

As additional support, the article stated: "Between 1919 and 1929 . . . the productivity of industry in the United States increased 50 percent, while real wages paid to workers increased only 27.5 percent."

VIII. The wages of capital and the wages of labor—The balance between consumption and production can only be restored at the expense of dividends.

This section differentiates between the *wages of capital* and the *wages of labor*: capital's wages (or costs) have a longer-lasting, ripple effect for the owner of the "machines" (e.g., by reinvesting in more and better equipment), while the laborer's wages are mostly gone soon after the work is completed (e.g., the paycheck is consumed for living expenses).

The piece then asserted "that a balance must be maintained between production and consumption"—which did not exist—and that balance should be maintained at the level of production. This section concluded that "this [rebalancing], as we have shown, can only be done at the expense of dividends [from the owners of the capital]."

IX. The issue is drawn between labor and capital— Solution of the problem rests primarily with industry and not with the Government.

In looking for potential solutions, this section posed the question: "Can the Government under the Constitution compel private industry, through the five-day work week, to reduce the share of benefits of the machine?" It assumed that the Constitution did not allow this because the right to set wages is primarily a private right, outside of the authority of the federal government to interfere. Thus, it concluded, the "problem of restoring the balance between production and purchasing power is primarily a problem of industry itself."

Next, it asked the questions: "Will industry act to save itself? Will it curb the thirst for more profits that in the final analysis is the cause of our depression?" In response, it (again) quoted Senator Couzens: "The business leaders of the country . . . have the ability to solve the problems of the depression. The problem is they have not been hurt. True, their profits have fallen off, but they are living just as comfortably as they were."

Charlie went on to say: "The control of the situation is in remarkably few hands . . . [where] . . . 200 corporations with fewer than

2,000 directors control 35 to 45 percent of the business wealth of the United States."

> X. But there are certain important things the Government can do—A possible program, covering taxation, the tariff (with a note on the plight of the farmer), the public utilities, the five-day week for Federal employees, prohibition, our part in world affairs.

After laying the framework for understanding the underpinnings of the Great Depression, the analysis next listed six concrete actions the federal government (including Congress) could do to alleviate the situation.

"First . . . the Government could help to check the drift of wealth into a few hands and at the same time obtain needed revenue for itself, by imposing heavy surtaxes on great fortunes, increasing death duties and reinstalling the gift tax."

"Second, it could reduce the tariff to schedules sufficient only to protect American business and American jobs from immediate destructive competition." The article further noted: "Reduction in the tariff would be reflected in lower prices to the consumer."

Third, the article advocated the government acquiring "the privately owned public utilities." Quoting Samuel Untermyer, a prominent attorney, the article notes that state commissions were inadequate to properly regulate private utilities. "If these utilities were publicly owned, the advocates of that policy argue, huge sums in profits would be diverted from the few hands into which they have been made to flow through the device of the holding companies. Profits could be distributed to the public through reduction in rates, or decreased taxes."

"Fourth, the Government could make itself a model employer by establishing the five-day week for Federal employees without a change in pay." The proposal concluded this would be "a great weapon of persuasion" and would be "a progressive influence in private industry."

"Fifth, the Government could repeal prohibition." Such action would "increase the revenue to the Government, decrease the expenses and aid general business . . ." Further, it was humorously noted: "In a business way, the principal if not sole sufferer from repeal would be the bootleg traffic."

"Sixth, the Government could promote international stability, and thereby contribute to the improvement of general conditions at home, by joining the League of Nations." Many reasons are cited for the economic advantages of joining. The high cost of maintaining the military, which is the cost of fighting "future wars," could be reduced by becoming a member and relying more on diplomacy. The United States would also be in a better position to trade off those war debts owed to it—many of which most likely would never be repaid—for a reduction in armaments by other nations. Stated otherwise: "Anything we might buy with the debts in the way of world peace and prosperity would be clear gain. Unquestionably the debts have a trading value."

The following and final section of the article is stated in its entirety.

> XI. Conclusion: Conceivably we can usher in a new prosperity through a readjustment of the distribution of the benefits of the machine—Amendment of "men's economic and social ideals" in the great need.

"Restoration of world prosperity would help us, but there would remain the great underlying problem that this article has sought to outline: the problem of how to bring about the readjustment made necessary by the concentration of too great wealth, with the aid of the machine, in comparatively few hands. Is the machine to be the servant or the master of the people? This is a question that each nation must answer for itself.

"Through a shorter work week without reduced pay, conceivably we in the United States could diffuse the benefits of the machine among the people that 'purchasing power' would be brought back to the production level of the nation set on the way to a new prosperity—a healthier prosperity than that of the vaunted Coolidge era. This, as we have shown, can only be done through the voluntary or enforced renunciation of excessive profits. The alternative is public or private relief, or both, for the workers displaced by the machine.

"Justice Brandeis once said: 'Instead of amending the Constitution, I would amend men's economic and social ideals.' And that, whatever else we may do or try to do, clearly must be accomplished if we are to solve the problem of the great depression."

The Reaction to "Our Country's Plight"

The effect of "Our Country's Plight" was dramatic. The *Post-Dispatch* was overwhelmed by a deluge of requests for copies, so much so that it reissued the piece in pamphlet form and mailed out thousands. "*Editor & Publisher*, the newspaper trade journal, called it 'the most thorough, scholarly, and candid roundup of the national depression, that has ever been our fortune to read in any newspaper, magazine or book.'"[455]

Intellectually, it was an important piece, in large part, because it identified the root cause of the Depression—the fundamental imbalance in wealth among the country's citizens caused by unrestrained (*laissez-faire*) capitalism. In addition, it pointed out that the government could (and should) selectively intervene to correct the imbalance, which, in turn, would lead to increased and healthier economic activity overall. It then listed six concrete ways that the government's involvement would help to turn around the economic slowdown.

Clearly, a piece as widely celebrated as "Our Country's Plight" had some influence on elected officials at the time. How much this was, we'll never know. However, it is noteworthy to see some of the actions that followed on the heels of its publication.

Taxation: Over the next ten years, the tax rates were raised, most pointedly on the more affluent citizens and on corporations. Starting with the Revenue Act of 1932, which was signed by President Hoover, a series of laws were enacted that increased taxes on upper-income individuals and on corporations. In addition, estate-tax rates were increased, and the gift tax was restored.

Tariffs: In 1934, President Roosevelt signed the Reciprocal Trade Agreements Act, reducing tariff levels and promoting trade liberalization and cooperation with foreign governments.

Public Utilities: In 1933, the Tennessee Valley Authority was created by legislation; it was—and remains today—a public utility owned by the federal government that provides electricity at reasonable rates to the citizens of seven states in the southeastern United States.

Five-day work week: The idea of the five-day (and 40-hour) work week slowly evolved during the early twentieth century. It began on the federal level in 1916, when Congress passed the Adamson Act, which applied only to the railroads. Then, in 1926, Henry Ford made it the standard at the Ford Motor Company. Finally, in 1938, the Fair Labor Standards Act came into effect; it was amended and finalized in 1940, by which time the five-day work week had become the national standard.

Repeal Prohibition: In December 1933, the Twenty-First Amendment repealed prohibition. It was generally considered a failed experiment whose burdens of enforcement outweighed its benefits.

The League of Nations: The United States never joined the League of Nations on account of the strong isolationist sentiment in Congress. However, its successor organization, the United Nations, was founded shortly after the end of World War II in 1945; the United States was one of its founding partners.

These remarkable changes, in part, reflect the platform of the Roosevelt Administration and the Democrats who were elected to office beginning in 1932. Although it would be over-reaching to say that the Democratic policies originated from Charlie's article, it's highly likely "Our Country's Plight" was one of the major influencers on the party's platform.

The Accolades and Professional Recognition

In 1932, the year following the publication of "Our Country's Plight," Charlie received a Pulitzer Prize for Journalism. The award, given by the Pulitzer Prize Board through Columbia University, recognized this article for its "discussion of the economic situation in the United States." Other accolades followed. In 1933 he was awarded the Missouri Honor Medal by the School of Journalism at the University of Missouri. In that same year, Charlie was elected President of the Gridiron Club, a by-invitation-only social organization made up of newspapermen in Washington, DC. It was then, and remains today, famous for its annual dinner where the members of the press and politicians get together socially for one evening and poke fun at one another. In 1935, Charlie received an Honorary Doctor of Laws Degree from George Washington University in Washington, DC.[456]

Suddenly, Illnesses in the Family

In 1932, Charlie, at age 47, had arrived at a good place. He enjoyed his work and his professional associations (e.g., the Gridiron Club and the Washington press corps). The Washington office of the *Post-Dispatch*, which he headed, had earned a solid reputation. Unlike many who suffered during the Depression, Charlie was well compensated and lived comfortably in Chevy Chase. His older son, John, was completing his freshman year at Dartmouth College, and the younger son, Walter, was graduating from Western High School in Washington. Florence continued her commitment to supporting Charlie's professional life and making the family's home a comfortable place. She was also noted for her meticulous flower beds. Unlike her agnostic husband, she was a devout parishioner at the Shrine of the Blessed Sacrament (known locally simply as "Blessed Sacrament"), the Catholic Church on nearby Chevy Chase Circle. It was all going very well for the Ross family—until the Ross boys were both struck with serious illnesses.

After Christmas vacation in 1932, John (then 18) returned to Dartmouth College to begin the second semester of his sophomore year. He returned to college after the Christmas vacation with some other Dartmouth students from Washington in a convertible sedan. (John later admitted: "I have never been so cold in my life.") After arriving at school in the bitter January cold, John began feeling poorly and eventually became seriously ill. Too sick to attend classes, he was diagnosed with hepatitis. The remedy prescribed by his doctors in Washington was absolute rest and "to eat well" in some healthful climate until he fully recovered. So, John and his mother traveled to Florida, where she personally took care of him during the winter of 1933 until he regained his health. Charlie remained at work in his Washington office.

Because he was only 16 years old when he graduated high school, Charlie and Florence were worried that Walter (who'd also been accepted to Dartmouth College) was too young to attend college immediately. At that time, Helen was living and studying in Vienna, Austria, and it was decided Walter would benefit from a year abroad. He could begin taking college courses at the University of Vienna, with his Aunt Helen close by. As it turned out, soon after Walter arrived, Hitler closed the University. So, Walter moved on to Switzerland and took courses at the University of Geneva. He also traveled around Europe, particularly France, in his spare time. Toward the end of one trip, he went to England, where he visited with Guy Innes, an old family friend from Australia. One evening Walter failed to show for a dinner as planned, so Guy went to Walter's hotel room to check on him. He found Walter collapsed on the bed with a ruptured appendix. He was rushed to the hospital, where complications developed. Charlie was notified and immediately set sail for England. Fortunately, with his father close by, Walter recovered in several weeks, and they were able to return together to the United States.

Both Charlie and Florence were devoted to their two sons and relieved that they were back on their feet. At the end of the summer, the family took its usual summer vacation to Rehoboth Beach, Delaware, where they all celebrated their return to good health.[457] After his recovery from hepatitis, John decided to remain in Washington, DC, and enrolled at Georgetown University. Walter, who had made a full recovery, went as planned to Dartmouth College for his freshman year.

Charlie Gets a Call from Mr. Pulitzer

At the beginning of 1934, Joseph Pulitzer, Jr., who inherited the *Post-Dispatch* from his father, believed the newspaper was leaning too far to the left. Pulitzer heard this drumbeat of criticism from his conservative businessmen friends, both in St. Louis and around the country. The current head of the editorial page was the brilliant Clark McAdams, who aggressively supported Roosevelt over Hoover in the 1932 election. O. K. Bovard also initially supported the policies of Roosevelt. However, as he became disillusioned with Roosevelt, friction developed between McAdams and Bovard. Pulitzer grew increasingly uneasy about the editorial management

A portrait of Charlie Ross from his time at the *Post-Dispatch*. Probably St. Louis, circa 1933. (Photo/Harris & Ewing and the Harry S. Truman Library)

of the *Post-Dispatch*, and he wanted to make a change. Who better to right the ship than the fair-minded and highly regarded Charlie Ross? Thus, early in 1934, Charlie was summoned to St. Louis, where Pulitzer offered him the job as the lead editor of the editorial page. Charlie didn't want the job, but he was loyal to the *Post-Dispatch*, and with severe arm-twisting by Pulitzer—which included a healthy salary increase—he relented and took the job. It began in mid-July of 1934.[458]

1934–1939—The St. Louis Years

When he walked into his new office in St. Louis as the Editor of the editorial page, Charlie was faced with two immediate problems. The first came as something of a surprise: the sudden political rise, with the support of the local Pendergast political machine, of Harry Truman, his old schoolmate and companion from Independence. The second he had known about: making sure the editorial perspective of the newspaper was balanced.

After Charlie had gone off to college in 1901, he and Harry Truman had gone their separate ways: Charlie into journalism, with Harry largely remaining in the Independence-Kansas City area, working at various jobs. Although they were most likely aware of each other's accomplishments through mutual friends, they had not kept in touch after high school. After his service in World War I, Harry found his way into local politics and, with the support of Tom Pendergast, was elected a county "judge," basically a county administrative position. Harry distinguished himself by spearheading an ambitious and much-needed road-building program in Jackson County. As a result, he earned a reputation as an excellent administrator and public servant and was easily re-elected to the county position in 1930. Looking for a candidate to run for the U. S. Senate in 1934, Pendergast encouraged Harry Truman to run. Harry was a true long-shot candidate with only local experience. However, Harry agreed and soon began campaigning around the state.

When Charlie returned to St. Louis, he learned about Harry's candidacy and his support by the Pendergast machine. Charlie knew all about the evils of machine politics (particularly the Pendergast variety) and he was immediately alarmed. Pendergast was the chairman of the Jackson County Democratic Party. He used his network of Irish family and friends to elect (sometimes using fraud) friendly politicians and handed out sweetheart contracts and patronage jobs to cement his connections. He also had a reputation as a gambler, which would be his downfall later in life.

Even though he knew and respected Harry personally, Charlie was convinced that this long-shot candidate would be too beholden to Pendergast. Charlie's instinct was to launch an editorial campaign against Harry's candidacy. After discussions with Pulitzer and the editorial staff, Charlie was persuaded to hold fire until after the primary election. Harry won the primary election with a plurality of 44,000 votes. After that election, the *Post-Dispatch* penned editorials decrying the Truman candidacy as one of "an obscure man scarcely known outside of the confines of Jackson County" who had been elevated by "the power of machine politics." But the newspaper chose to endorse neither candidate that year, and Truman, as the Democratic candidate running in the Depression year of 1934, easily beat his Republican opponent.[459]

Most of Charlie's time was dedicated to the editorial page. Joseph Pulitzer wanted it to be even-handed, and both he and Charlie had become concerned about the aggressive—and possibly unconstitutional—directions of the New Deal. Charlie, at the same time, worked to maintain a balance in the *Post-Dispatch's* editorial content and kept the other editors, most of whom had become staunch advocates of President Roosevelt, working toward a liberal-conservative balance. As time progressed, Charlie and Pulitzer became so concerned about the New Deal under Roosevelt that they steered the *Post-Dispatch* to endorse Alfred "Alf" Landon for President in 1936. The basis for this endorsement is summarized in the first sentence of the editorial announcing the paper's position:

> In the simplest terms, the overshadowing issue in the coming national election is whether or not we shall set up in America, in defiance of the American tradition and in defiance of the plain intent of the Constitution as it now stands, a government with vast and centralized authority over the economic life of the nation.[460]

Although Roosevelt convincingly won the election, the Landon endorsement molified Pulitzer's business friends and kept the political voice of the *Post-Dispatch* on an even keel.[461]

Working directly for Joseph Pulitzer often put Charlie at odds with the paper's other editors. O. K. Bovard resigned after the 1936 election, believing his authority and influence at the *Post-Dispatch* had been undercut by Pulitzer. Charlie spent much of his time justifying some of the paper's content to Pulitzer, and making sure that a "fair share" of the paper's attention supported business interests, particularly those of its advertisers. He spent time individually with the other editors giving assignments, reviewing their work, and addressing their concerns. By nature, Charlie was a low-keyed, rational man who liked to let well-presented facts speak for themselves; he wasn't a natural combatant who ruled by the force of his personality. This job did not play to Charlie's strengths, and, overall, he did not enjoy it, in spite of the title and authority that went with it.[462]

Charlie served as the Editor of the editorial page for more than four years, so it came as a welcome relief, in the final days of 1938, when Pulitzer granted Charlie's long-standing request to return to Washington as a political reporter. By then the editorial differences at the *Post-Dispatch* had been settled, the New Deal had not turned out to be as dire as Pulitzer and his business peers had feared, the Depression was beginning to fade, and Pulitzer had found a suitable replacement. Wanting a change, Pulitzer elevated Ralph Coghlan, a more intense man with a scrappy personality, who was already serving on the *Post-Dispatch's* editorial staff.[463]

Although Charlie and Florence had adjusted to living in St. Louis, they were thrilled to be returning to Washington, which they now considered home. Charlie was made a "contributing editor" for the *Post-Dispatch* with no decrease in salary, and, even more importantly for Charlie, he was given the freedom to write whatever he wanted without being edited. (Their agreement provided that the *Post-Dispatch* could choose not to publish a piece, but it would not edit it.) Thus, in January 1939, Charlie and Florence returned to Washington to begin the next chapter of their lives together.

17

A LADY AND A SCHOLAR

The Not-So-Roaring '20s

Helen's reflections on her life during most of the 1920s make it doubtful she would have categorized the time as a "roaring" decade. In her memoirs, Helen described the next step she took after her position at the railroad was eliminated: "Following the dissolution of the Railroad Administration, I made a brief investigation of industrial nursing for the Committee on Public Health Nursing for the Rockefeller Foundation."[464]

This investigation of nursing practices for the Rockefeller Foundation, not coincidentally, involved Helen's working with Pauline Goldmark's sister, Josephine, who in 1919 had been named secretary of the Rockefeller Foundation's Committee for the Study of Nursing Education. The study was headed by Doctor A. Winslow of Yale University. Josephine Goldmark was the principal investigator for the committee, which examined more than 70 nursing schools. The resulting report, entitled "Nursing and Nursing Education in the United States"—and commonly referred to as the Winslow-Goldmark Report—eventually led to the upgrading of nursing education throughout the country, particularly through the establishment of university affiliations and national accreditation standards and procedures.⁴⁶⁵ Helen never explained the reasons she worked for only a short period on that study. Most likely, once the work was underway, she decided that the relatively passive activity (researching) about a subject (nursing) to which she'd had scant exposure held little interest for her. After a few months she resigned and made other plans for the year. But first, she and Sis made their annual trip north to the Upper Peninsula of Michigan, where they operated their "darling," Camp Kechuwa, for a seventh consecutive summer.

Helen always enjoyed travel, and this led to her to the next step in her career and life. In her words:

"In 1920–1921, I made the first of many trips to Europe and studied one term at the London School of Economics under Graham Wallis, William Beveridge, and Harold Laski. The next several winters were spent in travel and in study."⁴⁶⁶

At age 30 Helen decided to study in London. This, of course, was a bold move, but Helen had embarked on risky adventures before. Moving to London became the latest in her ongoing quest to find a professional calling. For Helen, the risk was well worth taking.

The London School of Economics (LSE) was founded in 1895 by members of the Fabian Society. Its original purpose was to advance the principles of democratic socialism. It offered a variety of courses grounded in the social sciences, including economics, statistics, commercial and industrial law, political science, and sociology.

Not surprisingly, the heartbeat of the suffrage activity in the United Kingdom between 1906 and 1914 resided at the LSE.⁴⁶⁷ Helen studied at the LSE for only one term, but soon realized that, despite its progressive curriculum, the coursework wouldn't lead to a career that interested her. Her year in England held some exciting times; she later related that she: "Flew across the [English] Channel, [and] have been flying ever since."[468] Even though her term at the LSE didn't result in a new career, it was an interesting experience, one upon which she immediately traded.

Despite her challenging work and schedule, Helen Ross always made time for two months at Camp Kechuwa each summer. Lake Michigamme, MI, circa 1935. (Photo/Ross family collection)

By the middle of 1921, Helen found something in Europe that did interest her—and gave her an opportunity to continue traveling—as she cryptically noted years later:

"For two years [1922–1924] conducted European Travel School for girls." While no record of this school has survived, it allowed her to travel in Europe, and built on her interest in enhancing the lives of young women.

For the next five years (1924–1929) the search for a career direction continued. She and Sis maintained their Chicago residence just outside the gates of the University. Each June, they faithfully took the train north to Michigamme, Michigan. Camp Kechuwa was not only a summer getaway, but it was now a consistently profitable enterprise. During this period, she and Sis remained comfortably situated in Chicago, where they made friends who had ties to the neighboring University. They attended many receptions and lectures on campus. The friends and contacts they garnered during this period would become important in the years to come. Helen, thru her recruiting for Camp Kechuwa, had become very familiar with the private girls' schools in the Chicago area. From time-to-time she did substitute-teaching and counseling at these schools. Sis, who'd earned her undergraduate degree from the University of Chicago in March 1923, found work in food preparation in the Chicago area as well.

Good Luck with Good Timing

In 1929, weeks before the infamous stock-market crash, 39-year-old Helen attended a reception at the University of Chicago for Dr. Franz Alexander, a noted Hungarian-born physician and a graduate of the Berlin Psychoanalytic Institute. The University had recruited him to serve as its first professor of psychoanalysis, and the gathering was designed to encourage him to join the faculty of the University. Helen attended because of her contacts at the University and her European travel experience. At the reception, Helen and Dr. Alexander talked, and she told him she might be interested in learning more about psychoanalysis. According to Helen:

> "[Dr. Alexander] listened to my interests, and then, he said quite simply, 'Why don't you go to Vienna. Anna Freud is there and Helene Deutsch. This suggestion seemed sophisticated, almost absurd, to a novice with slim means. I have always felt grateful to Alexander for making such a fanciful undertaking seem a normal thing to do."[469]

Dr. Alexander's surprise suggestion came at a time when Helen was searching for a direction. It also addressed a fundamental question that had vexed Helen for a long time, one upon which she and Sis, in operating Camp Kechuwa, often disagreed. Helen explained the disagreement:

> "Sis, like Mammy, believed that 'explaining things' was all that was necessary to insure correct, logical conduct. If people know what is right, they will do it, she held firmly in her long association with children . . . [She] would often say to me in camp, 'Well, haven't you explained to Mary why she must not disturb others at night?' She thought all children would drink milk if she demonstrated its importance, and so, despite her repugnance, she set up cages of white mice, with and without milk in the diet; she put charts on the wall showing big puppies and little puppies, with 'Milk

made the Difference,' as a slogan. And the occasional child who did not succumb to her rational approach baffled her. 'Nonsense,' she would say, as I suggested the possibility of another kind of cause for refusing milk.

'I just don't understand why,' we just often said to each other in those early days of camp, and it was just this discovery that not everyone behaves in the way we were taught was rational and proper that led me to become interested in psychoanalysis."[470]

Helen soon answered Dr. Alexander's question—in the affirmative. In the late summer of 1929, after the last camper had left Camp Kechuwa, Helen returned to Chicago and then traveled to Vienna, Austria, where she enrolled as a student under the tutelage of Anna Freud and Helene Deutsche in the rigorous program at the *Psycho-Analytisches Institut* (known also as the Vienna Psychoanalytic Institute). Later in life, she summarized her intensive, five-year program in Vienna as follows:

"During this time, I was psychoanalyzed by Helene Deutsche; carried on therapeutic work, largely with children, under Anna Freud and August Aichhorn; and helped to translate Aichhorn's book *Wayward Youth*, published by Viking Press."[471]

Studying Psychoanalysis in Vienna

Helen's terse synopsis of her experiences belies the true character of the five busy and rich years she spent studying and learning in Vienna. Founded in 1922, the institution was created to serve as a psychoanalytic dispensary (the "Ambulatorium") for the local population of emotionally disturbed (or "troubled") youths in an outpatient setting. It was associated with the city's large general hospital (the AHK Hospital), where Sigmund Freud had begun his medical practice years before and where many of his students practiced medicine. The creation of the Ambulatorium was the realization of Freud's desire to make psychoanalysis accessible to people of modest means. The Ambulatorium, while keeping its clinical functions, soon evolved into the clinical and educational institution known as the Vienna Psychoanalytic Institute. By the time Helen arrived in 1929, it was training both domestic and international students in the theory and practice of psychoanalysis.[472]

In 1923 Anna Freud, the youngest of Sigmund's daughters and his intellectual protégé, assumed responsibility for the Ambulatorium after her father was diagnosed with cancer. The following year, Anna Freud recruited Helene Deutsch, one of the world's first female psychoanalysts, to take over as head of the clinic and training institute.

Helene Deutsch, born of Jewish parents in Poland in 1884, had come to Austria when she enrolled at the University of Vienna in 1907. She studied medicine there and became interested in psychiatry. When World War I broke out, Austria's military enlisted many of that country's (male) physicians, so Helene Deutsch, by then a qualified physician herself, was placed in charge of a neurological and psychiatric clinic in Austria. After the war ended in 1919, she underwent a personal psychoanalysis from Sigmund Freud in Vienna, which lasted for about one year. In 1923 she, then a disciple of Freud, became the first psychoanalyst to write a book about female psychology, called "Psychoanalysis of the Sexual Functions of Women." Highly sought after as a trainer and practical psychoanalyst, her seminars became remarkable and memorable experiences, and she trained many future psychiatrists and therapists. Two-thirds of her students were Americans, one of whom was Helen Ross.[473]

As part of her training, Helen underwent psychoanalysis by Helene Deutsch. About 40 years after her psychoanalysis, Helen made a telling reference to the analysis in a letter to a colleague, Dr. George Engel. In the letter, she expressed some of her thoughts about having a twin sister, and confided: "Helene Deutsche once remarked that I talked more of my [other] sisters and brother in my analysis than about my twin [Louise], and added, 'But when we reached the depths of your unconsciousness, Louise is there.'"[474]

Helen's study at the Vienna Psychoanalytic Institute included hands-on training with individual patients, both children and adolescents, as well as a wide variety of lectures. A small sample of the lectures offered included: "Analyzing Children" from Anna Freud, "Introduction to Psychoanalysis" from Eduard Hitschmann, "Clinical Psychoanalysis" from Wilhelm Reich, and "The Practice of Analyzing Abandoned Youth" from August Aichhorn.[475] (Sadly, the Vienna Psychoanalytic Institute was shut down in March of 1938 by the Nazis after the Annexation of Austria by the Third Reich).

In addition to her normal program, Helen worked directly with August Aichhorn, an innovative Austrian-born educator, considered one of the founders of psychoanalytic education and a pioneer in the field of working with juvenile delinquents and disadvantaged youths. As his student, Helen gained his trust and confidence to such an extent that they worked together to translate his influential book, *Wayward Youth*, into English. It became his best-known work, an international success, and a classic in its field.

These were busy and fulfilling years for Helen as she gained the professional training, knowledge, and credentials to pursue a new career—as a psychoanalyst and a therapist. When she returned permanently to the United States in 1934, she was qualified to use her newly acquired training.

1934

During Helen's absence in Europe, Dr. Alexander had remained fully occupied. He began his tenure at the University of Chicago as its first professor of psychoanalysis in 1930. His first book, *The Psychoanalysis of the Total Personality*, was also published that year. This was praised as an important "work developing the psychoanalytic theory of the super-ego and [it was immediately] praised by Sigmund Freud."[476] Then, two years later (1932), he established the Chicago Institute for Psychoanalysis (the CIP), where "under his leadership, the institute attracted many analysts and students who conducted extensive research on emotional disturbance and psychosomatic disease, identifying various disorders with particular unconscious conflicts."[477] So, not surprisingly, when she returned to Chicago in 1934, Dr. Alexander was the first person Helen contacted.

Dr. Alexander immediately offered her a position as a research associate under his direction. While not an upper-level post, Helen quickly accepted the offer, because the advantages clearly outweighed the shortcomings. The job offer came with two conditions: Helen would begin by working on a detailed study of asthmatic children, and her work would be under the direction (and scrutiny) of Dr. Alexander, who reputedly was an "authoritarian, albeit a benign despot."[478] However, the CIP's office was nearby, the work paid a dependable salary, and the annual schedule was structured so that Helen could be absent for two months each summer. It didn't take long for Helen and Dr. Alexander to establish a good working relationship. He appreciated her maturity, her past professional experiences, her energy, her tact, and her willingness to accommodate.

He discovered that Helen, with her well-honed interpersonal skills, could also effectively "engage in psychotherapeutic work with children and adolescents . . . in private practice."[479] In order to give herself and the CIP additional exposure in the local community, Helen was permitted to become "a psychiatric consultant for various social agencies—among others, the Illinois Institute for Juvenile Research, the Jewish Social Service Bureau of Chicago, and the Family Welfare Association of Evanston."[480]

Helen's workdays became busy, full, and satisfying. She had found a professional calling where she could help children to address their personal difficulties and make them more fulfilled human beings. She was working for Dr. Alexander, a knowledgeable, highly respected professional, at a growing cutting-edge psychoanalytic institution with the mission of helping others.

At Home with Sis and J. B. Ross

As Helen and Sis approached middle age, they realized it was unlikely they would marry or have children of their own. This realization came to them over time, and they accepted it and adjusted to it. In fact, neither ever married or had any children of her own. Yet throughout their professional lives, they helped hundreds of children, particularly girls. They stood out in their professions as experts on children. Perhaps their personal situations heightened their objectivity about raising children and made them uniquely qualified to render the help and advice they did.

Another facet of Helen's life changed in 1934. Her youngest sister and "charge," James Bruce Ross, (who was now going by her initials J. B.) was awarded a Ph.D. in history from the University of Chicago in the spring of 1934. To get her degree from Chicago, J. B. lived much of the time with Sis (and sometimes Helen) in the

Chicago apartment during the late 1920s and early 1930s. After receiving her Ph.D., J. B. left Chicago and relocated to Poughkeepsie, New York, where she'd taken a position as a substitute instructor in history at Vassar College. Though J.B. was 12 years younger than Helen, they remained close throughout their lives.

1941

Helen became increasingly comfortable in her work and demonstrated a talent for engaging people in both one-on-one settings and in group work. She spent an increasing amount of time working with various social agencies and family-welfare associations. She also found time to teach a course in personality development at the University of Chicago's School of Education,[481] and she began a course for social caseworkers at the Family Welfare Association of Omaha in Nebraska. She maintained her private counseling practice in conjunction with the CIP. Due to her high energy level, her flexibility, and her willingness to help others, Helen became a force for expanding the CIP out into the communities. This resulted in help for many people who otherwise might have gone without.

At that time, psychoanalysis was generally seen as something available only to rich people. Helen helped to create a new use of psychoanalysis that was based on practicality. Her engagement with everyday people and problems provided concrete evidence that psychoanalytic counseling and therapy worked and could be used to improve the lives of ordinary people.

Alice O'Brien and Captiva Island, Florida

In the 1930s, Helen met Alice M. O'Brien, the daughter of a Minnesota lumber baron, William O'Brien. Born in 1891 in St.

Paul, Minnesota, Alice was a free spirit by nature, she developed a fascination for the automobile and soon became a skilled driver and mechanic; one of her early experiences included driving a roadster from California to Minnesota. In 1918, during World War I, she went to France, where she joined the American Fund French Wounded, a humanitarian organization. During the war, she served as an ambulance driver, mechanic, and part-time nurse treating wounded soldiers. After the war, she returned to the United States and became involved in managing her family's sprawling and lucrative lumber business. During this period, she also sought relief from the bitter Minnesota winters by spending time on the west coast of Florida.[482]

The circumstances by which Helen and Alice met and became friends is unknown. However, by the early 1940s, Helen and Sis were spending part of each winter on Florida's west coast as Alice's guest at a resort known as The Captain's House. Those were welcome breaks from the frigid northern winters for Helen and Sis. Subsequently, Alice encouraged them to join her in establishing a winter residence on Florida's southwest coast on Captiva Island near the small city of Ft. Myers. In 1944, Helen and Sis purchased a lot on Captiva Island, and they built a house there in 1946, with Sis personally overseeing its construction. Alice also purchased a nearby lot, on which she built an impressive house of Florida cypress from her family's own timberlands. Alice convinced many of her friends from Minnesota to purchase lots nearby and build houses on them. These neighbors dubbed their seaside neighborhood "the Compound" and for many years enjoyed an active social life together during the winter months.[483]

J. B. Ross, who was also unmarried, joined her sisters for a part of each winter at their new home on Captiva Island. The sisters spent their winters collecting seashells on the beach each morning and tending to the flowering trees and shrubs on their property the rest of the day. They also pursued their professional reading and writing. As evenings approached, they would meet with neighbors for cocktails. This became for the Ross sisters a delightful way to spend their winter months, particularly since the alternative was the bitter northern cold in Chicago.

The neighbors in "the compound" on Captiva Island were mostly university-educated professionals. They all loved Helen, who they knew by her nickname "Hi." Some years after Helen and Sis had built their winter home, one of them authored and distributed a poem about Helen to the community. It read in part:

A LADY AND A SCHOLAR

> What's it that makes Hi, "Hi"?
> To define it takes better than I.
> If the rest of us thought that at
>   Seventy-eight
> Our comp'ny would others so elate
> We'd bow to the years with more of
>   grace—
> Still, to know that it happens is some
>   solace.
> Always courteous, always kind,
> Alive in spirit, body, and mind—
> An easy and warm responsiveness
> Of the mode in her thought and her speech
>   and her dress,
> A zest for just about everything
> And never bored or censuring.[484]

Administrative Director

After eight years under Dr. Franz Alexander, Helen became the Administrative Director of the Chicago Institute for Psychoanalysis in 1942. Her elevation reflected the confidence that Alexander and the board of directors had in her. She briefly describes the Administrative Director's position:

> "My duties in this position are multifarious: I raise money, help to supervise our training school of psychiatrists, help to organize and supervise the research, edit the publications, and perform many other administrative duties difficult to classify. During the past year, I have also edited a book written by the Staff of the Institute, tentatively entitled *Developments in Psychoanalytic Therapy*, to be brought out this [in 1945] fall by the Ronalds Press of New York."[485]

Fifty-two-year-old Helen assumed a broad array of new responsibilities. Using the management style she'd honed at Camp Kechuwa, she developed a collaborative approach that kept the institute operating effectively. And beyond her substantial administrative duties, she remained committed to the intellectual advancements of the CIP as an editor of many of its publications.

Activities Outside the CIP

Despite her heavy new responsibilities, Helen managed to keep a busy schedule of outside activities as well. She continued to work with welfare and social agencies and taught her course in personality development at the University of Chicago. She also found time to give short-term courses to groups interested in family welfare. In her words:

"In 1941, I began a course for social caseworkers of the Family Welfare Association of Omaha, which has developed into a seminar on the Psychiatric aspects of casework. This group meets for two-day sessions every five weeks. During the past two years, this work has been done jointly with Dr. Adelaide Johnson of the Institute. In addition, last year, Dr. Johnson and I gave a course at the Graduate School of Social Work at the University of Nebraska. Both the Omaha and Lincoln courses continue."[486]

Her teaching and training went beyond the Midwest. Helen traveled to other places as well. As she said in 1945:

"I have conducted many two-[day] or three-day 'institutes' for the Family Welfare Association of America in various parts of the country, for state welfare conferences, and other agencies concerned with the welfare of children, and have done a good deal of lecturing to parent, teacher, and social-worker groups. This work also continues."[487]

Board Memberships and Fundraising

In all her writings and correspondence, she never alluded to any situation where she experienced bias against her as a woman, although she must have experienced this. Rather, she accepted the society she lived in and made the best of it. In 1945, she said:

"At the present time I am a member of the Educational Council of the Francis Parker School of Chicago, and will this year [in 1945] act as a psychiatric consultant to the faculty. I shall also hold consultations with the Staff of the University

Nursery School of the University of Chicago. I am a member of the Board of the Chicago Home for Girls and a member of the Mayor's Committee on the Juvenile Court."[488]

Helen's responsibilities also included fundraising. She'd learned a few fundraising tricks from Dr. Alexander. As the founder of the CIP, he had skillfully cultivated wealthy donors, such as Alfred K. Stern, of the Julius Rosenwald Fund (Julius Rosenwald, a Chicago philanthropist, was an early owner of Sears, Roebuck & Company) as well as the Rockefeller and the Macy Foundations.[489] Helen, through her CIP experience as well as her work with the Goldmark sisters, became familiar with how large, charitable foundations worked—a perspective she would continue to draw upon in the years to come. She naturally gravitated toward a soft-sell fundraising approach that suited her understated personality.

One of the outside boards on which Helen served in the 1950s was the Francis Parker School. This nonprofit, private school founded in 1901 took the name of its founder, Colonel Francis W. Parker, a Civil War veteran. After the war, Parker became an educator whom his colleague, John Dewey, called "the father of progressive education." He incorporated progressive teaching principles, such as "learn by doing," and emphasized the student's citizenship as well as the related responsibilities each had within his or her community.[490] Beginning in 1945, Helen served as a "psychiatric consultant to the faculty,"[491] and this later evolved into her serving as a member of the school's Board of Trustees.[492]

Helen's Intellectual and Professional Growth

Initially, Helen's intellectual interest in psychoanalysis was focused on the one-on-one analysis of the individual. She wanted to learn the "other reasons" some campers at Camp Kechuwa struggled to follow simple rules. This desire to understand reasons for a behavior was fundamental to psychoanalysis. However, her positions at the CIP and at Camp Kechuwa required her to deal with groups of people. And even though she originally focused on and became an expert in her one-on-one counseling practice, she eventually began to increasingly appreciate the study of group dynamics as well. In her own words:

> "While most of the research work I have been able to do has centered about children, adolescents, and young adults as individuals—both in the camp and in my psychotherapeutic practice—I have had the opportunity to make observations on group psychology and have become increasingly interested in that branch of psychology."[493]

What motivated Helen to put so much of her time and effort into her work at the CIP? She answered that question, at age 55, when she wrote:

> "I am tremendously interested in the work of the Institute for Psychoanalysis, feeling that we have a great contribution to make to the development of psychiatry and thereby to the mental health of the country . . . It is in the wide application of these principles to education, to social work, to medicine—in short, to all those fields of work which deal primarily with human beings—that I am most interested."[494]

Helen, through her decades of experience, had observed children's behaviors for extended periods. This was the source of her belief that children who thought and acted in some detrimental (often anti-social) way had an underlying (and past) experience or a physical condition that caused their unusual (and undesirable) behavior. She became convinced that, by discovering those latent (triggering) thoughts or experiences, those children could be helped.

1950

In 1950, the final preparations were underway for the upcoming camping season. However, Sis began to feel poorly, and after a visit with her doctor learned she'd contracted cancer. Despite this, she and Helen soldiered through that 1950 season. By its end, Helen concluded it would be their last. Helen relied mightily on her older sister to operate their camp. Helen was able to fulfill her duties as the camp's director, but Sis struggled with her failing health; she performed her basic duties but spent a great deal of time in bed, resting. The camp season ended on a generally positive note, although with an overlay of sadness. Helen, at one point, believed she'd found a buyer, one who would give the camp a renewed life. Unfortunately, that sale fell through. So, when the camp's buildings, fixtures, and equipment were secured for the winter, its fate remained uncertain.

As 1951 began, Sis' health continued to decline. Her sisters gave Sis all the support they could in Chicago in her final days. As written by Helen in her memoirs, years later:

> "When Frances and J. B. and I could care for Sis in those last autumn days of her life (1951), it was a golden time outdoors, and the doors were open, so we could slip quickly outside to shed our tears, and we could share the recollections of the past, sometimes too far back for the younger sisters."[495]

Eventually, Sis succumbed to cancer on September 25, 1951, after which her body was transported to Independence, where she was buried. Her sisters found her a final resting spot in a grave next to their father and mother in the town's Woodlawn cemetery.

Losing her older sister—not to mention the uncertainty with the camp—were emotional and life-altering events for Helen. Helen threw herself into her work, vigorously applying herself to her profession. In 1951, at 61 years of age, Helen embarked on a decade of professional writing and communication that would be her most productive.

Author and Advisor

At this stage in her career, Helen realized that writing was the best way she could leverage her knowledge and her effectiveness. Her mission was to share her knowledge and experience and provide new and better ways to address many of the complicated problems in the lives of children. Helen became a prolific writer, lecturer, and advisor, especially for people and groups who cared for children.

A bibliography of Helen's published work written between 1938 and 1972 contains thirty-six contributions she made to professional journals and books, plus eleven additional articles and comments she contributed during that period—and there were other writings as well.[496] Some of these (e.g., an article entitled "Group Psychotherapy Related to Group Trauma") were professional works directed primarily to professionals in her field, but many (e.g., a pamphlet entitled "Fears of Children," discussed below) could be used by laypeople, such as teachers, parents, and social workers. Helen wanted her works to have the broadest possible audience, so she avoided professional jargon as much as possible. Instead, she chose language that was clear, simple, and down-to-earth.

The pamphlet entitled "Fears of Children" by Helen was published in 1951 and was one of her most popular. One in a series of "Better Living Booklets for Parents and Teachers," this 48-page pamphlet was copyrighted by Science Research Associates, Inc.

The first of the pamphlet's seven chapters begins in Helen's signature conversational style:

COMMON ATTITUDES TOWARD FEAR

"'Don't be afraid—come on, honey, walk to mommy,' says the mother, trying to coax her one-year-old to take his first step.

'I don't ever want to catch you walking on fences or climbing trees again. Do you realize what could happen to you if you fell?' says the mother of her daring five-year-old.

'I'm not afraid of the dark, but please leave the light on for a while yet,' says the little girl.

'Fraidy cat! Fraidy cat!' children yell at the youngster who wouldn't 'follow the leader.' And the accused answers tearfully, 'I'm not! I'm not!'

'Afraid,' 'scared,' and 'fear' are words that have mixed meaning for us. We associate them with childishness and cowardice. We condemn these feelings in others and deny them in ourselves. But all of us—adults and children alike—have some fears. They make us feel uncomfortable. We try to avoid them or get rid of them. We all try to master our fears.

We recognize, however, that some feelings of fear are useful and necessary. Parents and teachers know that they must teach children how to protect themselves, and that fear is a means of avoiding danger and harm. We teach fear of speeding automobiles, fear of fire, fear of unlabeled medicine bottles, fear of infection and disease, fear of strange men who offer candy or money. These are just a few of the lessons in sensible precautions that we teach our children . . .

HELPING CHILDREN WITH THEIR FEARS

In recent years, experts in human behavior—psychologists and psychiatrists—have learned a lot about what lies behind bravery and fear. They have learned much that can help parents understand why children are afraid, why they are brave, why they sometimes act foolishly. Perhaps most important, they have learned much that can aid parents, teachers, and children in facing life free of *crippling, disabling, irrational fears."*

In its six subsequent chapters, the booklet addresses the following topics:
2: What is fear?
3: Fear of the loss of love
4: Fear of bodily hurt
5: Fear of conscience
6: Fear of adolescence
7: How parents and teachers can help

The booklet's final chapter concludes with the following thoughts:

"GETTING 'IN TUNE' WITH YOUR CHILD

Many parents are so 'in tune' with their children that they know by intuition when a child is upset and what to do about it. These parents act spontaneously; they do not have to turn to a book! This intuition is not a magical or inborn trait. It is the product of the sensitiveness to the child's needs and readiness to respond. This awareness of the child's needs and this readiness are found in good teachers, too. But it has little to do with higher education. It is the result of warm feelings, which do not have to be taught.

But knowledge is helpful, too, and that is why such pamphlets as this are written—as guides to fathers and mothers and teachers who wish their children to grow up well.

We can't rear our children to be absolutely free of fear. This would not be wise, even if we could. But we can all help children grow to maturity unburdened by destructive anxiety, free to become spontaneous and creative adults with a greater capacity to enjoy themselves and to contribute to the happiness of others."[497]

Implicit in this and other books and articles written by Helen are her presumptions that the mother and father serve as the most fundamental unit for the support and rearing of a child. She also highlights the importance of teachers to a young person's psychological growth and development.

Her writings reveal the breadth of her expertise regarding children and families. Her writings include other practical pieces such as:

- "The Shy Child"[498]

- "The School Years: An Age of Discovery"[499]

- "Like Mother, Like Daughter?"[500]

- "A Contemporary Concept of Family Welfare"[501]

- "The Handicapped Child and His Family"[502]

Helen gained some access to a wider audience in the mid-1950s when she wrote a column in the *Sunday Chicago Sun-Times* entitled, "About Your Child." Although she was more than qualified to write this periodic column, it helped that Marshall Field III, who served with Helen on the board of The Francis Parker School in Chicago, owned that newspaper.[503] In any event, the column ran for about a year, after which it was discontinued.

Anna Freud and the Hampstead Clinic

Anna Freud and Helen Ross became friends when Helen studied at the Vienna Psychoanalytic Institute in the early 1930s, and they remained lifelong friends. In 1938, Anna and her father fled Nazi-dominated Austria, and made their home in London. (Sigmund Freud died in London in 1939.) Dorothy T. Burlingham moved to London with them. She was the granddaughter of Charles Lewis Tiffany, the founder of Tiffany & Co. Dorothy had been analyzed in Vienna by Sigmund Freud and had become good friends with Anna Freud.

During World War II, Anna worked in the London neighborhood of Hampstead in a nursery caring for young children separated from their families. There she witnessed firsthand the devastating effect of war on families, and particularly on the children. In 1947, Anna, as an outgrowth of what she'd experienced during the war years, founded the Hampstead Child Therapy Course and Clinic in London.[504] The purpose of the child-therapy course was to educate future teachers and psychoanalysts for disadvantaged children and to improve the methods of analyzing and caring for such children. By 1952, with the help of Dorothy Burlingham and Helen Ross, the organization became fully functional and was known as The

Hampstead Clinic, with Anna Freud serving as its director. It soon became famous as the world's first child psychoanalytic center for observational research, teaching, and learning.

The Hampstead Clinic made major contributions to research. The training-staff members were required to observe the interactions of the children and take notes. Those notes were organized, categorized, and recorded on index cards that could then be used to thematically correlate each situation in an analytical context. These notes later evolved into use as a "diagnostic profile." The diagnostic profile could then be used with the analysis and the treatment to help in diagnosis and treatment of future patients. Helen visited the clinic—and her friend, Anna Freud—in London on several occasions, and helped with its organization. However, her major contribution was bringing it financial support, most notably from Chicago's philanthropic Field Foundation. After the death of Anna Freud in 1982, the institution that had formerly been known as "the Hampstead Clinic" remained a vibrant enterprise, and in her honor was renamed The Anna Freud Centre.[505]

A New Life for Camp Kechuwa

After its closure at the end of the 1950 camping season, Helen decided the camp should remain closed, with no future in sight. It pained her to see the camp, where so many girls had learned to enjoy friends and outdoor life, lie fallow. She knew that, in the right hands, the camp had a future, but those hands proved to be few and elusive.

It eventually occurred to Helen that the three sons of her younger sister, Frances Ross Leake, had the experience and abilities to take over the camp. They had each worked for several summers at the camp. But there were significant hurdles. First, it was a girls' camp—and these were young men. Secondly, the "Leake boys," as they were called by Helen and Sis, were just beginning their own careers and couldn't afford to purchase a large summer camp. Helen determined that it was at least worth a conversation with her nephews to see if they might be interested.

After a great deal of thought about a possible arrangement, Helen contacted Charlie Leake, who had worked closely with Sis and seemed to her to be the most business-minded of the brothers. In their initial conversation, Charlie showed some interest in acquiring and operating the camp, provided that his younger brother, Bud, would partner with him. Helen took this as a favorable omen and put together a proposal which she hoped would work for her nephews. She offered to sell the camp's real estate, fixtures, and all the equipment (then appraised at $79,800) to Charlie for $40,000. He would then work out a joint-ownership arrangement with Bud. (The oldest brother, Jim, was by then a practicing physician and wasn't interested in the camp.) Helen's proposal included lending Charlie and Bud $2,000 for the start-up costs for reviving the camp. The $40,000 purchase price could be paid back over an extended period of 10–12 years and could be paid mostly out of the profits from the camp's operation. The Leake brothers shouldn't have to put down any money out of their own pockets. However, Helen insisted on two things. First, the terms of the final transaction, even though it was among family members, had to be in writing and drafted by her attorney. Second, one piece of the real estate, an island on Lake Michigamme called "Footprint Island," approximately one acre in size and located some distance away from the camp, would remain as Helen's private property and not included in the sale of the camp.[506]

The transaction his aunt proposed appealed to Charlie, who was then teaching school in the Chicago area. He immediately contacted Bud, then a graduate student in mathematics education at the University of Wisconsin. Bud also became excited and gave Charlie the "green light" to proceed with finalizing the purchase. Thus, in 1954, after the legal papers were signed, Camp Kechuwa again came to life. However, the Leake brothers, with Helen's blessing, made one major change—it reopened as a camp for boys!

Helen was delighted to see her darling Camp Kechuwa up and running again. Her nephews, whom she and Sis had trained years before, retained many of the camp's former characteristics and operations. The camp's emphasis on outdoor living continued into its new life, and this proved just as fun and engrossing for boys as it had been for girls. After Camp Kechuwa (for boys) resumed operation, Helen stepped away and simply made herself available to answer any questions her nephews might ask.

Helen, along with her sister, J. B., enjoyed spending a few weeks each summer on nearby Footprint Island. At first, the remote island had no buildings, or electricity, or running water. However, Helen, now over 60 years of age, had a small cabin built on the island's highest spot. It had a few basic amenities. This allowed Helen and J. B. to spend parts of each summer in that peaceful setting. For many years thereafter, Helen and J. B. enjoyed the clear lake, fresh air, glorious sunsets, and natural beauty of Lake Michigamme, just a long canoe ride away from the boys who were enjoying the revived Camp Kechuwa.

New York

Helen and Sis moved into their Chicago apartment in the 1920s and remained there until Sis' death from cancer in 1951. For Helen, Sis' death involved more than an emotional loss. They had joint economic arrangements as well, which needed to be sorted out and included Camp Kechuwa and the house on Captiva Island. J. B., their youngest sister, in the 1940s had joined the Vassar College faculty as a full-time professor and lived in Poughkeepsie, New York. She remained close to Helen, her "big sister."

In 1956, Helen's mentor, Dr. Franz Alexander, announced that he'd accepted a position as the head of psychiatry at the Psychiatric and Psychosomatic Research Institute at Mt. Sinai Hospital in Los Angeles, California.[507]

The departure of Dr. Alexander, Helen's professional mentor and guide for more than twenty years, profoundly affected Helen. She began to re-think her career at the CIP and decided she wanted to experience something different in her work. At this time an unexpected opportunity came to her attention. It was an interesting and challenging job offer from her profession's national organization.

By 1956, the American Psychoanalytic Association (APsA) had become the accepted national organization for those who practiced psychoanalysis in the United States. Founded in 1911 in Baltimore, Maryland (it later moved to New York City), the APsA was the nation's oldest national psychoanalytic organization. It focused on education, research, and membership development. It was part of the International Psychoanalytic Association, the largest worldwide psychoanalytic organization.[508] Most of its member teaching institutions were in the larger cities, and they operated independently. Although they generally practiced accepted principles of psychoanalysis, there was a wide inconsistency in the standards and practices among the members. Psychoanalysis was still a nascent field, and the APsA felt that the lack of consistency was holding back acceptance of the field. In 1956, the APsA decided it needed to address this issue, and determined that its first step should be a far-reaching, in-depth review of the actual practices of each of its members. Then, depending upon what was discovered, any issues could be addressed, and the practices improved.

The APsA commissioned one of its former presidents, Dr. Bertram D. Lewin, then a practicing psychiatrist in New York City, to do this major review and analysis. He immediately saw he would need a partner for this huge project. Lewin knew of Helen by reputation and approached her about joining the project. When Helen and Dr. Lewin met, they discussed the challenges of the project as well as its scope and the methods of inquiry and analysis that would be required. They soon realized that their outlook and personalities meshed well and that would make a good team. The APsA then made Helen an offer, and she signed on to the project. This meant she would have to leave Chicago and move to New York. She was looking forward to experiencing working in New York City, which had the added benefit of being close to J. B. in nearby Poughkeepsie.

As Helen had hoped, she and Lewin worked well together. Both proved to be affable and flexible, yet determined and methodical.

Helen Ross and her co-author, Bertram Lewin, with whom she wrote *Psychoanalytic Education in the United States*. New York City, 1970. (Photo/Ross Family collection).

They first organized what fundamentally would be a research project and collected vast amounts of information. This was followed by a categorization and an analysis of the information collected. In all, they visited fourteen institutions as well as three training centers, performed countless interviews, and collected and organized a mountain of information. They then offered cogent conclusions, which ultimately led to recommendations by the APsA. The project took more than three years. In the words of Dr. Lewin, even the physical work product of the project proved massive:

> "We had accumulated shelves of loose-leaf ring books, boxes, and filing cases bulging with documents of all sorts: records of interviews with faculty members, students, graduates, administrative staff; records of audits of classes and supervisory hours; extensive notes of observations in all fields of psychoanalytic education. We had correspondence and notes of consultations with experts outside of the narrower field. We had gathered syllabi, brochures, reports of institutes and committees, all sorts of records from institute offices, and answers to several questionnaires we had sent out to students."[509]

Once the research phase was complete, Helen and Lewin produced a highly readable final report. This became a book that was published by W.W. Norton in 1960: *Psychoanalytic Education in the United States*.[510] It contained thirty-three chapters covering a wide range of topics, including historical factors, data on enrollment (age, previous education, admissions data, selection process, length of training). It discussed the current practices for formal training of psychoanalysts, including teaching techniques, clinical supervision given to students, and the classroom experience. Other chapters covered topics such as curriculum, student progression and school problems, the clinic, child psychoanalysis, institute financing, and institutional facilities. In short, it presented a broad-based factual look at the entire educational process. And as an emphatic coda to the project, the appendix of the book contained a statement by the APsA on the minimal training standards for psychoanalysts.

Although primarily a technical study, the book was an immediate success in the psychoanalytic community. One key reason for its success was the stature of the authors. They were both well known and widely respected in the field. A second reason was the authors' objective analysis and the tact and discretion they used when presenting information from the many interviews.

The book ultimately led the APsA to establish accreditation standards for institutions teaching psychoanalysis. It also resulted in the much-needed standardization and overall improvement in psychoanalytic education in the United States.

Helen's co-authorship of the book brought her an elevated level of national recognition and stature beyond anything she'd enjoyed previously. Her many visits to psychoanalysis schools allowed her to meet most of the professors and instructors in the field. Her name and reputation became widely known, as did her practical expertise and personal warmth. This enhanced recognition and these additional professional contacts would be of significant value to Helen during the final stage of her career.

18

CHARLIE GETS THE CALL

1939—Charlie Returns to Washington

In January of 1939, Charlie and Florence happily returned to the Washington area. It was a welcome homecoming for them both—and the beginning of a halcyon six-year period.

For Charlie, this was an ideal assignment that came with handsome compensation. He worked downtown in the offices of the *Post-Dispatch* at 1422 F Street NW with the newspaper's other employees.[511] His protégé, Pete Brandt, who had replaced Charlie when he transferred to St. Louis, now served as the Chief Washington Correspondent for the *Post-Dispatch;* Charlie was provided an ample office in that suite.

Joseph Pulitzer, Jr., had given Charlie free rein to go about Washington, to observe and record the people and events he wished, and then to write about them in a regular column called, "Washington Letter." Pulitzer knew that Charlie's sense of what was important and what people wanted to know—or should know—would appeal to readers. Pulitzer's judgment of Charlie's abilities again proved sound as the "Washington Letter" became more and more widely read.

Charlie's duties and compensation had been worked out beforehand. Charlie, who would report directly to Pulitzer, would write the column—subject to rejection by Pulitzer, but not to any editing, and it would appear two or three times per week. Charlie would choose the topics for his column—which was reasonable given his superb connections and instinctive understanding of readers. In addition, Pulitzer charged Charlie with overseeing both the assignment and the editing of articles for the editorial section of Sunday's *Post-Dispatch*, referred to by journalists as its "dignity page." This section contained interpretive, thoughtful, and sometimes instructional pieces, and it reflected the editorial voice of the paper. Pulitzer took great pride in this section, so he gave Charlie the overall responsibility for it, even down to the selection of the headlines that appeared above each piece.[512] In his new position, Charlie was paid an annual salary of $35,000, a substantial sum in those days (equivalent to approximately $670,000 in today's dollars).

Changes had occurred in the political dynamics of Washington during the five years Charlie had been away. He noticed that the center of the news activity had shifted from the Congress to the White House. No longer did the likes of Senator William Borah of Idaho, a spellbinding orator, or Nebraska's Senator George W. Norris, an unflagging warrior for the welfare of the common man, command the attention of the reporters. Rather it was the Roosevelt White House and its "palace politicians," as Charlie referred to them, who had taken much of the spotlight. These "satellites whose sun is the President" fascinated Charlie, who wrote about them, in March of 1939:

> "The palace politicians are not interested in the success of the Democratic Party as such. They care little for the precedents and less of the party names and the old shibboleths. They say that theirs is the new 'politics of principle,' in contrast with the politics of expedience or partisanship. They say

they are interested only in the perpetuation of their ideas, not in their personal fortunes.

"That is as it may be. There can be no doubt that among them there are some men of the loftiest, most idealistic motives; equally there can be no doubt that among them are men whose desire, like that of nine-tenths of the officeholders of whatever degree, is to stay on the payroll."[513]

No matter what Charlie thought of the functionaries of the Roosevelt administration, he, like so many others, was impressed by the President himself. In one column, also written in March of 1939, Charlie devoted almost the entire column to his impressions of Roosevelt. It, in part, reads:

"Even one who saw him many times in action in the first two years of the New Deal, it [Roosevelt's] is a remarkable performance. The manifest confidence of the man in his own powers; his deftness of keeping out of traps; his quickness in retorts; the mobility of his features; above all his abounding vitality—these stand out from a medley of impressions of this astounding man."[514]

In addition to his salary, when Pulitzer thought that Charlie was doing a particularly good job—a frequent occurrence—Pulitzer would send Charlie a bonus check, often with a handwritten note.[515] In time, Charlie's "Washington Letter" became so highly regarded that Pulitzer realized he might be able to syndicate it, which would mean additional income for the *Post-Dispatch*. So, in the spring of 1940 he offered Charlie's column for syndication; it was immediately picked up by papers around the country, including the *Washington Star* and the *New York Post*.[516] At 55, Charlie found himself in an ideal professional position: living in the city he knew and loved, doing the work that best reflected his experience and talents, and being well-paid for his efforts. These were Charlie's Halcyon Days.

Florence

Florence loved their old house at 5 Primrose Street in Chevy Chase, which she and Charlie had to sell in 1934. Located a mile north of the District of Columbia, she had made the house into a comfortable home, made many friends, tended her gardens, and raised her two sons. Had it been on the market in 1939, when she and Charlie returned from St. Louis, they might have repurchased it. But things had changed. Her two sons were now out on their own, and she had to care for only Charlie and herself. They had more financial resources than ever, and with their sons having graduated from college, no large expenses loomed. Charlie and Florence were practical and didn't live above their means. But Florence always wanted to impress people, and now she had the opportunity to do it with a new home. Like most other people, Florence had her own definition of "thrift." She wasn't afraid to spend money, but she felt that large-dollar purchases should be for "things of lasting value"—a concept not objectively defined.[517] She enjoyed nice clothes, fine furniture, and jewelry. Not long after they returned to Washington, Florence found a house on the edge of Chevy Chase at 117 Kennedy Drive, in an area known as Kensington. It was a large, recently built, two-story house on an affluent street lined with similar stately homes. Now that she and Charlie could afford such an expansive showcase, she was going to have it.

The house had everything she wanted. It was located on the cusp of familiar, affluent Chevy Chase. Its location was within the boundaries of her former parish, the Shrine of the Blessed Sacrament

Catholic Church. It had an ample space for her gardening, as well as for a fishpond she would later put in. The house could accommodate large gatherings whenever she wanted to entertain. There was space for a live-in housekeeper. (Florence had live-in domestic help for years. These women served as housekeeper, cook, and laundress, as the situation required.) Florence set to work to make the new house an impressive home.

Charlie and Florence remained close to their two sons, who had set out on very different paths. John, the eldest, after graduating from college at Georgetown University in 1936, had decided to pursue a career in medicine. This was a path no one in the Ross family had previously taken. He entered Johns Hopkins Medical School in 1936, where he was set to graduate in 1940. Walter had graduated from Dartmouth College in 1937, after which he joined Charlie and Florence in St. Louis. He decided to follow in his father's footsteps, and had taken a job as a reporter for the *Post-Dispatch*. He remained in that job after Charlie and Florence left St. Louis for Washington.

Reconnecting with Harry Truman

At this time, Charlie rekindled his friendship with two old classmates from Independence High School, Harry and Bess Truman. Harry, despite not getting an endorsement from the *Post-Dispatch* in 1934, had been elected to the U. S. Senate that year. He served credibly as a junior senator and in 1940 won re-election, again despite opposition from the *Post-Dispatch*.[518] When Charlie and Harry renewed their friendship, Charlie was pleased to learn that Harry had become an avid reader of the "Washington Letter"[519] and that he didn't resent the lack of support from the *Post-Dispatch*.

In time, the Truman and Ross families became close and frequently saw each other socially. Florence enjoyed the company of Harry and Bess. Harry began referring to Florence as "Mrs. Charlie." To Margaret Truman, the Trumans' daughter, Charlie was always "Uncle Charlie."[520] Charlie took particular interest in Margaret's budding career as a concert singer. The Rosses and Trumans all hailed from Missouri—which they pronounced "Miz-ur-ah"—and shared similar interests. On one occasion, Harry was invited to the Ross home for breakfast. His punctuality impressed Florence, who later said: "When Harry Truman says he's going to be at your house at 7 a.m. for breakfast, he *arrives at* 7 a.m.!"[521]

1941

In 1941, Walter Ross was working for the *Post-Dispatch*. He saw the rising tide of fascism in the raging war in Europe. He decided he wanted to be ready in the (increasingly likely) event the U.S. entered the war, and he enlisted in the U. S. Naval Reserves. About the same time, he also met an attractive St. Louis young lady who also worked for the *Post-Dispatch*. Lucianna Gladney was a graduate of Smith College and the daughter of a successful local attorney. They became engaged and chose to be married in the Presbyterian Church. Charlie loved Lucianna, and was thrilled to finally have a daughter, albeit a daughter-in-law, in the family. However, Florence, a strict Roman Catholic, was troubled that the marriage was outside of the Catholic Church. Despite Florence's disapproval, Walter and Lucianna were married in a beautiful wedding held in a Presbyterian church in St. Louis in April 1941.

John graduated from Johns Hopkins Medical School in 1940, after which he began his hospital residency. While in his final year of college at Georgetown University, he had gone on a blind date with a young lady, Anne Moore, who attended Trinity College, a Catholic all-women's college in Washington. A romance ensued and continued until 1941, when John proposed. They were married in October of 1941 at Anne's parents' house in Yonkers, New York. As with Walter's bride, Charlie was very pleased to have Anne as part of the family. Florence also welcomed Anne, who, like John, had remained true to her Catholic upbringing.

But the joy of the growing Ross family was quickly tempered by world events that erupted on December 7, 1941, when the Japanese military attacked the U. S. Naval Base at Pearl Harbor, and a few days later, when Germany declared war on the United States—World War II for the United States had begun.

World War II

As with other American families, the sudden outbreak of the war dramatically affected the Ross family. Following the attack on Pearl Harbor, the Navy summoned Walter to active duty and assigned him to serve on a destroyer patrolling Alaska's Aleutian Islands. His brother, John, attempted to join the Navy Medical corps, but his application was declined for health reasons—stemming from his bout with hepatitis during his college days. For the next few years, he continued with internships and residency work at established hospitals, such as Massachusetts General Hospital in Boston and Barnes Hospital in St. Louis. He decided to pursue specialization in hematology. Walter, in the meantime, saw little combat action aboard his destroyer pounding the vicious seas in the frozen northern Pacific. Craving a more exciting assignment, he applied to become a Naval aviator. His request was granted, and he was sent to the naval flight school in Texas. He performed so well that after graduation he was assigned to remain in Texas and teach other navy pilots.

John, whose medical training was coming to an end, still wanted to serve his country, so in 1944 he again applied for the service, but, this time, to the Army. He was elated when he was accepted, and that summer began his basic training in the U. S. Army Medical Corps. After his officer training was completed, he was sent to Italy, where he served behind the front lines, managing the blood supplies, holding blood drives, and using his general medical skills for "patching up German prisoners of war."[522]

Charlie and Florence also adjusted their lives and routines during the war. Florence tended a "Victory Garden"—a 50' x 100' plot on a neighborhood lot, often with Charlie pitching in. Hired help had become scarce, so, Charlie would don old clothes after work and perform sundry outdoor and maintenance tasks in the garden and around the house. He enjoyed using his latent handyman skills he'd learned as a boy from his father.[523] Two days a week, Florence worked as a Red Cross Nurse's Aide at the Mount Alto Children's Hospital.[524]

Early in the summer of 1944, John was ordered to basic training at Pennsylvania's Indiantown Gap Military Reservation. Anne, at the time, was six months pregnant with their first child, so Florence and Charlie asked her to move in with them. Anne gladly did, and a few weeks later, on August 29, 1944, she gave birth to Charlie's and Florence's first grandchild, who was named Charles Griffith Ross after his grandfather. "Little Charlie" disrupted the household's routine but in the process brought great joy to his proud grandparents.

At the office, Charlie maintained a sizable workload throughout the war. Although the pace of news reporting, like everything in Washington, had accelerated, Charlie refused to fall behind. "I am keeping busy," he wrote in May 1944 to Mary Paxton Keeley, his one-time fiancée, now a journalist herself, with whom he had corresponded for the prior two decades.[525] In addition to his "Washington Letter" column, he helped produce a major series of new articles, plus he wrote two other series by himself. Early in 1943, he spearheaded the creation of a series of essays entitled "What Are We Fighting For?" These pieces were written by a variety of distinguished individuals such as Stuart Chase, a writer and economist; Harold E. Stassen, former governor of Minnesota; and Robert Moses, New York Parks Commissioner. In total, the collection included twenty independently written essays; Charlie wrote the final, summarizing essay himself. This collection was very popular, and the *Post-Dispatch* was overwhelmed with a legion of requests. They published them as a booklet and distributed 25,000 copies. The collection even received praise from the White House.[526]

Charlie himself wrote a staggering 22-article series entitled "Men and Jobs After the War." Utilizing the in-depth reporting technique and structure he used in "The Country's Plight," he identified and analyzed the measures that would be needed, after the war, to smooth the economic readjustments certain to take place in labor, industry, and business. In addition to that series, soon after the Democratic and Republican conventions in the summer of 1944, he wrote a set of articles entitled "Our Next President." In its four parts, this series dealt with the role of the next President as: (1) Commander-in-Chief of the armed forces, (2) post-war planner, (3) Chief Executive and politician, and (4) leader in charge of international political security.[527]

Charlie had attended every national political convention since 1920, yet he was as surprised as everyone else to see Harry S. Truman win the Democratic nomination for vice president in Chicago in July 1944. President Franklin Roosevelt, ever the crafty politician, decided not to support the inflexible and largely unpopular Henry Wallace as his running mate. Truman's unforeseen nomination startled many attendees who knew little about him. At that time, Roosevelt was only 62, and it was widely assumed he would serve out another four-year term. His serious health problems were a closely guarded secret. To no one's surprise, Roosevelt, in November 1944, was easily re-elected for an unprecedented fourth four-year term. In January 1945, both Roosevelt and Truman took their respective oaths of office. Roosevelt would serve in office for just another eighty-two days.

Truman Takes the Reins

American voters were reassured that the tide of the war in Europe had turned against Germany. The Japanese were also in retreat in the Pacific. These were the primary considerations on election day. Roosevelt's running mate, Senator Truman, remained a relative unknown, but, during the election, he campaigned enthusiastically and made no significant missteps. Only Roosevelt—and his inner circle—knew how tenuous his physical health was. After the election, astute observers could see the circles under his eyes and a noticeable decline in his condition. The public perception continued that the President was receiving excellent medical care and he would continue to carry on. No one cheats death. It came to President Roosevelt on Thursday, April 12, 1945, in Warm Springs, Georgia, where he suddenly died of a cerebral hemorrhage.

Roosevelt's death shocked most Americans, including Vice President Truman. Their relationship had been formal yet cordial. Roosevelt, who played his cards close to his vest, didn't inform his vice president of some extremely important matters, including the Manhattan Project to create the atomic bomb. It wasn't that Roosevelt didn't like or trust Truman. As a rule, Roosevelt preferred to keep his options open and reveal his long-range plans only to a tight inner circle. Truman, like many others who supported Roosevelt, fell outside that circle.

Late in the afternoon on Thursday, April 12, 1945, Truman was summoned to the White House. He was taken immediately to Eleanor Roosevelt, who said to him: "Harry, the President is dead." Truman hurriedly summoned the cabinet members to an impromptu meeting and gave them the news of the President's death. Then, shortly after 7 p.m., he was administered the oath of office by Chief Justice Harlan Stone, following which, Harry S. Truman became the 32nd President of the United States.[528]

The citizens of the United States, as well as the nation's allies were curious—and more than a little nervous—about this unknown man who'd suddenly become the President of the United States. Charlie, as a newsman, knew he was in a unique position based on his long friendship with Truman. He then did what he did best: he wrote a reflective, thoughtful piece about it. His article was published in the *Post-Dispatch* on April 15, 1945. It began with Charlie describing his high-school days with Truman, and then he reviewed Truman's unlikely political journey, about which Charlie concluded:

> ". . . The rise of Harry Truman to the Presidency is one of the amazing phenomena in American political history. Luck—or call it fate—time and again intervened to send him down the right road when another road would have stopped him at a dead end."

The article then described how Charlie thought Truman would perform as President. Charlie wrote:

> "What kind of President will Truman make? The answer is in the lap of the gods. In the writer's personal view,

unfortunate though it is that we must change leaders at this time, the Republic is in no danger from the accession of Harry Truman to the Presidency. He has shown the ability to rise to his responsibilities. He is impeccably honest. He takes advice but can be stubborn when he makes up his mind.

He gets along with people. Perhaps he is too amiable; that remains to be seen. But the ability to work out compromises is an invaluable trait in one charged with the day-to-day business of government. Truman has this ability in high degree . . .

Truman is genuinely a modest man. He came to the Senate, I believe, with a definite inferiority complex. He was a better man than he thought he was. His successes have been such that I doubt whether he feels now a sense of inferiority, but he remains, in the best sense, humble . . . He is a clubbable fellow. He likes to play poker, spin yarns, take an occasional drink. In the Senate, he was popular on both sides of the aisle. He got things done behind the scenes . . .

When Truman became Vice President, it was the most natural thing in the world for Senators of both parties to begin dropping in on him for a chat—or perhaps a sip of bourbon. Many of them observed on these occasions that they had never been in the Vice President's office when Henry Wallace was there. Wallace, to them, was otherworldly. He didn't speak their language; Truman does.

. . . Will Truman measure up? A firm answer cannot yet be given. But this can safely be said: Harry Truman has a lot of stuff—more stuff, I think, than he has generally been credited with. He has been called the average American, but he is better than average. He is no nonentity and no

Harding. He may not have the makings of a great President, but he certainly has the makings of a good President."[529]

Charlie Gets the Call

On April 18, 1945, three days after the *Post-Dispatch* published Charlie's piece about President Truman, Charlie was summoned to meet with Truman at the Blair House, across the street from the White House. Stephen T. Early, who had been Roosevelt's press secretary, had stayed on to help Truman through the initial days of the transition. He knew Truman wanted his own man as press secretary, so he suggested that Truman ask Charlie Ross. Truman replied: "Do you think he'll take it?"[530] Early replied that there is only one way to find out, so Truman requested the meeting.

Charlie arrived at the Blair House, pleasantries were exchanged, and then Truman asked Charlie to become his press secretary. Charlie listened to the request and then politely demurred. He had many serious misgivings. First, he fundamentally believed that the position of press secretary should be held by a politician and not a newspaperman. (In 1931, Charlie had written: "My advice to all Presidents is not to put up a newspaperman to meet the press. Choose a politician.")[531] Second, he thoroughly enjoyed his current job of authoring "think pieces" for the *Post-Dispatch*. Third, the annual salary of the President's press secretary was $10,000, less than one-third of the $35,000 annual salary he was paid by the *Post-Dispatch*—not to mention the bonuses that sometimes appeared from Pulitzer. Fourth, Charlie knew that the press-secretary position came with a lot of administrative and logistical duties. Charlie had learned the hard way from his days at the *Post-Dispatch* in St. Louis that management and administration were not his strengths. After listening to Charlie's reservations, Truman said: "But, Charlie, you aren't the kind of man who can say 'No' to the President of the United States." Truman was persistent, but Charlie remained noncommittal and requested time to think it over. Truman agreed, and the meeting ended.[532]

At home that evening, Charlie discussed the matter with Florence. "This man needs help," he said early on. Charlie knew Florence would be profoundly affected if he took this job. Their income would be slashed, and Charlie knew he'd be working even longer hours. He knew what the job entailed, and he knew he could do it. On the plus side, he knew that serving beside the President, he would witness world events as they unfolded, and "he would have his finger on an exciting piece of history."[533] In addition, he would be serving his country. Due to his life's circumstances, Charlie had never been drafted into the military, nor had he ever served his country by holding a government position. Truman had done so numerous times—and Charlie respected him for it. Now the weight of the U. S. government, then engaged in a global war, had fallen upon Truman, who had asked for his help. These and similar concerns swirled around Charlie's discussion with Florence that evening.

Florence turned out to be generally supportive. Then Charlie did something he rarely did—he prayed for guidance.[534] He wrestled with all the competing arguments that evening and, by the following day, had come to a decision. He would accept the position. After all, how could he turn down the President of the United States, particularly when he was a friend in need of help?

The following day at about 6:15 p.m., Charlie met with Truman and gave him the answer Truman hoped for. But it came with two qualifications. First, Charlie had to win agreement from the *Post-Dispatch's* Joseph Pulitzer, Jr., with whom Charlie had an ongoing business agreement. Truman and Charlie telephoned Pulitzer in

St. Louis, and Truman told Pulitzer that he had "drafted" Charlie for government work. Pulitzer hated the thought of losing Charlie and was immediately opposed to the idea. Truman pressed his case, and Pulitzer finally relented and he agreed to release Charlie to the Truman White House for two years.[535] Second, Charlie would begin working for the White House after he'd returned from the San Francisco Conference, an important step in the creation of the United Nations, and a conference for which Charlie had been preparing. Truman agreed. As a final compromise, Charlie's start-date as press secretary became May 15, 1945.[536] Once those details were agreed to, Charlie formally accepted; Truman was elated. The two men began discussing their childhood, and the conversation drifted to recollections of their favorite English teacher at Independence High School, Miss Matilda "Tillie" Brown.

"Say, won't this be news to Miss Tillie?" Charlie said.[537]

Truman laughed and ordered a long-distance call be made immediately to the retired, yet still spritely, 75-year-old Miss Tillie.

The telephone rang at Ms. Tillie's home; she answered.

"The President of the United States is calling," the speaker in Washington announced.

Truman then got on the phone, identified himself, and told Ms. Tillie: "Charlie has agreed to work with me as my secretary."[538]

Charlie then got on the phone and confirmed the arrangement.

"You and Harry have made good, and I'm proud of you," Miss Tillie told Charlie, bursting with pride.[539]

Harry took the phone back and asked her if she remembered their high-school graduation night when she gave Charlie a hug and a kiss. When she indicated she did, Harry added: "Yes, and the rest of us boys asked why you didn't pass that around."

Miss Tillie immediately responded: "Then you ought to remember that I told you when the rest of you did something worthwhile, you'd get your reward, too." And then she told him how proud she was of them and that the next time they met, she'd give Harry a kiss as well.[540]

It was a touching conversation that showed the respect Charlie and Harry had for their dedicated teachers, particularly Miss Tillie. She understandably was overwhelmed with pride. Fortunately, the outgoing press secretary, Stephen Early, was privy to the call and he immediately predicted that Miss Tillie wouldn't keep this call to herself. Miss Tillie, eager to share the story with others, acted predictably, and the story was quickly taken up by the local *Independence Examiner*. That paper, realizing it had a scoop, offered the story to other papers, including the *Post-Dispatch*. To avoid the perception of favoritism among the news outlets, Truman hurriedly called a news conference the next morning (April 20) at which he announced he had "drafted" Charlie Ross as the secretary in charge of press relations for a period of two years.[541] This innocent episode was an important object lesson for Charlie; he realized that *everything* the President does or says is news.

Keeping to his prior commitment, Charlie attended the United Nations Conference in San Francisco and wrote an uncharacteristically bland piece about it. His report was less than his best, in large part, because he was now Truman's press secretary-in-waiting, and he had to be careful what he said. On May 13, 1945, just before starting at the White House, he wrote a letter to his son John describing his recent experiences:

May 13, 1945
Dear John:

As you can well understand, I have been very busy; hence my long delay in writing.

In the last six weeks or so, it seems to me that I have lived about a year. On April 18 the President asked me to become his secretary in charge of press relations, and the following day, about 6:15 p.m., after much prayerful consideration, I accepted. About four hours later I was on my way to San Francisco to cover the United Nations conference as my last newspaper chore for some time to come. I do not say unqualifiedly my last, as Mr. Pulitzer kindly granted me a leave of absence so that I could accept the White House job without losing my standing in the *Post-Dispatch* pension system, which has just been inaugurated. He said that he hoped I would return to the P-D.

I was in San Francisco nearly two weeks and had a hectic time. I discovered that I had a great many friends that I didn't know I had. Between seeing and dodging people and doing a story a day and two radio broadcasts, I was on the hot foot all day and a good part of the night, each day and night . . .

I got home a week ago tomorrow (Monday). I had hoped for a bit of rest before going into the White House, but things have not panned out quite that way. However, I feel a lot better than I did when I arrived.

I am starting in at the White House tomorrow, but officially I shall not begin my new work until Tuesday [May 15], when I shall be sworn in.

I took the job because the President put it up to me in such a way that I could not in conscience say no. It will mean something of a come-down financially, but I can handle that part of it all right. The job will have plenty of headaches, but there will be many compensations, including that of having a grandstand seat at the greatest show in all the world.

A good part of the time since I got back I have spent in answering letters that poured in on me. I have done about 200 and I think there are about 300 to go. Anne has been very helpful. Some of the letters are from assorted crackpots, but most are genuine expressions of friendship, and all of these I intend to answer.

Charlie [John's infant son] has been and is a great joy to me. He is certainly a fine, lusty boy, and the most cheerful baby I have ever seen. I am also, as you know, extremely fond of his mother.

Your recent letters have been much appreciated. Of course, we are wondering what new assignment, if any, is in store for you now that V-Day has come to Europe.

President Truman has made a fine start. Throughout the country there has been an immense outpouring of good will toward him. Of course, the honeymoon will not last forever.

This is a poor letter, but the best I can do tonight . . .

The best to you, John. Drop in on me at the White House!

Affectionately,
Dad[542]

On May 15, 1945, two days after the above letter was written, Charlie, with Florence at his side, was sworn in by Wiley B. Rutledge, Jr., Associate Justice of the U. S. Supreme Court, using the same Bible Truman had used when he was sworn in a month before. Charlie took the oath, kissed the Bible, and then turned and kissed Florence. His stint as a public servant had begun.[543]

When his newspaper colleagues learned that Charlie had been chosen for press secretary, the reaction proved uniformly positive. The *United States News*, a national magazine at the time, said the following:

Mr. Ross personally. Mr. Ross, very tall, very gaunt and a little stooped, long has been popular with the Washington newspaper corps. The newsmen were virtually unanimous in applauding the appointment. They know him as a hard worker, and an agreeable companion. He is a man of great personal dignity, but no solemnity. He likes good talk and long luncheon sessions with his colleagues at the National Press Club, in which opinions, often barbed and witty, of men and events are exchanged. Like Mr. Truman, he has a Midwestern plainness and lack of ostentation and pompousness. As in schooldays, he still calls the President "Harry."[544]

Charlie Ross being sworn in as Press Secretary. Left to Right: Supreme Court Justice Wiley Rutledge, President Harry S. Truman, Charlie Ross, and Florence Ross. Washington, DC, March 19, 1948.
(Photo/The Associated Press)

Traveling with Truman

Charlie knew travel would be part of the job when he accepted his appointment. He'd traveled extensively throughout his career and generally enjoyed its stimulation as well as the breaks it provided from the routines of daily work. But now, as the President's press secretary, he'd be traveling more than he ever had in the past and nearly as much as the President. Truman often tried to make each trip enjoyable—or at least ensure there were enjoyable moments—and some of these moments benefited Charlie directly.

In June 1945, Charlie traveled with the President to San Francisco for the official signing of the new United Nations Charter, which had been years in the making and was one of Roosevelt's

President Harry S. Truman (left) and Charlie Ross shaking hands and greeting each other warmly while on a presidential trip. Circa 1946. (Photo/Harry S. Truman Library)

deepest wishes. Charlie's niece, Helen Holmquist—daughter of his sister Louise—was then in the Bay Area as a graduate student at Stanford. She had never met her Uncle Charlie. Knowing he would be in town, she contacted him to say "hello." Charlie asked her to meet him at the Fairmont Hotel, where he and the President were staying. When she arrived, she was ushered in. Charlie introduced himself, and after a few pleasantries, he told her "you bear a strong likeness to your mother." He then took her to the President's suite, where Truman was working. As they entered, Charlie said, "Mr. President, one of my relatives is here who I'd like you to meet."

"Charlie, I thought I'd already met all of your relatives," responded the President without missing a beat.

It was a pleasant, but brief, visit. Truman warmly recalled Helen's mother, Louise, from their childhood in Independence. Bess Wallace, now Mrs. Truman, had also been a close childhood friend of Louise Ross. Helen, of course, was thrilled to meet the President and always remembered that special event.[545]

The President showed Charlie an even greater courtesy the following month at the Potsdam Conference in July 1945.

Named after the Berlin suburb where it was convened, the Potsdam Conference (July 17–August 2, 1945) was the first meeting of the heads of the three major allies after the end of the fighting in Europe. Prime Minister Winston Churchill, Soviet Premier Joseph Stalin, and President Harry Truman had agreed to the meeting because their victorious troops were occupying different zones in the territory of defeated Germany. A conference was needed to address the huge question faced by the allies: "What next?"

Before Nazi Germany's defeat, the Allied leaders had met in Tehran and in Yalta, but now that the hostilities in Europe had ceased, they stood jointly in control. Primary issues included how to govern a defeated Germany, the boundaries of Poland, the occupation of Austria, the determination of reparations, as well as the prosecution of the war against Japan.[546] Also, importantly, it would be Truman's initial meeting with Stalin and Churchill.

For Charlie, the conference became his initial test in his new role. For security reasons, the conference, as well as its date and location, were kept confidential. Charlie had only limited room to accommodate members of the press on-board the cruiser *USS Augusta* that was taking the President to the meeting. The three chosen news reporters, who'd agreed to maintain confidentiality, came from the Associated Press, the United Press, and the International News Service—news outlets Charlie knew would cover virtually every daily newspaper and radio station in the country. No other reporters, including those from the leading big city newspapers, were informed. In early July, while the ship was *en route*, news of the upcoming conference somehow leaked to the press, and Charlie's well-intentioned strategy fell apart. As soon as the presidential party arrived in Potsdam, the press met them *en masse*. Those reporters who'd been left behind in Washington protested their exclusion and the perceived favoritism which had been shown to the news services. Eventually the furor receded when a press area was set up within the U. S. compound at Potsdam and daily briefings were held for the reporters. Charlie, however, had learned a harsh lesson about the jealousy and combative nature of his former news colleagues.

The brightest spot for Charlie at Potsdam occurred when his son, John, then serving in the Army Medical Corp in Italy, joined the U. S. delegation. Unknown to Charlie, President Truman had the Army issue temporary orders bringing Captain John Ross on temporary duty to the Potsdam Conference. Charlie, of course, was delighted to see his son. John enjoyed being with his father but felt self-conscious in receiving such special treatment. However, like a good soldier, he obeyed his orders and was happy to have this glimpse—at least for a few days—of world history in the making.[547]

While meetings at Potsdam ground on day after day, the conference itself had a few interesting moments and exchanges. The accommodations were barely adequate due to the devastation in Germany, but everyone understood and adjusted. On his way to Potsdam, the President was informed that Joseph Stalin had recently had a mild heart attack. Even so, the two men met before the conference for a couple of hours, and Truman came away with an overall positive impression ("I can deal with Stalin.").[548] President Truman got along well with both Winston Churchill and Joseph Stalin. Midway through the conference, however, the formal meetings came to a standstill for a couple of days because Churchill had been unexpectedly defeated in Britain's general election. He was immediately replaced by his successor, Clement Attlee. Days later, the President received a top-secret communication informing him of the success of the atomic bomb tests in New Mexico. He took this as an opportunity to tell Stalin that the United States had a powerful new weapon that it intended to use against the Japanese to shorten the war. Stalin's unemotional reaction to hearing this was likely due to the intelligence Soviet spies had already provided him about the bomb. It was one of Truman's objectives for the conference to gain Stalin's reassurance that the Soviet Union would more aggressively join in the war against Japan. Stalin agreed, reaffirming his yet-to-be-fulfilled Yalta promise, to promptly launch an invasion of Japanese-held areas near Russia's borders. After 17 days of the Potsdam Conference, many of the open issues were agreed to, including the establishment of four zones of occupation (among the three major powers, plus France), the setting of Poland's boundaries at the Oder and Neisse rivers, the establishment of a reparations scheme, and the creation of a council of the participants' foreign ministers to address additional matters. For Charlie, the conference highlighted the delicate balancing act he needed to walk to do his job for the President while also keeping the trust and confidence of his former press colleagues.

The Atomic Bomb

Charlie Ross, like Harry Truman, didn't believe it was right for a person to make a profit from his public service. Charlie, out of loyalty to the President, left few notes about any of their conversations. Certainly, they talked long and hard about the atomic bomb. Charlie was a trusted adviser. In addition, it was critical that the press's reaction to the bomb was positive. It was commonly held that Charlie was told of the bomb not long after Truman himself learned of it.

This perception of Charlie's ties to the President was so strong that when Metro-Goldwyn-Meyer (MGM) was planning to make a movie about the use of the atomic bomb, it created a script containing a fictional conversation between Charlie and the President. To ensure the script had at least some credibility, MGM sent a copy to the White House for review. Charlie read and vetoed at least one draft of the script stating that "it gave the impression that he [Truman] made a snap decision to use the bomb . . . [Rather the] decision [to use the atomic bomb] was taken only after the most prayerful consideration and upon the advice of all his leading military advisers."[549] Eventually, both Charlie and the President approved MGM's use of a fictional conversation between them, and this made-up dialogue became part of the movie entitled *The Beginning or the End?* The film was released in 1947.[550] This accommodation to MGM is strong evidence that Charlie and Harry discussed it—and most likely more than once and at some length.

The first atomic bomb was detonated over Hiroshima on August 6, 1945, while Charlie and the Presidential party were returning from Potsdam on-board the *USS Augusta*. After Japan failed to demonstrate any inclination to surrender, the second atomic bomb was detonated three days later over Nagasaki. Less than a week after that explosion, on August 15, 1945, Japan surrendered. The documents memorializing the terms of the surrender were signed aboard the battleship *USS Missouri* in Tokyo Bay on September 2, 1945.

Like all Americans, Charlie and Florence were elated the war was finally over. Their two sons had both served, but neither had seen combat. The family, unlike many American families, was unscathed and the boys were coming home. Walter decided not to return to journalism. Instead, he dove into a career in aviation using his Navy flying experience. Moving quickly, he formed a company called Ross Airplane Corporation, acquired land within the limits of the City of St. Louis, and had arranged to be the exclusive dealer and service center for Culver aircraft, a new company that built private airplanes.[551] After his tour in Italy, John was transferred to Walter Reed Hospital in Washington, where he continued working in his specialty, hematology, performing tests and discovering additional uses for the life-saving properties of blood.

Settling into His White House Role

As a news reporter, Charlie had scant administrative experience, and he knew from his St. Louis days that he was temperamentally ill-suited for this type of work. Harry Truman, by contrast, had worked for large organizations (e.g., a railroad and a bank). During World War I, he had joined the U. S. Army and was trained and served as an officer. His Army experience had a strong influence on his leadership skills. Truman started his meetings on time, valued conciseness and efficiency, realized the value of setting and meeting objectives, and believed that those working in government should honor its chain of command. Their markedly different styles complemented one another and, in the long run, helped both Harry and Charlie.

President Harry Truman was also vastly different from Roosevelt. President Roosevelt, as an extension of his larger-than-life personality and extraordinary communication skills, enjoyed holding press conferences. President Truman viewed press conferences as only a necessary (but unpleasant) way to inform the press. In this regard, the two chief executives proved dramatically different. The initial effect of this change for the White House press has been outlined by a veteran journalist as follows:

> "Truman had received good marks from the press in his debut. Copies of his first presidential address to Congress were ready almost an hour before delivery, instead of a few minutes before as issued under FDR. His first press conference drew a record of 348 correspondents, and Truman opened it precisely on time. He replaced Roosevelt's gadget-bedecked desk with a simpler one topped only with a few papers and some writing materials. He announced that he would hold press conferences once a week, instead of twice a week, as FDR did, and they would not be on fixed days. He would call them when there was news and would notify the correspondents sufficiently in advance. Not everyone was most likely pleased, but many reporters found the blunt-speaking chief executive a welcome change from his wily predecessor. There was, one said, 'no double talk.'"[552]

When Charlie reported to the White House as Truman's press secretary, he inherited Myrtle Bergheim as his administrative assistant. Born in April 1912 in rural South Dakota, she had graduated from Howard High School in Howard, South Dakota, in 1930 and eventually made her way to Washington, DC, where she found work at the Veterans Administration. In 1940 she began performing clerical and administrative duties in the White House press room under Stephen Early, Roosevelt's secretary for press relations.

Following the death of President Roosevelt, Ms. Bergheim stayed on in the press-relations office. When Charlie reported to the White House, she became his primary administrative support. Prim and neat in her appearance, she soon developed an excellent working relationship with Charlie. Both native Midwesterners, Myrtle Bergheim and Charlie appreciated each other's high standards, understood their respective roles, and communicated easily, often with a touch of light humor. She kept the office running smoothly and, when needed, acted as a buffer between Charlie and the hounding of White House reporters. They worked closely together, and their solid relationship lasted for Charlie's entire tenure as press secretary.[553]

Florence as Wife of the Press Secretary

Charlie's appointment as the presidential press secretary put him and Florence in the spotlight. On July 28, 1946, a cameo piece about Florence appeared in the Sunday edition of the *Washington Post* in a column entitled "Women of Washington" written by Bessie Hackett. A formal, flattering photograph of Florence appeared above the article, which began by highlighting Florence's gardening prowess. It began: "If Mrs. Charles G. Ross, wife of President Truman's press secretary, isn't digging in the grounds of their

Kensington home, she's probably curled up with a book about gardening. For, in a town overflowing with gardeners, few are more ardent than energetic, tanned Florence Ross—and few have become greater authorities."

Studio portrait of Florence Griffin Ross, wife of
Press Secretary Charlie Ross. Washington, DC, circa 1948.
(Photo/Harris & Ewing and Harry S. Truman Library)

This article about Florence mentions their victory garden during the war, and her love of gardening. ("I like everything that pertains to gardening—except pushing a lawn mower. . . . That's where I draw the line."). It also highlights some of her home's notable features (a "four-foot-deep water-lily pond" and "the coolest porch in Washington") as well as some of Florence's personal characteristics ("Natural and frank spoken, Mrs. Ross is a friendly person and easy to know. She shuns frills and furbelows and wears 'comfortable' clothes that match her personality.") Further, it gives background on her two sons, their military service, and her two-year-old grandson. "Superseding even the garden as 'the joy of our life' for Mr. and Mrs. Ross is John's little son—blond, blue-eyed Charles Griffith Ross 2nd." The article goes on to say that she and her husband "like the theatre and good music, scarcely ever miss a concert or play—that is, if they can help it." It quotes Florence as lamenting: "But now . . . well . . . my husband gets home later than ever before. We never can count on getting anywhere by 8 o'clock." The author concludes: "And newspapermen's wives the world over heave a sympathy sigh."[554]

About the same time Florence was featured in the *Washington Post* column, her son, Walter, and his wife, Lucianna, adopted two infant girls, whom they named Helen and Lucy. (Lucianna had previously miscarried, and her doctors told her it was unlikely she and Walter would ever be able to have children.) So, Charlie and Florence again became proud grandparents. Because Walter's family was living in St. Louis, Charlie made it a point to see his youngest son and family when his travel schedule allowed. On November 7, 1946, the Presidential party, traveling by train, stopped in St. Louis, where Charlie (and the President) had their picture taken with Charlie's "twin" granddaughters, Helen and Lucy Ross. A photograph of that event was taken showing the President smiling while holding the hand of baby Helen while Charlie, cradling both children, grinned and gazed fondly upon her sister, Lucy.

Charlie's Special Influence

By 1946, President Truman realized that a severe famine loomed, particularly in those war-torn countries previously occupied by the Nazis. A similar scenario could easily play out in many of the Asian countries formerly occupied by the Japanese. Truman needed someone with special expertise and skills to help avoid these disasters. He reached out to former President Herbert Hoover, whom he had never met. Hoover had been out of government—and had become a political pariah to both parties—since he had lost the election to Roosevelt in 1932.

President Truman knew that Hoover had an engineering degree from Stanford, that he knew his way around the government as a former Secretary of Commerce and U. S. President, and that he had been heavily involved in the economic-recovery efforts in Europe following World War I. It made sense to Truman that Hoover was the right man for the job. Truman and Hoover met, and Truman asked him if he'd be willing to help. Cautiously, Hoover agreed, but first suggested that he draft a series of memoranda outlining the situation as he saw it with his ideas of what should be done. Hoover soon drafted the promised reports. However, rather than send them to the White House through normal channels, he gave them to someone in the administration he trusted: Charlie Ross. Hoover had known Charlie since his presidential days when Charlie was covering the White House for the *Post-Dispatch*. The package of memoranda came directly to Charlie from Hoover with the following note: "I am sending it to you as I do not know how many hands these things go through under the present mechanism."[555] Hoover realized, as did many others, that Charlie was a trustworthy person who held a special place among Truman's top advisers.

Charlie's family sometimes used him to get the President's attention. For example, in May of 1945, the same month that Charlie began working at the White House, Helen Ross wrote Charlie on Chicago Institute of Psychoanalysis letterhead, asking him not directly for a "favor" but rather giving him a nudge, probably prompted by a mutual friend and noted surgeon, Dr. Evarts Graham. The pertinent part of that letter read:

> "I am not going to bother you with something every day, but here is something very important, concerning which your friend, Evarts Graham, is coming to see you soon, I happen to know.
>
> "In a nutshell the situation is this: In the past year, there have been virtually no new students in the pre-medical work in the entire country because of the Selective Service Act.
>
> "This means that we shall be behind almost a year's quota of doctors in the country four or five years from now, a serious state of affairs.
>
> "Of course, the Army and Navy are loath to defer healthy young men for any other pursuit, but a shortage of doctors will be a grave matter, especially in the next few years."

Louise, a few years later, had a more mundane request, one prompted by a "Colonel Rutherford," whom she apparently knew. The request and Charlie's response to it are summed up in the following paragraph, taken from the letter written on White House stationery by Charlie to Louise, dated July 8, 1948. It read:

> "Colonel Rutherford came in. He had four requests: (1) that the President sign his certificate of membership in the Shriners; (2) that I get him an autographed picture

of the President; (3) that I arrange for him to have his throat examined at Walter Reed Hospital; (4) that I arrange for him to meet the President. I will get his document signed. I think I will skip No. 2 and No. 4. I have arranged for Dr. Wallace Graham, the President's physician, to look at his throat—this despite the fact that his WHO'S WHO sketch, which you sent me, describes him as a Christian Scientist."

Charlie soon learned that requests like these came with the job—and sometimes through family members who had been approached by others. Although Charlie couldn't help pointing out the irony in Colonel Rutherford's requests, he always treated such inquiries judiciously, knowing that exercising a delicate diplomacy came with his White House territory.

Charlie appreciated and remained sensitive to the dignity of the Office of the President. In the presence of others, particularly in meetings, Charlie called Truman "Mr. President." In private social gatherings, such as those with close family members, he addressed Truman as "Harry."

Another episode involved the presidential aircraft. President Truman inherited his predecessor's official airplane when he took office. This outdated plane had been customized to accommodate wheelchair-bound President Roosevelt. Irreverent journalists had dubbed it the Sacred Cow. In 1947, it was replaced by a more-advanced DC-6 airliner, and Charlie breathed a sigh of relief. Charlie encouraged Harry to give the plane a more dignified name, and they agreed on *Independence*.[556]

Charlie's role included listening to and advising President Truman. Organizationally, Charlie reported to Truman, yet they were also friends who liked and respected one another. According to Ken Hechler, an aide who worked in the White House, typically when President Truman wanted to speak with someone who reported to him, such as the Secretary of Agriculture, that person was summoned to the Oval Office for the meeting. However, with Charlie, whose office was near the Oval Office, it was different—when Truman wanted to meet with Charlie, he went to Charlie's office. This accommodation, as seen by Mr. Hechler, was due to Truman's respect for Charlie as well as their long-time friendship.[557]

As soon as he learned of President Roosevelt's death, Truman immediately asked the Cabinet members to remain in place and carry on their duties. Predictably over the next few months, several Cabinet members departed, including Francis Biddle as Attorney General, Henry Morgenthau as the Treasury Secretary, and Frances Perkins as Secretary of Labor. The reasons for their leaving varied, but each was soon replaced, e.g., Tom C. Clark as Attorney General, Frederick Moore as the Treasury Secretary, and Lewis Schwellenbach as Secretary of Labor. Truman wanted and needed experienced help in one key position: Secretary of State. So, on July 3, 1945, he appointed James Byrnes to replace the retiring Edward Stettinius. Truman also retained the services of Roosevelt's Secretary of Commerce, Henry Wallace, who'd formerly served under Roosevelt as the Secretary of Agriculture and later as his Vice President. Both Byrnes and Wallace possessed invaluable experience working in the federal government.

As mentioned earlier, Roosevelt dropped the loyal Wallace from his ticket in 1944 and chose Harry Truman as the vice-presidential candidate. As an accommodation to Wallace, Roosevelt appointed him to the office of Secretary of Commerce in 1945, and he then became part of Truman's administration. Henry Wallace had markedly different views from Truman on how to deal with the Soviets. The get-tough approach of the Truman administration collided with Wallace's preference for a more conciliatory approach. Not content to keep his views to himself, Wallace drafted a lengthy speech outlining his views about the Soviets. He was scheduled to give it to a large left-wing audience at Madison Square Garden in September 1946. Just before giving this speech, he met with Truman and showed him a copy. Truman thumbed through the long docu-

President Truman with his White House Staff. Top row, Appointments Secretary Matthew J. Connelly, President Harry S. Truman, White House Counsel Samuel Rosenman. Bottom row: Press Secretary Charles Ross, naval aide Captain James Vardaman, and military aide General Harry Vaughan. Washington, DC, October, 1945.
(Photo/Hessler Studio, Harry S. Truman Library)

ment but didn't comprehend that it contradicted his current policy; Wallace orally assured him it did not. Wallace gave a copy to the press before speaking to the large New York audience—and even stated that Truman himself had read and approved it. Predictably, an uproar ensued. Secretary of State Byrnes, whose domain was foreign affairs, threatened to resign. The press and public were confused by the seeming about-face. Charlie immediately commenced damage control, which itself became a fiasco. As a result, Truman terminated Wallace from his cabinet position. However, a rift developed between Truman and Byrnes, and Truman suffered personal embarrassment (as did Charlie for his failed damage-control efforts). The prestige and popularity of the Truman administration plummeted.[558]

This embarrassing episode had serious repercussions, as the Democrats lost seats in Congress, and James Byrnes soured on working under Truman. However, the get-tough policy remained intact. This episode was a bitter learning experience for both Truman and Charlie, however, their working relationship remained unshaken and positive.

The relationship between Byrnes and Truman began to slide. Truman and Byrnes had become friends when they served together in the Senate. However, as a member of Truman's cabinet, Byrnes began (perhaps from a belief that he was more talented or qualified than Truman) to side-step informing Truman of his actions. In addition, he began to develop a more conciliatory approach toward the Soviets than Truman wanted. In any event, on January 21, 1947, he resigned as Secretary of State. Truman immediately accepted Byrnes' resignation and appointed the popular and talented war hero, General George C. Marshall, as the new Secretary of State.

The relationship between Truman and Byrnes continued to deteriorate even after Byrnes left office. In January 1950, Truman wrote that a "four-picture cartoon [had been published] in the *Evening Star*" showing Byrnes "as a much-mistreated man and a martyr to my very selfish treatment of him!" He wrote these words in a handwritten letter dated January 22, 1950, on White House letterhead to Charlie Ross. In this eight-page letter that begins "Dear Charlie," Truman recounted his view on the history between him and Byrnes, who, in conjunction with "Old (Bernard) Baruch was now attempting to discredit him (Truman)." This personal letter to Charlie was Truman's way of venting. He knew that by giving this letter only to Charlie, his thoughts—written in haste and fueled by emotion—wouldn't get him into undue

President Harry S. Truman (right) and Charlie Ross, viewing the activities at the Democratic National Convention via television in the Chief Executive's office. Washington, DC, July 13, 1948. (Photo/Harris & Ewing and Harry S. Truman Library)

trouble.⁵⁵⁹ Charlie, his trusted friend, became his filter when he needed to vent. Charlie would calm Truman down and then suggest a more constructive way to deal with the issue. This was a great asset for the emotional Truman, who realized that one misstep could result in disaster.*

19

THE FRIEND OF MY YOUTH IS GONE

1948

By almost any measure, 1948 was a watershed year for the Truman Administration. The Cold War stalemate in Europe intensified in February when the Soviets began jamming the *Voice of America* broadcasts. Two months later, Truman signed the Marshall Plan legislation, authorizing $15 billion in aid for the war-torn European countries to help them recover economically from the devastation of World War II. Two months after that, in June, the Soviets blocked the roads into Berlin to prevent the US and its allies from trucking food, medicine, and other vital goods and supplies into Berlin. In response, the U.S. and Great Britain immediately began airlifting those critical supplies into Berlin. Thus began the famous Berlin Airlift.

In May 1948, the U.S., despite resistance from Arab countries, recognized the new, independent nation of Israel, thus legitimizing its existence (and credibility) within the international community.

From June 21 to June 25, the Republican Party held its National Convention in Philadelphia, where Governor Thomas Dewey won the party's Presidential nomination. Then, from July 12 to July 14, in that same city, the Democratic Party held its National Convention, and its delegates elected Harry Truman as its candidate to continue as President. However, the Democratic Convention was disrupted by the walkout of the delegations from mostly southern states in protest of the party's (as well as Truman's) Civil Rights initiatives. This splinter group, known as the "Dixiecrats," held its own political convention a few days later in Birmingham, Alabama, where they nominated Governor Strom Thurmond of South Carolina as their Presidential candidate.

On July 26th, shortly after the Democratic National Convention had adjourned, Truman signed an Executive Order ending racial segregation in the military. Over the next three-plus months, the Presidential-election campaign consumed much of Truman's time—and Charlie Ross' as well.

Aboard the *Ferdinand Magellan* in June 1948

Following the Democratic Convention, the consensus among political commentators was that Truman's reelection prospects were decidedly bleak. The headwinds against him were fierce. The Dixiecrats had walked out and set up their own party, which promised to take important votes from the traditionally Democratic-leaning southern states. At the same time, Henry Wallace broke off from the Democratic Party and set up a new liberal party, the Progressive Party, which would potentially draw the support of liberal Democratic voters. The Republican Party, which controlled both houses of Congress, had nominated experienced and well-financed candidates in Governor Thomas E. Dewey and his running mate, Governor Earl Warren from California. It was no wonder the political soothsayers thought little of Truman's chances for reelection. However, the feisty Truman, who believed in the actions he'd taken as President and who, more importantly, believed in himself, refused to bow to the opinion of others.

In June, the month prior to the Democratic National Convention, Truman boarded the oversized Presidential railroad car—the *Ferdinand Magellan*—and headed west to speak at the commencement ceremony for the University of California at Berkeley. The *Ferdinand Magellan* had many stately comforts, including an oak-paneled living room, a first-class dining area, and five bedrooms with private baths. The other 16 cars on the train transported the 125 persons who traveled with the Presidential party, almost half of whom were reporters.[560] Originally built in 1928 by the Pullman Company, it had been appropriated by the government in 1942 for use by President Roosevelt. It weighed a hefty 142 tons and, with its added side armor and bulletproof windows, replicated a rolling fortress.[561]

Two months prior, in April 1948, Truman had accepted the invitation to speak at the University of California's graduation ceremony, and, much to the consternation of the Republicans, classified this cross-country trip as official Presidential business, which was funded as a government expense.[562] However, given the mode of transportation, the length of the trip, and the train's many stops, it was fairly transparent that this served as a test-run for the political campaigning that would take place once he was nominated at the Democratic Convention.

Charlie, as usual, traveled with the President. He also viewed this trip as an opportunity to visit three of his sisters. The trip had been tightly scheduled, and they left Washington on the evening of June 3rd. They would be gone two weeks. The initial stop was in Crestline, Ohio, a small town in the northern part of the state, and then it stopped twice at towns in Indiana. At all three stops, Truman spoke to local audiences of modest size about various topics, including foreign relations, the high cost of living, and the Republican Party's indifference to the common man.[563] The fourth stop was in Chicago, where Truman was to give a nationally broadcast speech in Chicago Stadium to the Swedish Pioneer Centennial Association. Charlie arranged a visit with his sisters, Sis and Helen, when the train stopped in Chicago. The following letter, dated May 28, 1948, was sent by Charlie to Sis:

Dear Sis:

Thanks for your note of the twenty-sixth. I shall look forward to seeing both you and Helen.

Our train is due to arrive at Union Station in Chicago at 4:50 p.m., Central Daylight Time, on Friday, June fourth. We shall drive direct to the Palmer House and remain there during the afternoon and evening. The President will leave the hotel at 8:50 p.m. and drive to the Chicago Stadium, where he is scheduled to begin speaking at 9:00 p.m.

Immediately after the address, we shall drive to the Chicago Northwestern Station and reboard the train.

I should very much like to see you and Helen and can do so if you will come to the Palmer House after our arrival there.

Please tell Helen that this supersedes my note to her about calling you up. Bess and Margaret will not be with us in Chicago. They are joining the train at Omaha on Sunday, June sixth.

With much love, as always,
[Handwritten signature]

P.S. Lest you may not have heard, this will tell you that John's and Anne's third baby was born about noon on Monday, the twenty-fourth. He weighed about seven pounds. He is a fine, well-formed boy, and both John and Anne are getting along splendidly. He is being named John Bruce Ross, Jr.[564]

[Author's note: Charlie's P.S. above caught my eye because it tells of my own birth.]

After the Chicago visit, the Presidential party boarded the train and headed west as scheduled. It arrived on June 12 in the San Francisco Bay Area, where Truman gave the commencement address at the University of California at Berkeley. In a lengthy, heartfelt speech, he reflected on the role of the U. S. in winning the war. He also focused on the importance of keeping the current global peace and outlined the recent actions taken by the Soviet Union that undermined that peace. After leaving the Bay Area, the Presidential train wended its way south, eventually traveling through Arizona on its way east. Charlie used the train's schedule to work in a visit with Louise.

Although they kept in communication through the years, mostly via letters, Louise had settled in far-off Arizona and rarely saw any of the family. Charlie was anxious see her, as was Bess Truman, who was now aboard the Presidential train. Eventually a plan took shape, which is reflected in the following telegram (reproduced verbatim below) sent by Charlie to Louise from the Presidential train as it passed through Wyoming in early June:

IN ALL PROBABILITY WE WILL COME THRU WINSLOW JUNE 15 MRS TRUMAN JOINS ME IN INVITATION TO YOU TO COME ON BOARD TRAIN AT WHAT EVER POINT IS CONVENIENT

TO YOU. SHE HOPES YOU WILL BRING FANNIE LOU MCCOY FINCH WITH YOU. WIRE OR WRITE ME YOUR PLANS CARE OF THE PRESIDENTS PARTY FAIRMONT HOTEL SAN FRANCISCO WHEN WE REACH ON JUNE 12=. CHARLIE[565]

Fannie Lou Finch was a childhood friend of both Bess and Louise. She had followed Louise to Arizona and moved from Independence to Phoenix decades earlier. She taught school in Phoenix, married L.R. Finch, and, with her husband, had become Arizonans.

Six days after the initial telegraph, Charlie sent a final one to Louise that updated the terms of their proposed meeting. It read as follows:

WE ARRIVE ASHFORK 7:20 A.M. TUESDAY. JUNE FIFTEENTH. BOARD TRAIN THERE WITH FANNIE LOU TO RIDE TO WINSLOW. ARRIVE THERE 10:55 A.M. BRING THIS TELEGRAM WITH YOU FOR IDENTIFICATION. LOVE= CHARLIE[566]

The Arizonans did their part to meet the Presidential train. Louise and her husband, Fritz, and their son, Lars, drove the 140 miles north from Phoenix to Ash Fork, Arizona, as did Fannie Lou (McCoy) Finch and her husband. They all met the train at the platform in Ash Fork at 7:20 a.m. Louise and Fannie Lou then boarded the Presidential train for the 110-mile trip to Winslow. This gave the old friends more than three hours to get reacquainted and catch up. The train stopped on schedule in Winslow, where the Arizonans disembarked; their husbands and Lars Holmquist were there at the platform, waiting for them.[567]

A smiling Louise introduced Fritz to President Truman, and then added:

"'Harry,' she said, 'I'll have to tell you there is a skeleton in the closet—my husband is a Republican.'"

President Truman naturally reacted with good humor, and later made sure both Louise and Fritz were invited to his Inauguration in Washington the following January.[568] After this warm and memorable visit, the Presidential train headed east, and the Arizonans drove 135 miles south to their homes in Phoenix.

The Whistle-Stop Tour

Truman's 1948 Presidential campaign has become one of the most iconic episodes in U. S. political history. Following the divisive Democratic National Convention, the election prognosticators almost universally predicted Truman would lose the election—and likely by a wide margin. But the determined Truman wanted to take his campaign to the voters, so he again requisitioned the *Ferdinand Magellan* and, as on his June trip to California, set out on a long journey that took him across a wide swath of the country. The Truman campaign train frequently stopped at small towns and cities along the way where he gave speeches from the *Magellan's* rear platform, mingled among the people, and shook as many hands as time allowed. The aggregate numbers from this campaigning-by-rail reflect its breadth. It lasted for just under two months—from Labor Day until the day prior to Election Day—and consisted of three different segments: a fifteen-day, cross-country leg to California; then a six-day jaunt to the Middle West; lastly, a ten-day swing through the heavily populated Northeast, and finally with a return trip to Truman's home in Missouri.[569] Along the way, Truman gave 275 speeches—in addition to the 76 he gave in June on his "non-political" west-coast trip. The results of the election startled most observers—and pundits—as Truman not only won the popular vote (49.5% to Dewey's 44.5%) but also the electoral votes (303 to Dewey's 189).

Charlie, one of Truman's primary advisers, traveled on-board the *Ferdinand Magellan* for the entire Whistle-Stop Tour. Not long after it was over and the results were in, Charlie did what he did best—he wrote an insightful piece about it. *Collier's*, a popular weekly magazine at that time, agreed to pay him for writing an article about the campaign. Charlie was agreeable, but prior to its publication, he had to get Truman's approval. Charlie believed it would be unethical to do otherwise. Truman reviewed Charlie's draft of the proposed article and readily agreed to it because it was fact-based and complimentary of Truman. He also knew that Charlie had taken a substantial reduction in pay to serve as his Press Secretary, and his fee for writing this article would help Charlie financially.[570]

"How Truman Did It"

The article Charlie wrote about the campaign, entitled "How Truman Did It," was published in the December 25, 1948 issue of *Collier's* and ran some 4,000 words. It featured, at the top of its first page, a photograph of Truman and Charlie each wearing a suit and tie and smiling a broad "victory smile." Below that picture, the following headline grabs the reader's attention:

> **The Presidential secretary analyzes the campaign. He had read all the reasons for Truman's surprising victory—as written by "experts." He scoffs. There was only one reason—Truman.**

Charlie's article starts with his seeing Truman in the early morning following Election Day—"fresh as a daisy and grinning broadly"—shortly after he learned of his victory. After those introductory paragraphs, Charlie sets the limits of the article "I intend to write here only about that part of the campaign which I personally saw—the President's part, and that of staff who traveled with him." Then the article hearkens back to the campaign's beginning, in mid-July after the nomination. Charlie writes that, in a regular 9:00 a.m. meeting of the White House staff, the President announced his intentions decisively:

> "We are going to win. I expect to travel all over the country and talk at every whistle stop. We are going to be on the road most of the time from Labor Day to the end of the campaign. It's going to be tough on everybody, but that's the way it's got to be. I know I can take it. I'm only afraid that I'll kill some of my staff—and I like you all very much and don't want to do that."

After this direct quote from the President, the article adds Charlie's assessment: "I don't believe it stretches the truth to say that the election was won then and there." He comments further: "If ever he [Truman] had any doubts about winning, he kept them to himself. He inspired us all to believe that he would win."

The remainder of the article is divided into five parts; some of the highlights are below:

THE PLANNING WASN'T EASY

The President alone planned the three legs of the trip. He wanted to campaign in the deep South as well, but a shortage of time and money prevented that. The trip's "schedules were being revised . . . [constantly and sometimes] . . . they were changed en route."

A PAIR OF FINE TROUPERS

Mrs. Truman and Margaret helped greatly and "were fine troupers" who, when "people saw them on the campaign trip, sensed the deep affection which binds them together, and liked it."

The President, who "writes good straight-away English" made the final decisions in drafting his speeches, which dealt with "issues in a down-to-earth way . . . in the words the President would naturally use."

FANCY WRITING NOT WANTED

Professional speechwriters weren't welcome, because the President himself could do a better job of expressing his ideas. Charlie editorially added: "I think the result was not bad." Also, the President often spoke "completely off-the-cuff."

Some speeches proved difficult to properly word, such as the one about the atomic bomb, but the President continuously found ways to make them work—and work well.

TOO LITTLE TRUMAN IN SPEECH

The President's final speech, scheduled to be delivered live on the radio the day before the election, had undergone four drafts, but was still considered "terrible" by his advisers and needed to be rewritten. So, Truman, just hours before its delivery, worked on it alone for one hour; it was then quickly edited by his advisers and delivered by Truman. Charlie's assessment: "To my mind, it was one of the best speeches the President made in the campaign, both in content and delivery. A little hoarseness in his voice didn't hurt. It gave his voice a heavier quality on the air."

A MAN OF AMAZING ENERGY

Charlie marveled at "the President's vitality." Even "after four-or five-hours' sleep—he rarely got more—he would again be vigorous and high spirited." Charlie humorously surmised: "He has the bounce of a rubber ball." The article noted two additional characteristics of the President: he "never failed in promptness" and "he drove himself unmercifully."

In concluding the article, Charlie gives two possible reasons that Truman launched his whistle-stop campaign. First: "The President made this kind of campaign because he was convinced that a Democratic victory was essential to the welfare of this country and of the world." The second reason is contained in the article's closing paragraph, which reads:

> "Finally, there was a purely personal motive behind his hard campaigning. He had been belittled and vilified. He had been described as a little man, fumbling, inept, not measuring up to the Presidential job. He had the human desire to prove his detractors wrong. He succeeded and, I think, he will continue to succeed in the years ahead."[571]

A Joyful Inauguration

Truman's second inauguration—the first occurred on April 12, 1945, in the Cabinet Room of the White House as the result of President Roosevelt's death—took place on Thursday, January 20,

1949; it was held on the East Portico of the U.S. Capitol building. The oath of office was administered by Supreme Court Chief Justice Fred Vinson, after which the President gave the inaugural address and then departed with the parade down Pennsylvania Avenue. As Truman wanted, it was a grand affair that, for the first time ever, was broadcast on television. He even gave the Federal employees a holiday so they could watch the proceedings.

President Truman made sure his family and friends had the opportunity to attend this historic event. He ensured that Charlie's family, including his sisters, received invitations. Of his six sisters, only the three who were married—Frances, Virginia, and Louise— were able to attend. Florence, John, and Anne also attended. They also received invitations to a host of parties and receptions held before and after the inauguration ceremony.

Louise's Impressions of the Inaugural Events

Fritz Holmquist—the "closet" Republican—didn't attend, but that didn't keep his wife, Louise, from going to Washington, enjoying the inauguration, and seeing her siblings and many old friends. In a series of letters written to her Arizona family, she reflected on the inaugural events. Her sister Virginia, who also attended many events, described Louise as "the somewhat dazed, and delightfully unsophisticated party-goer." In any event, Louise reported the following in her letters home about her whirlwind days at the inauguration.

Arriving by train at 9:00 a.m. on Monday, January 17th, Louise was met at the station by Florence in a White House car (with driver) and taken to Virginia's home in Washington for breakfast. Recovering from her long train ride, she spent that night at

Charlie's and Florence's home, where she stayed for the following three nights.

The following day (Tuesday) Florence again requisitioned a White House vehicle and driver and took Louise sightseeing to Mt. Vernon and then into Washington, where they viewed "most of the wonderful sights around the city." That evening she went with Charlie—Florence was unable to attend—to the Mayflower Hotel to a large dinner party given by the National Truman-Barkley Club. Before the dinner began, she and Charlie were ushered into a private room, which Louise described as "the Holy of Holies . . . a room reserved for the most high," where Bess and Margaret Truman, Mary Jane Truman, and "the Wallace men [Bess's relatives] and the wives" greeted them. Louise received celebrity treatment. ("Bess came to meet me and introduced me around. Margaret came, too, and expressed her pleasure that I was there. I met lots of old Independence friends. Some men in uniform came up and gave me an orchid . . .") After the reception, Louise and Charlie were directed to "a huge banquet room" where they sat at a table with some of the notable dignitaries in the administration, including the U. S. Solicitor General (Philip Perlman), the Secretary of the Navy (James Forrestal), the Secretary of the Air Force (Stuart Symington), the Presidential adviser (Matthew Connelly), and their wives. Louise reported: "Everyone was happy, and a feeling of good will was everywhere." After dinner, Louise and Charlie were invited to a small party at the Georgetown home of the incoming Secretary of State, Dean Acheson, where the "favored few" (Acheson, Clark Clifford, James Forrestal, and their wives) all enjoyed a "wonderful" time.[572]

The following day (Wednesday) she returned to Virginia's home for a visit, which included Frances Ross Leake and her husband,

Lowell, who had come in from New York. That evening she attended a "Gala" with Charlie and Florence where they saw entertainment from their seats in the Presidential balcony.

Inauguration Day (Thursday), as Louise experienced it, was explained in a letter she sent to her children about a month later, on March 4, 1949. She wrote:

> "Of course, Thursday was the big day. The big [White House] car came for us at 10:15 that morning. In this car were Charlie and Florence—Frances and Lowell—Anne Ross and I and Virginia and Carl. Later V[irginia] & C[arl] got in another car with some admiral and his wife. First, we went to Charlie's office and parked right in front of the White House. From there we had a police escort to the inaugural ceremony, which took place at noon on the Capitol Grounds. Then we were again escorted to the reviewing stand in front of the White House for the Inaugural Parade. It was a wonderful parade. Lasted over three hours. I am sure you've seen the pictures. From here, we went to the Presidential Reception at the National Gallery of Art. Again we were taken in ahead of a huge crowd and got in just before the President and Bess—Vice President Barkley and his daughter stopped the handshaking. It was here the President greeted me so informally and introduced me to Vice President Barkley saying—'This girl came all the way from Arizona to the celebration.' Barkley was so sweet. This is where he held my hand and expressed his appreciation. After the reception we rushed home and dressed for the ball. It was a beautiful affair."[573]

The following day (Friday) Louise reports that everyone was tired ("about dead") from the inauguration ceremonies and parties of the previous day; however "we kept going." That evening she attended a party for people from Independence, where she clearly enjoyed herself. ("This is where they will tell you your Mother had too much to drink. Believe it or not.")

The following day (Saturday) was another full day spent visiting and sightseeing. On Sunday "Virginia and Carl had a cocktail party for me" and the evening was concluded by a farewell supper at Virginia's." On Monday, Louise and Frances traveled to New York, where Frances and Lowell Leake reside.

By any measure, Louise had a full and memorable week. In her words: "I had a most wonderful trip and will have food for thought for many years."[574]

1949

Following Truman's frenetic Whistle-Stop Tour and the grueling Presidential Election of 1948, things returned a bit to "normal" for Charlie and the Truman administration in 1949. On the domestic front, Truman's push in early January for Congress to enact New Deal legislation—a broad program, where all Americans would receive health insurance, the minimum wage would be increased, and equal rights would be further guaranteed—was initially met with a tepid response by Congress.

By contrast, notable success was achieved in foreign affairs. In April, a dozen nations signed the treaty establishing the North Atlantic Treaty Organization (NATO), ensuring that its member countries would safeguard each other both politically and militarily. This treaty, as well as the permanent organization it spawned, united its member countries against the threat of aggression by the Soviet Union in the aftermath of World War II. The following month, the Soviet Union lifted the Berlin blockade and acknowledged the success of Truman's Berlin Airlift. The threat of Soviet influence remained, however, as the second Red Scare—the threat that subversive Communists, backed by the Soviet Union, were infiltrating the Federal government—was gaining momentum. Then, in September, Truman announced to the American people that the Soviet Union had exploded an atomic bomb, raising increasing concern about both the external and internal communist threat.

The administration did achieve a couple of key legislative victories in the second half of the year, when two pieces of Truman's Fair Deal were enacted. In July, the President signed into law The Housing Act of 1949—a sweeping expansion of the Federal role in mortgage insurance, urban renewal, and the construction of public housing. In October the Fair Labor Standards Act was amended, raising the minimum wage from 40 cents to 75 cents per hour and expanding those groups of individuals who qualify for it. All of this, of course, kept the President and Charlie busy, though thankfully not at the hectic pace of the Whistle-Stop Tour. Charlie began his fifth year under Truman in May of 1949. By then he was comfortable in his role and enjoyed the unfailing support of the President. However, as with anyone in a high-profile position, there were critics.

Charlie's Critics

The office of the Presidential press secretary has always been a demanding position. Charlie, of course, didn't seek the position, but it landed on him anyway. He was aware of the natural tension that existed between the White House reporters and Press Secretary. The reporters needed to get the news stories. The press secretary wanted to present news items that weren't inaccurate (or only partially accurate), premature, or otherwise misleading. He now knew the role and at one point described it as a "strange job."[575]

Two months after his tenure began, just after the Potsdam Conference, he was stung by the criticism he received from some newspapermen. He expressed his frustration in a memo to an assistant press secretary, Eben Ayers:

> "I am not clairvoyant. I cannot tell precisely what the President is going to do. At every step of the way, I have sought, however, to give the newspapermen, for their guidance, my idea of the probabilities. It would have been easier to impose a complete blackout, but we—you and I—have tried to be helpful. It seems the more we try, the more hell we get."[576]

Eventually Charlie accepted the challenges of the position. He said, "There is no other like it in the world, I am sure, that is even approximately like it"[577] He went on, "Sometimes it seems to me as if I'm just playing a game with my former colleagues."[578]

Charlie knew criticism would come with the job. W. Dale Nelson's book, *Who Speaks for the President?*, gives brief biographies of the press secretaries who served during the twentieth century. He noted the following complaints about Charlie's performance:

> "As usual, there were complaints from the press about the press secretary. He was not always aware of everything that was going on. He wasn't alert to the needs of wire services. He did not run his office well. He failed to coordinate news releases with the government departments and agencies. Some correspondents said they 'received the run around

and have been understandably exasperated at prolonged delays in getting answers to questions.' On top of that he was hard to hear."[579]

These may or may not have been fair—or even accurate. But it's clear that paperwork and administration weren't his strong suit.

Criticisms of a more personal nature were leveled against Charlie by a Truman biographer, Alonzo L. Hamby, when he wrote: "A year and a half younger than Truman, he nonetheless lacked the president's stamina, chain-smoked, and appeared constantly tired."[580] It is true Charlie "lacked the president's stamina"—but few measured up to Truman in that regard. Charlie did smoke cigarettes—and too many—and he may have "appeared" constantly tired. However, he was a man in his 60s whose body had always moved deliberately, and he suffered from arthritis. Notably, Charlie was never criticized by anyone in the Truman administration for failing to keep pace with the demands of his boss or of his job. During the final two years (1949–1950), Charlie suffered from (and was hospitalized for) severe arthritis and he had a couple of mild heart attacks.[581]

Charlie accepted criticism but recoiled at that which he believed was unfairly given, no matter by whom. He demonstrated this in a letter to the editor he wrote to *TIME* magazine. His letter, along with a head shot of him looking directly at the camera and somewhat professorial, was published in the magazine's November 22, 1948, issue and given the heading: "The Facts of Life." Charlie's letter, printed in the magazine in all capital letters as well as the editor's response read:

Sir: TIME, NOV. 8 SAYS THAT "ROSS . . . NEVER REALLY BELIEVED THAT HIS BOSS HAD A

CHANCE OF ELECTION." THIS STATEMENT IS ABSOLUTELY FALSE . . . *TIME* ALSO PERSISTS IN CALLING ME "OLD CHARLIE ROSS." IT HAPPENS THAT I WILL BE 65 YEARS OLD IN A FEW DAYS. SO WHAT? ANYWAY, I AM NOT "TIRED." COME DOWN TO WASHINGTON AND LEARN THE FACTS OF LIFE.

CHARLES G. ROSS
Secretary to the President
The White House
Washington, D.C.

TIME readily acknowledges that it is no position to argue the facts of life with an inhabitant of the White House. Ed.[582]

There were three other criticisms of Charlie's performance in the job. First, Charlie refused to interrupt and correct the President, even if he was making a misstatement, typically at a press conference. This is correct. Charlie believed any interruption of Truman while he was speaking publicly would have personally diminished the stature of the President and his position. Also, he knew the record could be corrected later—and it was, although sometimes awkwardly.

Secondly, Charlie never tried to market Truman or put him in a more favorable light. He wasn't concerned with the perception of the President's public image—or "selling" the President. Charlie viewed this as potentially deceptive and, as such, not part of his job. In an interview years later, Truman revealed he would have been insulted if Charlie had tried that.[583]

Third, Truman biographer Alonzo Hamby asserted that Charlie didn't like his job as Press Secretary. ["But like most individuals who accept assignment out of a sense of obligation, he was unhappy (and looked it) from his first day on the job."]584 Charlie, like most people in important positions had some "bad days" at work. However, there is no doubt Charlie enjoyed his job and working with Truman. This was explained by Walter Trohan, who was the Washington, DC, bureau chief for the *Chicago Tribune* and knew Charlie well. When asked about Charlie, he said the following: "I liked Charlie very much; he was a very agreeable fellow, and they say he killed himself in the White House. That's just strictly for the birds, because nobody ever enjoyed the White House press office as much as Charlie."585 Charlie served as the Press Secretary for five and a half years; he wouldn't have stayed that long if he disliked what he was doing.

1950

After a relatively placid 1949, the following year ushered in the decade of the 1950s and proved to be anything but normal. On the domestic front, in January, President Truman announced his decision to support the development of a hydrogen bomb, a much more powerful weapon than the two atomic bombs dropped on Japan to end World War II. Then, in February, the Red Scare began in earnest. Senator Joseph McCarthy of Wisconsin, in a speech to the Republican Women's Club announced that he had a list of 205 known members of the Communist Party who were working for the State Department. This and other allegations from Senator McCarthy ultimately led to Congressional Hearings—and much public angst—to sort through, and ferret out, his largely bogus allegations.

Internationally, the Cold War spread when Communist Mao Zedong, leader of the newly formed People's Republic of China, joined forces with Stalin to sign a bilateral agreement called the Treaty of Friendship, Alliance and Mutual Assistance. This alliance quickly had a profound effect in Korea, where ideologies—and armies—soon clashed.

The Korean War

Following the end of World War II, the Korean peninsula became divided politically and militarily into a northern region (North Korea) and a southern region (South Korea) along the 38th parallel. North Korea, controlled by the Soviet Union, soon installed a Communist regime. By 1950, the Soviet Union had handed influence over North Korea to Mao's Communist China. South Korea, in stark contrast, had adopted a constitution and formed a democratic government which operated under the aegis of the United States and the United Nations.

Beginning at the Potsdam Conference in 1945, it gradually became apparent that the Soviet Union's goal was to undermine democratic governments throughout the world and, in their places, install Communist regimes. To thwart this prospect of world domination by Communism, Truman adopted what he called the "containment policy." This provided non-communist countries support and aid to stop the spread of Communism in that country. The conflicts and tensions which followed became known as The Cold War. The 38th parallel in Korea became an important line in the sand in Asia to halt the spread of Communism.

The Korean War started on June 25, 1950, when North Korean troops, without warning, attacked and invaded South Korea. This aggression was spearheaded by Kim Il Sung, its Communist leader, who became emboldened by Mao's takeover of China the previous year. That was coupled with his (unfounded) fear that South Korea, backed by the U. S., would attempt an invasion of North Korea. He convinced both China and the Soviet Union that an attack into South Korea would be an easy victory, and Korea would become a single country under Communist rule. So, in June 1950, a ground war erupted on the Korean Peninsula.

In 1950, the U. S. had the most powerful military force in the world. It had won victories over Japan and Germany in World War II. It also had (and had used) the atomic bomb. The U.S. might use the atomic bomb again in this new war, which could trigger World War III. Great Britain, which had suffered severe economic losses in World War II, feared this. The fact that the outspoken and impetuous General Douglas MacArthur was the lead commander in Korea, did nothing to reassure our allies—particularly Great Britain.

December 4, 1950 (Monday)

When Charlie awoke on Monday morning, December 4, 1950, he could see it was a gray, windy, rainy day. His habit and a sense of duty made him rise, a bit slowly, from his comfortable bed. He no longer was a young man, having turned 65 less than a month before. His arthritis made his joints stiff, and his recent heart problems gave him caution.

As usual, he bathed, shaved, dressed in a conservative suit, and went downstairs, where Florence had breakfast laid out for him. This morning, he had a lot on his mind and dreaded what lay ahead. After breakfast, he had his usual morning cigarette and, shortly before he left the house, commented to Florence:

> "This will be a terrible week. Days like this, the tension is enormous. I don't see how I'll get thru [sic] them."[586]

She remembered this remark, because he seldom complained, and he found his work at the White House "extraordinarily interesting" and approached it as an honor he was fulfilling.[587] However, his schedule was full this week. Not only was the Korean War raging, but today Clement Attlee, the British Prime Minister, was arriving to question the President about Korea. Also, Helen was in town as a delegate to the White House's Mid-Century Conference on Children and Youth. To top things off, the President's daughter, Margaret, would be singing in concert at Constitution Hall. There were good reasons for him to be apprehensive about the week ahead.

A primary source of Charlie's pessimism about the stress of the upcoming week was the visit of Attlee. In his weekly press conference, President Truman was asked point blank if the use of the atomic bomb was under active consideration in North Korea. To this Truman responded: "Always has been. It is one of our weapons."[588] According to Margaret Truman and others, this direct answer—President Truman was notoriously direct—was designed to make the Chinese move more slowly in the war, knowing that their troops' annihilation was possible. Later in the same press conference, when asked about the role of the United Nations troops in this engagement, Truman said: "The action against Communist China depends on the action of the United Nations. The military commander in the field will have the use of weapons, as he always has." The President viewed this as a narrow question about the latitude of the field commander if the survival of his troops were at stake. However, the reporters viewed Truman's assertion differently; they presumed that the military commanders had the authority to use all weapons, including the atomic bomb. Following the press conference, the United Press issued a bulletin stating: PRESIDENT TRUMAN SAID TODAY THE UNITED STATES HAS UNDER CONSIDERATION USE OF THE

ATOMIC BOMB IN CONNECTION WITH THE WAR IN KOREA. The Associated Press, in the lead on its newswire, reported: HE [Truman] SAID . . . THE DECISION OF WHETHER OR NOT TO DROP ATOMIC BOMBS WAS ONE FOR THE COMMANDERS IN THE FIELD. This may or may not have caused the Chinese to be more cautious, but it certainly put our allies on edge.[589] In response to these headlines, Charlie Ross and Dean Acheson later that same day put together a clarifying statement, which was then issued by the White House. It read:

> "The President wants to make it certain that there is no misinterpretation of his answers to questions at his press conference today about the use of the atom bomb. Naturally, there has been consideration of this subject since the outbreak of the hostilities in Korea, just as there is consideration of the use of all military weapons whenever our forces are in combat.
>
> Consideration of the use of any weapon is always implicit in the very possession of that weapon.
>
> However, it should be emphasized, that, by law, only the President can authorize the use of the atom bomb, and no such authorization has been given. If and when such authorization should be given, the military commander in the field would have charge of the tactical delivery of the weapon.
>
> In brief, the replies to the questions at today's press conference do not represent any change in this situation."[590]

This statement did as much as it could to clarify the President's meaning and to calm fears. However, it wasn't enough to quell the concern in Great Britain. Atlee made a show of flying to the U. S.

the following Monday to speak directly to President Truman—a trip many in both countries thought unnecessary.[591]

After breakfast, Charlie drove through the rainy streets to the White House, where he faced the non-stop flow of work. (He told a close friend he found the volume crushing but the substance "extraordinarily interesting.") Toward the end of this busy day, at four o'clock that afternoon, Prime Minister Attlee arrived and was greeted by President Truman; then they met with General Omar Bradley (Chairman of the Joint Chiefs of Staff), Secretary of Defense George Marshall, and Secretary of State Dean Acheson. The Korean situation was reviewed in depth, after which the Prime Minister's concerns were addressed. After that meeting, Charlie received a debriefing from the President, who indicated he believed he had explained his press-conference remarks and satisfied Mr. Attlee to the point that there was now no longer any misunderstanding. Unfortunately, the London papers published a very garbled account of that meeting, leaving many questions for the White House press corps to field the following day.[592]

December 5, 1950 (Tuesday)

The next day, Tuesday, Charlie's relentless schedule continued. He arrived at work that morning and met briefly with the assistant press secretary, Eben Ayers. The White House press corps was clamoring for a more factual report about the prior day's meeting with Atlee. Charlie knew he would have to address those requests.

Then at 9:40 a.m., he left with the President to attend the White House Conference on Children and Youth, a national conference, held every ten years, which focused on issues related to young people. This year it convened in the spacious National Guard Armory because more than 5,000 people were attending, too many to hold it in the White House, where it had been held in the past. Charlie's sister, Helen, was in town and was a delegate to the conference. Truman spoke at the conference, after which he and Charlie returned to the White House for a few minutes.

Just after noon, Truman and Charlie departed for the Naval Gun Factory, where they boarded the Presidential yacht *Williamsburg*. A luncheon meeting to further review the Korean War situation and its United Nations' support was held aboard, primarily for the benefit of Prime Minister Attlee. This time, the President had invited select members of Congress along as well as some of the men from his administration who'd met with and spoken to Attlee the prior day. Charlie, as usual, didn't participate directly but kept himself informed on the substance of the meeting so he could report afterwards to the White House press.

Just before 5 p.m., Charlie returned to his office and again met with Eben Ayers, who informed him that one newspaper had reported that the President and Attlee had reached an agreement; Charlie told him this was not so. Charlie's response was characteristically precise, because although there had been a series of meetings at which the Prime Minister had been brought up to date on the circumstances surrounding the Korean War, no new agreement related to the war, the U.S., or its allies resulted from it.[593]

Although it was late in the day, Charlie knew he had a full evening ahead. That evening, he and his wife were scheduled to have dinner with his sister, Helen. Afterwards, Margaret Truman was going to sing in a solo concert in Constitution Hall, where he and Florence were to be guests of President and Mrs. Truman.

At about 5:30 p.m. the newspapermen were called into Charlie's office, where he gave a report about the luncheon meeting aboard the *Williamsburg*. He told them as much as he could (while remaining within the bounds of national security) about the meeting and provided the type of details print journalists craved, including the names of some of the food served at the luncheon. (He humorously gave the spelling and the pronunciation of the French words *bleu* and *jus*, reading directly from the menu.) The briefing was masterful, and he was "in good form and good nature" throughout.[594]

Press Secretary Charlie Ross informing reporters that Wake Island is to be the scene of a conference between President Truman and General Douglas MacArthur. Key West, FL, October 10, 1950. (Photo/Harry S. Truman Library)

At about 5:45 p.m., the update ended, and most of the newsmen left. Charlie and his secretary, Myrtle Bergheim, remained in his office, where, as an accommodation to Frank Bourgholtzer of NBC, he agreed to give a brief statement for the NBC radio audience about the President's meetings of the past two days. As the radiomen were setting up their equipment, Charlie lit a cigarette.

"Don't mumble," Ms. Bergheim jokingly admonished Charlie.

"You know I always speak very clearly," he good-naturedly retorted; then he slumped sideways in his high-backed leather chair as his lighted cigarette fell from his lips.

The men in the room initially thought Charlie was joking, but his secretary knew better and hurriedly called for Dr. Wallace Graham, the White House physician, who came immediately. He tried to revive Charlie, but it was too late. "He was gone before I got there," Dr. Graham pronounced. Charlie died at 5:50 p.m. from a heart attack.

Soon after, Florence and her son John arrived and went to Charlie's office in the White House. They, like everyone else close to Charlie, were shocked, although the heart attack wasn't a complete surprise. Charlie's heart problems were known to his family and close friends.[595]

President Truman, who was in the Blair House across the street from the White House when Charlie died, was immediately notified. He and Bess were both grief-stricken. Knowing that Margaret was also very fond of "Uncle Charlie," Truman made the decision that she should not be informed of Charlie's death until after her performance at Constitution Hall that evening. With heavy hearts Bess and Harry attended the concert. The British Ambassador, Oliver Franks, and his wife accompanied them as their guests.

The evening of Charlie's death, Harry penned a statement for the press. Afterwards he had it typed, and then he walked down the short corridor to where the newsmen were waiting for his remarks about his fallen friend. He began to read it aloud, but his voice faltered before he could complete the first sentence, so he stopped and collected himself. After a few seconds, he said:

"Ah, hell . . . I can't read this thing. You fellows know how I feel, anyway."

Then he tossed the page down on the table for the reporters to read for themselves, turned around, and walked back down the hall slowly with his head bowed. This was one of the few times Truman was ever at a loss for words, which reflected the depth of his grief. The statement was published in many newspapers the following day, including the *Washington Post*:

> "The friend of my youth, who became a tower of strength when the responsibilities of high office fell on me, is gone. To collect one's thoughts to pay tribute to Charles Ross in the face of this tragic dispensation is not easy. I knew him as a boy and as a man. In our high school years together he gave promise to those superb intellectual powers which he attained later in life. Teachers and students alike acclaimed him as the best all-around scholar our school had produced.
>
> His years of preparation were followed by an early maturity of usefulness. In the many roles of life he played his part with exalted honor and an honesty of purpose from which he never deviated. To him, as a newspaperman, truth was ever mighty as he pursued his work from Washington to the capitals of Europe to the far continents.
>
> Here at the White House, the scope of his influence extended far beyond his varied and complex and always-exacting duties as secretary to the President. He was in charge

of the press and radio, a field which steadily broadened in recent years, with continuous advances in the technique of communications. It is characteristic of Charlie Ross that he was holding a press conference when the summons came. We all knew that he was working far beyond his strength. But he would have it so. He fell at his post, a casualty of his fidelity to duty and his determination that our people should know the truth, and all the truth, in these critical times.

His exacting duties did not end with his work as press secretary. More and more, all of us came to depend on his counsel on questions of high public policy, which he could give out of his wealth of learning, his wisdom, and his far-flung experience. Patriotism and integrity, honor and honesty, lofty ideals and nobility of intent were his guides and ordered his life from boyhood onward. He saw life steady and he saw it whole. We shall miss him as a public servant and mourn him as a friend."[596]

December 6, 1950 (Wednesday)

Florence, Charlie's highly organized and frequently impatient spouse, wanted his funeral to move along quickly—and it did. Louise in Phoenix couldn't get to Washington on such short notice. In a letter written one month after the funeral, Florence semi-apologetically rationalized the reason the funeral was held less than 48 hours after his death. Florence wrote:

> "It was such a pity the weather was so bad you couldn't fly here at the time. I know it would have comforted the other sisters. But I knew what Charlie would have wanted in the way of having his funeral as soon as possible."[597]

Wednesday morning promptly at 9 a.m., she met with representatives of the Pumphrey Funeral Home on Wisconsin Avenue in Bethesda, Maryland, and planned the funeral arrangements. Charlie's body was taken from the White House and transported to the funeral parlor, where it was immediately prepared for burial, placed in "a wood burial case," and, that afternoon, taken to the Ross home in nearby Kensington. A public notice was prepared indicating the body would be taken to "his late residence where friends may call after 4 p.m., Wednesday, December 6th"—that same day—and that his funeral would be the following day and would be private. A plot was secured for Charlie's burial at the Roman Catholic Mount Olivet Cemetery in Washington, even though he did not practice that, or any other, faith.

The funeral announcement appeared in that afternoon's newspapers. It stated that funeral services the following day (Thursday) were private, and that, in lieu of flowers, potential mourners were asked to, "please send contributions to the Washington Heart Association or the Arthritis and Rheumatism Foundation of Washington." ("Charlie would have wanted it that way," Florence later said.) Florence received friends at her home beginning at 4 p.m. This whirlwind of planning and coordinating culminated in Charlie's funeral the following day.[598]

December 7, 1950 (Thursday)—The Funeral

Charlie's funeral took place on December 7, 1950, also the ninth anniversary of the infamous attack on Pearl Harbor. The weather accented the day's sadness; it was a foggy day with light wind and rain. The temperature reached just above 50 degrees. As planned, the funeral service was held at the Rosses' home. The President, of course, attended. He had canceled his regularly scheduled, Thursday press conference out of respect.

Monsignor Smyth, the priest at nearby Blessed Sacrament Church, for whom a car had been sent by Florence, presided over the funeral service, as well as the burial at the cemetery. He was a longtime family friend, both of Charlie and Florence. The private service at the Ross home started promptly at 2:30 p.m.[599] There was an open casket for viewing. No record was made of what was said at either service. However, in a handwritten letter the following month to Charlie's sister Louise, Florence reported:

> "There was never . . . a more distinguished gathering, and close friends were there, too. No one but the Pres. [Truman] was personally invited. We just let it be known that, though the notice said, 'Services Private' because of limitations of space in the house we wanted any of his friends who cared to come to do so. And of all the hundreds of callers, I never before saw so many men openly cry as they looked on him. He died without a moment's suffering, so there was no sign of pain or illness in his face. He looked absolutely natural. In fact, he had looked particularly well for the past month—not glowing, of course, but no strain of pain in his face and good color."[600]

An impressive array of family, friends, and colleagues came to the private service. Five of Charlie's six sisters attended, as did his two sons and their wives. (Even Charlie's eldest grandson—an exceptionally well-behaved little Charlie Ross—came with his mother.) Family friends served as pallbearers. Harry, Bess, and Margaret Truman were there. Others from the Truman administration included: Dean Acheson (Secretary of State), W. Averell Harriman (special assistant to President Truman), Charles Murphy (White House Counsel), as well as Clark Clifford, Matthew J. Connelly,

William Hassett, George Elsey, and others. Henri Bonnet, the French Ambassador, attended. The press, too, was well represented. Charlie's White House assistant, Eben Ayers, was there, as were a delegation of twenty-eight journalists sent by the National Press Club, of which Charlie had been a past president and a longtime member. These dozens of mourners filled the Rosses' spacious house as they paid their last respects to Charlie.

There is no record of what was said at the service. Florence made sure that the program moved along. Monsignor Smyth provided comforting words; short eulogies were likely given mentioning, as did his numerous published obituaries, some of Charlie's more salient virtues: intelligence, humanity, and kindness. The service lasted about a half-hour, after which Charlie's body was taken by the pallbearers to the waiting hearse. It then left the residence followed by a procession of three funeral cars (carrying mostly family members) as well as other passenger vehicles which drove the ten miles to the cemetery.

The graveside service and burial took place in Northeast Washington at Mount Olivet Cemetery. The weather had not changed: light rain, some fog, and light wind. It was a classically sad day for a funeral. Monsignor Smyth said the final words transitioning Charlie from this world into the next. Finally, his wooden casket was lowered into the grave as his family and friends said their final prayers, and then turned and walked away.[601]

December 8, 1950 (Friday)

Truman grieved for Charlie's family. The day after Charlie's funeral, he sent the following handwritten note to Florence:

> "Dear Mrs. Charlie: You'll never know how I miss Charlie. He and I understood each other completely. I don't think

I ever knew as ethical, as intellectually honest [a] man as Charlie.

You, of course, knew him better than anyone else could know him. But I grew up with him. We were pals in grade and high school. Charlie had a wonderful brain—and knew how to use it, use it honestly, in the public interest.

I wanted you and the boys [Charlie's two sons] to know my sentiments and my attachment to Charlie.

Sincerely,
Harry S. Truman.[602]

Bess Truman also felt the loss of Charlie Ross, whose six sisters had all been friends growing up in Independence. Five of the six sisters made it to Charlie's funeral. Ella ("Sis") Ross came from Chicago; Helen was already in Washington as a delegate at the White House's Mid-Century Conference; Virginia Ross Weston lived in Washington; Frances (Ross) Leake flew in from Florida; and his youngest sister, J.B. Ross, came down from Poughkeepsie, New York. Only Louise Ross Holmquist, in Phoenix, was unable to attend. While in Washington for the funeral, all Charlie's sisters stayed at Virginia's house, where on the morning after the funeral, Bess Truman visited to re-connect with her childhood friends. Sis wrote to Louise about the post-funeral meetings with Bess and Harry Truman:

"Helen says she told you that Bess came to V's [Virginia's] house and spent an hour with us Friday morning. She said to Helen the night before 'Harry lost a trusted friend.' Bess is very deeply grieved; also, I think she knows how much Harry needed him. In the aft. [afternoon] (Friday), the five of us went to the W.H. [White House]. A visit with the Pres [President] had been arranged. Five chairs were placed about his desk. He said, 'All of you except Louise.' We spent about 10 or 15 minutes with him. He tried to tell us what Charlie meant to him; I think he fully appreciated what a tremendous help C [Charlie] had been. Then we went through Charlie's office, where we were met by Steve Early (temporarily on duty until Joe Short of the *Baltimore Sun* takes over). Steve was under Roosevelt for about 11 yr. [years] and was Charlie's friend. Short is reputed to be a good newspaperman, but I doubt he is anywhere near Charlie's stature."[603]

Charlie Ross' empty office in the White House. Washington, DC. 1950.
(Photo/Harry S. Truman Library)

The letter continues with some news about family. It shows the deep feelings Harry and Bess had for Charlie and the Ross sisters. In turn, the Ross family, then and since, has held the Truman family in the highest regard.

Truman's Final Thoughts

Harry Truman never forgot the loss of Charlie Ross, his trusted friend. In his memoirs, written years later and noted for their objectivity, he wrote: "That evening, while he was still at his desk, Charlie suffered a heart attack and died. We had been friends since high-school days, and his loss grieved me very much. It struck me like the loss of my immediate family."[604]

20

HELEN'S FINAL DAYS

Helen's Retirement

Shortly after Helen's 70th birthday in 1960, W.W. Norton & Company, Inc. published the book Helen co-authored with Bertram Lewin, *Psychoanalytic Education in the United States*. Its 460 pages ended with a seven-page appendix that outlined a set of proposed criteria for member organizations of the American Psychoanalytic Association (APsA) to follow. The standards closely aligned with those eventually adopted by the APsA.[605] The book's publication also proved to be a milestone, albeit of another kind, for Helen—it ended her salaried employment.

Other professional women might have agonized over an upcoming retirement, with its naturally attendant questions: *Where do I go from here? What do I do next in life?* But not Helen. She'd seen this transition coming and prepared for it. Never having had any difficulty keeping busy, she adjusted to the new reality of retirement.

By the time Helen entered her life's eighth decade, she'd cemented many enduring relationships. Professionally, she'd made and nurtured many contacts beginning with her years studying in Vienna, then working at the CIP, and finally through her researching and writing the book. Children were her specialty in the field of psychoanalysis, and she knew this would keep her in demand. She had acquired enough personal assets and savings, so she could live comfortably in retirement. Her network of friends was both broad and deep, spanning not only her professional contacts but also people she knew from Camp Kechuwa and her winters in Captiva. During the hot Washington summers, she and J.B. would retreat for a few weeks to their cabin on Footprint Island on Lake Michigamee. During the cold winter months, they would go down to their comfortable home on Captiva Island, Florida. No, staying active and busy in retirement would not be a problem for Helen.

When J.B. retired from teaching history at Vassar College in 1966, she and Helen purchased a condominium unit in the newly constructed, nine-story, high-rise building known as The Colonnade in Northeast Washington, DC. Their large, upscale apartment overlooked the nearby, leafy neighborhood of Wesley Heights, where their sister, Virginia, and her husband, Carl, had lived for decades. Their upper-floor unit came with an impressive view of Washington. Washington appealed to both Helen and J. B for many reasons: it was a major city with good transportation options, and they wouldn't need to own a car. It had first-rate museums and cultural events. The Library of Congress, where J. B. could continue her research in her specialty, Medieval History, was around the corner. Across the street from the Colonnade was a community garden, where they rented a plot of ground and grew a variety of flowers and vegetables. The Colonnade proved to be a comfortable base of operations for them both over the next dozen years.

Teaching and Counseling

Helen had earned a reputation as a gifted teacher, and she knew that she wanted to continue teaching part-time during her retirement years. In 1963, she accepted the position as a supervisor and teacher at the Washington (DC) Psychoanalytical Institute. In addition, she instructed physicians in seminars held on a visiting basis at the medical schools at the University of North Carolina and at Duke University.[606] She received some compensation for her time and expertise, but the enjoyment she took from teaching meant more to her than the money. In 1965 she became a visiting lecturer in psychoanalysis at the newly formed Pittsburgh Psychoanalytic Institute, which had evolved out of the medical school at the University of Pittsburgh. She enjoyed the people and the professional arrangement in Pittsburgh, so she served for several years as a teacher and supervisor there.[607] She also found time to fit in many shorter-term assignments.[608]

A Special Pittsburgh Friendship

While working in Pittsburgh, Helen gave consulting advice to one of the pioneers of children's television, Fred Rogers, known to all children as "Mr. Rogers." Fred McFeely Rogers was born in Latrobe, Pennsylvania, near Pittsburgh, in 1928. In 1951 he graduated from Rollins College in Winter Park, Florida, with a degree in musical composition, after which he worked for NBC in New York City and then for WQED, the public television station in Pittsburgh. Initially he served as a writer, producer, and puppeteer for *The Children's Corner* on NBC, which aired in 1955–1956. In 1962, he shifted course and earned a divinity degree from the Pittsburgh Theological Seminary. He became an ordained minister in the United Presbyterian Church. Somewhat to his surprise, the leadership of the church encouraged him to continue his television work, which he did. In 1966 he returned to WQED where he wrote, produced, and hosted *Mister Rogers' Neighborhood*, which two years later became televised nationally on the National Educational

Television network, later known as the Public Broadcasting Service. Each of Mr. Rogers' shows began with its host, Mr. Rogers, changing into one of his trademark cardigan sweaters while singing the show's theme song, "Won't You Be My Neighbor?" The show then transitioned to the topic of the day—its key segment designed to teach "children how to get along with others, feel good about themselves, and cope with their fears."⁶⁰⁹ It became a hugely popular show, which aired on television for more than 30 years.

Fred later said that they hit it off from the beginning when they first met in the mid-60s. He said, "From the first time I met her, I felt her genuine interest in the kind of work I was doing."⁶¹⁰ He goes on, "Through the years of our friendship, Helen helped me in many ways—particularly in consultation with several projects of family communications."⁶¹¹ Eventually, Helen agreed to let Fred interview her on camera in his studio. Fred recalls, "I remember that day in 1975 with a lot of pleasure. There was a barn-like set in the studio, and Helen and I just sat down on two chairs in the middle of that barn and had a visit."⁶¹² The barn-like atmosphere must have reminded Helen of her early days in Independence. Fred relates, "Almost immediately she told me she felt quite at home there."⁶¹³ Fred was surprised and pleased that 85-year-old Helen was willing and able to appear on camera. He says, "Because of Helen's willingness to use the technology of television and film for teaching, we have records of her for all future generations to see and hear."⁶¹⁴ Fred and Helen's close friendship and professional relationship lasted for the remaining years until Helen's death.

Board Memberships

Beginning in the late 1940s, Helen began her decades of service as a board member for a variety of organizations focused on the needs of children. When she lived in Chicago, she became a board member of the Francis Parker School, a position she held for 15 years.[615] Beginning in 1946, she served as a Trustee for the Field Foundation, holding that position for more than 20 years. The Field Foundation, founded in 1940 by Marshall Field III, the grandson of the founder of the eponymous department store, supported a wide range of socially beneficial causes, particularly those with innovative approaches to solving social problems.[616] Helen realized that the Field Foundation could be a source of funding for a program helping children overseas. It wasn't long before she convinced its leadership that the Hampstead Clinic in London, founded by Anna Freud, would be worthy of its financial backing. Thanks to Helen's advocacy, it soon became a major interest of the Field Foundation.

The Hampstead Clinic, under Anna Freud's leadership, was dedicated to both the clinical practice of child welfare and the modernization of research techniques for the psychoanalysis of children. It was at the vanguard for the training a new generation of child psychotherapists. Helen, for years, received reports and letters from Anna Freud about the clinic's progress and accomplishments; she shared this information with her board colleagues at the Field Foundation who, in turn, provided generous financial support.[617] A fellow Field Foundation board member, Robert Coles, commented years later that the Hampstead Clinic became "a major interest of that foundation." He stated that to read Anna Freud's "accounts of how things went at her clinic was to learn not only about a child psychoanalyst's view of the young, but a strong leader's visionary interest in the next generation," and that so "many educators of all kinds (doctors, nurses, social workers, teachers) have taken their training at Hampstead [Clinic] and learned from Miss Freud not only the specifics of psychoanalysis but, more broadly, how to think about the possibilities in children as well as their inevitable times of trial."[618] Eventually, with Anna's encouragement, Helen took a seat on the Hampstead Clinic board as well.

Helen Holmquist Halnan and Anna Freud

Helen's friendship with Anna Freud began in Vienna in the 1930s and ran very deep. In the 1950s, after the closing of Camp Kechuwa, Helen had more time during the summer months and visited Anna at the clinic and provided help. Then, in 1962, Anna, who spent most of her time in England, named Helen a director of the Freud archives in New York City.[619] As Helen's health became weaker in the 1970s, the visits between the friends became fewer and fewer.

Helen's niece and namesake, Helen Holmquist Halnan, lived in Phoenix, Arizona, near her mother, Louise Holmquist. In 1976, Helen Halnan lived with her husband and children in Phoenix and was on the faculty of Phoenix College teaching psychology. Her aunt Helen contacted her and asked if she would be interested in going for a semester to the Hampstead Clinic to work with Anna Freud. Fortunately, Phoenix College had a liberal sabbatical policy, and her niece jumped at the opportunity. In 1977, she set her college teaching aside for a semester and travelled to London. Years later, she recalled her experience working under Ms. Freud as a "fascinating adventure." She wrote about the insights she experienced working with Anna Freud and included that information in the two scrapbooks she kept about her time there. Another prominent item in her scrapbook was a picture she'd had taken with the notoriously camera-shy Ms. Freud; it became one of her cherished keepsakes from her experience in London.[620]

The 1970s

As Helen began her ninth decade in 1970, her body slowed down—age forced it to—yet she doggedly maintained her correspondence with colleagues and friends. In 1971, she wrote short articles such as "Some Special Aspects of Psychoanalytic Educations" and "Anna Freud's Diagnostic Profile," both of which were published in the professional publication *Currents in Psychoanalysis*.[621] She also wrote a two-page letter to a psychiatrist colleague, Dr. George Engel, commenting on the professional paper he'd given about his relationship with his twin brother. Her letter praised his paper and provided some anecdotal insights into her relationship with her twin sister Louise. Helen showed her trademark efficiency (and frugality) in her correspondence to friends; she often responded to their letters and other inquiries by sending less-expensive postcards or by corresponding on small, light pieces of notepaper to save cost.

The Helen Ross Professorship

In 1972, in honor of Helen's years of helping others, the University of Chicago, recognized her professional accomplishments and contributions. In a ceremony held on June 7th, it announced the creation of an academic chair in her honor in its School of Social Service Administration. The chair was funded through an initial grant from The Ford Foundation with matching funds, not surprisingly, from The Field Foundation of Illinois. The brochure for the ceremony stated the reason for this recognition:

> "It is named honor of an American whose career has spanned a lifetime of communal and educational service. Helen

Ross is numbered among those who have made distinctive contributions to the life of this nation in the twentieth century."

The language of the beautifully printed brochure highlighted many of Helen's accomplishments. It singled out the following:

"In her own work and achievements, Helen Ross set a pattern for the application of psychoanalysis to those concerns of education and welfare that transcended the traditional organization of this new branch of medicine. For more than twenty-five years, while almost all of her colleagues were medically trained psychoanalysts, she gained the respect and admiration of an entire profession in whose ranks she came to hold honorary membership. In 1950, she was instrumental in establishing the Child Care Program of the Institute for Psychoanalysis of Chicago, the first program in the nation to provide post-graduate education in a psychoanalytic institute for teachers, social workers, pediatricians, clergymen, nurses, and other professional personnel who worked with children."

At the end of the brochure, a more personal note about the effect Helen had on her friends and colleagues was included:

"A woman of great wisdom, warmth, humor, and humane concern, Helen Ross is deeply beloved by friends and colleagues throughout the world. Counselor to many families, adviser to businessmen, to school administrators, foundation officers, and to professional associations, Helen Ross continues a rich and remarkable life."[622]

Helen and Children

All of Helen's professional and organizational work tends to overshadow her remarkable ability to make one-on-one connections with children. Helen had a special magic with children, which she refined through years of experience. One event in 1976 is a great illustration of this. Faye Sawyier, a good friend from Chicago, visited Helen in Washington, and they decided to go to the newly opened National Air and Space Museum. Helen wore a hat that day because she was from that generation of women who dressed more formally—and wore hats—to public events. Once inside the museum, Helen and Faye were seated in the huge amphitheater to see the introductory film about the museum. In that vast, open space, Helen was seated next to a little boy. Soon Faye noticed that Helen and the boy were "chatting happily away." Faye thought to herself: *"Isn't Helen amazing? Kids just gravitate to her."* As the film started, Helen whispered to Faye that the boy admired her hat. After the film concluded and the audience was filing out, Helen told Faye, "I think he was quite frightened by that huge place and all those odd sounds, so he settled down with a nice, plain close-at-hand object"—Helen's hat. Faye said, "Of course, she was right; when someone explains the calculus to you, you wonder how it is you yourself missed it. She didn't miss."[623] Helen's deep understanding of the desires, motivations, and needs of children was a hallmark of her success and a lifelong joy for her.

Helen's Final Days

Unlike with Charlie, Helen's final decline wasn't precipitous, and it didn't startle anyone. Her fatal illness was the same one that had claimed Sis 27 years before—cancer. In 1976, Helen received the diagnosis that cancer, then almost always a fatal disease, had taken root in her body. By then she'd begun to scale back her consulting and out-of-town travel. The trajectory of her fading health allowed her time to bring an orderly conclusion to her professional connections, many of which were carried on by mail. This included giving advice to colleagues who'd requested it. Her cancer's slow-moving nature also allowed her the time to say a proper goodbye to family and friends. It gave her time to think, to reflect on things, and deal with the struggle she was experiencing between life and death. Helen loved life, so seeing and feeling its end relentlessly approaching challenged her innate optimism. Her final days were not pleasant, yet she stoically made the most of them.

During her final months, Helen lived with J.B., then in her early 70s, in their comfortable condominium in Washington, DC. Virginia still lived just blocks away and remained in close touch as always, particularly after Helen's diagnosis. Her sister, Frances, occasionally visited from Ohio. She helped by typing some of Helen's correspondence once Helen was unable to do that for herself. Sadly, Louise in Arizona was frail and had such poor eyesight that she was unable to travel to see Helen during her final months. Throughout their lives, and no matter where each were living, the sisters kept in touch, mostly by mail (non-emergency telephone calls were too expensive for the thrifty Ross women). The sisters continued to support one another as they always had done. Caring for an elder sister during her final days was a natural extension of their lifelong love and support. When Helen lay dying in her Washington home, she did so with family nearby.

Helen was candid with friends about her pending death. One of Helen's professional colleagues, Dr. Doris M. Hunter, a psychiatrist from Pittsburgh, related:

"In April of last year [1977], I received a short note from Helen telling me of the progressive nature of her illness. It was a beautiful statement, written in her uniquely simple and forthright style and reflecting an admirable inner courage about what had become, in her eighty-seventh year of life, intimately inevitable. Her closing sentences were, 'Let it [this news] not cloud our communication. I have had a good life—remember.'"[624]

Then, three months prior to her death, Helen's good friend from Pittsburgh, Fred Rogers, on a visit to Washington stopped by to see her. He related this experience at her Celebration of Life ceremony held in Dahlgren Chapel at Georgetown University two months after her death. Fred said the following:

"The last time I saw Helen was in May of this year [1978], I had gone to Washington for some meetings and had called her sister, J.B., from the airport just to see how Helen was feeling. J.B. told me that she was having a pretty good day, and, after checking with Helen, she told me if I wanted, I was welcome to come to the apartment for a little visit.

Well, even as weak as Helen was, she still wanted to know about my family and my work and all her friends in Pittsburgh. We had such a good visit, and she spoke of many of you who are here today.

At one point I told her how helpful her films had been to so many people and how well the videotapes had turned out. She seemed very pleased to know that.

I held her hand a lot of the time, and we had some long silences, which were very comfortable. Somehow when you're with Helen, you get the clear message that you are *not guilty*—that you are marvelously accepted as you are . . . and that day in May was no exception.

At one point, after one of our silences, Helen said to me, 'Fred, do you ever pray for people?'

'Of course,' I answered, and I simply said, 'Dear God, Wilt Thou encircle us with Thy love wherever we may be.'

Helen looked at me and said ever so thoughtfully, 'That's what it's about, isn't it? Love is what it's all about.'

The more I've thought about that, the more I've realized that that's what Helen's major interest was. Helen's major in life was love.

In many uniquely different ways, her life and her love have blessed us all."[625]

Not all of Helen's final days were as peaceful and inspired as her visit from Fred Rogers. In letters to Dr. Doris Hunter, written during the final two months, she admitted she struggled to understand the uncertainty and finality of her impending death. Dr. Hunter related:

"There were two more letters, one in June, and one in late July [1978], both dictated to her sister, Frances. In these last months of her life, she was preoccupied with some ideas that had been developing in recent years about the concept of ambivalence. She had discussed them with me during one of her last visits to Pittsburgh, and now, as her life was coming to a close, she was struggling to order and integrate them with her idea that the ultimate ambivalence is between life and death. In her letter in June, she said, 'I really cry out for death, and then I find I am on the side of life.' Seven weeks later, in her last communication to me, she was still grappling with the ambivalence concept, and asking me to let her know the best thing I had ever read on the subject, saying she could agree with the views of many, but 'the ultimate fact is not there.' Calmly and with simple frankness, she wrote looking death squarely in the face, but not yet seeing him in his entirety, although feeling his presence, and of the importance of keeping in touch with one another as long as possible."[626]

Helen faced death as she had embraced life: bravely, inquisitively, and with an open mind—and fully understanding the need for love and for communication.

Helen's Unfinished Memoirs

Helen was an amazing personal communicator, but she was reluctant to talk about her own, remarkable life. She had come from a family—and a generation—that eschewed the spotlight and where showmanship was frowned upon. Lee Wilcox, the former camper and later "councilor" at the camp, urged Helen to write her life's story in the early 1950s. Helen reluctantly began the project, but the work progressed slowly. Periodically, Helen sent select segments she recalled about her life to Lee, written in longhand. Lee edited and typed Helen's handwritten notes. She believed Helen's life was not only fascinating, but could also serve as an inspiration to others, particularly women. This memoir project progressed slowly over many years—and in fits and starts.

In 1962, Lee Wilcox married Arthur Kneerim and had moved from Chicago to Connecticut. She continued to encourage Helen to work on her biography, but with little success. Hope was rekindled in the mid-1970s when Lee once again encouraged Helen to complete the project. Although Helen didn't want to disappoint her good friend, she clearly lacked enthusiasm for the project. Sadly, the memoir was never finished. As Helen's life came to an end, the manuscript was little more than 100 typed pages, and it mostly covered the first twenty-five years of Helen's life. Fortunately, these pages were saved and given to Ross family members by Lee. They became known within the family as "Aunt Hi's Memoirs." Many of its remarkable stories are included in this book.

Helen Ross passed away August 9, 1978 in Washington, DC.
This photo was used in her obituary.
(Photo/Ross family collection).

Helen's Funeral and Burial Service

Helen Ross died on Wednesday, August 9, 1978, and, as she requested, her body was cremated. In her obituary published in the *Washington Post*, a brief recap of some of the significant events in Helen's life were noted; however, the death notice made no mention of any funeral or burial service. That was intentional because Helen didn't want a fuss made over her remains, rather, she wanted the details of her funeral and burial to be private—and she left those practical decisions in the hands of her family. Her sister J.B. was keenly aware of Helen's affection for Anna Freud and the work she continued to do. The obituary concluded with the following brief statement: "The family suggests that expressions of sympathy be in the form of contributions to the Anna Freud Foundation in New York City."

Perhaps in response to the published notices, Anna Freud, three days after Helen's death, penned the following letter to J. B.:

August 12, 1978
Dear J. B. Ross,

I heard yesterday that Helen is dead. I have just lived through the same agonising [sic] experience with my sister, who was Helen's age and had the same ailment; therefore I know in every detail what it must mean for you.

For me it means that something inexpressively precious has gone and will never come again. Helen's rare combination of goodness and cleverness, firmness and gentleness, tolerance and sharpness of judgment, friendship and undemandingness, was hers alone.

I hope she knew how not only I, but many other people felt about her.

I wish I had seen her still.

With love,
yours,
Anna Freud

Helen's funeral service and burial took place days later, on Friday, August 18th. The arrangements were organized by three of her nephews, Jim, Bud, and Charlie Leake, sons of her sister, Frances. The "Leake boys," as Helen affectionately referred to them, had taken over Camp Kechuwa and had run it successfully for years. She knew them as fine young men who were the closest thing she had to sons. She had always been kind and understanding, and often generous, to them. The Leake boys, and their young families, were like her own, and no one, except her own sisters, was closer to her.

The Leake boys knew Helen as their "Aunt Hi." In a handwritten letter dated August 24, 1978, Jim Leake, the eldest of the Leake brothers, wrote an account of Helen's funeral service and burial and sent it to "Aunt Louise," who was then in ill-health and living in Arizona. The letter reads:

Thursday, August 24, 1978
Dear Aunt Louise

Dory [Jim's wife] and I returned from Camp Kechuwa on Lake Michigamee at the beginning of the week. We called Mom [Frances Ross Leake] back in Ada, Ohio, long distance from here . . . and told her about the beautiful service that we had for Helen, Aunt Hi, last Friday the 18th of August. The service was on Footprint Island, the spot she loved the most in the world. Mom [Frances] was very pleased and happy about the ceremony and was anxious that I write to you and tell you all about it.

Dory and I flew to Marquette, Michigan, one week ago and arrived just a few hours before Hi's ashes arrived from Washington, DC. At 11 a.m., we all left Camp Kechuwa [on Lake Michigamee] by motorboat for the two-mile trip to Footprint Island with Helen's ashes. All of us were Leake family members: Bud, his wife, Jane, and their two children, Kathy and Greg, Charlie, his wife, Sis, and two of their children, Don and Jerry, plus Doug and me.

It was a pretty but gray and overcast day, which seemed appropriate. We gathered up by a big shelf rock underneath the pine trees and looking out toward the beautiful lake. Bud was in charge of the service and first read a poem of Emily Dickinson's, which started out "the bustle in the house the morning after death" and spoke of "putting love away."

Then he read a portion of Chapter 3 of Ecclesiastes, which Helen had always loved and which was suggested by J.B. It starts out "to every thing there is a season and a time to every purpose under heaven. A time to be born and a time to die."

Next Charlie Leake spoke of Hi as a beautiful lady who was a second mother and a grandmother to us all and said, "God rest her soul in the place she loved." He continued:

> "I added that Hi had meant so much to the families of the three boys and that she had tied us all together with Camp Kechuwa, Lake Michigamee, and Footprint, and I finished by saying that we were all going to remember her forever."

Bud finished the service by reading another poem of Emily Dickinson's which includes the lovely line 'spreading wide my narrow hands to gather paradise.'

Finally, a few yards away, we buried Helen's ashes, each of us, including the children, putting on a handful of dirt and covering with the cool pine needles and leaves from the cliff.

Later, Bud will have a simple plaque placed on a rock over the grave for all of us to remember the spot when we visit in future years.

One of the nice things about coming back to Kechuwa in Hi's honor was that it brought the three Leake boys back together for a rare and wonderful reunion.

Louise, we want to extend to you our love and sympathy for the passing of your twin sister. We all love her and will miss her, too.

Much love,
Jim Leake"[627]

Helen Ross would have approved of this heartfelt remembrance.

21

THE FOUR SISTERS AND FLORENCE

Charlie's Family Legacy

When Charlie Ross died suddenly in 1950, he left behind his wife, Florence (age 56), sons John (age 36) and Walter (age 34), and five grandchildren. His absence left a hole in their lives, but they went on without him, some down unexpected paths.

Florence, still young, active, and in good health, decided that her large home on Kennedy Drive in Kenwood no longer suited her needs. Within a year, she'd sold that house and purchased a smaller home not far away on Drummond Avenue in Chevy Chase. After Charlie's funeral, Florence communicated less and less with his sisters, with whom she had little in common outside of their love for Charlie. She kept busy by volunteering as a Gray Lady at the local Red Cross, gardening, socializing with friends, and doting on her grandchildren, who lived nearby.

Florence's pleasant circumstances received a jolt in 1953, when her physician-son John decided to move to Jacksonville, Florida, where he'd taken a position as the Medical Director of the Jacksonville Blood Bank. Once her son and his family had left, Florence was left alone and at a crossroads.

Roy Roberts had been Charlie's friend and colleague since his early days reporting from Washington. They worked for newspapers on opposite sides of Missouri, Roy, at the *Kansas City Star* and Charlie, at the *St. Louis Post-Dispatch*. Each became the first reporters for their respective newspapers in Washington. In many ways, they pioneered how to report the news as a Washington correspondent and became good friends in the process. Roy, Charlie, and their wives also saw each other a lot socially during their time in Washington. Roy returned to Kansas City in 1928 to become his paper's managing editor and a member of its board of directors.

Although they were friends, they were very different in many ways. Roy was a conservative and a lifelong Republican, while Charlie's political views were more liberal, and he favored the Democratic Party. Roy's personality was decidedly outgoing and boisterous, while Charlie's was more reflective and thoughtful. Charlie was a proud graduate of the University of Missouri, while Roy was an equally proud alumnus of the rival University of Kansas. Charlie and Roy set up an annual wager on the outcome of the Kansas-Missouri football game. Each year, after the game was played, the winner would receive a five-dollar bill in the mail, always without any accompanying note.

Roy Roberts paid his respects to Florence and the family when Charlie died suddenly in 1950. In 1952, Roy's wife, Barbara, who'd been ill and wheelchair-bound for some time, passed away. In kind, Florence paid her respects to Roy for his loss. They kept in touch and eventually a courtship blossomed. Despite living in different cities, their courtship continued, and soon they decided to marry. Although Roy, like Charlie, was never a Catholic, the wedding took place at Blessed Sacrament in Chevy

Chase in May 1955. For the second time, Florence, a dedicated Catholic, had married a non-Catholic. The couple took an around-the-world honeymoon voyage lasting several months. Upon their return, Florence sold her house on Drummond Avenue in Chevy Chase, Maryland, and moved to Kansas City to live with Roy.

Florence and Roy turned out to be good for one another. When they started seeing each other, Roy was overweight, smoked Churchill cigars, enjoyed bourbon whiskey, and had experienced the inevitable health effects. Florence soon addressed this. Under her guidance, he ate healthier meals, mostly stopped drinking alcohol, and lost weight. One friend of his said that Florence "added ten years to his life," even though she couldn't stop him from smoking his beloved cigars.[628] Charlie had left Florence financially secure following his

Roy and Florence Ross Roberts seated at a table in what appears to be an outdoor cafe. Roy Roberts is the managing editor of the *Kansas City Star* and Florence is the widow of Press Secretary Charlie Ross. Circa 1958.
(Photo/Harry S. Truman Library)

death—mostly from his pensions and insurance policies—but, with Roy, she found herself married to a wealthy and generous man. She could now travel more, purchase items she otherwise couldn't afford, and give more to charities as well as to family members.

Roy became a welcome addition to the family for Florence's sons and their families. John thought highly of his new stepfather, who, he felt, was very good for Florence. Walter, who by the late 1950s, had become the news director and producer at the public-television station KETC in St. Louis and later served as the Executive Director of the St. Louis Teachers Association. Walter particularly enjoyed his telephone calls with Roy, who good-naturedly called him "Admiral," due to Walter's service in the navy.

Roy strongly believed in the value of a college education and encouraged all the Ross grandchildren to follow in Charlie and his sisters' footsteps. They all graduated from college.

Unfortunately, by the mid-1960s Florence and Roy found themselves facing the inevitable health problems that come with age. Roy's health problems finally caught up with him, and he passed away in his beloved Kansas City in 1967, at 79. At his request, his body was buried in Lawrence, Kansas, not far from the campus of the University of Kansas he loved so dearly. Just before Roy's death, Florence began experiencing heart problems, which turned out to be so serious that she had to have a pacemaker inserted. Florence, always active with her volunteer work and her gardening, chafed at the lack of energy and shortness of breath that came with her weakened heart. She passed away at age 77 in May 1971, as she was talking on the telephone to her parish priest.

Charlie would have been pleased that Florence lived a comfortable and useful life with Roy. He also would have been grateful that his (and his mother's) goal of getting a college education had rippled down through the subsequent generations of his family.

The Sisters' Legacies

After Helen's death in 1978, four of Charlie's sisters remained: Louise, Virginia, Frances, and J. B. Each had taken different paths. They had lived in different places, had pursued different interests, and each had made a life of her own. Each had been raised in Independence, in the same close family, with the same values. How did these remaining Ross sisters' lives play out? Did they all make themselves "useful"? Did they leave positive imprints on the world?

Louise

In many ways, Louise was the most adventurous and free-spirited of the sisters. Several stories capture this well.

When Louise arrived in Parker, then a mere outline of a town, she saw few permanent buildings (mostly tents and tarpaper shacks), and even fewer wagons and cars. Getting around was a challenge. She soon noticed that a group of feral donkeys roamed freely on the outskirts of the town. Louise, who daily had a long walk to the school where she taught, had an idea. She bought some carrots and began feeding the donkeys. In time she earned their trust, and they willingly went to her when she approached. Next, she made a crude bridle out of some clothesline, and placed it over the head of one donkey, who, surprisingly, didn't complain. Once the donkey became used to its new bridle, Louise found a sturdy box, climbed up on it, and sat on the donkey's back. Although initially skittish, it soon trusted Louise and she began riding around the town on her newfound friend. She decided to try to ride the donkey to school. She made it a point to arrive late so that the children would be out in front of the school, waiting for her to arrive. Her dramatic entrance had the desired effect. The impressed children crowded around her, laughing and giggling. At her request, one of the larger boys helped her down from the donkey and assisted her in tying it to a tree behind the school. The class then willingly filed into the schoolhouse, paying special attention that morning to their unconventional teacher as she walked them through their studies.[629]

After her move to Phoenix, she married Fred N. "Fritz" Holmquist, and they had four children together. During these early child-rearing years, Louise's mother, Ella, lived with them and provided welcome help to the growing Holmquist family. Louise needed her mother's help, and it was a blow when Ella passed away in December 1925, the last of her generation in the family. Ella's body was transported back to Independence where she was buried in the Woodlawn Cemetery next to her husband.

Following her mother's death, Louise remained fully occupied caring for her four small children. As told years later by her youngest son, an event occurred one beautiful spring morning in the late 1920s, when Louise decided it would be a good idea to take her twins Helen and Fred, then pre-school age, to Goldwater's Department Store in downtown Phoenix. This was an exciting adventure for the twins, but they wanted to play and to run, not watch their mother shop. Louise sat the twins down in a nook of the store and told them sternly to stay there until she was finished. Louise returned to her shopping. Soon, out of the corner of her eye, she noticed something streak by; she looked up and saw the twins heading for the store's large front door, with Helen in the lead and Fred following close behind. Louise ran toward the busy doorway only to see that her children had made it outside and were scampering down the sidewalk. Then she heard Helen yell to Fred: "You go that way, and I'll go this way—and let's see if mom runs after us." They then bolted in opposite directions.

A young man standing nearby, who'd seen what was happening, said to Louise, "I'll help you—I'll go after the boy if you go after the girl." The man dashed after Fred, while Louise chased Helen, catching up with her about a block away. Louise, with Helen in tow, returned to Goldwater's front door, where she saw Fred standing with the young stranger, waiting for her. She and the twins then walked hand in hand to the streetcar stop and boarded the next car home. The frightening experience gave Louise a renewed appreciation for her adopted hometown and for the friendly people of Phoenix.[630]

Fritz Holmquist enjoyed a healthy stream of business during the 1920s as his young family grew. However, the torrent of engineering work in the '20s slowed to a trickle in the next decade, as the Great Depression set in. Louise remained busy at home, tending to the needs of her children as best she could. Her youngest son recalled, "she kept house, cooked the meals, put the children to bed" and otherwise cared for her growing family.[631] She also continued her sewing on her "Singer sewing machine, which was black."[632] Fritz and Louise had to sell their home and move into a smaller, rented house. Louise's sister, Helen, sent boxes of used clothes for the Holmquist children.[633] Like many other American families, they adjusted and survived until better economic times arrived in the 1940s.

Fritz and Louise showed little interest in organized religion. Nevertheless, their youngest son recalled that one of his parents would sometimes take the children on Sunday to Trinity Episcopal Cathedral, near their home, and drop them off for Sunday school. He also recalled that his father on occasion made a "donation" to that church, particularly at Christmas time.[634]

Like many married couples, Fritz and Louise complemented one another. She was physically active and outgoing; he was quiet and studious. Louise excelled as a cook and a seamstress. Fritz mostly enjoyed reading, particularly poetry and professional journals, and generally kept his feelings to himself.[635] Louise on one occasion confided to her daughter: "The most difficult thing for your father to do is talk."[636] Fritz became widely known professionally and was considered "the dean of civil engineers" in Phoenix. According to an article written about him in 1955, Fritz "laid out more subdivisions here than any other person, among them Park Central, Biltmore Estates, GM Proving Ground, and Washington Street from Phoenix to Tempe.[637] Louise and Fritz made sure their children became conscientious students and received good educations. Louise never allowed her bright children to repeat her lackluster high-school performance.

Each of the Holmquist children graduated from Phoenix Union High School. Lars graduated in 1937 and then attended Phoenix College, a local, two-year college. During the Great Depression, in 1939, he traveled to Washington, DC, where he lived with his Aunt Virginia and Uncle Carl and attended nearby American University for a year. In 1940, he returned to Arizona and earned a bachelor's degree in mathematics in 1941 from the University of Arizona. He served in the U. S. Marine Corps in the war and returned to Arizona, where he was awarded a degree in Civil Engineering. Lars followed in his father's footsteps and enjoyed a long career as a civil engineer.

Helen Holmquist earned her undergraduate degree from Mills College and a Master's in psychology from Stanford University. She married Richard Halnan in 1945. Helen managed to balance an impressive career in psychology while also raising three children. For more than two decades, beginning in the late 1950s, she was a psychology professor at Phoenix College. In the 1960s, she appeared on a local Phoenix television station, KPHO-TV, and gave lectures on topics in psychology. And, as previously noted, she traveled to London in the late 1970s, where she assisted Anna Freud helping children at the Hampstead Clinic.

Helen's twin, Fred Nels Holmquist, Jr., after high school also attended Phoenix College. He graduated in 1942 and then studied at the University of Arizona, and later at the University of Washington, from which he received a bachelor's degree in 1944. He joined the U.S. Navy and saw action in the invasion of Iwo Jima, where he watched the U. S. flag raised over Mt. Suribachi. Following the war, he enrolled in graduate school and, in 1959, earned a Ph.D. in physics from the University of California at Berkeley. He enjoyed a long career as a physicist, doing important, often classified work, for such companies as the Livermore Labs, SW Center for Advanced Studies, GE, and TRW.[638]

The youngest brother, James Bruce Holmquist (who adopted the familiar moniker "J.B."), followed in his siblings' footsteps by attending Phoenix College. In 1943, he was drafted into the U. S. Navy, where he served much of the war on-board the battleship *USS Pennsylvania*. Upon his discharge in 1946, he studied at the University of Arizona, earning a degree in civil engineering in 1949. Upon graduation, he joined Holmquist Engineering with his father. Following his father's death in 1955, he left the firm and continued his career as a civil engineer for many years in both California and Florida.[639]

After a brief illness, Fritz Holmquist died in August 1955, at the age of 71, leaving behind his grieving spouse and four children. Louise remained in Arizona, where she enjoyed a wide circle of friends and the love of her family. Despite failing eyesight, she lived almost to her 90th birthday, passing away just five days shy of it on March 11, 1980.

Louise stands out as the most adventurous and unconventional sister among the Ross sisters. As a child, she chafed at the rigors of school and was a lackluster student; perhaps knowing she couldn't compete with her twin sister. Ironically, she became a very effective and innovative teacher. She also made sure her own children received good educations. She had struck out on her own and willingly left her friends and family far behind in 1910, when she had moved to wild and remote Parker, Arizona. This appealed to her free spirit and sense of adventure. Although unconventional by the Ross-family standards, Louise will always be remembered with love, pride, and, probably, a smile—and as an inspiration for future generations.

Virginia

Virginia, "the fire baby," was the first of Mama's "fall crop." She was always called "Ginny," or, more simply, "Gin." As related earlier, she graduated in 1919 from the University of Missouri, where her writings won her a fellowship for graduate study at Bryn Mawr College.[640] However, much like her sister Helen, years before, she realized she was too restless to pursue a graduate degree. After three days on campus, she gave up the fellowship and boarded a train south to Washington, D.C., where she arrived "with fifty cents in her purse and a box of candy under her arm."[641] She temporarily moved in with Charlie and his family. Never short of energy or gumption, she had a job with the Red Cross within a week and moved into a place of her own.

Virginia embraced the city and made social connections, one of which brought her to the Washington Canoe Club. There she met Charles H. "Carl" Weston, a Harvard-educated lawyer working at the U. S. Justice Department, in its anti-trust division. Both young, idealistic, and new to Washington, Carl and Virginia soon fell in love. This was the time of the infamous "Palmer Raids," when thousands of alien residents were arrested for "Communist leanings." These raids were considered by many, such as the American Civil Liberties Union, as high-handed and an affront to civil liberties. Carl became so disturbed by these raids that he resigned from the Justice Department in protest and moved to New York to practice law in a private firm.

Carl's move to New York didn't slow the budding romance with Virginia. On September 25, 1922, they were married and settled in New York City. Their first child, Amy Ross Weston, was born in 1924, followed two years later by the arrival of their second daughter, Virginia Burns Weston. Carl continued to practice law in New York until 1929, when he rejoined the post-Palmer Justice Department. The Weston family settled into a home on Hawthorne Street in the comfortable neighborhood of Wesley Heights near American University.

Carl Weston worked at the Justice Department for the next three decades. Virginia, as was customary at that time, became the primary homemaker, responsible for the daily housekeeping as well as the care of her two young daughters. Virginia, with her college education, organizational skills, and high energy, loved her family but felt she should contribute to the world outside of her home.

She decided to take a job working for the U. S. Children's Bureau. It was created in response to the dangerous working conditions and unsanitary living situations of children at the turn of the century. In 1912, Congress passed, and President Taft signed, legislation creating the U. S. Children's Bureau and charged it "to investigate and report . . . upon all matters pertaining to the welfare of children and child life among all classes of people." Today the Children's Bureau is under the Department of Health and Human Services, where it helps deliver services designed to protect children and strengthen families . . . [including] . . . adoption and foster care, as well as the prevention of child abuse and neglect.[642] The founders and early leaders of that organization—women such as Florence Kelley, Julia Lathrop, and Grace Abbott—were social trailblazers who greatly influenced Virginia. ("I grew up in a generation where there were many pioneers—all of them inspired me.")[643] Under the guidance of Julia Lathrop, Virginia used her economics training and management skills to help struggling families and children. Due to her family obligations, Virginia would never become one of those leaders she revered. ("I was young—at the bottom—and they were at the top," Virginia modestly asserted years later.)[644] Her work through the year improved the lives of many women and families around the country.

When they were young girls, Virginia's two daughters, Amy and "Burnsie"—the imaginative nickname her youngest daughter had adopted—both attended their aunts' Camp Kechuwa during the summers. Virginia's family, with Carl earning a good living at the Justice Department, stood on a relatively stronger financial footing than many other families, including the Holmquists in Phoenix. During the Depression, Virginia kept in touch with Louise and her other sisters to make sure their families got by and did not do without.

In the early 1940s, Virginia and Carl were surprised by a joyful, life-changing event when their third child arrived. The birth of Virginia's and Carl's unplanned son, Charles H. Weston, Jr., occurred on January 10, 1941, when she was forty-three years old. The baby arrived in good health, and they soon began to call him "Charlie." During World War II, Virginia, in addition to her domestic responsibilities, worked for the government at the Bureau of Labor Standards, and became an active volunteer in the League of Women Voters. After the war, she took on demanding government-consulting assignments in areas involving the working conditions and pay for railroad laborers and migrant workers. And, as previously noted, the Westons hosted many events for family and friends at their home, particularly during Truman's inauguration celebration.

By the early 1950s, Virginia and Carl had seen her daughters Amy and Burnsie graduate from Vassar College and the College of William & Mary, respectively. They each had married and moved away. With Carl deeply involved in the anti-trust litigation at the Justice Department and Charlie enrolled at the Sidwell Friends School in Washington, Virginia felt she had time to contribute more. ("Energy—that's what I have!" she stated in an interview in the 1950s.)[645] Her social consciousness and restlessness led her to a position on the District of Columbia Minimum Wage and Industrial Safety Board, on which she served for eight years, some as the Board's chairman. Her leadership was noted in a 1959 article which stated that "she was credited with a substantial strengthening of the board's activities . . . [and during her tenure] . . . the board revised minimum wage orders covering almost all women and minors in the District in industry." The article went on to summarize her success by asserting that, as "chairman of the D.C. Minimum Wage and Industrial Safety Board, a key position in which to help women workers, she found great satisfaction in seeing women's benefits from the board go up as the percentage of injured employees went down."[646]

In 1959, the year Virginia retired from the D.C. Wage Board, her son Charlie graduated from Sidwell Friends School and entered Earlham College in Indiana. Two years later, her husband, Carl, retired after more than three decades in the Justice Department. The couple never experienced boredom in their retirement. They traveled (visiting relatives and touring foreign countries), gardened, went on hiking trips with their club (The Hikers), played bridge (often at the Cosmos Club, where they had been longtime members), and generally enjoyed time with their family and friends.

Virginia passed away in 1983 at the age of 86, while her husband Carl lived to age 95, passing away in August of 1987 at his home in Washington, DC.[647]

Frances

Frances Bruce Ross was the second in Mama's "fall crop." Soon after graduation from the University of Missouri in April of 1921, she married her high-school sweetheart, Lowell Leake, in the *Kappa Kappa Gamma* sorority house near the campus. Lowell enjoyed the newspaper work he'd done in college, and he chose a career in journalism. Frances, who had no plans for a profession of her own, willingly followed and supported her husband as he pursued his dream. The couple traveled to Akron, Ohio, where Lowell had accepted a position as a sports reporter at $30 per week (equal to $497 in 2022) at *The Akron Press*, a member of the Scripps-Howard news organization.[648] Upon their arrival in Akron, the couple moved into a rented apartment and began their new life together as husband and wife.

By marrying right after graduation and relying on a husband for support, Frances had chosen a more conventional and traditional path. None of the other sisters had pursued this path, even though it was more the norm than exception at the time.

Beginning in June of 1921 and during their first years in Akron, Lowell and Frances succeeded in making a new home, found marriage to their liking, and prospered. Lowell soon rose to the position of City Editor and then, at age 24, became the Managing Editor of the *Akron Press*. On May 2, 1923, they welcomed their first child, James Ross Leake, into the world, and, less than two years later, on February 16, 1925, a second son, Charles Ervin Leake, was born. The young couple remained busy; with highly organized Frances running the household and Lowell doing well at work, their future looked bright.

The family's stable life was disrupted in December 1926 when the Scripps-Howard organization asked Lowell to move to Denver to serve as the Sunday editor of the *Rocky Mountain News*. The young family then moved to Denver, where they spent three years. During their time in Denver, a third son, Lowell Leake, Jr., nicknamed "Bud," was born on May 25, 1928. In the fall of 1929, Scripps-Howard transferred Lowell to Pittsburgh, Pennsylvania. Given the economic clouds on the horizon, he felt he couldn't decline the transfer. A few months later, in 1930, Lowell was transferred (again) to *The Buffalo Times* to serve as its Sunday editor. According to his autobiographical notes, he was soon promoted to Managing editor, and then, suddenly, on August 11, 1930, he was let go in a business reorganization. The Great Depression had arrived—and had altered the Leakes' lives forever.

In those early months of the Great Depression, Frances found herself living in unfamiliar Buffalo with her unemployed husband and her hands full caring for her three young boys. The behaviour of her husband, Lowell, began to worry her. About this time, probably due to his World War I combat experience, he had recurring nightmares and had difficulty sleeping through the night. He began to seek relief by drinking more.

Through the fall of 1930, with the help of Lowell's modest severance and Frances's common sense and organizational abilities, the family managed. Lowell looked for work, but potential employers were mostly out of town. After a few months, he was able to secure a position in New York City with United Press

International (UPI). Frances showed her grit late that fall when Lowell was in New York and she and the boys were left behind in Buffalo. As Lowell told it: "Frances and the boys were snowbound [in Buffalo], no gas, power lines down, snow six feet high around the doors. Frances fed the kids by heating food on a furnace surface, with canned heat, etc., and she had enough food because Larkins [grocery store] that Saturday had made a mistake and doubled her order for groceries and meat." Raised as one of the resourceful Ross women, Frances met adversity.

Lowell's acceptance of the position with UPI was the first in a series of jobs and relocations which continued throughout the Depression years. The family moved to Tenafly, New Jersey, and in 1933, they relocated again to Youngstown, Ohio. In 1936, when his position in Youngstown appeared secure, Sis lent the couple $2,000 to make a down payment on a house there. However, Lowell was soon laid off again. In need of work in the newspaper business, Lowell turned to his brother-in-law Charlie in Washington, DC.

Later that year, with Charlie Ross's help, Lowell was hired by the *Washington Post*, and the family moved to Chevy Chase, Maryland. Lowell's job with the *Washington Post* lasted three years. While in Washington, Frances became reacquainted with her friend, Bess Truman, whose husband, Harry, was a newly elected Senator from Missouri. Bess and Frances rekindled their friendship and played bridge every week in Bess's apartment. However, stability was only fleeting for the Leake family, particularly after Lowell decided that he'd rather *own* a newspaper than work for one.

In the summer of 1939, Lowell and an associate purchased what they thought was a promising newspaper, *The Courier*, published tri-weekly in Asheboro, North Carolina, a town of about 7,000 people. The family picked up and moved again. This time they relocated to a small, Southern town midway between Raleigh and Charlotte. According to Lowell, this was, from almost every perspective, "a disaster." His co-investor had a "family problem," and the paper's advertising person met an "untimely death." After a few months trying to right the ship, Lowell sold his interest in *The Courier*, putting him $7,000 in debt. Once again, he needed a job. Fortunately, the following year (1940), he found work in New York City at *PM*, a liberal magazine heavily funded by Marshall Field. It had adopted the unusual business model of not accepting advertising; an approach designed to foster unbiased reporting and opinions.

Frances became adept at moving the family from one place to another. Lowell had gone ahead to New York to begin his new job at *PM*, leaving Frances in charge of their three sons, packing up the family belongings, and dealing with the movers. Their financial situation was particularly tight. When the movers asked if she wanted to pay extra to have her family's goods insured, Frances declined. On the day of the move, the van was loaded early and headed north to New York City. Frances and the boys followed a short while later. On the road, Frances and the boys came across a burning truck on the side of the road. As they passed it, they saw it was the van carrying their worldly possessions, engulfed in flames. Eventually, Frances and the boys made it to Jackson Heights in Queens, New York City, where the family moved into an empty rented apartment. Over time, they slowly became a fully functioning household again.

By November 1941, Lowell had become "fed up with the editorial tactics and policies and quit *PM* to join the OSS [Office of Strategic Services] in the short-wave radio propaganda division." Lowell's dissatisfaction was short-lived because, shortly after the U.S. entered World War II, he was asked to return to *PM* to oversee its production and business operations. He remained at that magazine until 1948, which brought some much-needed stability to the family.

The Leake Boys and World War II

Beginning in 1940 and continuing throughout the decade, Frances and her sons helped Helen and Sis during the summers at Camp Kechuwa. These summers gave the Leakes an opportunity to leave their New York apartment and work outdoors. These were full summers, as Helen and Sis kept the boys and Frances continuously working. Later in life, the Leake boys recalled how their jobs at the camp taught them a great deal about the demands and rewards of hard work. These summers were a great break for Frances and gave her a chance to spend time with her sisters.

Jim was an eighteen-year-old college student when the war broke out in December of 1941. He received his draft notice early in 1942, while an undergraduate student at the University of Wisconsin. He was granted a deferment that allowed him to complete his spring semester. He then served in the military and continued his education after the war. Lowell Leake recalled, "Jim had been an infantryman, then an engineering student at Connecticut, then a medical student at Yale, and was destined for the University of Rochester." He ended up getting his medical degree from the University of Rochester, and later became a practicing physician. The middle brother, Charlie, was a sixteen-year-old high-school student when the war started. After graduation, he entered the Navy V-12 program, a special wartime program designed to educate and train future naval officers. The program sent him to Harvard, then to Bates College in Maine, and finally back to Boston to Tufts College, where he received his degree and a commission as an ensign in the U. S. Navy. Bud, only thirteen years old when the war started, graduated high school after the war ended. His father and mother attended his graduation, where according to his proud father, "Bud was honored as Mr. Personality . . . and won a war bond for the highest average in the sciences among the boys." He wanted to study engineering and applied to Cornell but was rejected, according to his father, "because of the influx of returning servicemen." Nevertheless, he received his college degree from Tufts in 1950 and later earned a master's and a Ph.D. from the University of Wisconsin in mathematics education. Frances, whose respect for education had guided her sons through their tough early years, was forever proud of their accomplishments.

In January of 1949, Frances and Lowell were the invited guests of President Truman to attend the inauguration festivities in Washington, DC. During the whirlwind of events, they went to a lunch at the Cosmos Club where, among other things, they "had a real visit with Gen. and Mrs. Omar Bradley." Frances described Bradley as "just about the nicest of all the so-called big shots I met." On Sunday, Virginia and Carl Weston gave a cocktail party for thirty family members and friends in honor of Virginia's "big sister," Louise, in from Arizona. The following day, Frances and Louise boarded a train for New York, where, over the next few days, Frances hosted her sister and toured New York. Frances recalled: "As I look back, the past two weeks were just about the most delightful I ever had." Her only lament was that three of her siblings did not attend: "It is a shame that Sis, Hi, and J. B. didn't go to Washington, too, for then all of the Rosses could have been together for once in a lifetime."[649]

In 1948, Lowell departed *PM* for the last time when he decided to go into the typesetting business for small publications. He lasted in that business for 18 months and, as Lowell told it in his memoir: "[I] lost all I had and some I didn't have." In 1950, Lowell found work in Florida with the *St. Petersburg Times* so he and Frances relocated to St. Petersburg. On the evening of December 5, 1950, Lowell was taking a nap. Frances was in another part of the house listening to the radio. Lowell heard her suddenly cry out. She had just heard the news that Charlie had died at his desk in the White House. She took a flight to Washington, DC, where she and all of her sisters except Louise attended the funeral.

The following summer, the *St. Petersburg Times* informed Lowell, as he put it, that he "was let go (the bulletin board said I resigned) on the basis of being last on the force of the department." Shortly thereafter, he found work in Akron, Ohio, with the Public Relations Service Co. of Akron as vice president in charge of sales. Frances eventually relocated to Akron with Lowell but first went to Chicago, to help care for her sister Sis, terminally ill with cancer.

Lowell and Frances lived for most of the 1950s in Akron, Ohio, although his inability to hold onto steady employment continued and his relationship with Frances suffered. During one particularly frustrating period, Frances went alone to Phoenix, Arizona, and stayed with her sister Louise, for several months. According to Helen Halnan, Frances came because she and Lowell were having marital difficulties due to Lowell's drinking. While there, Frances agreed to help sell children's clothes in a local store. At first, Frances showed her total lack of knowledge of sales and business but, after a few weeks, got better at it and enjoyed it. After a few months in Arizona, Frances returned to Lowell in Ohio.

By 1960, the couple had reconciled and moved to the small town of Ada, Ohio, located in northwestern Ohio midway between Toledo and Columbus. Frances taught elementary school and took classes at Northern Ohio University, courses most likely related to her teaching certification. Lowell worked at the *Ada Herald*. While in Ada, Frances became active in political and social affairs. This included speaking at the local Democrat Club dinner about growing up in Independence with the Trumans. In 1963, she wrote a letter to President John F. Kennedy in support of the nuclear test ban treaty and her approval of the Kennedy Administration's stand on civil rights.

Lowell, who'd often commented that eleven was his favorite number, passed away on March 11, 1976. Never noted as a religious man, he converted to Roman Catholicism shortly before his death. Four years later, in 1980, Frances left Ada and moved to Denver, Colorado, to be close to her oldest son, Jim, now a practicing physician.

In the 1970s, the Leakes converted Camp Kechuwa to a family-vacation property. Frances visited every summer until she was no longer physically able. In 1984, she organized a large family reunion there, making it possible for her three sons, their wives, all eleven of her grandchildren as well as several great-grandchildren to spend an entire week together. That year—as well as other years—the family organized a "Grandma Day" to celebrate Frances and her influence on her family. The celebration included a banquet dinner, with tributes to Frances, often written as "birch bark poems," a Camp Kechuwa tradition.

In the early 1990s, Frances moved into Sunny Acres retirement community. In her final years, she suffered from dementia and passed away on April 4, 1997, at the age of 98. She was the last of her generation of Rosses.

Five years before her death, Frances gave an interview to two junior-high-school students who were given the assignment of interviewing "a senior citizen" and writing that person's biography. The young students interviewed Frances at Sunny Acres and summarized their impressions: "Frances Leake is one of the strongest, bravest women I've [Sic] ever known. She has lived through many traumatizing events and is still in good health and happy. She has no regrets. She does have an overwhelming fear for today's children. What surprised us most is that she is not afraid to die. 'When I die—I don't expect to soon—I want to be cremated and my ashes spread over Mt. Evans. I feel that's the only way I'll get to the top.'"

After her death, in a tribute to his mother, Frances's oldest son, Jim, distributed her ashes in a brief ceremony at the Mt. Evans Wilderness Area in Colorado—making sure his mother made it to the top.

James Bruce "J. B." Ross

James Bruce Ross, born on July 3, 1902, was forever saddled with her father's first name. She was the youngest and the last of the "fall crop." Always a problem, she made her initial moniker work first as "Jamie," and then going by "J. B."

J. B. had a strong advantage to counterbalance her odd name. When Mama assigned the three older sisters their "charges," J.B. became Helen's responsibility. As noted earlier, Helen took her responsibility for J.B. seriously. One story involves a large dent made in the wall near the bottom of the staircase in the family home in Independence. One day Helen, carrying baby J. B. down the stairway, tripped and fell. She somehow was able to protect J. B. as they tumbled down the stairs. At the bottom, Helen's head caromed against the wall, leaving a large dent, but J. B. was unharmed. Luckily, Helen was not badly injured, but the dent in the wall remained and was viewed as a point of honor by Helen. It became J. B.'s good fortune that Helen, her successful, older sister, went on to finance a substantial part of J. B.'s college education as well as some of her early travel. J. B. attended Vassar and earned her undergraduate degree in history in 1925, graduating with *Phi Beta Kappa* honors, as many of her family had done before at the University of Missouri.

After college, J. B. enrolled in graduate school at the University of Chicago and lived with Sis and Helen. In 1927, J. B. was awarded a master's degree in history and published a scholarly article in *Classical Philology* entitled, "On the Early History of Leontius' Translation of Homer." During the summers, she helped at Camp Kechuwa. In 1928, J. B. traveled west and taught history at the Branson School, then a secondary school for girls that was located, coincidentally, in Ross, California. (Today, the Branson School still sits in Marin County, north of San Francisco, and operates as a college preparatory school, although now it's coed.) She returned to Chicago in 1930 and, with fellowship aid, resumed her graduate work in history at the University of Chicago. In 1934, she earned her Ph.D. in History from that university; her doctoral dissertation was entitled "A Study of the Medieval Attitude toward Antiquities." The next year, she began her college teaching career as a substitute instructor in history at her alma mater, Vassar College.

J. B.'s peaceful, academic life sustained two shocks during the late 1930s. Her interest in Medieval European history required her to research original texts located in Europe. This often required her to learn the language of the country, which she found easy to do. In the summer of 1936, she traveled to Granada, Spain. On July 19, the army of the fascist General Francisco Franco launched a coup d'etat and the Spanish Civil War began. J.B.'s hotel in Granada was bombed, and many of its guests were killed. Fifty years later, when interviewed about it, she said she could "still hear the whistling bombs." She and her traveling companion, Leila Barber, an art instructor from Vassar, remained trapped in the hotel in Granada for nineteen days, cut off from any communication with the outside world. J. B.'s family knew she was in Granada, at the time. Her brother and sisters were extremely worried. "I remember Mother being so worried about J. B.," recalled Burnsie Weston Slaughter. By mid-August, they were allowed to leave Spain, and J.B. returned to the United States.

In December 1938, the *Chicago News* announced that Miss J. B. Ross and Mr. Howard K. Beale were engaged to be married. According to family members, the wedding took place in the Westons' home in Washington, DC. The marriage was short-lived. While on her honeymoon, J.B. discoverd that Mr. Beale was a homosexual and the marriage ended abruptly. J. B. never remarried, and the family members refrained from ever mentioning Mr. Beale again.

College Professor

In 1937, J. B. accepted a teaching position as a history instructor at Wellesley College, which was twelve miles west of Boston. Like Vassar, it was one of the Seven Sisters all-women's colleges. After a couple of years at Wellesley, J.B. returned to Vassar, where she became a full-time history instructor. In 1943, she became an Assistant Professor and, in 1944, an Associate Professor and Assistant Dean. She held the position of Assistant Dean for four years, until 1948, at which time she returned full-time to teaching, research, and writing.

In 1948, J. B. took a leave of absence from teaching and returned to Europe to continue her research of medieval life. In 1949, she returned to Vassar. That same year, Viking Press published *The Portable Medieval Reader*, a compilation of original works translated and co-edited by J. B. and her friend and fellow historian, Mary McLaughlin. In 1953, J. B. and Mary McLaughlin translated and co-edited a second compilation of original works published by Viking, entitled *The Portable Renaissance Reader*. These books were widely used in college history courses for generations. Much of the content in these *Portable Readers* focused on the roles of women, children, and families in the Middle Ages, subjects largely overlooked in other texts at the time.

Vassar College, recognizing J. B.'s growing academic stature, promoted her to full Professor in 1955. The following year, she again took leave to continue her research, this time in Belgium. Her research and writing bore fruit with the 1959 publication of a book she translated and edited, *The Murder of Charles the Good, Count of Flanders,* originally written by Gilbert of Bruges. This told the story of an historically important slaying that occurred in a church in medieval Flanders in 1127. This was her third and final book. Her three books, coupled with the reviews and other articles she penned over her career, stand as an impressive body of scholarship.

In 1962, J. B. was awarded the Lucy Maynard Salmon Chair of History at Vassar College. She was a life-member of the Medieval Academy of America, the Renaissance Academy of America, the Society of Church History, and the American Historical Association. In 1966, she retired from teaching at Vassar, where she was named a Professor Emeritus of History.

In retirement, J. B. continued her work. She wrote several scholarly articles, including "Gasparo Contarini and His Friends (1970), "The Emergence of Gasparo Contarini" (1972), and "The Middle-Class Italian Child, Fourteenth to Early Sixteenth Centuries" (1974). She developed an interest in gardening. For many years, she lived with Helen in their spacious apartment in Washington, DC. Virginia's daughter (J. B.'s niece), Amy Weston Firfer was also a Vassar graduate, and Amy always remained close to her aunt.

J.B. and Helen went to their home on Captiva Island in the winter months and spent several weeks each summer on Footprint Island.

J.B. died of cardiac arrest on December 10, 1995, in the Collington Life Care Community in Prince Georges County, Maryland. Her life and accomplishments were richly noted in *Women Medievalists and the Academy*, a book published by the University of Wisconsin Press. An entire chapter is devoted to her life and work. In the chapter's final paragraph, her fellow historian and longtime friend, Mary McLaughlin, describes J. B. as "a gardener of the heart . . . [with] wise concern for the well-being of others, the generosity of spirit so variously bestowed on those whose lives she shared, her loving and unfailing devotion to her family and her friends." The article's author adds: "Her abiding interest in her students, her friends, and her colleagues, as well as her determination to understand rightly the history of men, women, and children who were the subjects of her research were gifts to us all."[650]

Like her brother and sisters, J.B. made significant contributions to our world and led a consequential life. She enlightened others, not only her (mostly female) students through her teaching, but also others who sought to learn the lessons of history as shown through her research and writing.

PARTING THOUGHTS AND EPILOGUE

Over a decade ago, I set out to discover the missing pieces of what I knew about the Ross side of my family. I had never known my famous grandfather Charlie, nor did I really know much about his six sisters. I'd met with three of the sisters (Great-Aunts Helen, J. B., and Virginia) briefly at various times in the 1960s and 1970s. However, it wasn't until I began researching this book that I realized there was a larger and more compelling picture that needed telling. This book centers around the remarkable life and accomplishments of Charlie Ross. However, the camera also swings to shows a story of a remarkable generation of Ross women . . . all of whom were born and raised in Independence, Missouri.

Over time, families tend to adopt their own set of shared values and guiding principles, perhaps as survival techniques or simply improvisation. These values might be things such as making money, taking care of the less fortunate, going to church, or simply staying ahead of the Joneses. The Ross family evolved their own shared values and guiding principles over the years. Below are the key ones that emerged from my research.

1. Get a College Education

JB Ross wasn't keen on an academic education beyond high school. However, he didn't stand in the way of the powerful vision of his wife, Ella, that their children would get a good education at a great university. This didn't begin with Ella, rather, it came from her mother, Rebecca Thomas, a family figure I knew little about before writing this book. Rebecca Thomas stands out as a true heroine in my story. She laid the groundwork for her grandson and later for her granddaughters to go on to higher education and rewarding lives. This was first achieved by Charlie, and then by his sisters, who would not settle for a subservient spot in the family.

2. The Christian Church (Disciples of Christ)

Like many small towns, the social strata of Independence was reflected in the congregations of its churches. The Episcopalians and Presbyterians were at the top; Methodists and the Christian Church were in the middle; and the Mormons and Baptists were toward the bottom (the Catholic Church was in a class apart on its own). Churches were a central part of life in the community, and most people attended.

The Ross family was heavily involved in the local Christian Church. The family of Rebecca Thomas founded that church in Independence. All the Ross children attended Sunday school at the Christian Church and absorbed its teachings, which were all based on the Bible. In the Christian Church, each member was allowed to interpret and follow the Bible's teachings in his or her own way. The Ross children were well-schooled in Christianity. Eventually, they all gravitated away from the church and became agnostics or atheists. However, they used their Bible teachings at the Christian Church as a moral compass throughout their lives.

3. Small Town Roots

As Charlie famously said, Independence was a small town "where everybody knew everybody." This meant, among other things, that there was easy proximity to the town's schools, library, churches, businesses, and government. All were modest, but they were easily accessible. Teachers, pastors, shop owners, and government employees were all approachable and provided help to young patrons, many of whom they had known for years. It's no accident that the first person Harry Truman and Charlie called to tell about his appointment as Press Secretary was Miss Tillie, their beloved high school teacher.

There were many relatives, particularly on Ella's side of the family, and close friends whom the family had known for decades. These relatives, friends, and neighbors helped to support the Ross family. This support was one reason, beyond Ella's thrifty ways, that enabled the family to survive when money was tight, and JB was off on one of his "mining trips."

Old friends with roots in Independence pop up in the stories of each of our characters. Most famous, of course, was President Harry S. Truman.

4. Support for Each Other

Within the close-knit Ross family, Charlie saw it as his duty to help his ambitious sisters achieve the core family value of a college education. But where did this duty to support his sisters come from? Clearly it came from Charlie's mother, Ella, and her mother Rebecca Thomas. And once that ball got rolling by Charlie, the other sisters—already neatly paired in a supportive structure—did the same for one another.

One of Ella's talents was that she was organized—very organized—as she needed to be, raising seven children. Charlie was given the duty of providing economic support for Helen so that she, like he, could attend college at the University of Missouri. Helen, in turn, provided economic support to Virginia and then J.B., so that they, too, could get a college education—and down the line it went.

The ethos of the siblings supporting one another throughout their lives became a binding Ross trait, and this applied to much more than just funding college. Throughout their lives they were always there for each other. In the case of Helen, Sis, and J.B. they shared homes and lives together.

5. Teach Others

With the influence of Ella and Rebecca, the Ross children looked at education not only as something to get, but also as something to give others through teaching. Charlie, Sis, Helen, Louise, Ginny, and J.B. were all teachers or professors at various points in their lives. This started when Helen founded her "school" in the barn on Main Street, where she and her sisters fashioned their playing around a make-believe classroom.

6. Advocacy for Women

Ella opened the door so that her "smart" daughters could achieve things that were very rare for women at the time. The goal for most girls in the Independence of that era was marriage—ideally, to someone from a well-connected family with promising prospects. Ella saw things differently. Charlie, of course, became the most famous. However, his journey was shaped by the influence of his six remarkable sisters and the family values that they all carried with them. Throughout their lives, almost all of the sisters advocated for improving the lives of women, and they each were an inspiration and role model for younger women.

ACKNOWLEDGMENTS

Publisher's Note: The following acknowledgments were compiled from unfinished handwritten notes made by the author, John Ross, before his death. The Ross Family has also added additional acknowledgments below that they feel reflect what John Ross would have wanted to say had he been able to finish his acknowledgments before he passed away.

Author's Acknowledgments: Beyond my wife, Patti Ross, to whom this book is dedicated, and my mother, who I amply mentioned in the Introduction, I would be beyond remiss not to acknowledge the following for their encouragement and support:

Previously Known Relatives

- Lucy Ross Natkiel, who sent me the 110 typed pages of our Aunt Hi's (Helen Ross') memoirs.

- Helen Ross (Lucy's sister), who met me in Missouri, and guided me through our long-lost family history.

- David, Shannon, and Katherine Ross, my three children, who gently nudged their dad from time-to-time throughout this long process, and for whom this book was largely written.

Somewhat Distant and Previously Unknown Relatives

- Charles H. Holman (grandson of Louise Ross Holmquist), a second cousin who had some of our family's history and who generously shared it with me, as well as his time (and accommodations in California). He helped me as I felt my way (often blindly) though this process.

- Helen H. Holman (daughter of Louise Ross Holmquist), enthusiastically received my telephone calls and generously answered all my questions. She provided important insights into this generation of Rosses, much of which found its way into this book.

- James Bruce "J.B." Holmquist (son of Louise Ross Holmquist), who provided insightful and often humorous anecdotes about his mother and their lives in Phoenix.

- Virginia "Burnsie" Weston Slaughter (daughter of Virginia Ross Weston), who not only housed and fed me at her home in Virginia but provided keen and useful insight about our family early on as I was beginning research for the book.

- Anna Davis (granddaughter of Louise Ross Holmquist), who was always cheerfully responsive to my many inquiries.

- Donald Leake (grandson of Frances Ross Leake) and his wife Julie Leake, who skillfully and generously guided me through the environs of Lake Michigamee, Michigan, including the grounds of Camp Kechuwa and Footprint Island. This provided much useful information about the family.

- Kathy Leake Weese (granddaughter of Frances Ross Leake), who has been invaluable in sharing a wealth of information about her grandmother's generation and in her remarks and comments on specific drafts I gave to her.

In-Laws

- Robert "Chip" Price and Barbara Price Percival (brother-in-law and sister-in-law), who were always upbeat and supportive of this project as if they were blood relatives.

- Pamela Tully Price (sister-in-law and Chip's spouse), who was a world class "fellow outlaw" in the Price family. She was also the former long-time owner of the Book Shop of Beverly Farms in Massachusetts and knows more about books than anyone I know. She has given me encouragement and support through the years.

Friends and Associates

- Claudette Mayer (family friend and college roommate of my sister-in-law Barbara), who not only gave me ongoing encouragement (and a few strategic nudges) but also generously introduced me to Bill Zinsser for additional, and much needed, support.

- William "Bill" Zinsser (1922–2015), a well-known writer, educator, and teacher who, along with his wife, Caroline, met with me one summer afternoon and let me tell them about my book project. After hearing me describe what I thought (in 2012) were the high points of the book, Bill pithily said,

"You may have something there." This "non-rejection" was all I needed, and my book remained alive.

- Kathryn Krause Rooney (wife of my college roommate and friend, Steve Rooney), who consistently demonstrated her infectious enthusiasm for telling this story, particularly for the sisters, who she found not only interesting, but inspirational. Her enthusiasm (and encouraging nudges) always left me thinking that this was a story worth telling and that others beyond my family might enjoy it as well.

To all those many people I have neglected to mention, and who, over the past decade this book has taken to complete, have provided encouragement and support, I say Thank You!! Please know that any mistakes and inconsistencies in this book are entirely my responsibility.

Ross Family Acknowledgments: The author's wife and children would like to thank the following people for all of their hard work, dedication, and support:

- As the author outlined in his introduction, the fine people at the Truman Library and Museum were instrumental in planting the seed for this book back in 2010 and helped throughout with research and support. We would like to thank Alex Burden (Executive Director) and Clifton Truman Daniel (Honorary Chairman, Truman Institute) for their kind help and support. In addition, special thanks go to Laurie Austin (Archivist) for her prompt and thorough help in researching photos for the book.

- Brooke C. Stoddard, who edited the manuscript and shared his own experience as a published author to coach John Ross on becoming a book author.

- Michele DeFilippo and her staff at 1106 Design, who worked with our publisher on this project. 1106 Design provided expert design, editing, proofing, and production services for the project. In particular, we would like to thank project managers Kayla Cook and Ronda Rawlins.

- James Singewald (Digital Imaging Specialist) at Full Circle Fine Art Services in Baltimore, who did a very professional job scanning, processing, and enhancing the old photographs from the Ross family collection.

- West Oak Associates, our publisher, who took the manuscript and made it into a living, breathing, book. We would especially like to thank Chip Price, who devoted himself to editing and producing the book that John envisioned. Pam Price proofread the final page proofs, and her experience and recommendations were invaluable.

ENDNOTES

1. Letter from Charles G. Ross to his sons, John B. Ross and Walter W. Ross, dated November 12, 1936, as edited by Charles G. Ross (hereafter referred to as CGR Letter of November 1936).
2. James Logan, *Clans of the Scottish Highlands*
3. 1790 U.S. Census data and 1800 U.S. Census data.
4. CGR Letter of November 1936.
5. 1850 Slave Enumeration for Henderson, Tennessee.
6. Helen Ross's memoirs.
7. Handwritten memoir notes of Virginia Ross Weston about her father, James Bruce Ross (circa 1982)
8. Letter from James Bruce Ross to his daughter, Miss Ella Ross, dated July 11, 1913.
9. Memoirs of Helen Ross (p. 27) [both griddle-cake adage and amethyst-ring episode].
10. Letter from James Bruce Ross to his daughter, Miss Ella Ross, dated July 11, 1913.
11. Memoirs of Helen Ross (p. 27) [both griddle-cake adage and amethyst-ring episode].
12. "Lockdown" by David W. Jackson and Paul Kirkman, 2009, pp. 44-46
13. "Lockdown," pp. 60-61.
14. "Jesse James," The *Biography Channel* website, http://www.biography.com/people/jesse-james-9352646, (accessed March 25, 2014).

15. Virginia Ross Weston's notes.
16. James Bruce Ross' (female) pedigree chart.
17. 1860 and 1870 Censuses.
18. Letter from Frances "Fannie" Thomas circa 1863.
19. Program announcement from Woodland College found in the archives of the Jackson County Historical Society.
20. Virginia Ross Weston's notes.
21. Letter from Charles G. Ross to his sons circa 1936, as edited in 1937.
22. Memoirs of Helen Ross p. 7.
23. Letter of Charles G. Ross dated Nov. 12, 1936, later hand-edited.
24. Virginia Ross Weston's handwritten memoirs, p. 10.
25. Memoirs of Helen Ross, pp. 88–90.
26. Letter of Charles G. Ross dated Nov. 12, 1936, later hand-edited
27. *Ibid.*
28. Memoirs of Helen Ross, p. 31.
29. Letter of Charles G. Ross dated Nov. 12, 1936, later hand-edited.
30. Author's note: It is interesting (and hopefully instructive for anyone who enjoys family history) to note that when I was a child, I was told almost nothing about J.B. Ross, my great-grandfather, *except*: "Your great-grandfather was a Marshal in Independence, Missouri, and he helped capture the James Brothers." Thinking that was an interesting piece of history I would sometimes mention it to my friends and schoolmates, none of whom, fortunately, had any information to the contrary.
31. "Lockdown," pp. 60, 61 and 70.
32. "Lockdown" by David W. Jackson and Paul Kirkman, pp. 69, 70, 86)
33. Memoirs of Helen Ross, p. 31.
34. Memoirs of Helen Ross, p. 3.
35. Memoirs of Helen Ross, p. 2.

36. CGR letter of November 12, 1936, as amended by his handwritten notes in 1936-1937.
37. *The Sunday School Evangelist* July 10, 1892 edition; Christian Publishing Company, St. Louis, Missouri; W. W. Dowling, Editor.
38. CGR's genealogy letter dated circa 1937, p. 13.
39. *The Reluctant Servant*, p. 14.
40. "Lockdown," p. 88.
41. HM, p. 21.
42. "Lockdown," p. 88.
43. HM, p. 21.
44. *Ibid.*
45. "Lockdown," p. 88.
46. Independence newspaper article
47. Letter of CGR dated November 12, 1936, later hand-edited.
48. Memoirs of Helen Ross, p. 9.
49. *Ibid.* p. 15.
50. *Ibid.* p. 16.
51. *Ibid.* p. 18.
52. *Ibid.*
53. *Ibid.* p. 19.
54. *Ibid.* Note in Helen Ross' memoirs, J.B. Ross' political boss is named "Mr. Kessler." In "Lockdown," he is referred to as "Mr. Keshlear."
55. *Ibid.*, p. 6.
56. *Ibid.*, p. 6.
57. Handwritten memoirs of Virginia Ross Weston.
58. Helen Ross' memoirs, p. 12.
59. *Ibid.*
60. Virginia Ross Weston's handwritten notes (undated), pp. 11-13.
61. Memoirs of Virginia Ross Weston [MVRW], p. 13 and Memoir notes of Helen Ross [MHR], p. 9

62. Charles Ross' genealogy letter, dated circa 1937, pp. 11-15.
63. MHR, pp. 7-8 and MVRW, p. 12A
64. MHR, p. 43
65. MHR, p. 9
66. *Ibid.*
67. *Ibid.*
68. *Ibid.*
69. MHR, p. 38
70. *Ibid.*
71. MHR, p. 39
72. MHR, p. 11
73. *Ibid.*, p. 10
74. *Ibid.*, p. 39
75. *Ibid.*, p. 36
76. *Ibid.*, p. 11.
77. *Ibid.*, p. 88.
78. *Ibid.*, p. 64
79. *Ibid.*, p. 51.
80. *The Reluctant Servant*, p.15.
81. MHR, pp. 42-51.
82. *Ibid.*, p.34
83. *Ibid.*, pp. 29-50.
84. *Ibid.*, p. 37.
85. *Truman*, by McCullough, p. 44
86. *Harry S. Truman*, Margaret Truman, p. 3.
87. Hi's Memoirs, p. 47 and *Man of the People* by Hamby, p. 6.
88. *Truman*, p. 58, and Ross family lore.
89. *Man from Missouri*, by Cyril Clemens, p. 27.
90. *Ibid.*, p. 26.
91. Hamby, pp. 4-5
92. *Ibid.*, pp. 4-5

93. *Ibid.*, p. 7
94. *Ibid.*, p. 8; MHR and MVRW
95. Hamby, p. 6
96. MHR.
97. Helen's memoirs, p. 1
98. *Ibid.*, pp. 2-3
99. *Ibid.* p. 3
100. *Ibid.* p. 22
101. See *Lock Down: Outlaws, Lawmen & Frontier Justice in Jackson County, Missouri* by David W. Jackson and Paul Kirkman, Jackson County (Mo.) Historical Society, 2009, Appendix E. (p. 137)
102. Helen's memoirs, p. 11
103. *Ibid.*
104. *Ibid.* p. 29.
105. *Ibid.* p. 30.
106. MHR, p. 16
107. *Man from Missouri* by Cyril Clemens, p. 26.
108. *Truman*, by David McCullough, p. 59
109. CGR's Ott School Report Card (JBR files)
110. CGR's Grammar Exam, May 23, 1898
111. CGR's Arithmetic Exam, May 24, 1898
112. *Man from Missouri*, p. 29.
113. *Plain Speaking* by Merle Miller, p. 57.
114. *Truman*, by David McCullough, p. 59.
115. Truman's memoirs, p. 118 (vol. I)
116. St. Louis *Post-Dispatch*, April 29, 1945.
117. *The Man from Missouri*, by Steinberg, pp. 27-28.
118. Hamby, pp. 15-16; Steinberg, p. 27.
119. MHR, p. 11.
120. *Plain Speaking*, by Merle Miller, p. 57.
121. MHR, p. 51

122. Memoir notes of Virginia Ross Weston, p. 23.
123. Memoirs of Helen Ross, p. 51.
124. Conversation with Katherine Leake Weese.
125. Memoirs of Helen Ross, p. 57.
126. Memoir of Helen Ross, p. 30.
127. *Ibid.*, p. 55.
128. Conversations with Helen, Virginia, and J.B. in the 1960s.
129. *Ibid.*, p. 50.
130. Memoirs of Helen Ross, p. 30.
131. *Ibid.*, p. 91.
132. *Ibid.*, pp. 73 and 75.
133. *Ibid.*, p. 18.
134. *Ibid.*, p. 90.
135. *Ibid.*, p. 16.
136. *Ibid.*, p. 18.
137. *Ibid.*, p. 18.
138. *Ibid.*, p. 90.
139. *Ibid.*, p. 51.
140. *Ibid.*, p. 52.
141. *Ibid.*, p. 87.
142. *Ibid.*, p. 50.
143. *Ibid.*, p. 39.
144. *Ibid.*, p. 50.
145. *Ibid.*, p. 91.
146. *Ibid.*, p. 91.
147. *Ibid.*, p. 54.
148. *Ibid.*, p. 91.
149. *Ibid.*, p. 53.
150. *Ibid.*, p. 54.
151. https://embryo.asu.edu/ and **Source URL:** https://embryo.asu.edu/pages/lydia-pinkhams-vegetable-compound-1873–1906

152. *Ibid.*, p. 88.
153. *Ibid.*, p. 57.
154. *Ibid.*, p. 64.
155. *Ibid.*, pp. 57-58.
156. Farrar, *Reluctant Servant: The Story of Charles G. Ross*, (Columbia, Missouri, University of Missouri Press, 1969), p. 24.
157. *Ibid.*, p. 25.
158. *Ibid.*, pp. 25–26.
159. Stephens, *A History of the University of Missouri*, (Columbia, Missouri, University of Missouri Press, 1962) pp. 360–361.
160. Academic transcript of Charles G. Ross for Degree of A. B. awarded June 1905.
161. Farrar, *Reluctant Servant*, p. 26.
162. *Savitar* [The Yearbook of the University of Missouri], Columbia, Missouri, 1903, p. 146.
163. *Savitar*, 1904–1905, p. 17.
164. *Missouri Alumnus*, "Eight Young Men of 1904–05," (1966) Columbia, Missouri, p.10–11.
165. Academic transcript of C.G. Ross.
166. *Savitar*, Vol. 11, p. 17.
167. Academic transcript of CGR.
168. Farrar, *Reluctant Servant*, p. 29.
169. Website of the Phi Beta Kappa Society (pbk.org)
170. A conversation with the son of Charles G. Ross (and father of this author) circa 1965.
171. *QEBH Fourth Memorial Directory*, University of Missouri, Columbia, Missouri, May 1940, from University Archives, University of Missouri-Columbia.
172. Farrar, *A Creed for My Profession: Walter Williams, Journalist to the World*. (Columbia, Missouri, University of Missouri Press, 1998: p. 30.
173. *Ibid.*, pp. 38–39.

174. *Ibid.*, pp. 49–50.
175. *Ibid.*, pp. 54–61.
176. *Ibid.*, p. 74.
177. *Ibid.* pp. 68–69.
178. *Ibid.*, pp. 81–85.
179. Farrar, *Reluctant Servant,* p. 32.
180. *Ibid.*, pp. 32–33.
181. Farrar, pp. 33–34.
182. Farrar, pp. 34–35.
183. Farrar. p. 36
184. *Ibid.*, p. 36
185. *Ibid.*, p. 61.
186. Helen's Memoirs, p. 66.
187. Helen's Memoirs, p. 91.
188. Helen's Memoirs, p. 64.
189. *Ibid.*, p. 96.
190. *Ibid.*, p. 58
191. *Ibid.*, pp. 64–65. Also, Mary Wollstonecraft (1759–1797) was an English writer who in 1792 wrote *A Vindication of the Rights of Woman*, which agreed that women were not inferior to men, but appear to be only because of lack of education. Her daughter, Mary Wollstonecraft Shelley (1797–1851), married the poet Percy Bysshe Shelley and edited her husband's works; she also wrote one of the earliest science-fiction novels, *Frankenstein,* published in 1818.
192. Helen's Memoirs, p. 84.
193. *Ibid.*, p. 97.
194. Helen's Memoirs, p. 56.
195. *Ibid.*
196. Essay by Virginia Ross Weston, entitled "Louise," dated February 1980.
197. Helen's memoirs, p. 91.

198. *Ibid.*, p. 87.
199. *Ibid.*, p. 87.
200. *Ibid.*, p. 90.
201. *Ibid.*, p. 90.
202. Handwritten notes of Virginia Ross Weston, circa 1980.
203. Essay by Virginia Ross Weston, entitled "Louise," dated February 1980, p. 2.
204. *Ibid.*, p. 3.
205. *Ibid.*
206. *Ibid.*, pp. 1–2.
207. *Ibid.*, p. 2.
208. *Ibid.*, p. 4.
209. *The Gleam*, 1909 issue, p. 14.
210. Helen's Memoirs, p. 91.
211. *The Arizona Republic*, May 17, 1945.
212. Essay by Virginia Ross Weston, entitled "Louise," dated February 1980, p. 4.
213. *Ibid.*, p. 7.
214. Helen's memoirs, p. 93.
215. *The Gleam*, 1915 issue, p. 21.
216. Handwritten notes of Virginia Ross Weston, circa 1980
217. Handwritten notes of Virginia Ross Weston, circa 1980.
218. Helen's Memoirs, p. 4.
219. Handwritten memoirs of Virginia Ross Weston (undated), p. 21.
220. *Ibid.*, p. 17.
221. *Reluctant Servant*, Farrar, p. 37.
222. "Did Yellow Journalism Fuel the Outbreak of the Spanish-American War?" by Lesley Kennedy, *The History Channel* (a/k/a history.com), A&E Television Networks, LLC, August 22, 2019.
223. *A Creed for My Profession*, Farrar, pp. 128–129.
224. *Ibid.*, p. 129.

225. *A Creed for My Profession*, Farrar, p. 50.
226. *Ibid.*, pp. 121–122.
227. *Ibid.*, pp. 114–118.
228. *Ibid.*, pp. 125–126.
229. *Ibid.*, p. 96.
230. *Collier's* (magazine), Vol. XLVII, September 2, 1911, p.18.
231. *A Creed for My Profession*, Farrar, p. 147.
232. *Ibid.*, p. 131.
233. *Ibid.*, p. 134.
234. *Ibid.*, p. 134.
235. *Ibid.*, p. 138.
236. *Ibid.*, p. 138.
237. *Ibid.*, p. 139.
238. *Ibid.*, p. 142
239. *Ibid.*, pp. 140, 146.
240. *Ibid.*, pp. 143–144
241. *Collier's: The International Weekly* [magazine], "Missouri's Journalist Factory: A Practical College Course, Which Included the Publication of an Eight-Page Newspaper" by Charles Phelps Cushing, Vol. XLVII No. 24. September 2, 1911, p. 18
242. *A Creed for My Profession*, Farrar, pp. 147–151.
243. *Ibid.*, p. 148.
244. *Ibid.*, p. 148.
245. *Ibid.*, p. 149
246. *Collier's*, p. 25.
247. *Ibid.*, p. 25.
248. *Ibid.*
249. *Ibid.*, pp. 18–19.
250. *Ibid.*, p. 18.
251. *Ibid.*, p. 19.
252. *Ibid.*, p. 25.

253. *Ibid.*, p. 25.
254. Mary Paxton Keeley Oral History Interview, National Archives, Harry S. Truman Library Museum. Columbia, Mo., July 12, 1966 by James R. Fuchs
255. Mary Paxton Keeley, State Historical Society of Missouri website, https://shsmo.org
256. *Ibid.*
257. Mary Paxton Keeley Oral History Interview, July 12, 1966 by James R. Fuchs.
258. *A Creed.* . . . Farrar, p. 165.
259. *Ibid.*, p. 165.
260. *Ibid.*, p. 165.
261. *Kansas City Star*, Sunday, July 17, 1975, p. 4C.
262. Mary Paxton Keeley, State Historical Society of Missouri website.
263. *A Creed.* . . . Farrar, p. 165.
264. *A Creed.* . . . Farrar, p. 166.
265. *A Creed.* . . . Farrar, p. 166.
266. For years, the portrait of Charlie Ross hung in Neff Hall at the School of Journalism. Across the archway in Walter Williams Hall, another journalism school building, Mary Paxton Keeley's portrait stood. In 1988 the school's dean, James D. Atwater, ordered the portraits be relocated and hung together in a prominent spot, in the Graduate Studies Center, side by side forever. *A Creed.* . . . Farrar, p. 238.
267. *A Creed.* . . . Farrar, pp. 202–203.
268. *A Creed.* . . . Farrar, p. 203.
269. *Ibid.*, p. 204.
270. Conversations with Virginia Ross Weston, circa 1969.
271. Helen's memoirs, p. 93.
272. See *Journalism's First Textbook: Creating a News Reporting Body of Knowledge,* by Joe Mirando, a paper presented at the Association

for Education in Journalism and Mass Communication, 76th convention, 14 August 1993, Kansas City, Missouri.
273. Website of the *Kansas City Star* in August 2021; www.kcstar.com/hemingway
274. William Strunk, Jr. and E. B. White, *The Elements of Style*, The Macmillan Company, 1959, Introduction, page ix.
275. ᵛ Helen's memoirs, p. 97.
276. *Ibid.*, p. 97.
277. Helen's memoirs, p. 96.
278. *Ibid.*, p. 99.
279. *Ibid.*, p. 99.
280. *Ibid.*, p. 99.
281. *Ibid.*, p. 98
282. Helen's memoirs, p. 98
283. *Ibid.*
284. *Ibid.*
285. *Ibid.*
286. *Ibid.*
287. *Ibid.*, p. 99.
288. *Ibid.*
289. Helen's memoirs, p. 100.
290. *Ibid.*
291. *Ibid.*
292. *Ibid.*
293. *Ibid.*, p. 99.
294. College transcript of Helen Ross at the University of Missouri (years: 1907 to 1911).
295. *Ibid.*, p. 97.
296. Helen's memoirs, pp. 96-97.
297. *Ibid.*
298. College transcript of Helen Ross (years: 1907 to 1911).

299. Helen's memoirs, pp. 95–96.
300. *Ibid.*, p. 97.
301. *Ibid.*
302. Conversations with Helen Ross, Virginia Ross Weston, and J.B. Ross 1966–1975.
303. Helen's memoirs, p. 102.
304. Helen's memoirs, p. 101.
305. *Ibid.*, p. 102.
306. Handwritten memoir of Virginia Ross Weston, circa 1982, p. 15
307. *Ibid.*, p. 16.
308. *Ibid.*
309. Stock certificate dated April 18, 1904.
310. Virginia's memoirs, p. 20.
311. Conversations with Helen and Virginia Ross Weston, circa 1966.
312. Virginia's memoirs, p. 17.
313. *Ibid.*
314. *Ibid.*
315. Town of Parker, Arizona, website; Historical Perspective; www.townofparkerarizona.com/history (2021)
316. *Ibid.*
317. Virginia's memoirs, p. 24.
318. Virginia memoirs, p. 24.
319. *Ibid.*
320. Virginia's memoirs, p. 24.
321. *Ibid.*
322. *Ibid.*
323. Memoir entitled "Louise," written by Virginia Ross Weston circa 1980. p. 4.
324. *Ibid.*
325. Virginia's memoirs, p. 24.

326. Memoir entitled "Louise," written by Virginia Ross Weston, circa 1980, pp. 4-5.
327. Conversation with Anne Moore Ross, daughter-in-law of Florence Griffin Ross (circa 1966).
328. *The St. Louis Republic,* Monday, January 22, 1906.
329. *The St. Louis Republic,* January 10, 1910.
330. Handwritten note by Florence G. Ross in the margin of the book *The Reluctant Servant,* by Farrar, p. 59.
331. When I was a child growing up, I was told by my mother: "It is exceptional that all four of your grandparents went to college." From that I inferred that all four had graduated from college. Fifty years later, I discovered that one—my grandmother Ross—had attended only one year, after which she was "dismissed by the dean." I've now learned oral history, particularly in a family, can be "tricky."
332. Conversations with Virginia Ross Weston and James Bruce Ross, sisters of Charlie Ross, circa 1967.
333. Conversations with Anne Moore Ross, daughter-in-law of Florence G. Ross.
334. Virginia Ross Weston's handwritten memoir notes, p. 24 (circa 1975)
335. *Ibid.*
336. Virginia Ross Weston's handwritten memoir notes, p. 24 (circa 1975).
337. "Typhoid Fever" from Mayo Foundation for Medical Education and Research; www.mayoclinic.org/diseases-conditions/typhoid-fever/symptons-causes (2021)
338. Virginia Ross Weston's handwritten memoir notes, p. 25.
339. *Ibid.*
340. Death Certificate of James B. Ross, issued by the Arizona State Board of Health, dated December 12, 1913.
341. Virginia Ross Weston's handwritten memoir notes, p. 27.

342. Newspaper article undated. Obtained from the HST Presidential Library. Article from most likely a newspaper in Columbia or St. Louis, Missouri. (circa November 1913).
343. Handwritten notation from Florence G. Ross in the margin on page 61 of the book *Reluctant Servant*, by Ronald T. Farrar, 1969.
344. *Ibid.*
345. Newspaper article, undated, for a Missouri paper.
346. Undated letter from John Griffin to Florence Griffin, postmarked October 9, 1911.
347. Letter from John Griffin to Florence Griffin, dated December 1, 1911.
348. Many years after John Griffin's death, rumors surfaced within the Ross family that, when Florence was growing up in the Griffins' home in St. Louis, that her father's "live-in mistress" lived there with them. This could have been a boarder or a live-in housekeeper, but those types of details were never revealed. Also, in the 1940s, one of Florence's daughters-in-law, who was also raised in St. Louis, became curious about Florence's father, so she hired a private investigator. The investigator reported back that Florence's father was "just an Irish drunk." None of these stories have been verified, but they are reasons that John Griffin's reputation has not fared well in Ross family lore.
349. Virginia Ross Weston's handwritten memoir notes, p. 26.
350. Memoirs of Helen Ross, p. 102.
351. *Ibid.*, p. 103. Helen tellingly omits Barbara's last name in her memoir, presumably to keep it confidential, due to the nature of their relationship.
352. *Ibid.*, p. 103.
353. Taken from Michigamee Township website: www.michigamee-township.com
354. Memoirs of Helen Ross, p. 103.
355. *Ibid.*
356. *Ibid.*

357. *Ibid.*, pp. 105–106.
358. Conversation on November 17, 2012, with Naomi Hult, former camper and councilor at Camp Kechuwa.
359. *Old Indian Days*, by C.A. Eastman, The McClure Company, New York, 1907, p. 26.
360. Conversations with Virginia Burns Weston Slaughter, circa 2012.
361. Memoirs of Helen Ross, p. 105.
362. *Ibid.*, p. 25.
363. Autobiographical Sketch—Helen Ross, dated September 1945.
364. Brochure from Camp Kechuwa for 1919 season states fee of $250.00 for eight weeks.
365. *Washington Post* July 26, 1982, column entitled "Washington Ways."
366. Autobiographical Sketch—Helen Ross, dated September 1945.
367. Conversation on November 17, 2012, with Naomi Hult.
368. *Associated Press* article of March 2, 1987.
369. *Washington Post*, July 26, 1982, column entitled "Washington Ways."
370. *The Reluctant Servant*, Farrar, p. 61.
371. *The Missouri Alumnus*, Volume II, No. 1, October 1913.
372. Handwritten note of Florence G. Ross at the bottom of page 61 of her copy of *The Reluctant Servant*, by Ronald T. Farrar (1969).
373. See *A Creed for My Profession*, Ronald T. Farrar, p. 169. (1998).
374. *The Reluctant Servant*, Farrar, p. 63.
375. *Ibid.*, p. 63.
376. When the School of Journalism began, it created its own newspaper, the *Missourian*, which, by design, operated as a standard, large-city newspaper. It sold advertising and subscriptions locally but incurred fewer actual expenses than the competing local newspaper, *e.g.*, salaries for editors and reporters. Over time, the *Missourian* made a profit. Much of the profit went into an account called the "Betterment Fund," to be used for "improvement and

advancement" in the School of Journalism. The Betterment Fund was controlled in these years by Dean Walter Williams. It is likely that this money paid for the sabbaticals for Frank Martin and Charlie Ross and their families. *A Creed for My Profession*, Farrar, pp. 154–155.

377. See walkergordononline.com/history.asp, p. 1.
378. *Ibid.*
379. *Ibid.*
380. See www.rawmilkinstitute.org/updates, p. 7.
381. *Ibid.*, p. 7.
382. Farrar, pp. 63 and 64. It must be noted that in *The Reluctant Servant*, the author incorrectly referred to the dairy not as Walker-Gordon, but as the Borden Company, which, more than a decade later, acquired Walker-Gordon, but was not involved in the Rosses' voyage in 1916. Also, the author incorrectly refers to the milk as "evaporated milk" instead of "raw milk." These two inaccuracies and their corrections were noted by Florence G. Ross in her handwritten notes in the margin of her copy of *The Reluctant Servant*.
383. *The Editor & Publisher and the Journalist*
384. Certificate of Registration of American Citizen (undated), signed by William C. Magelssen, U. S. Consul in Melbourne, Australia, with an expiration date of October 30, 1917.
385. Farrrar, *The Reluctant Servant*, p. 64.
386. *Ibid.*, p. 65.
387. *Ibid.*, p. 65.
388. *Ibid.*, p. 65.
389. *Ibid.*, p. 68.
390. *Ibid.*, p., 68. Citing Kingsbury, *Newspaper News.*
391. *Ibid.*, p. 66, citing Melbourne *Herald,* November 13, 1916.
392. *St. Louis Post-Dispatch*, December 24, 1916.
393. *Ibid.*, p. 68. Farrar, *The Reluctant Servant.*
394. *Ibid.*, p. 68.

395. *Ibid.*, p. 69. Farrar. [Note: Mr. Farrar in *The Reluctant Servant* on page 68 states that Charlie "had always detested teaching women students" and cites this as one reason for his dissatisfaction with continuing to teach at the School of Journalism. Further, he states on p. 68: "He was convinced that as far as women students were concerned, journalism, or any other course of study, was merely something to occupy their time until their wedding day, whereupon they would forget about their academic and professional training entirely." For this information, Farrar cites a conversation with Charlie's wife, Florence, in 1963. In my research, there is substantial evidence to dispute this claim. In her copy of *The Reluctant Servant*, Florence put two "X's" next to this assertion and to the footnote citing her alleged attribution. Charlie provided financial support to his sister, Helen, and most likely to a number of his other sisters so that they could obtain their college degrees. While it is true that Helen stated in her memoirs that Charlie dissuaded her from going into the field of journalism, he did that knowing her personally. Except for Farrar's discredited assertion, there is no evidence that he objected in any way to female college students generally or to the ones he taught each of the nine years he was teaching at the School of Journalism.]
396. Handwritten comment by Florence G. Ross in her copy of *The Reluctant Servant* on page 69.
397. Farrar, p. 68–69.
398. *Ibid.*, p. 70.
399. *Encyclopedia of Arkansas*; see encyclopediaofarkansas.net/entries/pauline-pfeiffer-11941.
400. Handwritten comment by Florence G. Ross noted on page 70 of her copy of *The Reluctant Servant*.
401. Farrar, *The Reluctant Servant*, pp. 71–72.
402. Handwritten notes from Diary of Charles G. Ross, January–March 1919.
403. Farrar, *The Reluctant Servant*, p. 73.
404. Memoirs of Helen Ross, p. 37.

405. Helen's Memoirs, p. 38.
406. *Ibid.*
407. *Ibid.*
408. Cited as https: // socialwelfare.library.vcu/edu/people/billikopf-jacob, pp. 1-5.
409. Biographical sketch of Helen Ross from University Archives, University of Missouri-Columbia: Collection, No. C:0/43/1, Box 3, p. 1.
410. Handwritten, undated letter, from Helen Ross to her sister, Virginia Ross, circa 1915.
411. Transcript of Virginia Ross from the University of Missouri, dated April 1919.
412. Conversation with Virginia Ross Weston in Washington, DC, circa 1967.
413. Biographical sketch of Helen Ross from University Archives, University of Missouri-Columbia: Collection, No. C:0/43/1, Box 3, page 2.
414. The grading scales were taken from the undated "Guide to Transcript Evaluation" provided by the Office of the University Registrar of the University of Missouri, in 2012. The grades cited herein are taken from the transcripts of the respective Ross-family members provided by the same office.
415. See college transcript of Virginia Ross, provided by the Office of University Registrar, University of Missouri-Columbia.
416. Helen's Memoirs, p. 92.
417. Virginia Ross Weston's memoir piece, entitled "Louise," circa 1980, pp. 5-6.
418. *Ibid.*, p. 6.
419. Memoirs of Helen Ross, p. 93.
420. Family story recounted by James B. Holmquist to John B. Ross in a telephone conversation on October 12, 2012.
421. Biographical sketch of Helen Ross, dated September 1945, made for her as the Administrative Director at the Institute of Psychoanalysis.

422. Biographical sketch of Helen Ross, dated June 7, 1949.
423. "Pauline Clara Goldmark," by Miriam Dinerman, Jewish Women's Archive; http://jaw.org/encyclopedia/article/goldmark-pauline.
424. "Josephine Clara Goldmark," by Kathryn Kish Sklar, Jewish Women's Archive; https://jaw.org/encyclopedia/article/goldmark-josephine-clara.
425. "Pauline Clara Goldmark," by Miriam Dinerman, Jewish Women's Archive, *ibid*.
426. Biographical sketch of Helen Ross, dated September 1945, made for her as the Administrative Director of the Institute of Psychoanalysis.
427. Memoirs of Helen Ross, p. 1.
428. See: www.history.com, and www.encyclopedia.com/history (Railroad Administration, U.S.)
429. "Pauline Clara Goldmark" by Miriam Dinerman, Jewish Women's Archive, *ibid*.
430. "Women in Railroad Operational Roles"—Final Report, June 2018, from the Institute of Transportation, University of Iowa, Ames, Iowa. (p. 2)
431. Memoirs of Helen Ross, p. 74.
432. *Ibid*.
433. *Ibid*., pp. 74–75.
434. *Ibid*., p. 75.
435. See college transcript of Virginia Ross, provided by the Office of the University Registrar, University of Missouri-Columbia.
436. Conversation with Virginia Ross Weston, circa 1969.
437. "She Champions The Cause Of Women," published in "Leaves" (a neighborhood newsletter of Wesley Heights in Washington, DC), May 1959, p. 7.
438. *Ibid*.
439. From unpublished typewritten notes entitled: "Lowell LaVerne Leake—an autobiography of his life written in 1957."

440. See college transcript of Frances Bruce Ross, provided by the Office of the University Registrar, University of Missouri-Columbia. [Note: The transcript does not reflect an award of the *Phi Beta Kappa* honor, but family lore and many relatives of Frances Bruce Ross have indicated she received that award.]
441. This account of Lowell Leake seeing his good friend killed in action is family lore; it was recalled by his grand-daughter, Katherine Leake Weiss. However, it was not mentioned by Mr. Leake in his unpublished autobiography referred to above.
442. From unpublished, typewritten notes entitled: "Lowell Laverne Leake—an autobiography of his life written in 1957."
443. Farrar, pp. 74-75.
444. Handwritten comment of Florence G. Ross in Farrar's *The Reluctant Servant*, p. 75.
445. Estelle Welsh was Florence's younger sister, whose husband was one of the children of the founder of the Welsh Baby Carriage Company of St. Louis. The couple had one daughter, Mary Estelle Welsh. In the 1920s, the couple separated, and Estelle came to Washington to be with her sister, and she lived and worked in Washington until her death in the early 1960s.
446. Farrar, p. 74; citing *St. Louis Post-Dispatch*, November 6, 1921.
447. Farrar, p. 80; *St. Louis Post-Dispatch*, August 7, 1923.
448. Farrar, p. 88.
449. Farrar, p. 88–89.
450. Farrar, p. 89.
451. Farrar, p. 81; *St. Louis Post-Dispatch*, January 31, 1926.
452. Farrar, pp. 91–92.
453. "What caused the Great Depression?" from *Foundation for Economic Education*, Feb. 2, 2018.
454. Farrar, p. 96.
455. Farrar, p. 98.
456. Farrar, p. 100–101.

457. Farrar, pp. 104–105.
458. Farrar, pp. 110–115.
459. Farrar, pp. 116–121.
460. Farrar, p. 125.
461. Farrar, p. 127.
462. Farrar, pp. 128–133.
463. Farrar, pp. 134–136.
464. See unpublished autobiographical sketch by Helen Ross, dated September 1945.
465. See *Encyclopedia Britannica*; www.britannica.com/biography/Josephine-Clara-Goldmark (December 11, 2021).
466. See unpublished autobiographical sketch by Helen Ross, dated September 1945.
467. Note: After a series of legal maneuvers—and 50 years of protests—in 1918, women in the United Kingdom 30 years of age and older were granted the right to vote. However, it wasn't until 1928 that another law was passed granting women over the age of 21 that right.
468. See unpublished autobiographical sketch of Helen Ross, dated August 7, 1949.
469. *The Washington Post*, August 11, 1978, p. C12.
470. Memoirs of Helen Ross, p. 94.
471. See unpublished autobiographical sketch by Helen Ross, dated September 1945.
472. See *Lehrinstitut Der Wiener Psychoanalytische Vereinigung*, from www.encyclopedia.com, March 2022.
473. Helene Deutsche, Jewish Women's Archive; http://jwa.org/encyclopedia/article/deutsche-helene, September 24, 2013.
474. Undated copy of a portion of a letter from Helen Ross to George Engel, circa 1970.
475. See *Lehrinstitut Der Wiener Psychoanalytische Vereinigung*, ibid.

476. *Encyclopedia Britannica*; https://www.britannica.com/biography/Franz-Alexander, 04 March 2020.
477. *Ibid.*
478. See "Chicago Institute for Psychoanalysis" by John Galbraith Simmons; www.encyclopedia.com/psychology/chicago-institute-psychoanalysis.
479. See unpublished autobiographical sketch by Helen Ross, dated September 1945.
480. *Ibid.*
481. *Ibid.*
482. See "About Alice," The Alice M. O'Brien Foundation; https://aobfoundation.org/about-alice, March 14, 2022.
483. From an unpublished pamphlet entitled, "Kernels from the Compound" by Elizabeth Pearsall, dated March 15, 1969.
484. *Ibid.*
485. See unpublished Biographical Sketch by Helen Ross, dated September 1945.
486. *Ibid.*
487. *Ibid.*
488. *Ibid.*
489. *See* https://www.encyclopedia.com/Chicago-Institute-Psychoanalyst/Encyclopedia.com
490. See website for the Francis Parker School, http//www.fwparker.org. (2022)
491. See unpublished Biographical Sketch by Helen Ross, dated September 1945.
492. See website for the Francis Parker School, http//www.fwparker.org; note Board of Trustees for 1958.
493. See unpublished Biographical Sketch by Helen Ross, dated September 1945.
494. *Ibid.*
495. Unpublished Memoirs of Helen Ross, p. 17.

496. See the unpublished "BIBLIOGRAPHY OF HELEN ROSS," dated March 31, 1972, compiled for the Pittsburgh Psychoanalytic Institute, Department of Psychiatry, University of Pittsburgh School of Medicine. Note: "The Shy Child" by Helen Ross, a Public Affairs Pamphlet (No. 239), copyrighted in 1956, was not included in that bibliography.
497. "Fears of Children" by Helen Ross, Copyright MCMLI by Science Research Associates, Inc., Grolier Incorporated, New York (1951)
498. "The Shy Child," by Helen Ross, Public Affairs Pamphlet No. 239, from Public Affairs Committee, Inc. (1956)
499. "The School Year: An Age of Discovery." *Child Study*, 32:11, 1955.
500. "Like Mother, Like Daughter?" In Davis, W.A., and Havighurst, R. J.: *Father of the Man*, Boston, Houghton Mifflin Co., 1947, p. 148.
501. "A Contemporary Concept of Family Welfare," *Marriage and Family Living*, 15:260, 1953.
502. "The Handicapped Child and His Family," *The Crippled Child*, 30: 8-10, No. 5, February 1953.
503. Noted in "The Shy Child." *Ibid*.
504. "Anna Freud," Britannica Online Encyclopedia; www.Britannica.com/biography/Anna-Freud (April 2022).
505. See: "Hampstead Clinic," www.encyclopedia.com/psychology; "Anna Freud," psychoanalysis.org.uk/anna-freud; "Anna Freud Centre" https://en.wikipedia.org/wiki/Anna_Freud_Centre.
506. Unpublished handwritten document from Charles Leake to his brother, Lowell "Bud" Leake, dated January 28th (circa 1954).
507. *New York Times*, March 9, 1964, p. 29.
508. American Psychoanalytical Association. APsA Mission & Vision, https://apsa.org/content/apsaa (April 7, 2022).
509. Lewin, B. D., The Consultation Service. *Journal of the American Psychoanalytic Association*. 1962; 10 (1), pp. 139–144.
510. Lewin, B. D., & Ross, H. (1960). *Psychoanalytic Education in the United States*, W.W. Norton & Co.

511. Draft registration card (Form D.S.S. Form 1) of Charles Griffith Ross dated April 27, 1942.
512. *Ibid.*, p. 145.
513. Farrar, pp. 138–139.
514. *Ibid.*, pp. 146–147.
515. *Ibid.*, p. 147.
516. *Ibid.*, p. 148.
517. Her daughter-in-law said to the author: "Your Grandmother [Florence] will go across town to save five cents on a pound of butter but won't bat an eye at spending $1,000 on jewelry."
518. W. Dale Nelson, *Who Speaks for the President? The White House Press Secretary from Cleveland to Clinton* (Syracuse University Press, 1998), p. 94.
519. *Ibid.*, p. 95.
520. *Ibid.*, p. 95, and Ross family lore.
521. Statement to John B. Ross, Jr., by Florence G. Ross, circa 1954.
522. Conversations between Dr. John B. Ross and the author, John B. Ross, Jr. (circa 1960).
523. Farrar, p. 149.
524. *Washington Post*, "Women of Washington," July 28, 1946.
525. Farrar, p. 148.
526. Farrar, pp. 149–150.
527. Farrar, p. 150.
528. Alonzo L. Hamby, *Man of the People: A Life of Harry S. Truman* (Oxford University Press, 1995), pp. 290–294.
529. Farrar, pp. 153–154; *St. Louis Post-Dispatch*, April 15, 1945.
530. W. Dale Nelson, *Who Speaks for the President?* p. 96.
531. *Ibid.*, p. 89.
532. Farrar, p. 156; M. Truman, *Harry S. Truman*, p. 227.
533. Raymond P. Brandt, "The President's Secretary," *Magazine of the Sigma Chi*, p. 136, July–August, 1945.

534. Handwritten letter from Charlie Ross to his son, John Ross, dated May 13, 1945.
535. Raymond P. Brandt, "The President's Secretary," *Magazine of the Sigma Chi*, p. 132–136. July–August 1945.
536. *Ibid.*
537. Farrar, p. 156.
538. Brandt, *Magazine of the Sigma Chi*, p. 132.
539. Farrar, p. 157.
540. *Ibid.*
541. Brandt, p. 135.
542. Handwritten letter from Charlie Ross to his son, John Ross, dated May 13, 1945.
543. Raymond P. Brandt, "The President's Secretary," *Magazine of the Sigma Chi*, p. 134.
544. *United States News*, "People of the Week," May 25, 1945, p. 66.
545. Telephone conversation with Helen Holmquist Halnan in April 2010.
546. *Encyclopedia Britannica*, "Potsdam Conference," www.britannica.com/print/article/4782799, May 2022.
547. Conversations between John B. Ross and John B. Ross, Jr., circa 1964.
548. Hamby, pp. 328–329.
549. Farrar, p. 171.
550. Farrar, pp. 170–173.
551. Letter from Charlie Ross to his sister, Louise Ross Holmquist, dated March 15, 1946.
552. W. Dale Nelson, *Who Speaks for the President?* (Syracuse University Press, 1998), p. 97.
553. *See Bergheim, Myrtle Papers.* Harry S. Truman Library. www.trumanlibrary.gov/library/personal-papers/myrtle-bergheim-papers#bio.May10,2022.

554. *Washington Post*, "Women of Washington" by Bess Hackett, July 28, 1946, p. 7S.
555. Nancy Gibbs and Michael Duffy, *The Presidents Club*, Simon Schuster (2012), p. 29.
556. Robert F. Dorr, "Air Force One: A History of Presidential Travel." DefenseMediaNetwork.com (November 10, 2016). https://www.defensemedianetwork.com/stories/air-force-one-a-history-of-presidential-air-travel/4.
557. Conversation between the author and Mr. Kenneth Hechler, Member of President Truman's White House Staff, in Key West, Florida, May 18, 2013.
558. Farrar, p. 182–187.
559. Unpublished, handwritten, eight-page letter, dated January 22, 1950 from Harry S Truman to Charles G. Ross.

* Author's note: The original of this letter was handed down from various items given originally to my mother, Anne Moore Ross, by my grandmother, Florence Griffin (Ross) Roberts, and then passed on to me. This letter, along with other family heirlooms inherited from my grandmother (Charlie's wife) was stored in an attractive wooden box and kept on the top shelf of my clothes closet at our home in Baldwin, Maryland. In the summer of 1994, when we were away on vacation, our home was burglarized, and the box, along with most of our silverware, was stolen. None of those items were ever recovered. Fortunately, the author had made a photocopy of that letter prior to the theft, and it is quoted herein.

560. Hamby, p. 441.
561. *Truman*, McCullough, p. 653.
562. Hamby, p. 441.
563. Farrar, p. 441.
564. Typed letter dated May 28, 1948, from Charles G. Ross to Miss Ella Ross.
565. Western Union Telegram, from Charles G. Ross to Mrs. Fred N. Holmquist, date-stamped June 7, 1948.

482 | TRUMAN'S TRUSTED FRIEND

566. Western Union Telegram, from Charles G. Ross to Mrs. Fred N. Holmquist date-stamped June 13, 1948.
567. Transcript dated Monday, June 14, 1948 of NEWSCAST OVER KTAR, KVOA, KYUM, KAWT, KGLU, KYCA, AND KWJB.
568. Unpublished recollections of her sister, Louise, by Virginia Ross Weston, dated February 1980.
569. *Truman*, McCullough, p. 654.
570. Conversation with Kenneth W. Hechler, May 18, 2013.
571. Charles G. Ross, "How Truman Did It," *Collier's* (December 25, 1948), pp. 13, 87.
572. Letter from Louise Ross Holmquist to her husband, Mr. F. N. Holmquist, dated Wednesday, January 19, 1949.
573. Letter from Louise Ross Holmquist to Helen and Fred Holmquist, dated March 4, 1949.
574. *Ibid.*
575. W. Dale Nelson, *Who Speaks for the President?* page 103.
576. *Ibid.*, p. 102.
577. *Ibid.*
578. *Ibid.*, p. 97.
579. *Ibid.*, p. 102.
580. Hamby, p. 301.
581. Nelson, p. 104.
582. Letters to the Editor, *TIME*, November 22, 1948, p. 8.
583. Farrar, pp. 236-238.
584. Hamby, p. 301.
585. Transcript of 1964 interview with Walter Trohan from the Harry S. Truman Library and Museum.
586. Letter dated January 6, 1951 from Florence G. Ross to Louise Ross Holmquist.
587. Margaret Truman Daniel, *Harry S. Truman* (copyright 1972) p. 498.
588. *Ibid.*, page 496.

589. *Ibid.*, page 497.
590. Harry S. Truman, *Memoirs*, pp. 395–396.
591. Harry S. Truman, *ibid.*, p. 498.
592. *Ibid.*, pp. 498–499.
593. Eben A. Ayers, *Truman in the White House*, copyright 1991, pp. 385–386.
594. Harry S. Truman, *Memoirs*, p. 499.
595. *Washington Post*, p. 1., December 6, 1950.
596. *Ibid.*, p. 13,; and Harry S. Truman, *Memoirs*, pp. 499-500.
597. Letter from Florence G. Ross to Louise R. Holmquist, dated January 6, 1951.
598. Records from the files of the Robert A. Pumphrey Funeral Home from December 1950.
599. *Ibid.*
600. Letter from Florence G. Ross to Louise R. Holmquist, dated January 6, 1951.
601. *Ibid.*
602. Note from Harry S. Truman to Florence G. Ross, dated December 8, 1950.
603. Letter from Ella Ross to Louise Ross Holmquist, dated Sunday, December 10, 1950.
604. Harry S. Truman, *Memoirs* Volume 2, p. 401.
605. At the time of the book's publication, the APsA's membership was limited to medical doctors. In 1989, it opened up its membership to include non-physicians who had undergone the rigorous training of and had graduated from APsA-approved institutions. See: website of the American Psychoanalytic Association, apsa.org.
606. *The National Cyclopedia of American Biography*, Vol. 61, p. 5, 1982.
607. *Ibid.*
608. *Ibid.*
609. Rogers, Fred, *Encyclopedia Britannica*, https://www.britannica.com/biography/Fred-Rogers (accessed June 16, 2022).

610. Unpublished copy of a presentation given by Fred Rogers at the "In Celebration of the Life of Helen Ross" ceremony at Georgetown University on December 4, 1978.
611. *Ibid.*
612. *Ibid.*
613. *Ibid.*
614. *Ibid.*
615. *The National Cyclopedia of American Biography*, Vol. *61*, p. 5, 1982.
616. *The National Cyclopedia of American Biography*, Vol. *61*, p. 5, 1982.
617. Robert Coles, *Anna Freud: The Dream of Psychoanalysis* (Addison-Wesley Publishing Company, Inc., 1991), xxiii.
618. *Ibid.*
619. *The National Cyclopedia of American Biography* Vol. *61*, p. 5, 1982.
620. Obituary of Helen Holmquist Halnan, February 19, 2013 (See www.legacy.com/obituaries/azcentral/obituary)
621. *Currents in Psychoanalysis*, New York, International Universities Press, Inc., 1971, pp. 3–13 and pp. 57–65, respectively.
622. Booklet provided by The University of Chicago School of Social Service Administration at the ceremony introducing The Helen Ross Professorship in Social Welfare Policy in Chicago, Illinois, June 7, 1972.
623. Unpublished eulogy written by Fay Horton Sawyer given at a memorial service for Helen Ross given at the Chicago Institute for Psychoanalysis *circa* 1977.
624. Helen Ross 1890–1978, *The Psychoanalytic Quarterly*, Vol. XLVII; 465-469, 1979.
625. Unpublished copy of a presentation given by Fred Rogers at the "In Celebration of the Life of Helen Ross" ceremony at Georgetown University on December 4, 1978.
626. *The Psychoanalytic Quarterly,* Vol. XLVII: 465-469, 1979. "Helen Ross 1890–1978."

627. Letter from Jim Leake to Louise Ross Holmquist, dated August 24, 1978.
628. Walter Trohan, oral history interview, Harry S. Truman Library, 1964.
629. Handwritten letter written by James Bruce Holmquist to John B. Ross; dated November 20, 2012.
630. *Ibid.*
631. Telephone conversation between the author and James Bruce Holmquist on October 12, 2012.
632. *Ibid.*
633. *Ibid.*
634. *Ibid.*
635. *Ibid.*
636. Quote taken from telephone conversation between the author and Helen Holmquist Halnan in 2010, one of several.
637. Obituary of F. N. Holmquist, published in the *Phoenix Gazette*, August 27, 1955.
638. Obituary of Fred Nels Holmquist, Jr., published in the *Dallas Morning News,* May 6, 2011.
639. Telephone conversation between the author and James Bruce Holmquist on October 12, 2012.
640. "She Champions the Cause of Women," *The Leaves*, an unpublished community newsletter issued by the Wesley Heights community in Washington, DC, May 1959, p. 7.
641. *Ibid.*
642. *United States Children's Bureau*, from website of the *Encyclopedia Britannica*, www.britannica .com/topic/United-States-Childrens-Bureau, date published: 09 February 2014 (access date: July 22, 2022).
643. "She Champions the Cause of Women," *The Leaves*, an unpublished community newsletter issued by the Wesley Heights community in Washington, DC, May 1959, p. 7.

644. *Ibid.*
645. *Ibid.*
646. *Ibid.*
647. "C.H. Weston Dies: Ex-Chief of Justice Antitrust Section," *Washington Post*, August 5, 1987.
648. The detailed information presented in this section (*"Frances"*) was taken from the unpublished memoir notes of Lowell L. Leake.
649. Unpublished letter from Frances Ross Leake to her son "Jim" and his wife "Dory," dated February 1, 1949.
650. Constance Hoffman Berman, "James Bruce Ross (1902–1995) and the Sources for Medieval and Renaissance History," *Women Medievalists and the Academy*, University of Wisconsin Press (2005), pp. 575–584.

www.ingramcontent.com/pod-product-compliance
Lightning Source LLC
Chambersburg PA
CBHW030335010526
44119CB00028B/404/J